PR, PS, PZ

English and American Literature and Juvenile Belles Lettres

Library of Congress Classification
2012

Prepared by the Policy and Standards Division
Library Services

LIBRARY OF CONGRESS
Cataloging Distribution Service
Washington, D.C.

LIBRARY OF
CONGRESS

This edition cumulates all additions and changes to subclasses PR, PS, and PZ through List 2012/06, dated June 16, 2012. Additions and changes made subsequent to that date are published in lists posted on the World Wide Web at

<http://www.loc.gov/aba/cataloging/classification/weeklylists/>

and are also available in *Classification Web*, the online Web-based edition of the Library of Congress Classification.

Library of Congress Cataloging-in-Publication Data

Library of Congress.
    Library of Congress classification. PR, PS, PZ. English and American literature and juvenile belles lettres / prepared by the Policy and Standards Division, Library Services. — 2012 ed.
        p. cm.
    "This edition cumulates all additions and changes to subclasses PR, PS, and PZ through List 2012/06, dated June 16, 2012. Additions and changes made subsequent to that date are published in lists posted on the World Wide Web ... and are also available in   *Classification Web*, the online Web-based edition of the Library of Congress classification." — T.p. verso.
    Includes index.
    ISBN 978-0-8444-9555-2 (alk. paper)
    1. Classification, Library of Congress. 2. Classification—Books—English literature.
3. Classification—Books—American literature. 4. Classification—Books—Children's literature. I. Library of Congress. Cataloging Policy and Support Office. II. Title. III. Title: English and American literature and juvenile belles lettres. IV. Title: English and American literature. V. Title: Juvenile belles lettres.

    Z696.U5P83 2012
    025.4'682—dc23

                            2012028371

For sale by the Library of Congress Cataloging Distribution Service,
101 Independence Avenue, S.E., Washington, DC 20541-4912.
Product catalog available on the Web at **www.loc.gov/cds**.

PREFACE

The first edition of Subclasses PR, PS, and PZ, *English and American Literature and Juvenile Belles Lettres*, was published in 1915, together with subclass PN. That edition was reissued in 1964 with supplementary pages. The second edition was published in 1978, and the third edition in 1988. Beginning with the 1998 edition, subclass PN was no longer included, having been published separately since 1997. A 2005 edition cumulated additions and changes made since the publication of the 1998 edition. Another edition was published in 2008. This 2012 edition includes additions and changes made since the 2008 edition was published.

In editions of the Library of Congress classification schedules published since 2004, classification numbers or spans of numbers that appear in parentheses are formerly valid numbers that are now obsolete. Numbers or spans that appear in angle brackets are optional numbers that have never been used at the Library of Congress but are provided for other libraries that wish to use them. In most cases, a parenthesized or angle-bracketed number is accompanied by a "see" reference directing the user to the actual number that the Library of Congress currently uses, or a note explaining Library of Congress practice.

Access to the online version of the full Library of Congress Classification is available on the World Wide Web by subscription to Classification Web. Details about ordering and pricing may be obtained from the Cataloging Distribution Service at

<http://www.loc.gov/cds/>

New or revised numbers and captions are added to the L.C. Classification schedules as a result of development proposals made by the cataloging staff of the Library of Congress and cooperating institutions. Upon approval of these proposals by the editorial meeting of the Policy and Standards Division, new classification records are created or existing records are revised in the master classification database. Lists of newly approved or revised classification numbers and captions are posted on the World Wide Web at

<http://www.loc.gov/aba/cataloging/classification/weeklylists/>

Janis L. Young, senior subject cataloging policy specialist in the Policy and Standards Division, is responsible for coordinating the overall intellectual and editorial content of class P and its various subclasses. Kent Griffiths and Ethel Tillman, assistant editors of classification schedules, create new classification records and their associated index terms, and maintain the master database.

Barbara B. Tillett, Chief
Policy and Standards Division

July 2012

	English literature
	Literary history and criticism
1	Periodicals. Serials
(3)	Yearbooks
	see PR1
5	Societies
7	Congresses
9	Museums. Exhibitions
	Subarrange by author
	Catalogs of slides
10	General
10.5.A-Z	Catalogs of public institutions. By name of institution, A-Z
	Collections of monographs, studies, etc.
	For collected essays, studies, etc., of individual authors
	see PR99
13	Series. Monographs by different authors
14	Minor collections. Festschriften
19	Encyclopedias. Dictionaries
	Communication of information
20	General works
20.3	Information services
20.5	Computer network resources
	Including the Internet
	Theory and principles of the study of English literature
21	General works
25	Relation to English history
27	History of literary history
	Study and teaching
31	Periodicals. Societies. Serials
33	General works. Treatises, etc.
	Outlines, syllabi, etc. see PR87
35	General special
37	Addresses, essays, lectures
	By period
41	Middle ages to 1600
43	17th-18th centuries
45	19th century
47	20th century
51.A-Z	By region or country, A-Z
53.A-Z	By school, A-Z
	Biography of teachers, critics, and historians
54	Collective
55.A-Z	Individual, A-Z
	Subarrange each by Table P-PZ50
56	Literary research
	Criticism
	Cf. PN80+ General literary criticism

	Criticism -- Continued
57	General works
61	Addresses, essays, lectures
63	History
65.A-Z	Special topics, A-Z
65.D57	Discourse analysis
65.M38	Marxist criticism
65.T48	Textual criticism
67	Collections of essays in criticism
	For collections by individual authors see PR99
	By period
	Medieval to 1600
	Including Elizabethan
69	Treatises. Theory, history, etc.
70	Specimens. Selections
	17th century
71	Treatises. Theory, history, etc.
72	Specimens. Selections
	18th century
73	Treatises. Theory, history, etc.
74	Specimens. Selections
	19th century
75	Treatises. Theory, history, etc.
76	Specimens. Selections
	20th century
77	Treatises. Theory, history, etc.
78	Specimens. Selections
	History of English literature
	Periodicals see PR1
	General works
	English
81	Early works through 1800
	1801-
83	Treatises
85	Compends
86	Comic histories of English literature
87	Outlines, syllabi, tables, charts, questions and answers, etc.
89	Indexes of poems and stories for schools
91	Juvenile works. Stories of English literature
	French
93	Treatises. Compends
94	Addresses, essays, lectures
	German
95	Treatises. Compends
96	Addresses, essays, lectures
	Other languages

	History of English literature
	General works
	Other languages -- Continued
97	Treatises. Compends
98	Addresses, essays, lectures
99	Collected essays, studies, etc., of individual authors
	Cf. PR13+ Literary history and criticism
101	Individual addresses, essays, lectures, etc.
	Biography, memoirs, letters, etc.
	Collected biography
103	Early through 1800
105	1801-1900
106	1901-
107	Collected memoirs, letters, etc.
108	Miscellany: Satire, humor, etc.
	Literary landmarks. Homes and haunts of authors
109	General works
110.A-Z	By place, A-Z
	Special classes of authors
	Women authors
	For women of specific occupations, ethnic groups, etc. see PR120.A+
111	General works
113	Through 1800
115	1800-1900
116	1900-
119	Women and literature. Feminine influence
120.A-Z	Other classes of authors, A-Z
120.A75	Asians
120.B55	Blacks
120.C3	Catholics
120.C55	Children
120.G38	Gays
120.J48	Jews
120.K54	Kings and rulers
120.L33	Laboring class. Working class
120.L4	Lawyers
120.L45	Lesbians
120.M45	Men
120.M47	Mentally ill
120.M55	Minorities
120.M87	Muslims
120.P6	Physicians
120.P73	Prisoners
120.P75	Protestants
120.P87	Puritans
120.Q34	Quakers

	History of English literature
	Special classes of authors
	Other classes of authors, A-Z -- Continued
120.S64	Soldiers
121	Anonymous literature
	Relations to other literatures and countries
	Cf. PN851+ Comparative literature
125	General works
127	Ancient
128	Medieval
129.A-Z	Modern. By region or country, A-Z
	Translation of foreign literature into English
	Collections see PN6019+
131	General works
133	Ancient classics
135.A-Z	By region or country, A-Z
	Translations of English literature
137.A1	General works
137.A5-Z	By language, A-Z
	Collections see PR1112+; PR1179.A+
138	English literature by foreign authors
	Class here general works only
	For individual authors (in their respective chronological sections) see PR1803+
(138.5)	Foreign literature by English authors
	For reference only, e.g. Lettres sur les Anglais qui ont écrit en Français par S. Van de Weyer, PQ144.5
	For individual authors, see the authors of the respective foreign literature
	Special topics not limited to, or identified with, one period or form
	For treatment of special topics by a specific class of author see PR111+
	Treatment of special subjects
	Cf. PN56+ General literature
	Cf. PN683+ General literature (Medieval)
	Cf. PN1010+ General literature (Poetry)
	Cf. PR275.A+ English literature (Medieval)
	Cf. PR317.A+ English literature (Poetry)
	Classical antiquity see PR127
140	Classicism
143	Nature
145	Religion. Mysticism
146	Romanticism
147	The supernatural
149.A-Z	Other, A-Z
149.A3	Absurdity

History of English literature
  Special topics not limited to, or identified with, one period or form
    Treatment of special subjects
      Other, A-Z -- Continued

149.A37	Africa
149.A647	Allegory
149.A67	America
149.A7	Animals
149.A74	Apocalyptic literature
149.A79	Arthurian romances
149.A798	Astrology
149.A8	Astronomy
149.B35	Bars (Drinking establishments)
149.B5	Bible
149.B62	Body, Human
149.B87	Business
149.C34	Camp (Style)
149.C5	Chivalry
149.C53	Cities and towns
149.C58	Collaborative authorship
149.C63	Color
149.C65	The comic
149.C66	Conformity
149.C665	Consciousness
149.C67	Costume
149.D47	Devil
149.D57	Disasters
149.D68	Doubles
149.D96	Dystopias
149.E28	East (Far East)
149.E29	Economics
149.E3	Education
149.E55	Emotions
149.E84	Ethiopia
149.E87	Evil
149.E89	Exoticism
149.F3	Fairies
149.F32	Falconry
149.F34	Family
149.F35	Fantastic literature
149.F46	Femininity
149.F64	Folklore
149.G36	Gardens
149.G39	Gaze
149.G54	Globalization
149.G58	Golden age (Mythology)

History of English literature
   Special topics not limited to, or identified with, one period or
     form
     Treatment of special subjects
      Other, A-Z -- Continued

149.H37	Harmony (Aesthetics)
149.H57	History
149.H65	Holy, The
149.H86	Humanism
149.I58	Incubi
149.I6	India
149.I65	Interracial marriage
	Irony see PR931+
149.I8	Islam
149.I82	Islands
149.L35	Landscape
149.L37	Language
149.L39	Latin America
149.L47	Lesbianism
149.L58	Local color
149.L6	Love
149.M33	Manners and customs
149.M35	Marriage
149.M53	Middle Ages
149.M56	Mirrors
149.M65	Monsters
149.M87	Museums
149.M95	Mythology
149.N27	Narration (Rhetoric)
149.N3	Nationalism
149.O18	Object (Philosophy)
149.O2	Obsessive-compulsive disorder
149.O44	Old age
149.P26	Pacifism
149.P3	Pastoral literature
149.P4	Philosophy
149.P45	Pilgrims and pilgrimages
149.P53	Place (Philosophy)
149.P6	Politics
149.P66	Popular literature
149.P68	Power (Social sciences)
149.P72	Prophecy
149.P78	Psychoanalysis
	Pubs see PR149.B35
149.R43	Reality
149.R45	Relation (Philosophy)
149.R47	Repetition

History of English literature
　Special topics not limited to, or identified with, one period or
　　form
　　Treatment of special subjects
　　　Other, A-Z -- Continued

149.R65	Romances
149.S4	Science
149.S46	Seasons
149.S47	Secret societies
149.S48	Sequels
149.S5	Sex. Sex customs
149.S64	Skepticism
149.S7	Social ideals
149.S75	Space and time
149.S8	Stereotype (Psychology)
149.S95	Sympathy
149.T33	Taboo
149.T7	Tragic, The
149.T83	Tuberculosis
149.U8	Utopias
149.V55	Vitalism
149.W3	Wales
149.W54	Wills
151.A-Z	Treatment of special classes. By subject, A-Z
151.A53	Anglo-Saxons
151.A95	Authors
151.C37	Capitalists and financiers
151.C5	Children
151.C54	Clergy
	Financiers see PR151.C37
151.H4	Hermits
151.I53	Indians
151.J5	Jews
151.K55	Kings and rulers
151.L3	Labor
151.L37	Lawyers
151.L5	Libertines
151.L53	Librarians
151.M46	Men
151.M68	Mothers
151.O94	Outsiders
151.P8	Preachers
151.S25	Saints
151.S3	Seamen
151.S45	Servants
151.V3	Vagabond
151.V56	Villains

	History of English literature
	Special topics not limited to, or identified with, one period or form
	Treatment of special classes. By subject, A-Z -- Continued
151.W6	Women
153.A-Z	Special characters, A-Z
153.B58	Bluebeard
153.B63	Boadicea, Queen, d. 62
153.C73	Cressida
153.F57	Fortunatus
153.L33	Lady of the Lake
153.M47	Merlin
153.S48	Shore, Jane, d. 1527
	By period
161	Works covering more than one period
163	Origins. Celtic period, Roman period, etc.
166	Early English (Beginnings through 1500)
	Anglo-Saxon (Beginnings through 1066)
	For special works, authors, and collections of Anglo-Saxon literature see PR1490+
171	Collections of monographs, studies, etc.
	Treatises. Compends
173	English
175	Other
176	Addresses, essays, lectures
177	Outlines, quizzes, tables, etc.
179.A-Z	Special topics, A-Z
179.C45	Chronology
	Darkness see PR179.L54
179.D43	Death
179.D48	Devil
179.F66	Food habits
179.G63	Gods
179.H65	Homosexuality
179.L54	Light and darkness
179.L57	Literacy
179.M38	Maxims
179.M53	Migrations of nations
179.O7	Oral-formulaic analysis
179.P35	Paradise
179.P4	Peace
179.P44	Penance
179.P73	Prayer
179.R32	Race
179.S5	Shamanism
179.T48	Textual criticism
179.V4	Versification

History of English literature
By period
Anglo-Saxon (Beginnings through 1066)
Special topics, A-Z -- Continued

179.W37	War
179.W65	Women
181	Collected essays of individual authors
182	Relations to other literature
	Cf. PR125+ General literary history

Special regions

183	Northumbrian
185	West Saxon
187	Mercian
189	Kentish

By period

191	Before Alfred
195	10th and 11th centuries

Special forms
Poetry

201	General works
203	General special
205	Epic. Historical
207	Elegiac
208	Hagiographical
210	Lyric
215	Didactic. Gnomic
217	Other

Prose

221	General works
226	Religious
231	History, science, etc.
236	Translations (from the Latin, etc.)

Medieval. Middle English (1066-1500)

251	Collections of monographs, studies, etc.

Treatises. Compends

255	English
257	Other
260	Addresses, essays, lectures
265	Outlines, quizzes, tables, etc.
275.A-Z	Special topics, A-Z
275.A4	Allegory
275.A47	Animals
275.A5	Antichrist
275.A77	Art
275.B4	Beauty
275.B47	Bestiaries
275.B5	Bible

History of English literature
   By period
      Medieval. Middle English (1066-1500)
         Special topics, A-Z -- Continued

275.C42	Characters and characteristics
275.C45	Charity
275.C48	Childbirth
275.C5	Chronicle
275.C55	Clergy
275.C56	Clothing and dress
275.C58	Contradiction
275.C6	Courtly love
275.C65	Courts and courtiers
	Daughters and mothers see PR275.M64
275.D4	Deadly sins
275.D43	Death
275.D53	Didactic literature
275.E66	Eroticism
275.E7	Eschatology
275.E77	Ethics
275.E8	Etiquette
275.F34	Faith
275.F6	Fortuna (Goddess)
275.F75	Friendship
275.F95	Future life
275.G44	Gender identity
275.G49	Giants
275.G67	Gossip
275.H47	Heroes. Heroines
275.H5	Historiography
275.H6	Honor
275.H83	Human-animal relationships
275.H85	Hunting
275.I3	Iconoclasm
275.I34	Identity (Psychology)
275.J4	Jesus Christ
275.L3	Laments
275.L35	Law
275.L54	Life cycle, Human
275.L6	Lord's Supper
275.L66	Love
275.M3	Marriage
275.M34	Mary, Blessed Virgin, Saint
275.M35	Masculinity
275.M4	Medicine
275.M44	Mental illness
275.M5	Mirrors

History of English literature
By period
Medieval. Middle English (1066-1500)
Special topics, A-Z -- Continued

275.M6	Monasticism
275.M615	Monsters
275.M62	Moon
275.M64	Mothers and daughters
275.M9	Mysticism
275.N27	Narration
275.N29	National characteristics
275.N3	Nature
275.N54	Nightingales
275.N63	Nobility
275.N66	Nominalism
275.N8	Nuns
275.O72	Oral tradition
275.O78	Outlaws
275.P34	Paganism
275.P43	Peasants
275.P45	Pilgrims and pilgrimages
275.P5	Plato
275.P63	Politics
275.P65	Popular literature
275.P67	Power (Social sciences)
275.P7	Preaching
275.R37	Rape
275.R4	Religion
275.S49	Sex differences
275.S56	Sin
275.S63	Social history. Society
275.S82	Sublime
275.T45	Textual criticism
275.T73	Travel
275.T74	Troy
275.T95	Typology (Theology)
275.W36	Wales
275.W5	Wisdom
275.W6	Women
275.W67	Work

By period
Before Chaucer. Anglo-Norman (1066-1400)
Cf. PC2941+ Anglo-Norman literature

281	General works
283	Collected essays
285	Addresses, essays, lectures
	Special topics see PR275.A+

	History of English literature
	By period
	Medieval. Middle English (1066-1500)
	By period -- Continued
	15th century
291	General works
293	Collected essays
295	Addresses, essays, lectures
	Special topics see PR275.A+
	By form
	Poetry
	General
	Cf. PR1972.G35+ Gawain-poet (Collected works)
311	Treatises
313	Collected essays
315	Addresses, essays, lectures
317.A-Z	Special topics, A-Z
317.A52	Allegory
317.A55	Alliteration
317.A73	Architecture
317.B4	Beauty
317.C65	The comic
317.D4	Death
317.D42	Debate poetry
317.D7	Dreams
317.E64	Epistolary poetry
317.F7	Frame stories
317.F75	Friars
317.G4	Gesture
317.G83	Guardian and ward
317.H56	Historical poetry
317.J48	Jews
317.L38	Laudatory poetry
317.L68	Love poetry
317.M34	Manuscripts
317.M53	Middle age
317.M57	Mirrors
317.N28	Narrative poetry
317.N3	National characteristics
317.O72	Oral tradition
317.P38	Pastoral poetry
317.P6	Politics
317.P73	Preaching
317.R6	Romanticism
317.S3	Satire
317.S36	Science
317.S4	Seasons

History of English literature
  By period
    Medieval. Middle English (1066-1500)
      By form
        Poetry
          General
            Special topics, A-Z -- Continued

317.S48	Sex
317.S53	Sieges
317.S6	Social life and customs
317.S82	Subjectivity
317.T48	Textual criticism
317.T53	Theology
317.V58	Visions
	Ward and guardian see PR317.G83
317.W66	Women

          Metrical romances. Epics

321	General works
	Special classes
	Classical romances
322	General works
323	Troy
324	Alexander
326	Other
	English
327	General works
328	Arthurian
	Including later versions and versions in prose
329	Other
	French
330	General works
331	Charlemagne
333	Other
335	Miscellaneous romances of chivalry
339	Northern (Scandinavian, German, etc.)
345	Oriental
347	Fables. Beast epics
	Religious, Christian see PR365
	Lyric
351	General works
352	Memoirs, letters, etc.
353	Collected essays
354	Addresses, essays, lectures
355.A-Z	Special, A-Z
	e. g.
355.C5	Chansons d'aventure
355.C68	Courtly love

	History of English literature
	By period
	Medieval. Middle English (1066-1500)
	By form
	Poetry
	Lyric
	Special, A-Z -- Continued
355.I74	Irony
365	Didactic and religious
369	Satirical and humorous
	Drama see PR641+
	Prose see PR251+
	Modern
	General
401	Treatises. Compends
402	Memoirs, letters, etc.
403	Collected essays
404	Addresses, essays, lectures
408.A-Z	Special topics, A-Z
408.A36	Adoption
408.A4	Allegory
408.A58	Apocalyptic literature
408.A66	Architecture and literature
408.A68	Art and literature
408.A7	Arthurian romances
408.A9	Autobiography
408.B53	Bible
408.B67	Boredom
408.C38	Cassandra (Legendary character)
408.C47	Christian literature
408.C6	The comic
408.C63	Conversation
408.C65	Country homes
408.C66	Country life
408.C75	Criminals
408.D47	Deviant behavior
408.D49	Didactic literature
408.D5	Dido, Queen of Carthage
408.D57	Dissenters, Religious
408.D65	Don Juan (Legendary character)
408.D7	Dreams
408.E47	Elizabeth I, Queen of England
408.E77	Error
408.E85	Evil
408.E94	Eye
408.F34	Fantastic literature
408.F36	Fathers

History of English literature
By period
Modern
General
Special topics, A-Z -- Continued

408.F4	Fear
408.F5	Figures of speech
408.F55	Finn MacCumhaill, 3rd cent.
408.G56	Gnosticism
408.G66	Gossip
408.G68	Gothic literature
408.H35	Hand
408.H65	Homosexuality
408.I5	Imagination
408.I53	Imperialism
408.I55	Implication
408.I57	Influence
408.I59	Intercultural communication
408.L38	Law
408.L53	Liberty
408.L57	Literary form
408.L66	London
408.M4	Melancholy
408.M45	Memory
408.M47	Merline (Legendary character)
408.M55	Mimesis
408.M66	Monologue
408.M68	Mountains
408.M7	Mourning customs
408.N37	Narration
408.N38	National characteristics
408.N65	Nonsense literature
408.P28	Parody
408.P3	Pastoral literature
408.P32	Patriotism
408.P4	Pessimism
408.P54	Pilgrims and pilgrimages
408.P6	Plagiarism
408.P62	Plague
408.P63	Plato
408.P65	Politics
408.P67	Popular literature
408.P76	Prometheus (Greek deity)
408.P8	Psychoanalysis
408.P83	Psychology
408.R34	Race
408.R36	Radicalism

History of English literature
 By period
  Modern
   General
    Special topics, A-Z -- Continued

408.R43	Regionalism
	Religious dissenters see PR408.D57
408.R6	Rogues and vagabonds
408.R7	Medieval romances
408.S34	Science
408.S43	Seafaring life
408.S45	Seduction
408.S47	Separation
408.S49	Sex role
408.S57	Slavery
408.S64	Society and literature
408.S66	Space and time
408.S665	Spice trade
408.S67	Sports
408.S74	Stoics
408.S83	Subjectivity
408.S85	Surrealism
408.T37	Taste
408.T72	Tragic, The
408.V54	Violence
408.W35	Walking
408.W37	War
408.W65	Women
408.W67	Working class
(409)	Treatment of special subjects
	see PR408

Renaissance and Reformation. 16th century

411	General works
412	Memoirs, letters, etc.
413	Collected essays
414	Addresses, essays, lectures
418.A-Z	Special topics, A-Z
418.A4	Allegory
418.B66	Books
418.C35	Christian literature
418.C66	Combat
418.D5	Dido, Queen of Carthage
418.D55	Divorce
418.E45	Eloquence
418.H8	Humanism
418.I42	Identity (Psychology)
418.L57	Literary form

History of English literature
By period
Modern
Renaissance and Reformation. 16th century
Special topics, A-Z -- Continued

418.M4	Melancholy
418.M45	Merlin (Legendary character)
418.N35	Nationalism
418.N37	Natural law
418.P3	Pastoral literature
418.P34	Patriotism
418.P6	Plagiarism
418.P65	Politics
418.R6	Rogues and vagabonds
418.R7	Romances, Medieval
418.S52	Shades and shadows
418.S64	Society and literature
418.S74	Stoics
418.T48	Textual criticism
418.U76	Utopias
418.W65	Women
(419)	Treatment of special subjects
	see PR418

Elizabethan era (1550-1640)
Including Elizabethan and Jacobean periods combined

421	General works
422	Memoirs, letters, etc.
423	Collected essays
424	Addresses, essays, lectures
427	Euphuism
428.A-Z	Other special topics, A-Z
428.A44	Alchemy
428.A45	Alienation (Social psychology)
428.A47	Amazons
428.A52	Anatomies
428.A74	Archaeology
428.A76	Art
428.A77	Astronomy
428.A8	Authorship
428.B55	Biography
428.B6	Boadicea, Queen, d. 62
428.B63	Body, Human
428.C24	Cannibalism
428.C25	Capitalism
428.C26	Carnival
428.C27	Castles
428.C28	Casuistry

History of English literature
  By period
    Modern
      Elizabethan era (1550-1640)
        Other special topics, A-Z -- Continued

428.C3	Catholic authors
428.C35	Chiasmus
428.C45	Chivalry
428.C48	Christian literature
428.C6	Classical literature
428.C63	Climate, Influence of
428.C633	Color
428.C635	Commerce
428.C638	Courage
428.C64	Courts and courtiers
428.C74	Crime. Criminals
428.C78	Crying
428.D4	Death
428.D47	Desire
428.D57	Disguise
428.D74	Dreams
	Eastern Europe see PR428.E88
428.E37	Eating disorders
428.E39	Economics
428.E42	Education
428.E43	Elizabeth I, Queen of England
428.E56	Emotions
428.E85	Ethics
428.E88	Europe, Eastern
428.E95	Exorcism
428.E97	Exoticism
428.F45	Feminism
428.G37	Gardens
428.G43	Gender identity
428.G45	Generosity
428.G54	Gifts
428.G74	Grief
428.H43	Heart
428.H57	History
428.H66	Homosexuality
428.H8	Humanism
428.I33	Identity
428.I54	Imperialism
428.I57	Incest
428.I58	Indians
428.I59	Invective
428.I75	Islam

History of English literature
By period
Modern
Elizabethan era (1550-1640)
Other special topics, A-Z -- Continued

428.I8	Italian literature
428.K55	Kings and rulers
428.L29	Labyrinths
428.L35	Language and languages
428.L37	Law
428.L53	Libel and slander
428.M35	Manners and customs
428.M355	Maps
428.M36	Marriage
428.M364	Martyrdom
428.M37	Masculinity
428.M375	Master and servant
428.M38	Material culture
428.M4	Melancholy
428.M44	Memory
428.M55	Minorities
428.M63	Moderation
428.M66	Money
428.M8	Music
428.M9	Mysticism
428.N34	Names
428.N37	Nationalism
428.N39	Nature
428.N46	Neoplatonism
428.N65	Nonsense
428.O24	Ocean travel
428.O43	Old age
428.O73	Oral tradition
428.P36	Pastoral literature
428.P37	Patrons
428.P5	Philosophy
428.P53	Pilgrims and pilgrimages
428.P56	Place (Philosophy)
428.P6	Political science
428.P65	Popular literature
428.P66	Population
428.P67	Prefaces
428.P68	Privacy
428.P7	Proverbs
428.P75	Psychoanalysis
428.P76	Psychological aspects
428.Q44	Queens

History of English literature
  By period
    Modern
      Elizabethan era (1550-1640)
        Other special topics, A-Z -- Continued

428.R35	Race
428.R37	Rape
428.R43	Reason
428.R46	Religion
428.R63	Rogues and vagabonds
428.R65	Romances
428.S45	Self
	Servant and master see PR428.M375
428.S48	Sex
428.S54	Silence
428.S58	Skepticism
	Slander see PR428.L53
428.S64	Social change
428.S65	Social classes
428.S75	Sports
428.S82	Subjectivity
428.T43	Technology
428.T7	Translations
428.T73	Travel
428.T75	Triumph
428.T77	Trust
428.W5	Wit
428.W63	Women
(429)	Treatment of special subjects
	see PR428

     17th century

431	General works
432	Memoirs, letters, etc.
433	Collected essays
434	Addresses, essays, lectures
435	Puritan era (1620-1660)
437	Restoration
438.A-Z	Special topics, A-Z
438.A53	Ancients and moderns, Quarrel of
438.C45	Character sketches. Character books
438.C65	Conformity. Nonconformity
438.D44	Death
438.D48	Devotional literature
438.D53	Didactic literature
438.D54	Digression (Rhetoric)
438.D56	Diseases
438.D57	Dissenters, Religious

History of English literature
  By period
    Modern
      17th century
        Special topics, A-Z -- Continued

438.E363	East Asia
438.E39	Ecology
438.E56	Elizabeth I, Queen of England
438.E95	Exile (Punishment)
438.G37	Gardens
438.H43	Heart
438.H85	Humanism
438.I36	Idolatry
438.I67	Intellectuals
438.M43	Medicine
	Nonconformity see PR438.C65
438.N85	Numismatics
438.P37	Parody
438.P47	Perspective
438.P53	Pirates
438.P54	Plagiarism
438.P65	Politics
438.R42	Realism
438.R45	Religion
438.S25	Salvation
438.S37	Science
438.S45	Self
438.S63	Society
438.S65	Solomon, King of Israel
438.T42	Textual criticism
438.T72	Travel
(439)	Treatment of special subjects see PR438

      18th century

441	Treatises. Compends
442	Collected essays
443	Addresses, essays, lectures
445	Classicism (1700-1750/1800)
447	Romanticism. Return to nature (1750-1880)
448.A-Z	Special topics, A-Z
448.A25	Abnormalities, Human
448.A37	Aesthetics
448.A44	Allegory
448.A55	Animals
448.A75	Architecture
448.A77	Art and literature
448.A87	Authors and patrons

History of English literature
By period
Modern
18th century
Special topics, A-Z -- Continued

448.B53	Bible
448.B63	Body, Human
448.B67	Book reviewing
448.B74	Breeding
448.C34	Capitalism
448.C52	Characters and characteristics
448.C55	Children
448.C58	Clothing and dress
448.C63	Collaborative authorship
448.C64	Colonies
448.C65	Conversation
448.C68	Country homes
448.C7	Courtesy
448.C75	Crime
448.C87	Curiosities and wonders
448.D45	Demythologization
448.D53	Didactic literature
448.D57	Diseases
448.D66	Domestics
448.E36	Economics
448.E43	Emigration and immigration
448.E46	Emotions
448.E57	Enthusiasm
448.E58	Environmentalism
448.E75	Erotic literature
448.E85	Exoticism
448.F34	Fables
448.F45	Feminism
448.F55	Flirting
448.G46	Generosity
448.G6	Gothic literature
448.H65	Homosexuality
	Human abnormalities see PR448.A25
448.I49	Illegitimacy
	Immigration see PR448.E43
448.I52	Imperialism
448.I53	Impressment
448.I534	India
448.I536	Indians
448.I54	Industries. Industrial revolution
448.I73	Italy
448.L53	Life cycle, Human

History of English literature
By period
Modern
18th century
Special topics, A-Z -- Continued

448.L57	Literary forgeries
448.L65	London (England)
448.L66	Loneliness
448.M37	Masculinity
448.M42	Medicine
448.M44	Melancholy
448.M45	Mental illness. Mentally ill
448.M47	Mentoring
	Mentally ill see PR448.M45
448.M57	Misogyny
448.M66	Motherhood. Mothers
	Mothers see PR448.M66
448.N38	National characteristics
448.N54	Night
448.N66	Nonsense Club
448.N67	Nostalgia
448.O75	Orientalism
448.O77	Orphans
448.P28	Passivity (Psychology)
448.P3	Pastoral literature
	Patrons see PR448.A87
448.P47	Personal belongings
448.P5	Philosophy
448.P55	Plagiarism
448.P6	Politics
448.P64	Popular literature
448.P68	Praise
448.P75	Psychology
448.R33	Race
448.R43	Realism
448.R45	Religion
448.R54	Rhetoric
448.S33	Scriblerus Club
448.S34	Seduction
448.S35	Self
448.S4	Sentimentalism
448.S45	Sex differences
448.S5	Sincerity
448.S53	Skepticism
448.S55	Slavery
448.S62	Smallpox
448.S64	Society and literature

History of English literature
  By period
    Modern
      18th century
        Special topics, A-Z -- Continued

448.S69	Space and time
448.S72	Speech
448.S75	Spontaneity (Philosophy)
448.S94	Symbolism
448.S95	Sympathy
	Time and space see PR448.S69
448.T45	Theology
448.V55	Virginity
448.V57	Virtue
448.W37	Waste (Economics)
448.W54	Wild men
448.W65	Women authors
(449)	Treatment of special subjects
	see PR448

      19th century

451	General works
452	Memoirs, letters, etc.
453	Collected essays
454	Addresses, essays, lectures
457	Early 19th century. Romanticism. Lake School

        Victorian era

461	General works
462	Memoirs, letters, etc.
463	Collected essays
464	Addresses, essays, lectures
466	Preraphaelitism
468.A-Z	Special topics, A-Z
468.A29	Adventure
468.A33	Aestheticism
468.A5	Anarchism
468.A54	Anglo-Saxon Revival
468.A56	Animals
468.A58	Anorexia nervosa
468.A66	Apocalyptic literature
468.A72	Archetype (Psychology)
468.A74	Aristocracy
468.A75	Armed Forces
468.A76	Art
468.A78	Arthurian romances
468.A82	Avant-garde (Aesthetics)
468.B45	Belief and doubt
468.B5	Biblical criticism

History of English literature
  By period
    Modern
      19th century
        Special topics, A-Z -- Continued

468.B53	Blacks
468.B55	Blasphemy
468.B58	Blindness
468.B68	Boundary disputes
468.B83	Buddhism
468.C3	Catholicism
468.C42	Celts
468.C5	Children
468.C6	Classicism
468.C65	The comic
468.C66	Consciousness
468.C68	Consumption (Economics)
468.C73	Creation
468.D36	Dandies
468.D42	Death
468.D43	Decadence
468.D57	Diseases
468.E36	Economics
468.E45	Emigration and immigration
468.E65	Epiphanies
468.E93	Examinations
468.F32	Fables
468.F35	Fantastic literature
468.F46	Feminism
468.F56	Finance
468.F72	Fraud
468.F74	Free trade
468.F75	Friendship
468.G37	Geneva
468.G38	Geology
468.G4	German literature
468.G5	Girls
468.G68	Gothic revival (Literature)
	Gypsies see PR468.R63
468.H35	Hair
468.H57	History
468.H63	Home
468.H65	Homosexuality
468.I45	Imagination
	Immigration see PR468.E45
468.I49	Imperialism
468.I517	India

History of English literature
  By period
    Modern
      19th century
        Special topics, A-Z -- Continued

468.I52	Infanticide
468.I53	Influence
468.J49	Jews
468.K56	Knowledge, Theory of
468.L3	Laboring class authors
468.L35	Landscape
468.L38	Law. Lawyers
468.L52	Liberalism
468.L65	London (England)
468.L68	Love
468.M34	Magic
468.M36	Man-woman relationships
468.M38	Masculinity
468.M385	Mass media
468.M39	Material culture
468.M42	Medicine
468.M45	Memory
468.M47	Mesmerism
468.M53	Middle Ages
468.M55	Minstrels
468.M56	Misanthropy
468.M57	Missing link
468.M59	Monsters
468.M596	Mothers. Mother and child
468.M6	Mottoes
468.M63	Mourning customs
468.M85	Murder
468.M86	Music halls (Variety theaters, cabarets, etc.)
468.M87	Mystery
468.N29	Narration (Rhetoric)
468.N293	National characteristics
468.N3	Nature
468.N4	Needlework
468.N6	Nonsense literature
468.N64	Nostalgia
468.O6	Opium
468.O74	Orientalism
468.O77	Outsiders
468.O8	Oxford
468.P15	Pain
468.P19	Parodies
468.P35	People with disabilities

History of English literature
By period
Modern
19th century
Special topics, A-Z -- Continued

468.P37	Periodicals
468.P42	Persephone (Greek deity)
468.P46	Photography
468.P48	Physiology
468.P53	The picturesque
468.P535	Pirates
468.P54	Plagiarism
468.P55	Play
468.P57	Politics
468.P6	Pornography
468.P65	Proverbs
468.P68	Psychology
468.R3	Race
468.R33	Radicalism
468.R35	Railroads. Railroad travel
468.R42	Realism
468.R44	Religion
468.R46	Renaissance
468.R53	Riddles
468.R63	Romanies
468.R65	Romanticism
468.S34	Science
468.S43	Self
468.S46	Sentimentalism
468.S47	Setting
468.S48	Sex
468.S52	Silence
468.S55	Slavery
468.S6	Social conditions
468.S63	Socialism
468.S68	Sound
468.S75	Stereotype (Psychology)
468.S8	Style
468.S83	Sun
468.S86	Supernatural
468.S9	Symbolism
468.T4	Technology
468.T48	Textual criticism
468.T49	Thought and thinking
468.T73	Transportation
468.V35	Vampires
468.V54	Vikings

PR

History of English literature
By period
Modern
19th century
Special topics, A-Z -- Continued

468.V57	Virginity
468.V59	Visual perception
468.V86	Vulgarity
468.W34	Wagner, Richard, 1813-1883
468.W35	Walking
468.W37	War
468.W38	Waterloo (Belgium), Battle of, 1815
468.W5	Wholeness
468.W6	Women
(469)	Treatment of special subjects
	see PR468

20th century

471	General works
472	Memoirs, letters, etc.
473	Collected essays
474	Addresses, essays, lectures
	The Irish revival see PR8750+
478.A-Z	Special topics, A-Z
478.A43	Alchemy
478.A53	Anarchism
478.A87	Authors
478.B46	Bloomsbury group
478.C38	Causation
478.C65	Consciousness
478.D35	Dance
478.D43	Decadence
478.E76	Erotic literature
478.F35	Fantastic literature
478.F45	Feminism
478.F87	Futurism
478.H57	History and literature
478.H65	Homosexuality
478.I53	Imperialism
478.I54	Inklings (Group of writers)
478.I83	Italy
478.J34	Jack the Ripper
478.J68	Journalism
478.L38	Latin America
478.L66	London (England)
478.M34	Masculinity
478.M37	Mass media
478.M6	Modernism

History of English literature
  By period
    Modern
      20th century
        Special topics, A-Z -- Continued

478.M94	Mysticism
478.M96	Myth
478.N37	National characteristics, English
478.O83	Oxford University
478.P33	Palestine
478.P36	Pastoral literature
478.P45	Photography
478.P64	Politics
478.P66	Popular literature
478.P665	Postcolonialism
478.P67	Postmodernism
478.R33	Radicalism
478.R43	Regionalism
478.R58	Rivers
478.S26	Science
478.S57	Society and literature
478.S6	Spanish Civil War
478.S64	Spiritualism
478.S66	Sports
478.S78	Style
478.T47	Terrorism
478.V56	Violence
478.V68	Voyages to the otherworld
478.W37	War
478.W65	World War I
478.W67	World War II
(479)	Treatment of special subjects
	see PR478

      21st century

481	General works
488.A-Z	Special topics, A-Z

Poetry

500	Periodicals. Societies. Serials

  General works

501	Early to 1850
502	Recent
503	Collected essays
504	Addresses, essays, lectures
504.5	Study and teaching

  Special classes of authors see PR111+
  Special topics

505	Laureates

	History of English literature
	Poetry
	Special topics -- Continued
507	Popular poetry. Ballads
	For traditional folk poetry and ballads see PR976+
508.A-Z	Other, A-Z
508.A44	Allusions
508.A45	Alphabet
508.A54	Anthologies
508.A66	Archetype (Psychology)
508.A7	Art
508.A76	Astronomy
508.A88	Authority
508.B5	Birds
508.C65	Christianity
508.C66	Cities and towns
508.C68	Classical literature
508.C7	Color
508.C79	Crime
508.D5	Diction
508.D57	Discourse analysis
508.D8	Dreams
508.E55	Epitaphs
508.F34	Fairies
508.F36	Fantasy
508.H28	Hallucinations and illusions
508.H3	Happiness
508.H45	Hermetism
508.H5	History and politics
508.H6	Homosexuality
508.I45	Imagination
508.I48	Inspiration
508.I49	Intention
508.I5	Introductions
508.J4	Jesus Christ
508.K56	Knowledge, Theory of
508.L3	Language
508.L5	Liberty
508.L58	Literary form
508.L7	Love
508.M35	Masculinity
508.M43	Metaphor
508.M75	Music
508.M8	Mysticism
508.M87	Myth
508.M9	Mythology
508.N2	National characteristics

History of English literature
  Poetry
    Special topics
      Other, A-Z -- Continued

508.N3	Nature
508.N84	Numbers
508.P34	Parentheses
508.P35	Personification
508.P84	Point of view
	Politics see PR508.H5
508.P9	Psychology
508.Q3	Quaker poets
508.R4	Religion
508.R5	Repetition
508.R55	Ritual
508.R84	Ruins
508.S27	Satire
508.S3	Science
508.S4	The Sea
508.S43	Secret societies
508.S65	Space and time
508.S95	Syntax
508.T56	Time
508.T72	The Tragic
508.T74	Trees
508.U6	Uneducated poets
508.V45	Versification
508.V55	Violence
508.V63	Vocabulary
508.W6	Women
509.A-Z	Special forms, A-Z
509.A6	Allegories
509.B53	Blank verse
509.C45	Children's poetry
509.D5	Didactic
509.D7	Doggerel
	Dramatic monologues see PR509.M6
509.E4	Elegiac
509.E7	Epics
509.E73	Epigrams
509.F2	Fables
509.F7	Free verse
509.H4	Heroic verse
509.L8	Lyrics
509.M6	Monologues. Dramatic monologues
509.N6	Nonsense verse
509.O24	Occasional verse

	History of English literature
	Poetry
	Special forms, A-Z -- Continued
509.O3	Odes
509.P3	Pastorals
509.P7	Prose poems
509.S7	Sonnets
509.U53	Unfinished poems
509.V54	Villanelles
	By period
	Anglo-Saxon see PR171+
	Medieval see PR311+
521-529	15th-16th centuries (1485-1550) (Table PR1)
531-539	Elizabethan era (1550-1640) (Table PR1)
	Including Elizabethan and Jacobean periods combined
	17th century
541-549	General (Table PR1 modified)
545.A-Z	Special topics, A-Z
545.C4	Charles I
545.C56	Civil War, 1642-1649
545.C674	Conscience
545.J2	Jacobean poets
545.M4	Metaphysical poets
	18th century
551-559	General (Table PR1 modified)
559.A-Z	Special forms, A-Z
559.E7	Epics
559.M63	Mock-heroic poetry
561-569	Restoration and Augustan era (1660-1750) (Table PR1)
571-579	Romanticism. Return to nature (1750-1830) (Table PR1)
	19th century
581-589	General (Table PR1)
590	Early 19th century
	Including Romanticism, Lake School, and the Age of Wordsworth
	Victorian era
591-599	General (Table PR1 modified)
595.A-Z	Special topics, A-Z
595.C55	City and town life
595.D42	Decadence (Literary movement)
595.P7	Preraphaelitism
595.R54	Rhymers' Club
595.R6	Romanticism
	20th century
601-609	General (Table PR1 modified)

	History of English literature
	Poetry
	By period
	20th century
	General -- Continued
605.A-Z	Special topics, A-Z
605.F39	Fathers
605.M63	Modernism
605.M68	The Movement
605.O85	Otherworld
605.P67	Postmodernism
605.R64	Romanticism
605.S44	Self
605.S63	Spanish Civil War
605.S87	Surrealism
605.W65	World War I
605.W66	World War II
610	Through 1960
611	1961-2000
	21st century
612	General works
613.A-Z	Special topics, A-Z
	For list of Cutter numbers for special topics not limited to the 21st century, see Table PR1 5.A+
614.A-Z	Special forms, A-Z
	For list of Cutter numbers see Table PR1 9.A+
618	Dialogue
	Drama
621	Periodicals. Societies. Collections
623	Dictionaries
625	General works
627	Addresses, essays, lectures
	Special classes of authors see PR111+
	Special topics and forms
631	Comedy
633	Tragedy
635.A-Z	Other, A-Z
635.A3	Adaptations
635.A78	Arthur, King
635.A8	Astrology
635.B8	Burlesque
635.B83	Businessmen
635.C47	Characters and characteristics
635.C5	Children's plays
635.C54	Chronology
635.C6	Church
635.C65	Cleopatra, Queen of Egypt, d. 30 B.C.

History of English literature
　　Drama
　　　Special topics and forms
　　　　Other, A-Z -- Continued

635.C67	Closure (Rhetoric)
635.C69	Consciousness
635.C7	Court life
635.D48	Devil
635.D65	Domestic drama
635.E86	Evil
635.F33	Family
635.F35	Farce
	Folk drama see PR979+
635.G4	Gentry
635.H4	Heroes
635.H5	Historical drama
635.H65	Homosexuality
635.I5	Interludes
635.I67	Irish
635.I7	Irony
635.L47	Letters
635.L6	Lost plays
635.M27	Magic
635.M4	Masques
635.O53	One-act plays
635.P3	Pastoral drama
635.P45	Pilgrims and pilgrimages
635.P5	Plots
635.P66	Professions
635.P7	Prose drama
635.P73	Proverbs
635.R4	Religious drama
635.R44	Repentance
635.S28	Satire
635.S38	Self
635.S4	Sentimental drama
635.S62	Soldiers
635.S64	Soliloquy
635.T45	Theater
635.T55	Timur, 1336-1405
635.T7	Tragi-comedy
635.V4	Verse drama
635.W6	Women

　　By period
　　　Medieval

641	General works
643.A-Z	Special, A-Z

History of English literature
  Drama
    By period
      Medieval
        Special, A-Z -- Continued

643.C67	Comedy
643.C7	Corpus Christi pageants
643.D47	Devil
643.I57	Interludes
643.J83	Judgment Day
643.M37	Mary Magdalene, Saint
643.M5	Miracle plays
643.M7	Moralities
643.M8	Mysteries
643.P64	Political plays
643.S3	Satiric plays
644.A-Z	Individual plays, cycles, and locales, A-Z
644.C32	Castle of perseverance
644.C4	Chester
644.C6	Coventry Corpus Christi plays
644.C7	Coventry plays (i.e. Ludus Coventriae or N-Town plays)
644.E28	East Anglia
	Ludus Coventriae see PR644.C7
	N-town plays see PR644.C7
644.T6	Towneley
644.W3	Wakefield
644.W58	Wisdom (Morality play)
644.Y6	York

      16th century
        Including Tudor period in general

646	General works
647	Collected essays
648	Addresses, essays, lectures
649.A-Z	Special topics, A-Z
649.B5	Bible
649.C6	Court life
649.D53	Didactic drama
649.H86	Humanism
649.K55	Kings and rulers
649.M37	Marriage
649.M38	Masques
649.P6	Politics
649.R4	Religious drama
649.R46	Rhetoric
649.W37	War

	History of English literature
	Drama
	By period -- Continued
651-658	Elizabethan era (1550-1640) (Table PR5)
	Including Elizabethan and Jacobean-Caroline periods combined
	17th century
671-678	General (Table PR5)
680	Puritan era (1620/40-1660)
691-698	Restoration (1660-1700) (Table PR5)
	18th century
701-708	General (Table PR5)
	Augustan era. Classicism (1700-1750/80)
711	General works
712	Collected essays
713	Addresses, essays, lectures
714.A-Z	Special topics, A-Z
714.C6	Comedy
714.M37	Masculinity
714.P6	Politics
714.S2	Satire
714.S6	Society
714.T68	Tragedy
714.T7	Translations
714.W6	Women
	Romanticism. Return to nature (1750/80-1830)
716	General works
717	Collected essays
718	Addresses, essays, lectures
719.A-Z	Special topics, A-Z
719.C47	Characters and characteristics
719.G68	Gothic revival
719.I45	Imperialism
719.P65	Politics
719.V4	Verse drama
719.W66	Women
	19th century
721-728	General (Table PR5)
	Victorian era
731	General works
732	Collected essays
733	Addresses, essays, lectures
734.A-Z	Special topics, A-Z
	For list of Cutters, see Table PR5 8.A+ Use insofar as applicable
734.F3	Failure
734.N3	Naturalism

History of English literature
 Drama
  By period
   19th century
    Victorian era
     Special topics, A-Z -- Continued

734.P4	Pessimism
734.P65	Popular drama
734.V47	Verse drama

   20th century

735	Periodicals. Societies. Serials
736	General works
737	Collected essays
738	Addresses, essays, lectures
739.A-Z	Special topics, A-Z
739.A27	Absurd (Philosophy). Theater of the absurd
739.A33	Adaptations
739.A35	Adultery
739.A44	Alienation
739.A77	Art. Artists
739.C63	Cognitive dissonance
739.C65	Comedy
739.C77	Cruelty
739.D42	Death
739.D48	Detective and mystery plays
739.D58	Diseases
739.E38	Education
739.F36	Family
739.F37	Farces
739.F45	Femininism
739.H5	Historical drama
739.H65	Homosexuality
739.I33	Identity (Psychology)
739.L3	Language
739.M37	Marriage. Married people
739.M44	Melodrama
739.M6544	Monologue
739.M68	Motherhood
739.M87	Music-halls
	Mystery plays see PR739.D48
739.N83	Nuclear warfare
739.P56	Place (Philosophy)
	Poetic drama see PR739.V47
739.P62	Poets
739.P64	Politics
739.P73	Prejudices
739.R33	Radio plays

	History of English literature
	Drama
	By period
	20th century
	Special topics, A-Z -- Continued
739.R37	Realism
739.R4	Religion
739.S45	Sex role
739.S62	Socialism
	Theater of the absurd see PR739.A27
739.T7	Tragicomedy
739.V47	Verse drama
739.W67	World War II
	21st century
740	Periodicals. Societies. Serials
741	General works
744.A-Z	Special topics, A-Z
	Prose
750	Periodicals. Societies. Serials
751	General works
753	Collected essays
754	Addresses, essays, lectures
	Special classes of authors see PR111+
756.A-Z	Special topics, A-Z
756.A38	Aesthetics
756.A5	Animals
756.A9	Autobiography
756.B56	Biography
756.C48	Children
756.C56	Confession
756.C9	Country life
756.D52	Dialogues
756.D58	Divorce
756.H57	History
756.H95	Hysteria
756.I4	Illegitimacy
756.I46	Infanticide
756.M36	Masculinity
756.N38	Natural history
756.O43	Oedipus complex
756.P55	Philosophy
756.P64	Polemics
	Rhythm see PE1561
756.R65	Romanticism
756.S33	Science
756.S38	Self
756.S39	Sentimentalism

	History of English literature
	Prose
	Special topics, A-Z -- Continued
756.S46	Social history
756.S47	Social ideals
756.S62	Social problems
756.T45	Theater
756.T72	Travel
756.U86	Utopias
756.W65	Women
756.W67	World War I
	By period
	Anglo-Saxon see PR221+
	Medieval see PR251+
767	Through 1600
769	17th and 18th centuries
771-778	19th century (1780-1900) (Table PR6)
781-788	Victorian era (Table PR6)
801-808	20th century (Table PR6)
811-818	21st century (Table PR6)
	By form
	Prose fiction. The novel
821	General works
823	Collected essays
824	Addresses, essays, lectures
824.5	Study and teaching
825	Digests, synopses, etc.
	Special topics
826	Theory, philosophy, aesthetics. Technique
829	The short story
830.A-Z	Other special topics, A-Z
830.A27	Abused women
830.A32	Actors
830.A36	Adolescence
830.A37	Adultery
830.A38	Adventure stories
830.A39	Africans
830.A394	Aging
830.A397	Alchemy
830.A4	Alcoholism
830.A42	Alienation
830.A44	Allusions
830.A46	Alternative histories (Fiction)
830.A49	Amnesia
830.A52	Androgyny (Psychology)
830.A53	Anglo-Indians
830.A54	Animals

History of English literature
    Prose
       By form
          Prose fiction. The novel
             Special topics
                Other special topics, A-Z -- Continued

830.A7	Architecture
830.A72	Arctic regions
830.A74	Art
830.A76	Arthurian romances
830.A78	Artists
830.A79	Authors and readers
830.A794	Authorship
830.A8	Autobiography
830.B35	Bankruptcy
830.B4	Beauty, Personal
830.B44	Belief and doubt
830.B47	Betrothal
830.B52	Bildungsromans
830.B54	Biographical fiction
830.B56	Blondes
830.B58	Blushing
830.B62	Body fluids
830.B63	Body, Human
830.B66	Boredom
830.B68	Botany
830.B72	Brainwashing
830.B75	British Museum
830.B77	Brothers and sisters
830.C25	Capitalism
830.C47	Characters and characteristics
830.C475	Charity
830.C48	Childbirth
830.C5	Children
830.C513	Children's stories
830.C516	Chivalry
830.C52	Christmas
830.C527	Cinderella
830.C53	City and town life
830.C56	Clergy
830.C58	Clerks
830.C587	Closure (Rhetoric)
830.C59	Clothing and dress
	Colleges see PR830.U5
830.C6	Colonies
830.C63	The comic
830.C633	Commerce

History of English literature
  Prose
    By form
      Prose fiction. The novel
        Special topics
          Other special topics, A-Z -- Continued

830.C634	Commitment
830.C636	Communication
830.C64	Conduct of life
830.C65	Conspiracies
830.C66	Conversation
830.C67	Country life
830.C68	Courtroom fiction
830.C69	Courtship
830.C74	Crime
830.C75	Crowds
830.C84	Cultural relations
830.C92	Cycles
830.D35	Dance
	Daughters and fathers see PR830.F36
830.D37	Death
830.D372	Decadence
830.D373	Degeneration
830.D377	Democracy
830.D38	Demonology
830.D39	Description
830.D4	Detective and mystery stories
830.D44	Developing countries
830.D49	Dialogue
830.D52	Diary fiction
830.D53	Didactic fiction
830.D56	Disasters
830.D57	Dissenters
830.D65	Domestic fiction
830.D68	Doubles
830.D96	Dystopias
830.E25	Eavesdropping
830.E37	Economics
830.E38	Education
830.E46	Emotions
830.E6	Epic
830.E64	Epiphanies
830.E65	Epistolary fiction
830.E67	Ethics
	European War, 1914-1918 see PR830.W65
830.E85	Evangelicalism
830.E95	Evolution

History of English literature
  Prose
    By form
      Prose fiction. The novel
        Special topics
          Other special topics, A-Z -- Continued

830.E97	Exiles
830.E98	Experience
830.E982	Experimental fiction
830.E985	Explorers
830.F27	Fairy tales
	Falsehood see PR830.T78
830.F29	Family
830.F3	Fantastic fiction. Fantasy
830.F33	Fascism
830.F35	Fate and fatalism
830.F36	Fathers and daughters
830.F37	Fathers and sons
830.F45	Feminism
830.F46	Femmes fatales
830.F47	Festivals
830.F48	Fetishism
830.F64	Folklore
830.F65	Food
830.F67	Free will and determinism
830.F7	French Revolution
830.G32	Gambling
830.G33	Gardens
830.G34	Gay men
830.G35	Gender identity
830.G354	Genealogy
830.G357	Gentry
830.G36	Germany
830.G45	Ghost stories
830.G57	Girls
	God, Providence and government of see PR830.P734
830.G59	Gossip
	Gothic tales see PR830.T3
830.G6	Governesses
830.G67	Grief
830.G7	Grotesque
830.G84	Guilt
830.H4	Heroes and heroines
830.H5	Historical novels
830.H6	Holocaust, Jewish (1939-1945)
830.H65	Home

                    History of English literature
                      Prose
                        By form
                          Prose fiction. The novel
                            Special topics
                              Other special topics, A-Z -- Continued

830.H67	Homosexuality
	Horror tales see PR830.T3
830.H72	Horses
830.H8	Humanism
830.H85	Humorous stories
830.H93	Hysteria
830.I3	Identity (Psychology)
830.I4	Illustrations
	Imaginary voyages see PR830.V6
830.I54	Imperialism
830.I55	Impostors and imposture
830.I57	Impressionism
830.I59	Incest
830.I593	Inclosures
830.I6	India
830.I615	Individualism
830.I62	Industry
830.I63	Intellectuals
830.I64	Intimacy (Psychology)
830.I65	Inventions
830.I7	Irony
830.I75	Islands
830.J4	Jews
830.K54	Knowledge, Theory of
830.L3	Labor. Working class
830.L34	Landscapes
830.L35	Language
830.L38	Latin America
830.L39	Law. Lawyers
830.L43	Legal stories
830.L46	Lesbians
830.L47	Letters
830.L54	Life cycle, Human
830.L58	Liverpool
830.L65	London
830.L69	Love
	Manners and customs see PR830.S615
830.M34	Marginality, Social
830.M36	Marriage
830.M367	Masochism
830.M37	Masquerades

History of English literature
  Prose
    By form
      Prose fiction. The novel
        Special topics
          Other special topics, A-Z -- Continued

830.M38	Material culture
830.M42	Medicine
830.M44	Memory
830.M45	Men
830.M46	Mental illness
830.M47	Mentoring
830.M475	Metaphor
830.M48	Mexico
830.M53	Middle class
830.M63	Modernism
830.M65	Money
830.M67	Morals
830.M69	Mothers
830.M73	Motion pictures
830.M85	Museums
830.M87	Music. Musicians
830.M93	Mysticism
830.M95	Myth
830.N35	Names
830.N353	Napoleonic Wars, 1800-1815
830.N355	Narcissism
830.N3554	Narratees
830.N3557	National characteristics
830.N356	Nationalism
830.N357	Naturalism
830.N36	Nature
830.N49	Newspapers
830.N65	Nonverbal communication
830.N66	Nostalgia
830.N68	Novelists
830.N87	Nurses
830.O28	Obsessive-compulsive disorder
830.O33	Occultism
830.O46	Odors
830.O64	Openings (Rhetoric)
830.O74	Orient
830.P28	Parodies
830.P3	Pastoral fiction
830.P34	Patriarchy
830.P44	Performing arts
830.P444	Pessimism

History of English literature
   Prose
     By form
       Prose fiction. The novel
         Special topics
          Other special topics, A-Z -- Continued

830.P45	Philosophy in fiction
830.P455	Phobias
830.P46	Physicians
830.P47	Physiognomy
830.P49	Picaresque literature
830.P5	The Picturesque
830.P52	Pilgrims and pilgrimages
830.P525	Place (Philosophy)
830.P53	Plots
830.P54	Pluralism (Social sciences)
830.P57	Point of view
830.P59	Police
830.P6	Politics
830.P66	Poor
830.P68	Popular literature
830.P69	Postmodernism (Literature)
	Primitive society see PR830.S63
830.P7	Prisons
830.P72	Privacy
830.P726	Professions
830.P73	Prostitutes
830.P734	Providence and government of God
830.P74	Psychoanalysis
830.P75	Psychology
830.P78	Publishers and publishing
830.P8	Puritanism
830.Q45	Quests
830.R34	Race
830.R4	Realism
830.R45	Regionalism
830.R5	Religious element in fiction
830.R53	Repetition
830.R54	Repression (Psychology)
830.R56	Return motif
	Robinsonades see PN3432
830.R7	Romances
830.R73	Romanticism
830.R75	Rosicrucians
830.S317	Scandals
830.S32	Scapegoat
830.S34	Science

History of English literature
  Prose
    By form
      Prose fiction. The novel
        Special topics
          Other special topics, A-Z -- Continued

830.S35	Science fiction
830.S4	Sea
830.S42	Seafaring life
830.S423	Secrecy
830.S424	Secretaries
830.S425	Seduction
830.S427	Self
830.S43	Self-deception
830.S44	Sensationalism
830.S45	Sentimentalism
830.S47	Servants
830.S48	Setting
830.S49	Sex
830.S5	The Sick
830.S52	Sisters
830.S53	Skepticism
830.S56	Small groups
830.S58	Snobs and snobbishness
830.S6	Social classes
830.S615	Social life and customs
	Social marginality see PR830.M34
830.S62	Social problems
830.S625	Socialism
830.S63	Primitive society
830.S635	Soliloquy
	Sons and fathers see PR830.F37
830.S64	Speech
830.S65	Spy stories
830.S76	Stream of consciousness fiction
830.S82	Subjectivity
830.S824	Sublime, The
830.S83	Success
830.S84	Suicide
830.S85	Supernatural
830.S87	Suspense
830.S9	Symbolism
830.S93	Symbolism of numbers
830.T3	Tales of terror. Gothic tales. Horror tales
830.T47	Terrorism
830.T5	Time
830.T64	Toleration

	History of English literature
	Prose
	By form
	Prose fiction. The novel
	Special topics
	Other special topics, A-Z -- Continued
830.T67	Totalitarianism
830.T7	The Tragic
830.T73	Tragicomedy
830.T75	Travel
830.T76	Triangles (Interpersonal relations)
830.T78	Truthfulness and falsehood
(830.U48)	Underdeveloped areas
	see PR830.D44
830.U5	Universities and colleges
830.U7	Utopias
830.V3	Vampires
830.V56	Visions
830.V6	Voyages, Imaginary
830.W34	Wagner, Richard, 1813-1883
830.W37	War
830.W47	Wessex (England)
830.W5	Widows
830.W53	Windows
830.W6	Women
830.W63	Work
	Working class see PR830.L3
830.W65	World War I
830.W66	World War II
830.Y68	Young adult fiction
	By period
833	16th century (1485-1550)
	Elizabethan era (1550-1640)
	Including Elizabethan and Jacobean combined
836	General works
837	Collected essays
838	Addresses, essays, lectures
839.A-Z	Special topics, A-Z
839.A86	Authorship (as a theme)
839.G46	Geography. Geographical discoveries
839.G7	Greek romances
839.L3	Labor. Working class
839.L67	Love
839.W65	Women
	Working class see PR839.L3
	17th century
841	General works

History of English literature
  Prose
    By form
      Prose fiction. The novel
        By period
          17th century -- Continued

842	Collected essays
843	Addresses, essays, lectures
844.A-Z	Special topics, A-Z
844.P52	Picaresque romances

          18th century

851	General works
852	Documents, contemporary records, etc.
853	Collected essays
854	Addresses, essays, lectures
855	Sources, relations, foreign influences
858.A-Z	Special topics, A-Z
	For list of Cutter numbers see PR830.A+

          19th century

861	General works
862	Documents, contemporary records, etc.
863	Collected essays
864	Addresses, essays, lectures
865	Sources, relations, foreign influences
868.A-Z	Special topics, A-Z
	For list of Cutter numbers see PR830.A+

          Victorian era

871	General works
872	Documents, contemporary records, etc.
873	Collected essays
874	Addresses, essays, lectures
875	Sources, relations, foreign influences
878.A-Z	Special topics, A-Z
	For list of Cutter numbers see PR830.A+

          20th century

881	General works
882	Documents, contemporary records, etc.
883	Collected essays
884	Addresses, essays, lectures
885	Sources, relations, foreign influences
	Study and teaching see PR824.5
888.A-Z	Special topics, A-Z
	For list of Cutter numbers see PR830.A+

          21st century

889	General works
890.A-Z	Special topics, A-Z
	For list of Cutter numbers see PR830.A+

History of English literature -- Continued
    Oratory

901	General works
902	Addresses, essays, lectures
	By period
903	To 1600
904	17th century
905	18th century
906	19th century
907	20th century
907.2	21st century
908	Diaries
	Letters
911	General works
912	Addresses, essays, lectures
	By period
913	To 1600
914	17th century
915	18th century
916	19th century
917	20th century
918	21st century
	Essays
921	General works
922	Addresses, essays, lectures
	By period
923	To 1600
924	17th century
925	18th century
926	19th century
927	20th century
928	21st century
	Wit and humor
	For collections see PN6172.2+
931	General works
932	Addresses, essays, lectures
	By period
933	To 1600
934	17th century
935	18th century
936	19th century
937	20th century
938	21st century
	Miscellany. Curiosa. Eccentric literature
941	General works
942	Addresses, essays, lectures
	By period

	History of English literature
	Miscellany. Curiosa. Eccentric literature
	By period -- Continued
943	To 1600
944	17th century
945	18th century
946	19th century
947	20th century
948	21st century
	Folk literature
	For general works on folk literature, see GR
	Cf. PZ8.1 Juvenile literature (Folklore, legends, romance)
(951)	General works. Histories. Treatises
(953)	Collected essays
(957)	Addresses, essays, lectures
	By period
961	To 1600
(963)	17th century
(965)	18th century
(967)	19th century
(968)	20th century
(971.A-Z)	Special topics, A-Z
(971.E7)	Eulenspiegel
	Special forms
	Chapbooks
972	General works. History
	Collections
973	Reprints. By editor
974	Originals
975	Separate issues
	Poetry. Ballads (Broadsides, etc.)
976	General works. History
977	Collections
	For early texts see PR1181+
978.A-Z	Special ballads, etc., A-Z
	e. g.
	Thomas Rhymer (Ballad)
978.T5	Texts
978.T52	Criticism
	Drama. Folk drama, mumming plays, etc.
979	General works. History
980	Collections
981.A-Z	Special plays, A-Z
	Under each:
	.x *Texts*
	.x2 *Criticism*
	Proverbs see PN6400+

History of English literature -- Continued
990   Juvenile literature (General)
             For special genres, see the genre
          Collections of English literature
1098   Periodicals. Societies. Serials
          General collections
             Including collections not comprehensive, but covering greater
                periods than PR1119+
1101   Collections published before 1801
1105   Collections published after 1801
1109   Selections, anthologies, etc.
            Cf. PN6075+ Selections for daily reading
1110.A-Z   Special classes of authors, A-Z
1110.B5   Blacks
1110.C5   Children
1110.C6   College students
1110.G39   Gays
1110.J48   Jews
1110.L33   Laboring class
1110.M55   Minorities
1110.P65   People with disabilities
1110.S65   Soldiers
1110.W6   Women
1111.A-Z   Special topics (Prose and verse), A-Z
            For collections on special topics by a specific class of
               author see PR1110.A+
1111.A6   Animals
1111.A85   Arthurian romances
1111.A9   Autumn
1111.B47   Biography
1111.B5   Birds
1111.C2   Cats
1111.C515   Chartism
1111.C52   Children
1111.C53   Christmas
1111.C56   Coal mines and mining
1111.C58   Cornwall, England
1111.C6   Country life
1111.C67   Cricket
1111.C7   Crime
            Dedications see PR1111.P7
1111.D4   Devon
1111.D6   Dogs
1111.D64   Don Juan (Legendary character)
1111.D7   Dreams
1111.D75   Drinking customs
1111.E25   Easter

Collections of English literature
　General collections
　　Special topics (Prose and verse), A-Z -- Continued

1111.E35	Edinburgh (Scotland)
1111.E38	Education
1111.E5	England
1111.E57	Entertaining
1111.E74	Erotic literature
1111.F27	Fall of man
1111.F3	Family
1111.F33	Fantasy
1111.F453	Feminism
1111.F53	Fishing
1111.F54	Flagellants and flagellation
1111.F7	France
1111.G3	Gardens
1111.G48	Ghosts
1111.G67	Gothic revival
1111.G7	Grotesque
1111.H45	Herbs
1111.H5	History and patriotism
1111.H57	Homosexuality
1111.H6	Horses
1111.I57	Indians
1111.I58	Industrialization
1111.I59	Infants
1111.L3	Lake District, England
1111.L6	London
1111.L63	Loneliness
1111.L7	Love
1111.M45	Men
1111.M55	Monsters
1111.M57	Mothers
1111.M95	Mythology
1111.N28	Narcotics
1111.N29	Nationalism
1111.N3	Nature
1111.N45	Negation
1111.N5	Night
1111.N66	Nonsense literature
1111.O24	Ocean
1111.O25	Ocean travel
1111.O74	Orient
1111.P35	Parent and child
1111.P38	Parodies
	Patriotism see PR1111.H5
1111.P6	Politics

	Collections of English literature
	General collections
	Special topics (Prose and verse), A-Z -- Continued
1111.P7	Prefaces, prologues, dedications, etc.
	Prologues see PR1111.P7
1111.R35	Railroad travel
1111.S25	Sacraments
1111.S3	Science
1111.S43	Seafaring life
1111.S45	Seduction
1111.S49	Sin
1111.S53	Soccer
1111.S55	South Africa
1111.S57	Spain
1111.S58	Spirituality
1111.S7	St. Andrews (Scotland)
1111.S78	Supernatural
1111.S9	Switzerland
1111.T35	Teddy bears
1111.T87	Tuscany (Italy)
1111.V47	Venice (Italy)
1111.V54	Villages
1111.W33	Walking
1111.W37	War
1111.W43	West Country, England
1111.W6	Women
1111.W7	Work
1111.Y56	Yorkshire
	Translations from foreign literatures (including translations with texts) see PN6019+
	Translations of English literature into foreign languages
	Cf. PR1179.A+ Translations of English poetry
1112	Polyglot collections
1113	French
1114	German
1115	Italian
1116.A-Z	Other, A-Z
	By period
	Anglo-Saxon see PR1490+
	Early English Text Society
1119.A2	Original series
1119.E5	Extra series
	Medieval (to 1600)
1120	General collections
	Special (Metrical romances) see PR2064+
	Special (Prose romances) see PR2115
	Renaissance. 15th-16th centuries

	Collections of English literature
	By period
	Renaissance. 15th-16th centuries -- Continued
1121	General collections
1125	Elizabethan era
	Seventeenth century
1127	General collections
1129	Puritan era
1131	Restoration
	Eighteenth century
1134	General collections
1136	Augustan era. Classicism
1139	Romanticism. Return to nature
	Nineteenth century
1143	General collections
1145	Victorian era
	Twentieth century
1148	General collections
1149	Through 1960
1150	1961-
1151	Twenty-first century
	Poetry
1170	Periodicals. Societies. Serials
1171	Collections published before 1801
1173	Collections published 1801-1960
1174	Collections published 1961-
1175	Selections
1175.3	Anthologies of poetry for children
1175.5	Digests, synopses, etc.
1175.8	Concordances, dictionaries, indexes, etc.
1176	Selections for the days or months of the year
	For selections from a single author, see the author's works, e.g. PR4203, Browning yearbooks
	For literary almanacs and calendars, see AY68, AY756, AY836, etc.
1177	Selections from women poets
1178.A-Z	Special classes of authors, A-Z
1178.B55	Blacks
1178.C5	Children
1178.C64	College students
1178.G39	Gay men
1178.J48	Jews
1178.M45	Mennonites
1178.M46	Mentally ill
1178.N8	Nuns
1178.P6	Poets laureate
1178.P75	Prisoners

	Collections of English literature
	Poetry
	Special classes of authors, A-Z -- Continued
1178.Q3	Quakers
1178.R7	Royalty
1178.S25	Sailors
1178.S3	School verse
1178.V4	Veterans
1178.W67	Working class
	Translations from foreign languages
	see the language in PQ, etc.
	Translations of English poetry
1179.A2	Polyglot collections
1179.A5-Z	By language
	Subarrange by title or editor, etc.
	Cf. PN6110.A+ General collections of poetry
1180	Adaptations, prose versions, etc.
	Special forms and subjects
	Class here collections strictly limited to English authors
1181	Ballads
	For traditional folk ballads see PR977
1184	Love poems. Love and marriage
	Lyrics. Songs
1187	General collections
1188	Songbooks
	Including popular and minor
1191	Religious poetry
	For hymns see BV343+
	Sea and sailors see PN6110.S4
1194	Minor forms
	Including ballads, rondeau, chant royal, sestina, etc.
1195.A-Z	Other special. By subjects or class, A-Z
1195.A2	Aberfan, Wales
1195.A37	Aeronautics, Military
1195.A44	AIDS (Disease)
1195.A46	Air
1195.A5	America
1195.A64	Animals
1195.A7	Art
1195.A75	Arthur, King
1195.B28	Bahai poetry
1195.B33	Balaklava (Ukraine), Battle of, 1854
1195.B43	Beatles (Musical group)
1195.B5	Birds
1195.B7	Boys, Poetry for
1195.B84	Bunting, Basil
1195.C18	Canada

Collections of English literature
  Poetry
    Special forms and subjects
      Other special. By subjects or class, A-Z -- Continued

1195.C19	Canterbury tales
1195.C2	Carols
1195.C4	Catholic poetry
1195.C45	Cats
1195.C453	Causley, Charles, 1917-
1195.C455	Chartism
1195.C46	Childbirth
1195.C47	Children
	Christ see PR1195.J4
1195.C48	Christian poetry
1195.C49	Christmas
1195.C53	Clerihews
1195.C55	Colonies
1195.C56	Colors
1195.C6	Concrete poetry
1195.C62	Conduct of life
1195.C63	Conservation of natural resources
1195.C64	Cornwall, England
1195.C67	Country life
1195.C7	Cricket (Game)
1195.D3	Dancing
1195.D45	Derbyshire (England)
1195.D6	Didactic poetry
1195.D63	Dinosaurs
1195.D65	Dogs
1195.D67	Dorset, England
1195.D7	Drinking customs
1195.D72	Drug abuse
1195.D73	Dryden, John
1195.E17	Earth
1195.E5	Elegies
1195.E52	England
1195.E53	Epic poetry
	Epilogues see PR1195.P7
1195.E6	Epithalamia
1195.E7	Erotic verse
1195.E9	Europe
1195.F34	Fairies
1195.F343	Fairy tales
1195.F35	Family
1195.F36	Fantastic poetry
1195.F38	Farm life
1195.F45	Feminism

Collections of English literature
  Poetry
    Special forms and subjects
      Other special. By subjects or class, A-Z -- Continued

1195.F5	Flowers
1195.F66	Food
1195.F68	France
1195.F7	Freedom
1195.F73	Friendship
1195.F8	Fugitive verse
1195.G2	Gardens
1195.G25	Geology
1195.G47	Ghosts
1195.G485	Gipsy poetry. Romany poetry
1195.G5	Poetry for girls
1195.G58	Golden age (Mythology)
1195.G6	Gordon family
1195.G65	Gothic poetry (Literary genre)
	Gypsy poetry see PR1195.G485
1195.H25	Haiku
1195.H3	Hebrew poetry
1195.H35	Heroic verse
1195.H4	Highlands of Scotland
1195.H5	Historical poetry. Patriotic poetry
1195.H55	Hitchhiking
1195.H57	Hodgson, Ralph
1195.H574	Holly, Buddy
1195.H58	Homosexuality
1195.H59	Hong Kong
1195.H6	Hospitals
1195.H8	Humorous poetry
	Cf. PR1195.S3 Satire
1195.I53	Infants, Death of
1195.I55	Inspiration
1195.I58	Invective
1195.I7	Ireland
1195.J4	Jesus Christ
1195.J6	Jonson, Ben
1195.K4	Kerouac, John
1195.K48	Kilpeck (Hereford and Worchester)
1195.L3	Labor. Working class
1195.L33	Lake District, England
1195.L34	Landscape
1195.L36	Laudatory poetry
1195.L37	Law and lawyers
1195.L6	London
1195.L8	Lullabies

Collections of English literature
  Poetry
    Special forms and subjects
      Other special. By subjects or class, A-Z -- Continued

1195.L85	Luther, Martin
1195.M15	Machinery
1195.M18	Maclean, John
1195.M2	Madrigals
1195.M22	Magic
1195.M24	Manners and customs
1195.M33	Medicine
1195.M36	Melancholy
1195.M53	Mice
	Military aeronautics see PR1195.A37
1195.M6	Monsters
1195.M63	Mothers
1195.M65	Mountains
1195.M67	Muktananda Paramhamsa, Swami
1195.M8	Mythology
1195.N2	Narrative poetry
1195.N3	Nature
1195.N52	Night
1195.N53	Nightingales
1195.N64	Nonsense verse
1195.N8	Nuns
1195.O3	Odes
1195.O64	Operas
1195.O8	Outdoor life
1195.P2	Painter poets
1195.P25	Parents
1195.P27	Parodies
1195.P3	Pastorals
	Patriotic poetry see PR1195.H5
1195.P47	Pets
1195.P55	Philosophy
1195.P63	Poetry as a topic
	Political poetry see PR1195.H5
1195.P66	Preraphaelitism
1195.P665	Presley, Elvis
1195.P67	Printing
1195.P7	Prologues and epilogues
1195.P74	Prose poems
1195.P76	Proverbs
1195.R28	Radicalism
1195.R3	Railroads
1195.R33	Raising of Jairus' daughter (Miracle)
1195.R47	Revolutionary poetry

Collections of English literature
　Poetry
　　Special forms and subjects
　　　Other special. By subjects or class, A-Z -- Continued

1195.R55	Rivers
	Romany poetry see PR1195.G485
1195.R6	Roses
1195.R66	Royal Canadian Mounted Police
1195.R83	Rugby football
1195.S27	Sappho
1195.S3	Satire
	Cf. PR1195.H8 Humorous poetry
1195.S4	Science
1195.S414	Scotland
1195.S417	Sea poetry
1195.S42	Seasons
1195.S43	Shaw, Bernard, 1856-1950
1195.S44	Slavery
1195.S5	Sonnets
1195.S65	Soul
1195.S68	Sound poetry
1195.S7	South Africa
1195.S73	Sports
1195.S74	Spring
1195.S86	Sunday
1195.S87	Surrealism
1195.T55	Time
1195.T63	Toasts
	Tobacco see GT3020+
1195.T73	Trees
1195.T76	Trout
1195.U6	United States
1195.V2	Vagabond verse
1195.V3	Vers de société
1195.V68	Voyages and travel
1195.W25	Wallingford, England
1195.W33	War
1195.W34	Warwickshire
1195.W37	Water
1195.W45	Whales
1195.W5	Williamson, David
1195.W54	Winter
1195.W6	Women
1195.W64	Wordsworth, William
	Working class see PR1195.L3
1195.W65	World War I
1195.W66	World War II

Collections of English literature
  Poetry -- Continued
    By period
      Anglo-Saxon see PR1490+

1203	Medieval
	Cf. PR1972.G35+ Gawain-poet (Collected works)
	Cf. PR2064 Metrical romances (Collected)
1204	Early modern (1250-1700)
1205	16th (-17th) century
1207	Elizabethan era
	17th century
1209	General collections
1211	Puritan era
1213	Restoration
	18th century
1215	General collections
1217	Augustan era. Classicism
1219	Pre-Romanticism. Return to nature
	19th century
1221	General collections
1222	Early 19th century. Romanticism
1223	Victorian era
1224	Late 19th and early 20th centuries (Recent. Late Victorian to present)
	20th century
1225	General collections
1226	Through 1960
1227	1961-2000
1228	21st century
	Drama
	Comprehensive
1241	Early through 1800
1243	1801-
1245	Selected plays. Anthologies, etc.
1246.A-Z	Special classes of authors, A-Z
1246.B53	Blacks
1246.W65	Women
	Special
1248	Comedies
1251	Farces
1253	Fairy plays. Masques
1255	Historical plays. Chronicle plays
1257	Tragedies
1259.A-Z	Other, A-Z
1259.B87	Burlesques
1259.C57	College and school drama
1259.C6	Courtroom drama

Collections of English literature
Drama
Special
Other, A-Z -- Continued

1259.D4	Detective and mystery plays
1259.H65	Homosexuality
1259.H67	Horror plays
1259.I5	Interludes
1259.L47	Lesbianism
1259.M4	Melodrama
1259.M6	Moralities
	Mumming plays see PR981.A+
	Mystery plays see PR1259.D4
1259.O5	One-act plays
1259.P46	People with disabilities
1259.P64	Political plays
	Prologues and epilogues see PR1195.P7
	Punch and Judy see PN1972+
1259.R33	Radio plays
	School drama see PR1195.C6
1259.S93	Suffragists
1259.W65	Women

By period
Medieval: Mysteries, miracle plays, moralities
Cf. PR641+ English literary history

1260	General collections
1261.A-Z	Individual plays and cycles, A-Z
1261.C3	Castle of perseverance
1261.C54	Chester plays
1261.C59	Coventry Corpus Christi plays
1261.C6	Coventry plays (i.e. Ludus Coventriae or N-town plays)
1261.D4	Deluge
1261.E8	Everyman
1261.M3	Mankind
1261.M34	Mary, Blessed Virgin, Saint
1261.P38	Passion play
1261.P75	Pride of life
1261.T68	Towneley plays
1261.W5	Wisdom
1261.Y67	York plays
1262	Early modern. Pre-Shakespearian drama
1263	Elizabethan era (1550-1640)
	Including Elizabethan and Jacobean periods
	17th-18th century
1265	General works
	17th century

	Collections of English literature
	Drama
	By period
	17th-18th century
	17th century -- Continued
1265.3	General collections
1265.5	Jacobean-Caroline
1265.7	Puritan era
1266	Restoration
1269	18th century
1271	19th century
1272	20th century
1272.2	21st century
1272.5.A-Z	Translations of English drama. By language, A-Z
	Minor material of individual authors
	Class here mostly unbound and uncataloged material
1273.Z9A-.Z9Z	Copyright deposit and other pamphlet plays, 19th-20th
	centuries, in part uncataloged
	A collection to be later reclassified and catalogued
1273.Z99A-.Z99Z	Plays in typewritten form
	Prose (General)
	For prose fiction cataloged before July 1, 1980, see PZ
	General collections
1281	Early to 1800
1283	1801-
1285	Selections, anthologies, etc.
1286.A-Z	Special classes of authors, A-Z
1286.B53	Blacks
1286.C3	Catholics
1286.P75	Prisoners
1286.W6	Women
	By period
	Anglo-Saxon see PR1490+
	Medieval see PR1120+
1293	16th century (Elizabethan)
1295	17th century (Puritan era)
1297	18th century
	19th century
1301	General works
1302	Early 19th century (Romanticism)
1304	Victorian era
1307	20th century
1307.2	21st century
1307.5.A-Z	Translations of English prose fiction. By language, A-Z
1309.A-Z	Special subjects and forms, A-Z
1309.A38	Adventure stories
1309.A42	Aeronautics

Collections of English literature
  Prose (General)
    Special subjects and forms, A-Z -- Continued

1309.A53	Animals
1309.B52	Bible
1309.C33	Calcutta (India)
1309.C36	Cats
1309.C47	Characters and characteristics
1309.C48	Children
1309.C5	Christmas
1309.C58	Contract bridge
1309.C6	Country life
1309.C7	Crime. Criminals
1309.D36	Deadly sins
1309.D38	Degeneration
1309.D4	Detective and mystery stories
	Dime novels see PR1309.P45
1309.D63	Dogs
1309.D67	Doppelgängers. Doubles
1309.D78	Drugs
1309.D84	Dwellings
1309.E75	Erotic stories
1309.E85	Extrasensory perception
1309.F26	Fairy tales
1309.F3	Fantastic fiction
1309.F35	Fathers and sons
1309.G5	Ghost stories
1309.G63	God
1309.G73	Greek civilization
1309.H45	Historical fiction
1309.H55	Holmes, Sherlock (Fictitious character)
1309.H57	Homosexuality
1309.H6	Horror stories
1309.H64	Horses. Horse racing
1309.I44	Imaginary letters
1309.I45	Immigrants
1309.I46	Imperialism
1309.I47	India
1309.I5	Industry
1309.I57	Internet
1309.I74	Ireland
1309.L3	Labor. Working class
1309.L43	Legal stories
1309.L47	Lesbianism
1309.L64	London
1309.L68	Love
1309.M54	Millennium celebrations (Year 2000)

	Collections of English literature
	Prose (General)
	Special subjects and forms, A-Z -- Continued
1309.M6	Months
1309.M88	Music
1309.N3	Nature
1309.N65	Noir fiction
1309.O64	Opera
1309.P45	Penny dreadfuls
1309.P6	Poland
1309.P64	Politics
1309.P67	Popular literature
1309.R3	Railroad stories
1309.R47	Revenge
1309.R58	Robin Hood (Legendary character)
1309.R6	Rock music
1309.R64	Rogues and vagabonds
1309.S2	Satires
1309.S3	Science fiction
1309.S4	Sea stories
1309.S43	Seasons
1309.S5	Short stories
1309.S62	Social isolation
1309.S63	Social problems
	Sons and fathers see PR1309.F35
1309.S68	Sports stories
1309.S7	Spy stories
1309.S75	Steampunk fiction
1309.S8	Students
1309.S9	Supernatural
1309.T42	Teddy bears
1309.T5	Theater
1309.T73	Travel
1309.V36	Vampires
1309.V4	Venus (Planet)
1309.W37	War stories
1309.W4	Western stories
1309.W5	Witchcraft
	Working class see PR1309.L3
1309.W7	Women
	Oratory
	General collections
1321	Early through 1800
1322	1801-
1323	Selections, etc.
	By period
1324	Through 1600 (1640)

Collections of English literature
  Oratory
    By period -- Continued
1325   17th-18th centuries
1326   19th century
1327   20th century
1328   21st century
1329.A-Z   Special, A-Z
1329.C3   Catholic authors
1330   Diaries
      Letters
        General collections
1341   Early through 1800
1342   1801-
1343   Selections, etc.
       By period
1344   Through 1600 (1640)
1345   17th-18th centuries
1346   19th century
1347   20th century
1348   21st century
1349.A-Z   Special, A-Z
1349.C4   Children's letters
1349.C5   Letters to children
1349.L8   Love letters
           Cf. HQ801.3 How to write love letters
      Essays
        General collections
1361   Early through 1800
1362   1801-
1363   Selections, etc.
       By period
1364   Through 1600 (1640)
1365   17th-18th centuries
1366   19th century
1367   20th century
1368   21st century
1369.A-Z   Special, A-Z
         e. g.
1369.E5   The Englishman
1369.G8   The Guardian
1369.R3   The Rambler
1369.S7   The Spectator
1369.T2   The Tatler
     Wit and humor see PN6146.2+
     Folk literature see PR951+
     Other miscellaneous collections see PN6233+

	Anglo-Saxon literature
	Collections
	Including collections of Anglo-Saxon and Early English
	Contemporary
1490	Exeter book (Codex Exoniensis) (Table P-PZ41)
	For individual works from the Exeter book see
	PR1509+
	Cf. PR1760+ Riddles
1495	Vercelli book (Codex Vercellensis) (Table P-PZ41)
1500.A-Z	Other contemporary collections, A-Z
	Caedmon manuscript (Oxford. University. Bodleian
	Library. MSS. Junius 11) see PR1600+
1500.N67	Nowell codex
1502	Modern
	Selections. Anthologies
1505	General works
1506	Concordances, indexes, etc.
1508	Modern English translations
1508.2.A-Z	Other languages, A-Z
	Subarrange by translator
1508.2.G4	German
	Individual authors and works
1509.A	A - Ad
	Address of the soul to the body see PR1774
1519.A	Ad - Ael
1519.A45	Aegidius (Legend)
1519.A5	Aelfheah (St. Alphege)
	Aelfric
	Collected works
1520	By date
1521	By editor
1522	Selections
	Separate parts see PR1525+
	Translations
1523	Modern English. By translator
1524	Other. By language
	Subarrange by translator
	Separate works
	Homilies
1525	General works
1526.A-Z	Special homilies, A-Z
1526.G8	St. Gregory's day (Table PR10)
1526.S4	Sevenfold gifts of the spirit (Table PR10)
1527	Lives of the saints. Passions of the saints (Table PR9)
1528	Sigewulf's Interrogations on Genesis (Table PR9)
1529	Virelai (Table PR9)

	Anglo-Saxon literature
	Individual authors and works
	Aelfric
	Separate works -- Continued
1530.A-Z	Other special, A-Z
	Subarrange each by Table PR10
1531	Dictionaries, indexes, etc.
1533	General works
	Criticism
1534	General
1535	Textual. Manuscripts, etc.
	Sources
1536	General works
1537.A-Z	Other, A-Z
1538	Language, grammar, style
1539.A	Aelfr - Alf
	e. g.
1539.A5	Alexander's letter to Aristotle
	Alfred, the Great
	Including works connected with his name
	Collected works
1540	By date
1541	By editor
1542	Selections
	Translations
1543	Modern English. By translator
1544	Other. By language
	Subarrange by translator
	Separate works
1545	Translation of St. Augustine's Soliloquies (Table PR9)
1547	Translation of Bede's Ecclesiastical history (Table PR9)
1549	Translation of Boethius's Consolatio philosophiae (Table PR9)
1551	Translation of Gregory's Cura pastoralis (Table PR9)
1552	Translation of Gregory's Dialogues (Table PR9)
1553	Laws of the Anglo-Saxons (Table PR9)
1555	Translation of Orosius (Table PR9)
1556	Translation of Proverbs (Table PR9)
1557	Translation of Psalms (Table PR9)
1560	Periodicals. Societies. Collections
1561	Dictionaries, indexes, etc.
	Biography see DA153
	Criticism
1564	General works
1565	Textual. Manuscripts, etc.
	Special
1566	Sources

	Anglo-Saxon literature
	Individual authors and works
	Alfred, the Great
	Criticism
	Special -- Continued
1567.A-Z	Other, A-Z
1568	Language, grammar, style
1569.A	Alf - Ang
	Alfred aethelings's death
	Alphege, St. see PR1519.A5
	Andreas see PR1644+
	Anglo-Saxon Chronicle see DA150+
1572.A	Ang - Az
1572.A7	Apollonius of Tyre
	Apostles' Fates see PR1703
	Apuleius. Herbarium see PR1726
1575	Azarias (Table P-PZ37)
	Cf. PR1601 Caedmon
1576.A-.B	Az - Be
	Battle of Brunanburh see PR1592
	Battle of Maldon see PR1594
	Be domes daege (De die judicii)
1578	Beda Venerabilis (Table P-PZ37)
	Cf. PR1547 Alfred's Translation of Bede
	Beowulf
1580	Texts. By editor or date
1581	Selections. By editor or date
1583	Modern English versions. By translator
1584.A-Z	Translations into foreign languages. By language, A-Z
	Subarrange by translator
	Criticism
1585	General works
	Including authorship
1586	Textual
1587.A-Z	Special subjects, A-Z
1587.A7	Archaeology
1587.C3	Cain (Biblical figure)
1587.C4	Celtic literature
1587.C43	Ceremonial exchange
1587.C47	Christianity
1587.D43	Death
1587.D7	Dragons
1587.E5	Elegiac poetry
1587.F85	Funeral rites and ceremonies
1587.G43	Geats
1587.H45	Heroes
1587.I76	Irony

	Anglo-Saxon literature
	Individual authors and works
	Beowulf
	Criticism
	Special subjects, A-Z -- Continued
1587.K55	Kings and rulers
1587.M65	Monsters
1587.M9	Mythology
1587.P75	Proverbs
1587.P77	Psychology
1587.S28	Scandinavia
1587.T7	Translations
1587.W43	Wealhtheow, Queen of the Danes
1587.W54	Wiglaf
1588	Language, grammar, etc.
	Bestiary see PR1752+
1590	Blickling homilies (Table P-PZ41)
1591	Breviary (Benedictine)
1592	Brunanburh. Athelstan's victory (Table P-PZ41)
1594	Byrhtnoth's death. The battle of Maldon (Table P-PZ41)
1597.B-.C	By - Ca
	Caedmon
	Collected works
1600	By date
1601	By editor
1602	Selections
	Translations
1603	Modern English. By translator
1604	Other. By language
	Subarrange by translator
	Separate works
	Christ and Satan see PR1630+
1607	Daniel (Table PR11)
	Works formerly ascribed to Caedmon are retained here in order not to separate the literature of the subject
	Dream of the Rood; Ruthwell cross see PR1680+
1609	Exodus (Table PR11)
	Works formerly ascribed to Caedmon are retained here in order not to separate the literature of the subject
	Including Exodus and Daniel
1611	Genesis (Table PR11)
	Works formerly ascribed to Caedmon are retained here in order not to separate the literature of the subject
1613	Hymn (Table PR11)
	Judith see PR1730+
1620	Periodicals. Societies. Collections
1622	Dictionaries, indexes, etc.

	Anglo-Saxon literature
	Individual authors and works
	Caedmon -- Continued
1623	General works
	Criticism
1624	General works
1625	Textual. Manuscripts, etc.
	Special
1626	Sources
1627.A-Z	Other, A-Z
1628	Language, grammar, style
1629.C	Cae - Chr
	e. g.
1629.C5	Ceadda, Saint, Bp. Legend
1630-1634	Christ and Satan (Table P-PZ34)
	Fall of the Angels
	Christ's Harrowing of Hell
	Christ's Temptation
	The Chronicle see DA150+
	Cf. PR1519.A Aelfheah
	Cf. PR1569.A Alfred aetheling's death (1036)
	Cf. PR1592 Brunanburh (957)
	Cf. PR1594 Byrhtnoth (991)
	Cf. PR1686 Eadgar's coronation (973)
	Cf. PR1687 Eadgar's death (975)
	Cf. PR1689 Eadmund (942)
	Cf. PR1691 Edward the Martyr's death (978)
	Cf. PR1693 Edward the Confessor's death (1066)
1637.C	Chr - Cy
	Creation, Wonders of see PR1792
	Cross of Ruthwell see PR1680+
	Cynewulf
	Collected works
1639	By date
1640	By editor
1641	Selections
	For separate parts see PR1644
	Translations
1642	Modern English. By translator
1643.A-Z	Other languages, A-Z. By translator
	Separate works
1644	Andreas (Table PR12)
1645	Christ (Table PR12)
	Dream of the rood see PR1680+
1647	Elene (Table PR12)
	Fates of the apostles see PR1703
	Gifts of men (Bi mauna craeftum) see PR1746

	Anglo-Saxon literature
	Individual authors and works
	Cynewulf
	Separate works -- Continued
	Guthlac see PR1722
	Judith see PR1730+
1652	Juliana (Table PR12)
	Phoenix see PR1750
	Riddles see PR1760+
1660	Periodicals. Societies. Collections
1662	Dictionaries, indexes, etc.
1663	General works
	Criticism
1664	General
1665	Textual. Manuscripts, etc.
	Special
1666	Sources
1667.A-Z	Other, A-Z
1667.A93	Authorship
1667.P6	Plots
1668	Language, grammar, style
	Daniel see PR1607
1672-1676	Deor's lament (Table P-PZ34)
1678.D	De - Dr
1678.D65	Dōmes daege
1680-1684	Dream of the rood (Table P-PZ34)
1686	Edgar's coronation (Table P-PZ41)
1687	Edgar's death (Table P-PZ41)
1689	Edmund. Liberation of the five boroughs (Table P-PZ41)
1691	Edward the Martyr's death (979) (Table P-PZ41)
1693	Edward the Confessor's death (1066) (Table P-PZ41)
1698	Evangelium de virginibus (Table P-PZ41)
	Exeter book see PR1490
	Exodus see PR1609
1700.E-.F	Ex - Fa
	Falsehood of men see PR1742
1703	Fates of the apostles (Table P-PZ41)
1705.F	Fates - Father
	Fates of men see PR1744
1707	Father's instruction (Table P-PZ41)
1709.F	Father - Finn
1709.F56	Finding of the True Cross
1710-1714	Finnsburh (Table P-PZ34)
	Cf. PR1580 Beowulf
	Genesis see PR1611
1718.G	Gen - Gno
	Gifts of men see PR1746

Anglo-Saxon literature
Individual authors and works -- Continued

1720	Gnomic verses (Table P-PZ41)
1722	Guthlac (Table P-PZ41)
1724.G-.H	Guth - Herb
	Harrowing of Hell see PR1630+
1726	Herbarium of Apuleius (Table P-PZ41)
	Cf. QK75 Botany
1728	Husband's message (Table P-PZ41)
	Cf. PR1790 The wife's complaint
1730-1734	Judith (Table P-PZ34)
1735.K	K
1735.K44	Kentish Psalm 50
1736	Leechbook (Laece boc) (Table P-PZ41)
1738.L-.M	Leech - Man
	Maldon, Battle of see PR1594
1742	Man's falsehood (Bi manna lease) (Table P-PZ41)
1744	Man's fate (Bi manna wyrdum) (Table P-PZ41)
1746	Man's gifts (Bi manna craeftum) (Table P-PZ41)
1748	Man's mind (Bi manna mode) (Table P-PZ41)
1749.M-.P	Man - Ph
1749.M28	Margaret, of Antioch
1749.M3	Martyrologium
1749.M43	Medicina de quadrupedibus
	Cf. PA6567 Latin texts
	Cf. R127.A+ Medicine
1749.M5	Menologium
1750	Phoenix (Table P-PZ41)
1752-1756	Physiologus (Table P-PZ34)
1757.P	Physiologus - Pz
	Placitus, Sextus. Medicina de quadrupedibus see
	PR1749.M43
1757.P7	Psalter (Paris psalter)
1758.Q	Q
1759.R	R - Rid
1760-1764	Riddles (Table P-PZ34)
	Cf. PR1490 Exeter book
1765.R	Rid - Ruin
1765.R55	The riming poem
1766	The ruin (Table P-PZ41)
1768.R-.S	Ru - Sa
1768.R83	Rune poem
	Ruthwell cross see PR1680+
1770	Salomon and Saturn (Table P-PZ41)
1772	Seafarer (Table P-PZ41)
1773.S	Seaf - Soul
1773.S68	Soul and body

	Anglo-Saxon literature
	Individual authors and works -- Continued
1774	Soul's address to the body (Table P-PZ41)
1775.S	Soul - Sz
1776.T	T
1777.U	U
1778.V	V
1779.W	W - Wal
1780-1784	Waldere (Table P-PZ34)
1786	Wanderer (Table P-PZ41)
1788	Widsith (Table P-PZ41)
1790	Wife's complaint (Table P-PZ41)
	Cf. PR1728 Husband's message
1792	Wonders of creation (Table P-PZ41)
1793.W	Won - Wul
1795-1799	Wulfstan (Table P-PZ35)
	Latin literature of the Anglo-Saxon period
	see subclass PA
	Anglo-Norman period. Early English. Middle English
	Individual authors and works
	For plays and play cycles see PR1261.A+
	For metrical romances see PR2065.A+
1803.A	A - Al
1804	Alexander of Hales (Table P-PZ39)
1805.A	Al - An
1806-1810	Ancren riwle (Table P-PZ34)
1812	Andrew of Wyntoun (Table P-PZ39)
1813.A54	Anne (Mother of the Virgin Mary), Saint, Stanzaic life of
1813.2	Aquinas, St. Thomas
	see class B
1815.A	Aq - As
1817	Assumptio Mariae
1818.A	As - Au
1818.A55	Assembly of gods
1818.A93	Audelay, John, fl. 1426
1820-1828	Aungerville, Richard (Richard of Bury) (Table P-PZ33)
1829.A	Au - Ay
	Ayenbite of inwyt see PR2085.M3
1831	Bacon, John (Table P-PZ39)
1833	Barbour, John (Table P-PZ37)
1834.B	Barb - Bes
1836	Bestiary (Table P-PZ41)
1837.B	Bes - Blz
1837.B6	Bible
	Class here poetical paraphrases and Bible stories
	For other works, see subclass BS
	Blind Harry see PR1989.H6

Anglo-Norman period. Early English. Middle English

Individual authors and works -- Continued

1840.B48	Boke of stones
1840.B5	Bokenham, Osbern (Table P-PZ40)
1841	Bradwardine, Thomas (Table P-PZ39)
1842	Buke of the chess (Table P-PZ41)
1843	Canute song (Table P-PZ41)
1845	Capgrave, John (Table P-PZ39)
1846.C	Cap - Cax
1846.C27	Castleford's chronicle
1846.C3	Catharina, Saint of Alexandria. Legend
1846.C35	Catonis disticha

Class here Middle English versions only

For modern English translations of the Latin text see PA6273.A+

1847-1848	Caxton, William (Table P-PZ36)
1849.C3	Cecilia, Saint. Legend
1849.C4	Chandos, the herald
1849.C6	Charles, Count of Angouleme, Duke of Orleans (Table P-PZ40)

Cf. PQ1553.C5 Old French literature

Chaucer, Geoffrey

Collected works

1850	Original editions and reprints. By date
1851.A-Z	Editions with commentary. By editor, A-Z
1852	Selections. Anthologies
1853	Minor poems. Collected fragments
1854	Translations. By language

Subarrange by translator

1855	Adaptations, modernization, etc.

For the Canterbury tales see PR1872

Separate works

1856-1857	Anelida and Arcite (Table PR13)
1859-1860	Boethius's De consolatione philosophiae (Table PR13)
1862-1863	Book of the Dutchess (Table PR13)

Canterbury tales

Texts

1865	By date
1866	By editor
1867	Selections
1868.A-Z	Special parts, A-Z

Under each text:

	.x	By date
	.x2	By editor
	.x3	Criticism
1870.A-Z	Translations. By language, A-Z	

Subarrange by translator

	Anglo-Norman period. Early English. Middle English
	Individual authors and works
	Chaucer, Geoffrey
	Separate works
	Canterbury tales
	Translations -- Continued
1870.A1	Modern English
	Including literal prose
1872	Miscellaneous: Adaptations, versions for children, etc.
	For foreign languages see PR1870.A+
	Indexes see PR1903
	Criticism
1874	General works
1875.A-Z	Special topics, A-Z
1875.A44	Allegory and symbolism
1875.B63	Body, Human
1875.C65	Contests
1875.E84	Ethics
1875.F67	Folklore
1875.F7	Franklin
1875.H66	Homosexuality
1875.H67	Host
	Human body see PR1875.B63
1875.L6	Love
1875.M3	Manuscripts
1875.M34	Masculinity (Psychology)
1875.O26	Occupations
1875.O73	Oral interpretation
1875.P4	Peasants
1875.P45	Performing arts
1875.P5	Philosophy
1875.P55	Play
1875.P79	Psychology
1875.P85	Puns and punning
1875.R45	Religion
1875.R65	Romances
1875.S45	Self. Self-consciousness
	Self-consciousness see PR1875.S45
1875.S63	Social problems
1875.S75	Storytelling
1875.T48	Textual criticism
1875.T55	Time
1875.V34	Value
	Other works
1877-1878	House of fame (Table PR13)
1881-1882	Legend of good women (Table PR13)

	Anglo-Norman period. Early English. Middle English
	Individual authors and works
	Chaucer, Geoffrey
	Separate works
	Other works -- Continued
1885-1886	Parlament of foules (Table PR13)
1888-1889	Romaunt of the rose (Table PR13)
1891-1892	Treatise on the astrolabe (Table PR13)
1895-1896	Troilus and Criseyde (Table PR13)
1897.A-Z	Other works, A-Z
	e. g.
1897.A2	The ABC (Hymn to the Blessed Virgin)
1898.A-Z	Doubtful and spurious works, A-Z
1901	Periodicals. Societies. Collections
1903	Dictionaries. Indexes, etc.
	Biography, criticism, etc.
1905	General works
1905.1	Family. Ancestors. Descendants
1906	Relations to contemporaries
1906.5	The age of Chaucer
1907	Homes and haunts. Landmarks, etc.
1908	Anniversaries. Celebrations
1909	Portraits, monuments, etc.
1910	Miscellaneous. Relics, etc.
1911	Authorship
	Sources
1912.A2	Collections
1912.A3	General works
1912.A5-Z	Indebtedness to special works or authors
1913.A-Z	Influence on other writers, A-Z
1914	Influence on English literature
1915.A-Z	Influence on other literatures. By region or country, A-Z
1921	Chronology of works
	Criticism and interpretation
1924	General works
	Characters
1927	General works
1928.A-Z	Special classes, A-Z
1928.J48	Jews
1928.M45	Men
1928.W64	Women
1931	Plots. Scenes. Time, etc.
1933.A-Z	Treatment and knowledge of special subjects, A-Z
1933.A44	Allegory and symbolism
1933.B57	Birds
1933.C65	Complaint poetry
1933.D74	Dreams

Anglo-Norman period. Early English. Middle English

  Individual authors and works

    Chaucer, Geoffrey

      Criticism and interpretation

        Treatment and knowledge of special subjects, A-Z --

          Continued

1933.E74	Ethics
1933.F43	Feces
1933.F7	Frame stories
1933.G37	Gardens
1933.G45	Geography
1933.G47	Gesture
1933.H57	History
1933.H85	Humor
1933.I75	Irony
1933.K58	Knights and knighthood
1933.K6	Knowledge, Theory of
1933.L38	Law
1933.M4	Medicine
1933.M96	Mythology
1933.N27	Narration
1933.N3	Naval art and science
1933.O75	Orient
1933.P46	Philosophy
1933.P64	Politics
1933.P79	Psychology
1933.R4	Religion
1933.S24	Saint Valentine's Day
1933.S27	Satire
1933.S3	Science
1933.S35	Sex. Sex role
1933.S59	Social conditions
1933.S73	Speech
	Symbolism and allegory see PR1933.A44
1933.T73	Tragic, The
1933.W37	War
1939	Textual criticism, commentaries

Language. Style, etc.

1940	General works
1941	Dictionaries. Concordances

    Grammar

1943	General works

      Special topics

1945	Pronunciation
1946	Use of words
1948	Syntax
1951	Versification

	Anglo-Norman period. Early English. Middle English
	Individual authors and works
	Chaucer, Geoffrey
	Language. Style, etc. -- Continued
1954	Dialect, etc.
1955.C	Chaucer - Chro
1955.C5	Chestre, Thomas
(1961.A-Z)	Chronicles
	Benedict of Peterborough see DA209.T4
	Bok, Thomas
	see subclass DA
	Eadmer see DA190+
	Florence of Worcester see DA150+
	Geoffrey of Monmouth see DA140+; DA150+
	Gervase of Canterbury
	see subclass DA
	Gesta regum Britanniae see DA140+
	Gesta Stephani
	see subclass DA
	Giraldus Cambrensis see DA725; DA930+; DA933+
	Henry of Huntingdon see DA190+
	Jocelin of Brakelond
	see subclass DA
	Ordericus Vitalis
	see subclass DA
	Paris, Matthew see DA220+
	Ralph of Coggeshall
	see subclass DA
	Ralph of Diceto
	see subclass DA
	Richard of Devizes see DA150+
	Robert de Monte
	see subclass DA
	Roger of Hoveden see DA200+
	Roger of Wendover see DA220+
	Simeon of Durham
	see subclass DA
	William of Malmesbury see DA190+
	William of Newburgh see DA200+
1964	Cleanness (Table P-PZ41)
1965.C	Cleanness - Cursor mundi
1965.C6-.C63	Cocke Lorell's bote (Table P-PZ43)
1965.C65-.C653	Court of Sapience (Table P-PZ43)
1965.C7-.C73	Croxton play of the sacrament (Table P-PZ43)
1966	Cursor mundi (Table P-PZ41)
1968.D2-.D3	Dame Siriz (Table P-PZ43a)
1968.D4	Davy, Adam (Table P-PZ38)

Anglo-Norman period. Early English. Middle English
Individual authors and works -- Continued
De Taystek, John. Lay folks' catechism see PR2019.L37

1968.D5-.D52	Debate of the carpenter's tools (Table P-PZ43a)
1968.D6-.D63	Debate of the body and soul (Table P-PZ43)
1968.D65	Demaundes off Love
	Duns Scotus, John
	see class B
1968.E3-.E33	Editha, Saint. Legend (Table P-PZ43)
1968.E4-.E43	Erkenwald, Saint. Legend (Table P-PZ43)
1968.E5-.E53	Erthe upon erthe (Table P-PZ43)
1968.E68-.E683	Estorie del Evangelie (Table P-PZ43)
1969	Fabyan, Robert (Table P-PZ39)
1971	Fortescue, Sir John (Table P-PZ37)
1972.G2-.G23	Gamelyn (Table P-PZ43)
	Gawain-poet
	Class here the works treated collectively
	For individual works, see PR1964, PR2065.G3, PR2110, PR2111
1972.G35	Texts. By date
1972.G353	Criticism
1972.G42	Genesis and Exodus (Middle English poem)
1972.G5	Geoffrey of Vinsauf
1972.G54	Gesta Romanorum
	Class here early versions only
	For later English translations of the Latin text see PA8323
1974	Gildas
	Giraldus Cambrensis see DA725; DA930+; DA933+
1978	Godric
1980-1988	Gower, John (Table P-PZ33)
1989.G2	Gregorius (Legend)
1989.G4	Grey, William (Table P-PZ40)
1989.G6	Grosseteste, Robert (Table P-PZ40)
1989.G8	Guilforde, Sir Richard (Table P-PZ40)
1989.H2-.H23	Hali Meidenhad (Table P-PZ43)
1989.H3	Harrowing of Hell
1989.H35	Hay, Gilbert, Sir, fl. 1456 (Table P-PZ40)
1989.H6	Henry, the minstrel ("Blind Harry") (Table P-PZ38)
	Henry of Bracton
	see classes J, K
1990.H4	Henryson, Robert (Table P-PZ40)
1990.H45	Herebert, William, ca. 1270-1333 (Table P-PZ40)
1990.H8	Higden, Ranulf (Table P-PZ40)
1992.H	Hig - Huc
1992.H47	Hoccleve, Thomas, 1370?-1450? (Table P-PZ40)
1992.H5	Holland, Sir Richard, fl. 1450 (Table P-PZ40)

Anglo-Norman period. Early English. Middle English

Individual authors and works -- Continued

1994	Huchowne of the Awle Ryale (Table P-PZ37)
	Cf. PR1964 Cleanness
	Cf. PR2065.G3+ Sir Gawayne
	Cf. PR2110 Patience
	Cf. PR2111 Pearl
1995.H	Hu - Hw
1998	Hwon holy chireche is under uote (Table P-PZ41)
1999.H8	Hylton, Walter (Table P-PZ40)
1999.I3	Idle, Peter, d. 1474? (Table P-PZ40)
1999.I38	Imitatio Christi
1999.I5	Isle of ladies
2000-2004	James I of Scotland (Table P-PZ35)
2006	John of Sailsbury (Table P-PZ39)
2007.J67	Joseph, of Arimathea
2007.J7	Juliana (Middle English) (Table P-PZ38)
2007.K4	Kempe, Margery, b. ca. 1373 (Table P-PZ40)
2008	The land of Cokayne
	Langland, William (Piers Plowman)
2010	Texts. By editor or date
2011	Selections. By editor or date
2013	Modern English versions. By translator
2014.A-Z	Translations into foreign languages. By language, A-Z
	Subarrange by translator
	Criticism
2015	General works
	Including authorship
2016	Textual
2017.A-Z	Special subjects, A-Z
2017.A5	Allegory
2017.A53	Ambiguity
2017.A55	Anti-clericalism
2017.A65	Apocalyptic literature
2017.B44	Belief and doubt
2017.D45	Desire
2017.D73	Dreams
2017.E53	England
2017.F33	Faith
2017.F73	Franciscans
2017.G63	God
2017.H6	Hope
2017.I37	Illustrations
2017.L35	Language and languages
2017.L38	Law
2017.M37	Marriage
2017.M8	Mysticism

Anglo-Norman period. Early English. Middle English
  Individual authors and works
    Langland, William (Piers Plowman)
      Criticism
        Special subjects, A-Z -- Continued

2017.N38	Nature
2017.P47	Personification
2017.P54	Play on words
2017.P64	Politics
2017.P67	Poor
2017.P74	Prophecies
2017.Q67	Quotations
2017.S24	Salvation
2017.T48	Textual criticism
2017.T53	Theology
2017.W54	Will
2018	Language, grammar, etc.
2019.L37	Lay folks' catechism
2020-2028	Layamon (Table P-PZ33)
2029.L2	Libell of Englishe policy
2029.L24	Life of Christ (Middle English poem)
	Cf. PR2063.M44 Metrical life of Christ
2029.L3	Lives of the saints
2029.L5	Lofsong of Ure Lefdi
2029.L6	Lovelich, Henry, fl. 1450 (Table P-PZ40)
2029.L7	Lutel soth sermun
2030-2038	Lydgate, John (Table P-PZ33)
2039.L-.M	Ly - Ma
2039.M34	Maidstone, Richard, d. 1396
	Malory, Sir Thomas (Le Morte d'Arthur)
	Texts
2040	By date
2041	By editor
2042	Selections
	Translations
2043.A-Z	Modern English. By editor, adaptor, etc., A-Z
	Including adaptations, abridgments, etc.
2044	Other. By language
	Criticism
2045	General works
2046	Sources
2047	Characters and other special
2048	Language
2049	Authorship
2050-2054	Mandeville, John (Table P-PZ35)
2056	Mannyng, Robert (Table P-PZ37)
2058	Map, Walter (Table P-PZ39)

	Anglo-Norman period. Early English. Middle English
	Individual authors and works -- Continued
2059.M	Map - Marsh
2059.M63	Margaret, Saint. Legend
	Marsh, Adam (Ada, de Marisco)
	see subclasses DA, PA
2061.M	Marsh - Merlin
2061.M38	Mary, Blessed Virgin, Saint. Legends
2061.M4	Mary Magdalene, Saint. Legend
2061.M6	Meditations on the life and passion of Christ
2061.M63	Meditations on the Supper of our Lord
2062	Merlin
2063.M34	Metham, John, fl. 1448 (Table P-PZ40)
2063.M4	Metrical chronicle of England
2063.M44	Metrical life of Christ
	Cf. PR2029.L24 Stanzaic life of Christ
	Metrical romances
2064	Collections
	Cf. PR1203 Medieval poetry
2065.A-Z	Special, A-Z
2065.A15-.A153	Alexander (Table P-PZ43)
2065.A16-.A163	Alexander and Dindimus (Table P-PZ43)
2065.A18-.A183	Amadas (Table P-PZ43)
2065.A2-.A23	Amis and Amiloun (Table P-PZ43)
2065.A38-.A383	Arthur (Table P-PZ43)
2065.A4-.A41	Arthur and Merlin (Table P-PZ43a)
2065.A56-.A563	Athelston (Table P-PZ43)
2065.A6-.A63	Avowing of Arthur (Table P-PZ43)
2065.A8-.A83	Awntyrs of Arthur at the Terne Wathelyne (Table P-PZ43)
2065.B2-.B23	Barlaam and Josaphat (Table P-PZ43)
2065.B4-.B43	Beves of Hamtoun (Table P-PZ43)
2065.B57-.B573	Boke of Mawndevile (Table P-PZ43)
2065.B6-.B63	Le Bone Florence of Rome (Table P-PZ43)
2065.C39-.C393	Cheuelere Assigne (Chevalier au Cygne) (Table P-PZ43)
2065.C4-.C43	Chevy chase (Table P-PZ43)
2065.C57-.C573	Clariodus (Table P-PZ43)
2065.C6-.C63	Cleges (Table P-PZ43)
2065.E2-.E23	Eger and Grime (Table P-PZ43)
2065.E3-.E33	Eglamour (Table P-PZ43)
2065.E4-.E5	Emare (Table P-PZ43a)
2065.E7-.E73	Erle of Tolous (Table P-PZ43)
2065.F4-.F42	Ferumbras (Table P-PZ43a)
2065.F6-.F63	Floire and Blancheflor (Table P-PZ43)
2065.G3-.G31	Gawain and the grene knight (Table P-PZ43a)
2065.G4-.G43	Generides (Table P-PZ43)

Anglo-Norman period. Early English. Middle English
Individual authors and works
Metrical romances
Special, A-Z -- Continued

2065.G5-.G51	Golagros and Gawain (Table P-PZ43a)
	Guillaume de Palerne see PR2065.W7+
2065.G6-.G63	Guy of Warwick (Table P-PZ43)
2065.H3-.H4	Havelok the Dane (Table P-PZ43a)
2065.I5-.I53	Ipomedon (Table P-PZ43)
2065.I6-.I63	Ipomedon, Lyfe of (Table P-PZ43)
2065.I8-.I83	Isumbras (Table P-PZ43)
2065.K5-.K53	King Alisaunder (Table P-PZ43)
2065.K6-.K63	King Horn (Table P-PZ43)
2065.K65-.K653	King of Tars (Table P-PZ43)
2065.K88-.K883	Knight of Curtesy (Table P-PZ43)
2065.L19-.L193	Lancelot of the Laik (Table P-PZ43)
2065.L2-.L23	Landeval (Table P-PZ43)
	Launfel see PR1955.C5
2065.L5-.L53	Libeaus Desconus (Table P-PZ43)
	Mandeville, John. Itinerarium (Metrical version) see PR2065.B57+
2065.M3-.M33	Morte Arthure (Alliterative poem) (Table P-PZ43)
2065.M5-.M53	Morte Arthure (Rhymed poem) (Table P-PZ43)
	For Malory's work see PR2040+
2065.O3-.O33	Octavian (Table P-PZ43)
2065.O6-.O63	Orfeo (Table P-PZ43)
2065.O8-.O83	Otuel (Table P-PZ43)
2065.P2	Partonope of Blois (Table P-PZ43)
2065.P4-.P5	Perceval of Galles (Table P-PZ43a)
2065.R4-.R43	Richard Coeur de Lion (Table P-PZ43)
2065.R6-.R62	Robert of Sicily (Table P-PZ43)
2065.R8-.R82	Roland and Vernagu (Table P-PZ43a)
2065.S3-.S33	The seven sages of Rome (Table P-PZ43)
2065.S5-.S53	Siege of Jerusalem (Table P-PZ43)
2065.S6-.S63	The siege of Troy (Table P-PZ43)
	Sir Cleges, Sir Eglamour, etc. see PR2065.C6+; PR2065.E3+
2065.S7-.S73	Sowdone of Babylone (Table P-PZ43)
	Speculum Gy de Warewyke see PR2143.S6
2065.S8-.S81	The squire of low degree (Table P-PZ43a)
	Swan-knight see PR2065.C39+
2065.T4-.T43	Titus and Vespasian (Table P-PZ43)
2065.T6-.T63	Torrent of Portugal (Table P-PZ43)
2065.T7-.T73	Triamour (Table P-PZ43)
2065.T8-.T82	Tristan (Table P-PZ43a)
2065.T83-.T833	Troy book (Laud MS. Misc. 595) (Table P-PZ43)
2065.W3-.W32	Wars of Alexander (Table P-PZ43a)

	Anglo-Norman period. Early English. Middle English
	Individual authors and works
	Metrical romances
	Special, A-Z -- Continued
2065.W5-.W53	Wedding of Sir Gawain (Table P-PZ43)
2065.W7-.W73	William of Palerne (Table P-PZ43)
2065.Y7-.Y73	Ywain and Gawain (Table P-PZ43)
2070.M	Metr - Mich
2085.M3	Michel, Dan, of Northgate (Table P-PZ40)
2085.M46	Ministry and passion (Middle English poem)
2085.M5	Minot, Laurence (Table P-PZ40)
2085.M57	Mirk, John, fl. 1403? (Table P-PZ40)
2085.M6	Mirror of man's salvation
2085.M84	Mum and the sothsegger
2085.N35	Nativity of Mary and Christ (Middle English poem)
2085.N4	Nicholas of Guildford (Table P-PZ40)
2085.N59-.N6	Northern homily cycle
2085.N7	Northern passion
2087.N-.O	No - Oc
(2090-2098)	Occleve, Thomas, 1370?-1450?
	see PR1992.H47
	Orleans, Charles, Duke of see PR1849.C6
2100-2108	Orm. The Ormulum (Table P-PZ33)
2109.O7	The owl and the nightingale
2109.P2	Paris and Vienne
2109.P3	The parliament of three ages
2109.P5	The passion of Our Lord
	Paston letters
	see subclass DA
2109.P56	Patrick, Saint
2110	Patience (Table P-PZ41)
	Patrick, Saint see PR2109.P56
2111	Pearl (Table P-PZ41)
	Pearl-poet see PR1972.G35+
2112	Peblis, to the play
2113	Pecock, Reginald (Table P-PZ37)
2114.P4-.P43	Pilgrimage of the lyf of the manhode (Table P-PZ43)
2114.P73	Prick of conscience
2115	Prose romances (Collections)
2117	Proverbs of Alfred (Table P-PZ41)
2118.P	Proverbs - Pz
	Pryam, Denis see PR2065.P2
2119.Q	Q
2119.Q27	Quare of jelusy
2119.Q3	Quatre fils Aimon
2119.Q34	Quatrefoil of love
2120.R	R - Richard

	Anglo-Norman period. Early English. Middle English
	Individual authors and works
	R - Richard -- Continued
2120.R3	Ralph Collier
	Rauf, Collyear see PR2120.R3
2120.R42-.R423	Regius poem (Table P-PZ43)
	Renaut de Montauban see PR2119.Q3
2121-2122	Richard de Holand (Table P-PZ36)
2123.R	Rich - Robin
	Richard of Bury see PR1820+
2123.R53	Richard the Redeless
	Robin Hood
	Class here ballads, chapbooks, etc., in verse
2125	General works
2127	Prose versions, adaptations, imitations
	For juvenile literature see PZ8.1
2129	History and criticism
2135-2136	Rolle, Richard (Table P-PZ36)
2137.R6	Russell, John, fl. 1450 (Table P-PZ40)
2138.R	Rus - Rz
2139.S	Sai - Sir
	Saint Cecilia see PR1849.C3
	Saints, Legends of
	see the forename, e. g. Editha, Erkenwald, etc.
2139.S25	Salomon et Marcolphus
2139.S3	Sawles wards
2139.S5	Scot, Michel
2139.S58	Simonie (Poem)
2139.S6	Sinners beware
2139.S8	Sir Patrick Spens
2141	Sir Thopas (Table P-PZ41)
2143.S4	The song against the king of Almaigne
2143.S54	South English legendary
2143.S55	Southern passion
2143.S6	Speculum Gy de Warewyke
2145.S-.T	Spec - Thom
2148.T3	Thomas de Hales (Table P-PZ40)
2148.T5	Thomas, of Erceldoune (Poem)
	Cf. PR978.T5+ Thomas Thymer (Ballad)
	Cf. PR2065.T8+ Sir Tristem, by Thomas, The Rhymer
	Three kings' sons see PQ1581.T76+
2148.T7	Trevisa, John (Table P-PZ40)
2148.T8	Tundal's vision
2148.T9	Turnament of Totenham
2148.U75	Usk, Thomas, d. 1388 (Table P-PZ40)
2148.V2	The vengeaunce of Goddes deth
2148.V3	Virgilius

	Anglo-Norman period. Early English. Middle English
	Individual authors and works -- Continued
2148.V5	Visio Pauli
	Visio Tnugdali see PR2148.T8
	Wace see PQ1545.W2
2148.W2	Walton, John (Table P-PZ40)
2148.W3	William of Ockham (Table P-PZ40)
2148.W4	William of Shoreham (Table P-PZ40)
2148.W6	William of Wadington (Table P-PZ40)
2148.W8	Wirecker, Nigel (Table P-PZ40)
2148.W9	The woman of Samaria
2149.W	Wom - Wyc
2150-2158	Wycliffe, John (Table P-PZ33)
	Cf. Class B, Religion
2159.W	Wyc - Wyn
2163	Wynners and watere
2165	Yonge, James (Table P-PZ39)
	English renaissance (1500-1640)
	Prose and poetry
2199.A-Z	Anonymous works, A-Z
	Individual authors and works
2200	A - As
	Ascham, Roger
	Collected editions
2201.A1	By date
2201.A2	By editor
2201.A5-Z	Single works
2202	Criticism
2203.A3	Austin, Henry, fl. 1613
2203.A45	Austin, William, 1587-1634
2203.A5	Aylmer, John
2203.A7	Ayton, Sir Robert
	Bacon, Francis
	For biography see B1197
	Cf. B1150+ Philosophy (General)
	Collected works see B1153+
2205	Selected works (English literature)
	Separate works
	Essays
2206.A3	Texts. By date
2206.A5-.Z29	Texts. By editor
2206.Z3-.Z9	Translations. By language, A-Z
2207.A-Z	Other works, A-Z
2208	Criticism
2209.B14	Baker, Robert, fl. 1562-1563
2209.B15	Baldwin, William
2209.B2	Bale, John

English renaissance (1500-1640)
   Prose and poetry
      Individual authors and works -- Continued

2209.B26	Bancroft, Thomas
2209.B28	Bannatyne, George
2209.B3	Barclay, Alexander
2209.B4	Barclay, William
2209.B6	Barnes, Barnabe
	For dramatic works see PR2209.B6
2209.B8	Barnfield, Richard
2211.B2	Basse, William
2211.B3	Beaumont, Sir John
2211.B4	Beedome, Thomas, d. 1641?
2211.B5	Bellenden, John
2211.B8	Bodenham, John
2212-2213	Bouchier, Sir John (Lord Berners) (Table P-PZ36)
2214.B17	Bracegirdle, John, d. 1614
2214.B2	Bradshaw, Henry
2214.B3	Brathwaite, Richard
2214.B4	Breton, Nicholas, 1545?-1626? (Table P-PZ38)
2214.B6	Broke, Arthur
2215-2216	Brooke, Fulke Greville, Lord (Table P-PZ36)
2217.B5	Browne, William
2218-2219	Buchanan, George (Table P-PZ36)
2220.B84	Bullein, William, d. 1576
2223-2224	Burton, Robert (Table P-PZ36)
2228-2229	Campion, Thomas (Table P-PZ36)
2231-2232	Carew, Richard (Table P-PZ36)
2233.C2	Cartwright, Thomas
2233.C26	Cavendish, George, 1500-1561?
2233.C35	Chapman, George
	For his dramatic works see PR2440+
2233.C4	Cheke, Sir John
2233.C6	Chester, Robert
2233.C8	Chettle, Henry
2234	Churchyard, Thomas (Table P-PZ37)
2235.C5	Constable, Henry
2235.C7	Copland, Robert, fl. 1508-1547
2235.C8	Copley, Anthonie
2236.C	Copley - Coryate
2237	Coryate, Thomas
2239	Coverdale, Miles
	Cf. BS145+ Texts and versions of the Bible
2240.C5	Craig, Alexander
2240.C8	Cranmer, Thomas
	Cf. DA317.8.C8 Tudor history, 1485-1603
2240.C84	Crowley, Robert, 1518?-1588

English renaissance (1500-1640)
　　Prose and poetry
　　　Individual authors and works -- Continued

2240.D15	Daborn, Robert
2241.D4	Daniel, Samuel, 1562-1619 (Table P-PZ40)
2242.D19	Davies, John, 1565?-1618
2242.D2	Davies, Sir John
2243	Dekker, Thomas
	For his dramatic works see PR2480+
2244.D2	Deloney, Thomas
2244.D4	Derricke, John
2244.D45	Dickenson, John, romance writer
2245-2248	Donne, John (Table P-PZ35a)
2249.D6	Dorset, Thomas Sackville, 1st Earl of
2250-2253	Douglas, Gavin (Table P-PZ35a)
2255-2258	Drayton, Michael (Table P-PZ35a)
2260-2263	Drummond, William (of Hawthornden) (Table P-PZ35a)
2265-2269	Dunbar, William (Table P-PZ35)
2270.E15	Earle, John, Bp. of Salisbury, 1601?-1665
2270.E2	Edwards, Richard
2270.E3	Edwards, Thomas
2270.E5	Elyot, Sir Thomas
2270.F37	Feltham, Owen, 1602?-1668
	Fisher, John
	see class B
2271-2272	Fletcher, Giles (Table P-PZ36)
2273.F5	Fletcher, Joseph
2274-2275	Fletcher, Phinease (Table P-PZ36)
2276.F5	Florio, John
2276.F6	Forrest, William
2276.F7	Foxe, John
2276.F77	Fraunce, Abraham, fl. 1587-1633
2276.G3	Garden, Alexander
2277-2278	Gascoigne, George
	For his dramatic works see PR2535+
2279.G2	Gifford, Humfrey
2279.G4	Googe, Barnabe
2279.G6	Gosson, Stephen
2279.G8	Grafton, Richard
2280.G44	Greene, Robert, 1558-1592
2280.G5	Gresham, James
	Grimald or Grimoald, Nicholas see PR2549.G5
2283.H2	Hake, Edward
	Hakluyt, Richard see G69.H2
	Hall, Edward
	see subclass DA
2283.H7	Hall, Joseph

English renaissance (1500-1640)
    Prose and poetry
        Individual authors and works -- Continued

2283.H8	Hannay, Patrick
2284-2285	Harrington, Sir John (Table P-PZ36)
	Cf. DA1+ History of Great Britain
	Cf. HX1+ Socialism
2287-2288	Harvey, Gabriel (Table P-PZ36)
2290-2291	Hawes, Stephen (Table P-PZ36)
2293	Henry VIII
	Herbert, George, 1593-1633 see PR3507+
2294.H2	Herbert of Cherbury, Edward Herbert, 1st baron
	Cf. B1201.H3+ Philosophy (General)
2294.H3	Heywood, Jasper
2294.H33	Heywood, Thomas, d. 1641
	For dramatic works see PR2570+
	Hollinshed, Raphael
	see subclass DA
2294.H5	Holland, Sir Richard
2294.H58	Hoskins, John, 1566-1638
2294.H6	Howell, James
2294.H7	Howell, Thomas
2294.H8	Hume, Alexander
2295	James I of England
2296.J2	James, Richard
2296.J4	Jewell, John
2296.J6	Johnson, Richard, 1573-1659?
2296.J7	Johnson, Robert
	Jonson, Ben, 1573?-1637 see PR2625.A2+
2296.K3	Kendall, Timothy
	Knox, John
	see BR, BX
2296.L24	Lane, John, 16th/17th cent.
2296.L27	Lanier, Emilia
	Latimer, Hugh
	see subclass BX
2296.L6	Lindsay, Sir David
	For dramas, interludes, etc. see PR2659.L5
2296.L7	Lindsay, Robert
2296.L85	Lock, Anne Vaughan, ca. 1534-ca. 1590
2297-2298	Lodge, Thomas (Table P-PZ36)
	For Wounds of civil war (Marius and Scilla) see
	PR2659.L6
2299.L	Lodge - Lyly
2300-2303	Lyly, John (Table P-PZ35a)
2304.L4	Lyly, William
2304.M3	Markham, Gervase

English renaissance (1500-1640)
  Prose and poetry
    Individual authors and works -- Continued

2304.M5	Major, or Mair, John
	Martin Marprelate pamphlets see PR2199.A+
2308	Mennis, Sir John
2311-2312	Meres, Francis (Table P-PZ36)
2315.M	Me - Mo
2315.M48	Middleton, Christopher, 1560?-1628
	Mirror for magistrates see PR2199.A+
2315.M65	Moffett, Thomas, 1553-1604
2315.M7	Montgomerie, Alexander, 1545?-1611
2321-2322	More, Sir Thomas (Table P-PZ36)
	For biography and general works on More see
	DA334.M8
2323.M67	Moulsworth, Martha
2324-2325	Munday, Anthony (Table P-PZ36)
	Cf. PR2719.M6 English Renaissance drama
2326.N2	Napier, John (Table P-PZ38)
2326.N3	Nash, Thomas
2326.N4	Niccols, Richard
2326.N6	North, Sir Thomas
2326.N8	Norton, Thomas
2326.O5	Overbury, Sir Thomas
2326.O7	Owen, John
2326.O8	Oxford, Edward De Vere, Earl of, 1550-1604
2327-2328	Painter, William (Table P-PZ36)
2329.P125	Palmer, Thomas, Sir, 1540-1626
2329.P13	Parkes, William, fl. 1612
2329.P14	Parry, Robert, fl. 1540-1612
2329.P15	Peacham, Henry, 1576?-1643
2329.P2	Pembroke, Mary (Sidney), Countess of
2329.P4	Phaer, Thomas
2329.P6	Pole, Reginald, cardinal
	Cf. B, Religion
	Cf. DA, History of Great Britain
2329.P85	Proctor, Thomas, fl. 1578
2331-2332	Puttenham, Richard (Table P-PZ36)
2334-2335	Raleigh, Sir Walter (Table P-PZ36)
	Cf. D, History (General)
	Cf. DA, History of Great Britain
	Cf. E, History of America
	Randolph, Thomas see PR2739.R3
2336.R4	Rastell, John
2336.R6	Reynolds, John
2336.R8	Rich, Barnaby (Table P-PZ40)
2337.R2	Ripley, George

English renaissance (1500-1640)
   Prose and poetry
      Individual authors and works -- Continued

2337.R6	Robinson, Clement
2337.R7	Robinson, Thomas
2337.R75	Rolland, John
2337.R8	Rous, Francis
2337.R9	Rowlands, Samuel
2337.R98	Roy, William, fl. 1527-1531
2337.S2	Sabie, Francis, fl. 1595
2338	Sandys, George
2339.S2	Scot, Thomas
2339.S3	Selden, John
2339.S5	Sempill, Sir James, and Robert
2339.S52	Shepherd, Luke
2339.S54	Shirley, James, 1596-1666
	Sidney, Mary, Countess of Pembroke see PR2329.P2
2340-2343	Sidney, Sir Philip (Table P-PZ35a)
	For Defense of Poesy see PN1031+
2344.S35	Sidney, Robert
2345-2348	Skelton, John (Table P-PZ35a)
2349.S3	Smith, Thomas, Sir, 1513-1577
2349.S35	Smith, William, fl. 1596
2349.S49	Southwell, Anne, Lady, 1573-1636
2349.S5	Southwell, Robert
2349.S7	Speed, John
2349.S74	Speght, Rachel
2350-2368	Spenser, Edmund (Table P-PZ32 modified)
	Separate works
2355	Astrophel (Table P-PZ41)
2356	Colin Clouts come home again (Table P-PZ41)
2357	Complaints (Table P-PZ41)
2358	Faerie Queene (Table P-PZ41)
2359	Shepheardes calendar (Table P-PZ41)
2360.A-Z	Other, A-Z
	Subarrange each by Table P-PZ43
2369.S47	Stewart, John, of Baldynneis
2369.S5	Stirling, William Alexander, 1st Earl of
	Cf. PR3157.S75 Drama
2369.S7	Stubbs, Philip
2370-2373	Surrey, Henry Howard, Earl of (Table P-PZ35a)
	Including works of Surrey and Wyatt combined
2375-2378	Sylvester, Joshua (Table P-PZ35a)
2380-2383	Taylor, John (the water-poet) (Table P-PZ35a)
2384.T45	Telney, Edmund, d. 1610
2384.T47	Tofte, Robert, 1561-1620
2384.T5	Turberville, George (Table P-PZ38)

English renaissance (1500-1640)
  Prose and poetry
  Individual authors and works -- Continued

2384.T7	Tusser, Thomas
2384.T9	Tyndale, William
	Cf. B, Religion
2384.U4	Udall, John
2384.W3	Warner, William
2384.W5	Watson, Thomas
2384.W7	Webbe, William
2384.W75	Weever, John, 1576-1634
2386-2387	Whetstone, George (Table P-PZ36)
2388.W4	Whitney, Geoffrey, 1548?-1601?
2388.W6	Wilson, Thomas
2390-2393	Wither, George (Table P-PZ35a)
2394.W	Wi - Wo
2395-2398	Wotton, Sir Henry (Table P-PZ35a)
2399.W	Wo - Wy
2399.W7	Wroth, Mary Sidney, Lady, fl. 1621
2400-2404	Wyatt, Sir Thomas (Table P-PZ35)
2405.W-Z	Wyatt - Z

The drama

2411.A-Z	Anonymous plays, A-Z
	Collections see PR1262
	Individual authors
2417	Armin, Robert (Table P-PZ39)
2419.B2	Bale, John, 1495-1563 (Table P-PZ38)
2419.B3	Barnes, Barnabe (Table P-PZ40)
	For biography, etc. see PR2209.B6
2420-2438	Beaumont, Francis, and Fletcher, John (Table P-PZ32 modified)
	For collected and separate plays by John Fletcher (and by him and others in collaboration, Beaumont excepted), see PR2500+, or the dramatist to whom the play is mainly credited
	Separate works
2425.A-.G	A - G
	e. g.
2425.C6-.C63	Coxcomb (Table P-PZ43)
2425.C8-.C82	Cupid's revenge (Table P-PZ43a)
2426.H-.K	H - K
	e. g.
2426.K5-.K53	A king and no king (Table P-PZ43)
2427	Knight of the burning pestle (Table P-PZ41)
2428.K-.P	K - P
	e. g.
2428.M3-.M33	Maid's tragedy (Table P-PZ43)

	English renaissance (1500-1640)
	The drama
	Individual authors
	Beaumont, Francis, and Fletcher, John
	Separate works -- Continued
2429	Philaster (Table P-PZ41)
2430.P-Z	P - Z
	e. g.
2430.S3-.S33	Scornful lady (Table P-PZ43)
2430.T6-.T7	Triumph of honor (Table P-PZ43a)
2430.W6-.W63	Woman-hater (Table P-PZ43)
2439.B14	Berkeley, William, Sir, 1608-1677 (Table P-PZ40)
2439.B3	Bower, Richard (Table P-PZ40)
2439.B4	Brandon, Samuel, fl. 1598 (Table P-PZ38)
2439.B5	Brome, Richard (Table P-PZ40)
2439.B7	Buchanan, George (Table P-PZ40)
	Campion, Thomas see PR2228+
2439.C4	Carlell, Lodowick (Table P-PZ40)
2439.C8	Cartwright, William (Table P-PZ40)
	Cary, Elizabeth, Lady, 1585 or 6-1639 see PR2499.F3
2440-2458	Chapman, George (Table P-PZ32 modified)
	Separate works
2446.A3	All fools (Table P-PZ43)
2446.A6	Andromeda liberata (Table P-PZ43)
2447.B2	The Ball (Table P-PZ43)
2447.B4	Blinde beggar of Alexandria (Table P-PZ43)
2447.B7	Bussy d'Ambois (Table P-PZ43)
2447.C2	Caesar and Pompey (Table P-PZ43)
2447.C6	Conspiracie of Charles, Duke of Byron (Table P-PZ43)
2447.E2	Eastward hoe (Table P-PZ43)
2448.G5	Gentleman usher (Table P-PZ43)
2448.H7	Humerous dayes myrth (Table P-PZ43)
2448.M2	May day (Table P-PZ43)
2448.M5	Memorable masks of the two honourable Inns of Court (Table P-PZ43)
2448.M7	Monsieur d'Olive (Table P-PZ43)
2448.R3	Revenge for honour (Table P-PZ43)
2449.R4	Revenge of Bussy d'Ambois (Table P-PZ43)
2449.S3	Second maiden's tragedy (Table P-PZ43)
2449.T3	Tragedie of Alphonsus, Emperor of Germany (Table P-PZ43)
2449.T5	Tragedie of Chabot, Admirall of France (Table P-PZ43)
2449.T7	Two wise men and all the rest fools (Table P-PZ43)
2449.W5	Widowes teares (Table P-PZ43)
	Prose works and poetry see PR2233.C35

	English renaissance (1500-1640)
	The drama
	Individual authors
	Chapman, George -- Continued
	Translations by Chapman
	Hesiod
	see subclass PA
	Homer's Iliad and Odyssey
	see subclass PA
	Juvenal's Satire on Nero
	see subclass PA
	Musaeus
	see subclass PA
2459.C4	Chettle, Henry (Table P-PZ40)
2459.C46	Clavell, John, 1601-1643 (Table P-PZ40)
2459.C6	Cooke, Jo., fl. 1614- (Table P-PZ40)
2460-2468	Daniel, Samuel (Table P-PZ33)
2470-2478	D'Avenant, Sir William (Table P-PZ33)
2479.D3	Davenport, Robert
2479.D5	Day, John
2480-2498	Dekker, Thomas (Table P-PZ32 modified)
	Prose works and poetry see PR2243
	Separate plays
2485.A-.H	By title, A-Hom
	Subarrange each by Table P-PZ43
2486	Honest whore (Table P-PZ41)
2487.H-.O	By title, Hoo-Olc
	Subarrange each by Table P-PZ43
2488	Old Fortunatus (Table P-PZ41)
2489.O-.S	By title, Ole-Shn
	Subarrange each by Table P-PZ43
2490	Shoemaker's holiday (Table P-PZ41)
2491.S-Z	By title, Shof-Z
	Subarrange each by Table P-PZ43
2499.D5	Dorset, Thomas Sackville, 1st Earl of (Table P-PZ40)
2499.D7	Drayton, Michael (Table P-PZ40)
2499.E4	Edwards, Richard (Table P-PZ40)
2499.F25	Fage, Mary (Table P-PZ40)
2499.F3	Falkland, Elizabeth Tanfield Cary, viscountess, 1585-1639 (Table P-PZ40)
2499.F4	Field, Nathan (Table P-PZ40)
2500-2518	Fletcher, John (Table P-PZ32 modified)
	Cf. PR2420+ Beaumont and Fletcher
	Separate works
	Bonduca
2505.B5	Texts
2505.B6	Adaptations

	English renaissance (1500-1640)
	The drama
	Individual authors
	Fletcher, John
	Separate works
	Bonduca -- Continued
2505.B7	Criticism
	Chances
2505.C4	Texts
2505.C5	Adaptations
2505.C6	Criticism
	Custom of the country
2505.C7	Texts
2505.C8	Adaptations
2505.C9	Criticism
	Demetrius and Enanthe, being The Humorous lieutenant
2505.D3	Texts
2505.D4	Adaptations
2505.D5	Criticism
2506	Faithful shepherdess (Table P-PZ41)
	Island princess
2507.I7	Texts
2507.I8	Adaptations
2507.I9	Criticism
	Loyal subject
2507.L6	Texts
2507.L7	Adaptations
2507.L8	Criticism
	Mad lover
2507.M3	Texts
2507.M4	Adaptations
2507.M5	Criticism
	Monsieur Thomas
2507.M6	Texts
2507.M7	Adaptations
2507.M8	Criticism
	Pilgrim
2507.P4	Texts
2507.P5	Adaptations
2507.P6	Criticism
	Rule and wife and have a wife
2508.R7	Texts
2508.R8	Adaptations
2508.R9	Criticism
	Sir John van Olden Barnavelt
2508.S3	Texts

English renaissance (1500-1640)
The drama
Individual authors
Fletcher, John
Separate works
Sir John van Olden Barnavelt -- Continued

2508.S4	Adaptations
2508.S5	Criticism
	Spanish curate
2508.S6	Texts
2508.S7	Adaptations
2508.S8	Criticism
	Thierry and Theodoret
2508.T3	Texts
2508.T4	Adaptations
2508.T5	Criticism
	Valentinian
2509.V3	Texts
2509.V4	Adaptations
2509.V5	Criticism
	Wife for a month
2509.W23	Texts
2509.W24	Adaptations
2509.W25	Criticism
	Wild-goose chase
2509.W3	Texts
2509.W4	Adaptations
2509.W5	Criticism
	Wit without money
2509.W6	Texts
2509.W7	Adaptations
2509.W8	Criticism
	Woman's prize
2510.W3	Texts
2510.W4	Adaptations
2510.W5	Criticism
	Women pleased
2510.W6	Texts
2510.W7	Adaptations
2510.W8	Criticism
2520-2528	Ford, John (Table P-PZ33)
2529.F7	Fulwell, Ulpian (Table P-PZ40)
2529.G3	Gager, William (Table P-PZ40)
2535-2536	Gascoigne, George (Table P-PZ36)
	For biography see PR2277+
2539.G5	Glapthorne, Henry (Table P-PZ40)
2539.G6	Goffe, Thomas, 1591-1629 (Table P-PZ40)

	English renaissance (1500-1640)
	The drama
	Individual authors -- Continued
2539.G7	Golding, Arthur (Table P-PZ40)
2540-2548	Greene, Robert (Table P-PZ33)
	For prose works see PR2280.G44
2549.G5	Grimald, Nicholas (Table P-PZ40)
2549.H3	Hackett, John (Table P-PZ40)
2549.H5	Halliwell, Edward (Table P-PZ40)
	Harding, Samuel, b. 1618 see PR2747.S17
2549.H6	Haughton, William (Table P-PZ40)
2549.H65	Hausted, Peter, d. 1645 (Table P-PZ40)
2549.H8	Heming, William (Table P-PZ40)
2560-2568	Heywood, John (Table P-PZ33)
2570-2578	Heywood, Thomas (Table P-PZ33)
	For prose works and poetry see PR2294.H33
2585.H4	Hughes, Thomas (Table P-PZ40)
2585.H7	Hunnis, William (Table P-PZ40)
2591.I4	Ingelend, Thomas (Table P-PZ40)
2592.J45	Jeffere, John (Table P-PZ40)
	Johnson, Ben
	Collected works
2600	By date
2601.A-Z	Editions with commentary, etc. By editor, A-Z
2602	Selected works, unedited works, fragments, etc.
2603	Selections. Anthologies. Extracts
2604.A-Z	Translations. By language
2604.F4	French
2604.G5	German
2604.I5	Italian
2604.S5	Spanish
2604.Z5	Other
	Separate works
2605	Alchemist (Table P-PZ41)
2606	Bartholomew fair (Table P-PZ41)
2607	The case is altered (Table P-PZ41)
2608	Catiline (Table P-PZ41)
2609	Cynthia's revels (Table P-PZ41)
2610	The devil is an ass (Table P-PZ41)
2611	Eastward ho (Table P-PZ41)
2612	Epicoene, or The silent woman (Table P-PZ41)
2613	Every man in his humor (Table P-PZ41)
2614	Every man out of his humor (Table P-PZ41)
2615	The magnetic lady (Table P-PZ41)
2616	The new inn (Table P-PZ41)
2617	Poetaster (Table P-PZ41)
2618	Sad shepherd (Table P-PZ41)

	English renaissance (1500-1640)
	The drama
	Individual authors
	Johnson, Ben
	Separate works -- Continued
2619	Sejanus (Table P-PZ41)
	The silent woman see PR2612
2620	Staple of news (Table P-PZ41)
2621	Tale of a tub (Table P-PZ41)
2622	Volpone (Table P-PZ41)
	Masques. Entertainments
2624.A2	Collected
2624.A5-Z	Special
	Poetical works
2625.A2	Collected
2625.A5-Z	Special
2626	Other works
2627	Doubtful or spurious works
2628	Imitations, etc.
2629	Illustrations to the works
	Biography, criticism, etc.
2630	Dictionaries, indexes, etc.
	Class here general encyclopedic dictionaries only
	For concordances and dictionaries see PR2645
2630.5	Historical sources and documents of the biography or author
	For sources of literary works see PR2636+
	Autobiographical works
2631.A2	Autobiography. By date
2631.A3-.A39	Journals. Memoirs. By title
2631.A4	Letters (Collections). By date
2631.A41-.A49	Letters to and from particular individuals. By correspondent (alphabetically)
2631.A5-Z	General works
2632	Special periods of the author's life
	Including early life, education, love and marriage, relation to women, relation to men, later life
2633	Relations to contemporaries. Times, etc.
2634	Homes and haunts. Local associations. Landmarks
2635	Anniversaries. Celebrations. Memorial addresses. Iconography. Monuments. Relics. Museums, exhibitions, etc.
	Authorship
	Including manuscripts, sources, etc.
	For textual criticism see PR2643
2636	General works
2637	Chronology of works

English renaissance (1500-1640)
The drama
Individual authors
Johnson, Ben -- Continued
Criticism and interpretation
History

2637.3	General works
2637.4.A-Z	By region or country, A-Z
2638	General works
2639	Characters
2641	Technique, plots, scenes, time, etc.
2642.A-Z	Treatment and knowledge of special subjects, A-Z
	For list of Cutter numbers, see Table P-PZ31 42.A+
2643	Textual criticism, commentaries, etc.
	Language, style, etc.
2644	General works
2645	Dictionaries. Concordances
2646	Grammar
2647	Versification, meter, rhythm, etc.
2648	Dialect, etc.
2649.K4	Kirchmeyer, T. (Table P-PZ40)
2650-2658	Kyd, Thomas (Table P-PZ33)
2659.L3	Legge, Thomas (Table P-PZ40)
2659.L4	Lenton, Francis, fl. 1630-1640 (Table P-PZ40)
2659.L5	Lindsay or Lyndsay, Sir David (Table P-PZ40)
	Cf. PR2296.L6 Prose and poetry
2659.L6	Lodge, Thomas (Table P-PZ40)
	Cf. PR2297+ Prose and poetry
2659.L8	Lupton, Thomas (Table P-PZ40)
2659.L9	Lyly, John (Table P-PZ40)
	Cf. PR2300+ Prose and poetry
2659.M3	Markham, Gervase, 1568?-1637 (Table P-PZ40)
	Marlowe, Christopher
	Collected works
2660	By date
2661	By editor
2662	Selected works. Selections
	Subarrange by editor, if given, or by date
2663.A-Z	Translations. By language, A-Z
	Separate works
	Dido see PR2670.D5+
2664	Doctor Faustus (Table P-PZ41)
2665	Edward II (Table P-PZ41)
	Hero and Leander see PR2670.H6+
2666	Jew of Malta (Table P-PZ41)
2668	Massacre at Paris (Table P-PZ41)
2669	Tamburlaine the Great (Table P-PZ41)

	English renaissance (1500-1640)
	The drama
	Individual authors
	Marlowe, Christopher
	Separate works -- Continued
2670.A-Z	Other, A-Z
	Subarrange each by Table P-PZ43 unless otherwise specified
2670.D5-.D6	Dido (Table P-PZ43a)
2670.H6-.H63	Hero and Leander (Table P-PZ43)
2671	Apocryphal, spurious works, etc. (Collections only)
	Illustrations
	Class at N8215, or with the special artists in NC-NE as the case may be
	Class illustrated editions with other editions
	Class portraits, etc., of the author with his biography
	Biography, criticism, etc.
2672.A1-.A5	Periodicals. Societies. Serials
2672.A6-Z	Dictionaries, indexes, etc.
2673.A3-.A39	Autobiography, journals, memoirs. By title
2673.A4	Letters (Collections). By date
2673.A41-.A49	Letters to and from particular individuals. By correspondent (alphabetically)
2673.A5-Z	General works
	Criticism
2674	General works
2675	Textual. Manuscripts, etc.
	Special
2676	Sources
2677.A-Z	Other, A-Z
	For list of Cutter numbers, see Table P-PZ32 17
2678	Language. Grammar. Style
2690-2698	Marston, John (Table P-PZ33)
2699.M5	Mason, John (Table P-PZ40)
2700-2708	Massinger, Philip (Table P-PZ33)
2709.M3	May, Thomas (Table P-PZ40)
	Mayne, Jasper see PR3548.M4
2709.M8	Medwall, Henry (Table P-PZ40)
2710-2718	Middleton, Thomas (Table P-PZ33)
2719.M6	Munday, Anthony (Table P-PZ40)
	Cf. PR2324+ Prose and poetry
2719.N3	Nabbes, Thomas (Table P-PZ40)
	"Nero" see PR2411.A+
2729.N7	Norton, Thomas (Table P-PZ40)
	Pedler's prophecy see PR2411.A+
2730-2738	Peele, George (Table P-PZ33)
2739.P4	Pickering, John (Table P-PZ40)

	English renaissance (1500-1640)
	The drama
	Individual authors -- Continued
2739.P5	Porter, Henry, fl. 1599 (Table P-PZ40)
2739.P7	Preston, Thomas (Table P-PZ40)
2739.R3	Randolph, Thomas (Table P-PZ40)
2739.R4	Redford, John, d. 1547 (Table P-PZ38)
	"Return from Parnassus" see PR2411.A+
2739.R7	Rickets, J. (Table P-PZ40)
2739.R8	Rowley, Samuel (Table P-PZ40)
2740-2744	Rowley, William (Table P-PZ35)
2747.S17	S.H. (Samuel Harding), b. 1618 (Table P-PZ40)
	Sackville, Sir Thomas see PR2499.D5
2747.S2	Sampson, William (Table P-PZ40)
2749	Se - Sh
	Shakespeare, William
2750	Original quartos and facsimiles and reprints
2750.A01-.A73	Original editions
	Arranged and numbered like PR2801+
2750.B01-.B73	Facsimiles and reprints
	Arranged like .A1-.A73
2750.C01-.C9	Collected reprints
	Arranged chronologically
	Collected works
2751.A1	First folio edition (1623)
2751.A15	Facsimiles. By date of reprint
2751.A1501-.A1540	Separate works (Table PR3)
2751.A2	Second folio edition (1632)
2751.A25	Facsimiles. By date of reprint
2751.A2501-.A2540	Separate works (Table PR3)
2751.A3	Third folio edition (1664)
2751.A35	Facsimiles. By date of reprint
2751.A3501-.3540	Separate works (Table PR3)
2751.A4	Fourth folio edition (1685)
2751.A45	Facsimiles. By date of reprint
2751.A4501-.4540	Separate works (Table PR3)
	Collations, notes, descriptions, etc., of the folio
	editions see PR3070+
	Bibliography of folios see Z8813
	Modern editions
2752.A-Z	18th century. By editor, publisher, etc., A-Z
2753.A-Z	19th century. By editor, publisher, etc., A-Z
2754.A-Z	20th century. By editor, publisher, etc., A-Z
	Class here editions first edited in the 20th century
2755.A-Z	21st century. By editor, publisher, etc., A-Z
	Partial editions. Selected works, etc.
	Subarrange by editor, if given, or date

	English renaissance (1500-1640)
	The drama
	Individual authors
	Shakespeare, William
	Partial editions. Selected works, etc. -- Continued
	General
2757	Early to 1800
2759	Recent
	By form
2761	Comedies
2762	Histories
2763	Tragedies
	Poems see PR2841+
	Selections. Anthologies, etc.
	Subarrange by editor, if given, or date
	Dictionaries of quotations see PR2892
2767	Through 1800
2768	1801-
	Minor collections: Almanacs, Birthday books, Thoughts, etc.
2770	Through 1800
2771	1801-
2773	Wit and humor
2774	Selections arranged in drama form
	Cf. PR2879 Imitations, paraphrases, adaptations
	Translations
	For translations of pseudo-Shakespearian plays see PR2851+
2775	Dutch
2776.A-Z	Separate works, A-Z
	Subarrange by translator
	Poems
2776.X1	Collected poems
	Subarrange by editor, if given, or date
2776.X2	Selections. Anthologies
2776.X3	Songs
	Special poems or songs
2776.X5	Venus and Adonis
2776.X6	Rape of Lucrece
	Passionate pilgrim see PR2873.P3
	Sonnets
2776.X8	Collections. Selections
2776.X8A4	Separate sonnets. By number
	e.g.
2776.X8A4 no. 91	Sonnet number 91
2776.X9	Other
	French

English renaissance (1500-1640)
The drama
Individual authors
Shakespeare, William
Translations
French -- Continued

2777	Early to 1800
2778	Recent
2779.A-Z	Separate works, A-Z
	Subarrange by translator
2779.X1-.X9	Poems
	Subarrange like PR2776.X1+
	German
2780	Early to 1800
2781	Recent
2782.A-Z	Separate works, A-Z
	Subarrange by translator
2782.X1-.X9	Poems
	Subarrange like PR2776.X1+
2783	Italian
2784.A-Z	Separate works, A-Z
	Subarrange by translator
2784.X1-.X9	Poems
	Subarrange like PR2776.X1+
2785	Russian
	For other Slavic languages see PR2795.S3+
2786.A-Z	Separate works, A-Z
	Subarrange by translator
2786.X1-.X9	Poems
	Subarrange like PR2776.X1+
	Scandinavian
2787	Danish. Norwegian
2788.A-Z	Separate works, A-Z
	Subarrange by translator
2788.X1-.X9	Poems
	Subarrange like PR2776.X1+
2789	Icelandic
2790.A-Z	Separate works, A-Z
	Subarrange by translator
2790.X1-.X9	Poems
	Subarrange like PR2776.X1+
2791	Swedish
2792.A-Z	Separate works, A-Z
	Subarrange by translator
2792.X1-.X9	Poems
	Subarrange like PR2776.X1+
2793	Spanish and Portuguese

English renaissance (1500-1640)
The drama
Individual authors
Shakespeare, William
Translations
Spanish and Portuguese -- Continued

2794.A-Z	Separate works, A-Z
	Subarrange by translator
2794.X1-.X9	Poems
	Subarrange like PR2776.X1+
2795.A-Z	Other European. By language, A-Z
2795.C3-.C32	Catalan (Table PR4a)
2795.I7-.I72	Irish (Table PR4a)
	Slavic
2795.S3-.S32	Bohemian. Czech (Table PR4a)
2795.S33-.S332	Bulgarian (Table PR4a)
2795.S35-.S352	Croatian (Table PR4a)
2795.S37-.S372	Macedonian (Table PR4a)
	Montenegrin see PR2795.S6+
2795.S4-.S42	Polish (Table PR4a)
(2795.S5-.S52)	Russian
	see PR2785
(2795.S55-.S56)	Ruthenian
	see PR2795.S76+
2795.S6-.S62	Serbian. Montenegrin (Table PR4a)
2795.S7-.S72	Slovak (Table PR4a)
2795.S75-.S752	Slovenian (Table PR4a)
	Sorbian see PR2795.S77+
2795.S76-.S762	Ukrainian. Ruthenian (Table PR4a)
2795.S77-.S772	Wendic. Sorbian (Table PR4a)
2795.Y5-.Y52	Yiddish (Table PR4a)
	Other languages
2796.A-Z	Asia
	Arabic
2796.A69	Collected works. By translator
2796.A7A-.A7Z	Separate works, A-Z
	Subarrange by translator
2796.A9-.A92	Azerbaijani (Table PR4a)
2796.C5-.C52	Chinese (Table PR4a)
2796.H4-.H42	Hebrew (Table PR4a)
2796.K3-.K32	Kannada (Table PR4a)
2796.K6-.K62	Korean (Table PR4a)
2796.P45-.P452	Persian (Table PR4a)
2796.S26-.S262	Sanskrit (Table PR4a)
2796.T5-.T52	Thai (Table PR4a)
2796.V53-.V532	Vietnamese (Table PR4a)
2797	Polynesia. Oceania

	English renaissance (1500-1640)
	The drama
	Individual authors
	Shakespeare, William
	Translations
	Other languages -- Continued
2798	Africa
2799	American Indian
2800.A-Z	Mixed languages (Pidgin or creole), A-Z
	Artificial languages see PM8001+
	Esperanto see PM8285.A5+
2800.5.A-Z	English texts for foreign students with notes, glossaries, etc. By language, A-Z
	Subdivide by special plays
	e. g.
2800.5.S7J8	Julius Caesar for Spanish students
	Separate works
2801	All's well that ends well (Table PR4)
2802	Antony and Cleopatra (Table PR4)
2803	As you like it (Table PR4)
2804	Comedy of errors (Table PR4)
2805	Coriolanus (Table PR4)
2806	Cymbeline (Table PR4)
2807	Hamlet (Table PR4 modified)
2807.A7	Corpus Hamleticum
2808	Julius Caesar (Table PR4)
2809	King Henry IV, parts 1 and 2 (Table PR4)
2810	King Henry IV, part 1 (Table PR4)
2811	King Henry IV, part 2 (Table PR4)
2812	King Henry V (Table PR4)
2813	King Henry VI, parts 1, 2, and 3 (Table PR4)
2814	King Henry VI, part 1 (Table PR4)
2815	King Henry VI, part 2 (Table PR4)
2816	King Henry VI, part 3 (Table PR4)
2817	King Henry VIII (Table PR4)
2818	King John (Table PR4)
2819	King Lear (Table PR4)
2820	King Richard II (Table PR4)
2821	King Richard III (Table PR4)
2822	Love's labour's lost (Table PR4)
2823	Macbeth (Table PR4)
2824	Measure for measure (Table PR4)
2825	Merchant of Venice (Table PR4)
2826	Merry wives of Windsor (Table PR4)
2827	Midsummer night's dream (Table PR4)
2828	Much ado about nothing (Table PR4)
2829	Othello (Table PR4)

English renaissance (1500-1640)
The drama
Individual authors
Shakespeare, William
Separate works -- Continued

2830	Pericles (Table PR4)
2831	Romeo and Juliet (Table PR4)
2832	Taming of the shrew (Table PR4)
2833	Tempest (Table PR4)
2834	Timon of Athens (Table PR4)
2835	Titus Andronicus (Table PR4)
2836	Troilus and Cressida (Table PR4)
2837	Twelfth night (Table PR4)
2838	Two gentlemen of Verona (Table PR4)
2839	Winter's tale (Table PR4)
2840	Lost play: Love's labour's won (Table PR4)
	Poems
2841	Collected poems
	Subarrange by editor, if given, or date
2842	Selections. Anthologies
2843	Songs
	Special poems or songs
2845	Venus and Adonis (Table PR4)
2846	Rape of Lucrece (Table PR4)
	Passionate pilgrim see PR2873.P3
2848	Sonnets (Table PR4 modified)
2848.A4	Separate sonnets. By number
	e. g.
2848.A4 no. 91	Sonnet number 91
2849	Other
	Doubtful, spurious works. "Shakespeare apocrypha"
2851	Collected works
2852	Selections, extracts
	Special works
	For original quartos, facsimiles or reprints see PR2750
2854	Arden of Feversham (Table PR4)
2855	Arraignment of Paris (Table PR4)
2856	Birth of Merlin (Table PR4)
2857	Bottom the weaver (Table 0548)
2858	Double falsehood (Table PR4)
2859	Edward III (Table PR4)
2860	Fair Em (Table PR4)
2861	Fifth of November (Table PR4)
2862	Locrine (Table PR4)
2863	London prodigal
2864	Merry devil of Edmonton (Table PR4)

English renaissance (1500-1640)
  The drama
    Individual authors
      Shakespeare, William
        Doubtful, spurious works. "Shakespeare apocrypha"
          Special works -- Continued

2865	Mucedorus (Table PR4)
2866	Puritan (Table PR4)
2867	Sir John Oldcastle
2868	Sir Thomas More (Table PR4)
2869	Thomas, Lord Cromwell (Table PR4)
2870	Two noble kinsmen (Table PR4)
2871	Vortigern (Table PR4)
2872	Yorkshire tragedy (Table PR4)
2873.A-Z	Others. By title, A-Z
	e. g.
2873.P3	Passionate pilgrim
2875	Criticism, etc.
	Imitations, paraphrases, adaptations
2877	Collected works
2878.A-Z	Adaptations, etc. of special Shakespearian works, A-Z
	Cf. .A25 under "Separate works"
2879	Other special works
	History and criticism of adaptations, etc.
2880.A1	General works
2880.A5-Z	Special authors
	e. g.
2880.D7	Dryden
	Translations
	Class here studies, etc. only
	For texts of translations see PR2775+
2881	General works
2881.5.A-Z	By language, A-Z
2883	Illustrations
	For illustrated editions see PR2752+
	For Shakespeare portraits, etc. see PR2928+
	For Shakespearean women see PR2991
	Shakespeare and music
	Works about music in relation to Shakespeare's poems and plays see ML80.S5
	Shakespeare's knowledge and treatment of musical subjects see PR3034
	Criticism, biography, etc.
	Bibliography see Z8811+
	Discussions of folios, quartos, etc. see PR3070+
2885	Periodicals

English renaissance (1500-1640)
The drama
Individual authors
Shakespeare, William
Criticism, biography, etc. -- Continued
Societies

2887	American
2888	English
2889	Other
2890	Collected works
2891	Collected prints, etc.

e.g. Folger Shakespeare Library prints
For special subjects, see PR2883, PR2915+, PR2929, etc.

2892	Concordances, dictionaries, indexes, quotations
2893	Historical sources and documents of the biography of Shakespeare

Cf. PR2952+ Sources of authorship
General treatises, essays, etc.
Class here literary biography, popular accounts, "Life and works"
Comprehensive
English

2894	General works
2895	Outlines, primers, etc.

Cf. PR2987 Study and teaching

2896	French
2897	German
2898.A-Z	Other, A-Z
2899	Addresses, essays, lectures
2900	General works
2901	Family. Ancestry. Name
2903	Youth. Education
	Love and marriage. Relation to women
2905	General works
2906	Anne Hathaway
2907	London: Creative period
2908	Return to Stratford. Death. Will
2909	Autobiographical and biographical allusions

Including "Keys" to personal references in the works, etc.
Cf. PR2848 Sonnets
Cf. PR2959 Allusions in works of contemporaries

2910	The age of Shakespeare. Elizabethan England

Cf. PR3000+ Shakespeare's treatment and knowledge of special subjects

English renaissance (1500-1640)
   The drama
     Individual authors
       Shakespeare, William
         Criticism, biography, etc. -- Continued
           Relations to contemporaries, etc.
             For literary relationships see PR2952+

2911	General works
2912.A-Z	English. By name, A-Z
2913	Other
	Homes and haunts
2915	General works
2916	Stratford and Warwickshire
	London
2918	General works
2920	Theaters
2923	Anniversaries. Celebrations
	Memorials. Testimonials to his genius
2924.A-Z	Monuments, windows, fountains, gardens, etc. By place, A-Z
	Cf. PR2930 Iconography
2925	Literary memorials
2926	Poetry
2927	Prose
	Iconography
	For illustrations to Shakespeare see PR2883
2928	General works, history, etc.
	Illustrations by special artists see NC1+
2929	Portraits
2930	Monuments
	Relics, museums, collections, exhibitions
2931	General works
2932	Stratford
2933.A-Z	Other, A-Z
2933.F64	Folger Shakespeare Library
2933.G35	Gallery Stratford (Ontario)
2933.H3	Halliwell-Phillipps collections
2933.H46	Henry E. Huntington Library and Art Gallery
2933.H52	Hickmott (Allerton Cushman) Collection
2933.L37	Lehigh University. Library. Rare Book Room
2933.M45	Meisei Daigaku. Toshokan
2933.O8	Oxford University
2933.U55	University of Illinois Library
2933.Y34	Yale Center for British Art
2935	Fiction, drama, etc., based upon Shakespeare's life
	Shakespeare in particular countries see PR2971.A+
	Authorship

English renaissance (1500-1640)
  The drama
    Individual authors
      Shakespeare, William
        Authorship -- Continued

2937	General works
	Bacon-Shakespeare controversy
2939	Pro-Shakespeare
	Including histories of the controversy and judicial estimates
	Baconian theory
2941	Periodicals. Societies. Collections
	Controversial literature
2943	Early to 1880
	Recent
2944	English
2945	Other
2946	Addresses, essays, lectures
2947.A-Z	Other hypotheses, A-Z
2948	Satire, humor, etc.
	Manuscripts. Writing. Signatures
2949	General works
2950	Ireland forgeries. By author
2951	Collier controversy
	Cf. PR3071 Textual criticism
	Sources
2952	General works
2952.5	Collections
2953.A-Z	Special. By subject, A-Z
2953.A7	Archpriest controversy
2953.E6	Emblem literature
2953.M54	Middle Ages
2953.M65	Moralities
2953.R4	Renaissance
2953.W5	Wit and humor. "Shakespeare jest books"
2954.A-Z	Literatures of other countries, A-Z
	e. g.
2954.I7	Italian
2954.S7	Spanish
2955.A-Z	Special authors or works, A-Z
2955.A68	Apuleius
2955.C53	Chaucer
2955.H7	Holinshed's Chronicles
2955.L8	Lyly
2955.M8	Montaigne
2955.O86	Ovid
2955.P6	Plutarch

English renaissance (1500-1640)
The drama
Individual authors
Shakespeare, William
Authorship
Sources
Special authors or works, A-Z -- Continued

2955.S45	Seneca
2956	Forerunners
	Cf. PR651+ Elizabethan era treatises
	Relations to his contemporaries
2957	General works
2958.A-Z	Special, A-Z
	e. g.
2958.B4	Beaumont and Fletcher
2958.J6	Jonson
2958.M3	Marlowe
2959	Allusions
2961	Chronology of works
	Criticism and interpretation
	History of Shakespearian criticism
2965	General
	By period
2967	17th century
2968	18th century
2969	19th century
2970	20th century
2971.A-Z	By region or country, A-Z
	e.g. Shakespeare in France, Germany, etc.
	Cf. PR3105+ Dramatic representations of
	Shakespeare's plays
2972.A-Z	Biography of Shakespeare scholars, A-Z
	e. g.
2972.C76	Crosby, Joseph
2972.F7	Furness, Horace Howard
2972.M3	Malone, Edmond
	Influence on special authors
	see the author, e.g. de Musset in PQ; Heine in PT;
	etc.
	Treatises, essays, etc.
	Cf. PR2894+ General treatises in English
	English
2975	Early to 1800
2976	Recent
2977	French
2978	German
2979.A-Z	Other, A-Z

	English renaissance (1500-1640)
	The drama
	Individual authors
	Shakespeare, William
	Criticism and interpretation -- Continued
	Special forms
	For criticism of individual works, see the work
2981	Comedies
2981.5	Tragicomedies (Romances)
2982	Histories. English chronicle plays
2983	Tragedies
	Including Roman history plays
2984	Poems
	For the sonnets see PR2848
2986	Philosophy, aesthetics, etc
	e.g. Idealism, naturalism
	Cf. PR2894+ General criticism, biography, etc.
	Cf. PR2975+ General criticism and interpretation
2987	Study and teaching
	Including outlines, syllabi, synopses, etc.
	Cf. PR2895 Outlines, primers, etc., of general criticism, biography, etc.
	Characters. Treatment of life
	Class here works dealing with characters from several plays only
	For works on the characters of a particular drama see PR2801+
	Cf. PR2997.A+ Technique (Special subjects)
2989	General works
	Special
	Groups. Classes
2991	Women
2992.A-Z	Other, A-Z
2992.C4	Children
2992.C6	Comic characters
2992.D38	Daughters
2992.F3	Fathers
2992.F6	Fools
2992.H4	Heroes
2992.K5	Kings and rulers
2992.M28	Men
2992.M3	Mentally ill
2992.M53	Midwives
2992.M65	Monsters
	Rulers see PR2992.K5
2992.S25	Satirists
2992.S47	Servants

English renaissance (1500-1640)
   The drama
      Individual authors
         Shakespeare, William
            Criticism and interpretation
               Characters. Treatment of life
                  Special
                     Groups. Classes
                       Other, A-Z -- Continued

2992.T74	Trickters
2992.V5	Villains
2992.W4	Welshmen
2993.A-Z	Individual, A-Z
	e. g.
	Cf. PR2801+ Shakespeare's separate works
2993.F2	Falstaff
2994	Wit and humor
	Technique. Dramatic art
	Cf. PR2894+ General criticism, biography, etc.
	Cf. PR2975+ General criticism and interpretation
	Cf. PR3070+ Textual criticism
2995	General works
2997.A-Z	Special. By subject, A-Z
	Action see PR2997.G4
2997.A53	Allegory
2997.A63	Ambiguity
2997.A8	Asides
2997.C55	Closure
2997.G4	Gesture. Action
2997.I46	Imitation
2997.N37	Narration
2997.O65	Openings
2997.P37	Parody
2997.P6	Plots
	Cf. PR2877 Collected paraphrases, etc.
	Cf. PR2987 Study and teaching
2997.P7	Proverbs
2997.P8	Puns
2997.R4	Reported events
2997.S3	Scene structure
2997.S55	Silence
2997.S7	Soliloquies
2997.S75	Sound
2997.S8	Suspense
2997.S87	Symbolism
2997.T5	Time
2997.U5	Unities

English renaissance (1500-1640)
The drama
Individual authors
Shakespeare, William
Criticism and interpretation -- Continued
Treatment and knowledge of special subjects

3000	General works
3001	Philosophy
3004	The supernatural. Folklore, etc.
3007	Ethics
3009	Mythology
	Religion
3011	General works
3012	The Bible
3014	History. Geography
3017	Politics
3021	Economics. Laboring classes, etc.
	Sociology
3024	General works
3026	Crime and statistics
3028	Law. Legal knowledge
3031	Education
3034	The arts: Music, painting, theater, etc.
3036	Crafts. Technical arts
	e.g. Printing
3037	Literature. The classics
	Nature
3039	General works
3041	Botany
3044	Zoology. Animals
	Science
3047	General works
3049	Mathematics
3053	Astronomy. Astrology
3056	Physics
3059	Chemistry
	Medicine
3062	General works
3065	Psychology. Psychiatry
	Including insanity
	Cf. PR2992.M3 Mentally ill in Shakespeare's works
3067	Sports
3069.A-Z	Other special subjects, A-Z
3069.A37	Africa
3069.A38	Aging
3069.A42	Ambition

English renaissance (1500-1640)
  The drama
    Individual authors
      Shakespeare, William
        Criticism and interpretation
          Treatment and knowledge of special subjects
            Other special subjects, A-Z -- Continued

3069.A425	Androgyny
	Animals see PR3044
3069.A6	Archery
3069.B5	Birds
3069.B58	Body, Human
3069.B6	Books and reading
3069.C37	Carnival
3069.C45	Choice (Psychology)
3069.C53	Conduct of life
3069.C56	Conscience
3069.C57	Constancy
	Contrariety see PR3069.P64
3069.C6	Costume
3069.D42	Death
3069.D55	Dilemma
3069.D57	Disguise
3069.D64	Dogs
3069.D67	Dreams
3069.D7	Drinking
3069.E37	East. Orient
3069.E87	Europe
3069.E92	Executions and executioners
3069.E94	Exile (Punishment)
3069.F35	Family
3069.F36	Farewells
3069.F37	Fathers
3069.F64	Food
3069.F66	France
3069.F73	Friendship
3069.H4	Heraldry
3069.H6	Honor
3069.H64	Horses
3069.H85	Hunting
3069.I57	Incest
3069.I69	Iran. Persia
3069.I7	Ireland
3069.I8	Italy
3069.L3	Languages
3069.L46	Letter-writing. Letters
3069.L6	Love

English renaissance (1500-1640)
  The drama
    Individual authors
      Shakespeare, William
        Criticism and interpretation
          Treatment and knowledge of special subjects
          Other special subjects, A-Z -- Continued

3069.M27	Management
3069.M3	Manners and customs
3069.M32	Marriage
3069.M34	The Marvelous
3069.M43	Measurement
3069.M44	Mediterranean Region
3069.M46	Memory
3069.M47	Middle Ages
3069.M5	Military life
3069.M68	Mourning customs
3069.N8	Numismatics
	Orient see PR3069.E37
	Persia see PR3069.I69
3069.P64	Polarity. Contrariety
3069.P67	Poverty
3069.P74	Pregnancy
3069.R33	Race
	Reading see PR3069.B6
3069.R36	Reconciliation
3069.R4	Repentance
3069.R44	Resurrection
3069.R46	Revenge
3069.R55	Rites and ceremonies
3069.R59	Role playing
3069.R6	Rome
3069.S36	Scotland
3069.S4	Self-knowledge
3069.S45	Sex role
3069.S55	Solitude
3069.S58	Spain
3069.S6	Speech
3069.S94	Swearing
3069.T5	Time
3069.V55	Violence
3069.W37	War
3069.W53	Widows
3069.W65	Wonder
3069.W67	Work

English renaissance (1500-1640)
The drama
Individual authors
Shakespeare, William
Criticism and interpretation -- Continued
Textual criticism, commentaries, emendations, etc.
Cf. PR2894+ General criticism, biography, etc.
Cf. PR2975+ General criticism and interpretation

3070	Early works
3071	Recent
	Language, style, etc.
3072	General works
	Dictionaries see PR2892
	Grammar
3075	General works
3077	Use of words
3078	Syntax
3081	Other special (not A-Z)
	Including pronunciation
3085	Versification
3087	Prose
3088	Dialect
	Dramatic representation of Shakespeare's plays
	General works
3091	English
3092	Other
3093	Motion-picture and video productions of Shakespeare's plays
	By period
3095	Elizabethan
3097	17th-18th centuries
3099	1800-1950
3100	1951-
	By region or country
	Cf. PR2971.A+ Shakespeare in particular countries
3105	America
3106	Great Britain
3107	France
3108	Germany
3109.A-Z	Other regions or countries, A-Z
3112	Famous actors of Shakespearian parts
3135.S3	Sharpe, Lewis (Table P-PZ40)
3135.S5	Sharpham, Edward (Table P-PZ40)
3137.S7	Shirley, Henry (Table P-PZ40)
3140-3148	Shirley, James (Table P-PZ33)
	Cf. PR2339.S54 Prose and poetry

	English renaissance (1500-1640)
	The drama
	Individual authors -- Continued
3153.S3	Smith, Wentworth (Table P-PZ40)
3153.S5	Sparrow, Thomas (Table P-PZ40)
3157.S7	Stevenson, William (Table P-PZ40)
3157.S75	Stirling, William Alexander, 1st Earl of (Table P-PZ40)
3157.S8	Strode, William (Table P-PZ40)
3157.S9	Stub, Edmund (Table P-PZ40)
	Suckling, Sir John see PR3718
3167.T3	Tailor, Robert (Table P-PZ40)
3167.T7	Tomkis, Thomas (Table P-PZ40)
3170-3174	Tourneur, Cyril (Table P-PZ35)
3175.T5	Townshend, Aurelian (Table P-PZ40)
3176.U3	Udall, Nicholas (Table P-PZ40)
3176.V4	Verney, Francis (Table P-PZ40)
3176.W2	Wager, Lewis (Table P-PZ40)
3176.W22	Wager, William (Table P-PZ40)
3176.W25	Wapull, George (Table P-PZ40)
3180-3188	Webster, John (Table P-PZ33)
3190.W3	Wever, Richard (Table P-PZ38)
3190.W4	Whetstone, George (Table P-PZ40)
3190.W5	Wilde, George (Table P-PZ40)
3190.W6	Wilkins, George (Table P-PZ40)
3190.W63	Wilmot, Robert (Table P-PZ40)
3190.W64	Wilson, Arthur (Table P-PZ40)
3190.W7	Wilson, Robert (Table P-PZ40)
3190.W8	Wingfield, Anthony (Table P-PZ40)
3193.W5	Woodes, Nathaniel (Table P-PZ40)
3194.Y3	Yarington, Robert (Table P-PZ40)
3195.Z7	Zouche, Richard (Table P-PZ40)
	Translations from foreign literatures
	Collections see PN6011+
	Individual authors and works
	see subclasses PQ - PT
	17th and 18th centuries (1640-1770)
3291	Anonymous works (Table P-PZ28)
	Individual authors
	Subarrange by Table P-PZ39 or Table P-PZ40 unless otherwise specified
3300-3308	Addison, Joseph (Table P-PZ33 modified)
	Collected works
3300	By date
3300.D00-.D99	1700-1799
3300.E00-.E99	1800-1899
3300.F00-.F99	1900-1999
3300.G00-.G99	2000-2099

17th and 18th centuries (1640-1770)

Individual authors -- Continued

3310-3314	Akenside, Mark (Table P-PZ35)
3315.A3	Allibond, John (Table P-PZ40)
3315.A35	Alsop, Anthony (Table P-PZ40)
3315.A4	Amhurst, Nicholas (Table P-PZ40)
3315.A45	Amory, Thomas (Table P-PZ40)
3315.A48	Anderson, Edward, 18th cent. (Table P-PZ40)
	Anderson, Edward, 1763-1843 see PR3315.A48
3315.A5	Andre, (Major) John (Table P-PZ40)
3315.A65	Annesley, James, 1715-1760 (Table P-PZ40)
	Ansbach, Elizabeth, Margravine of see PR3388.C15
3316.A3	Anstey, Christopher (Table P-PZ40)
3316.A36	Antrobus, Benjamin (Table P-PZ40)
3316.A4	Arblay, Mme. Frances (Burney) d' (Table P-PZ40)
3316.A46	Arbuckle, James (Table P-PZ40)
3316.A5	Arbuthnot, John (Table P-PZ40)
3316.A6	Armstrong, John (Table P-PZ40)
3316.A65	Arrowsmith, Joseph, fl. 1673 (Table P-PZ40)
3316.A68	Aubin, Penelope, 1679-1731 (Table P-PZ40)
3316.A685	Austen, Katherine, 1628-1683 (Table P-PZ40)
3316.A7	Aylet, Robert (Table P-PZ40)
3316.B13	Bacon, James, fl. 1795 (Table P-PZ40)
3316.B17	Baker, Daniel (Table P-PZ40)
3316.B2	Bampfylde, John (Table P-PZ40)
3316.B25	Banks, John, fl. 1696 (Table P-PZ40)
3316.B27	Barber, Mary, ca. 1690-1757 (Table P-PZ40)
3316.B28	Barker, Jane (Table P-PZ40)
3316.B3	Baron, Robert (Table P-PZ40)
3316.B36	Baxter, Richard (Table P-PZ40)
3316.B4	Beattie, James, 1735-1803 (Table P-PZ38)
3316.B5	Beaumont, Joseph (Table P-PZ40)
	Beckford, William see PR4091+
3316.B7	Beckingham, Charles (Table P-PZ40)
3317	Behn, Aphra (Table P-PZ39)
3318.B2	Belon, Peter (Table P-PZ40)
3318.B3	Bentley, Richard (Table P-PZ40)
	For collected works see PA27
3318.B35	Berington, Simon, 1680-1755 (Table P-PZ40)
3318.B4	Bickerstaffe, Issac (Table P-PZ40)
3318.B42	Bicknell, Alexander, d. 1796 (Table P-PZ40)
3318.B45	Biddulph, John, 1725?-1774? (Table P-PZ40)
3318.B5	Blackmore, Sir Richard (Table P-PZ40)
3318.B7	Blair, Robert (Table P-PZ40)
	Blake, William see PR4140+
3318.B75	Blamire, Susanna, 1747-1794 (Table P-PZ40)
3324.B4	Boaden, James (Table P-PZ40)

	17th and 18th centuries (1640-1770)
	Individual authors -- Continued
	Bobbin, Tim, 1708-1786 see PR3349.C8
3325	Boswell, James, 1740-1795 (Table P-PZ37)
3326.B2	Bourne, Vincent (Table P-PZ40)
	Bowdler, Harriet see PR3326.B24
3326.B24	Bowdler, Henrietta Maria (Table P-PZ40)
3326.B25	Bowdler, Jane (Table P-PZ40)
3326.B257	Boyd, Elizabeth (Table P-PZ40)
	Boyle, Charles see PR3607.O4
3326.B277	Bramston, James, 1694?-1744 (Table P-PZ40)
3326.B3	Brewer, Anthony (Table P-PZ40)
3326.B35	Bristol, George Digby, 2d Earl of (Table P-PZ40)
3326.B36	Brome, Alexander, 1620-1666 (Table P-PZ40)
3326.B37	Brooke, Frances Moore, 1724?-1789 (Table P-PZ40)
3326.B4	Brooke, Henry (Table P-PZ40)
3326.B6	Broome, William (Table P-PZ40)
3326.B9	Brown, James (Table P-PZ40)
3326.B92	Brown, John, 1715-1766 (Table P-PZ40)
3326.B93	Brown, Thomas, 1663-1704 (Table P-PZ40)
3327	Browne, Sir Thomas (Table P-PZ37)
3328.B3	Bruce, Michael (Table P-PZ40)
3328.B5	Buckingham, George Villiers, 2nd Duke of (Table P-PZ38)
3328.B6	Buckingham, John Sheffield, 1st Duke of (Table P-PZ40)
	Bunyan, John
	Collected works see BR75
3329.A1	Collected allegorical works
	Special works
	Divine emblems
3329.D1	English texts. By date
	Translations
3329.D4	Dutch
3329.D5	French
3329.D6	German
3329.D7	Scandinavian
3329.D71-.D89	Other languages, A-Z
3329.D9	Criticism
	Grace abounding
3329.G1	English texts. By date
	Translations
3329.G4	Dutch
3329.G5	French
3329.G6	German
3329.G7	Scandinavian
3329.G71-.G89	Other languages, A-Z
3329.G9	Criticism
	Holy war

17th and 18th centuries (1640-1770)
Individual authors
Bunyan, John
Special works
Holy war -- Continued

3329.H1	English texts. By date
	Translations
3329.H4	Dutch
3329.H5	French
3329.H6	German
3329.H7	Scandinavian
3329.H71-.H89	Other languages, A-Z
3329.H9	Criticism
	Life and death of Mr. Badman
3329.L1	English texts. By date
	Translations
3329.L4	Dutch
3329.L5	French
3329.L6	German
3329.L7	Scandinavian
3329.L71-.L89	Other languages, A-Z
3329.L9	Criticism
	Pilgrim's progress
	English editions
3330.A1	By date
3330.A2	By editor or illustrator
3330.A22	Selections
3330.A25	Juvenile versions
3330.A3	Metrical versions
3330.A33	Dramatizations
	Translations. By date
3330.A35	Dutch
3330.A4	French
3330.A5	German
3330.A55	Greek
3330.A6	Italian
3330.A65	Scandinavian
3330.A7	Spanish and Portuguese
3330.A71-.A89	Other languages (alphabetically)
	e. g.
3330.A72	American Indian
3330.A75	Hawaiian
3330.A77	Hungarian
3330.A782	Lushai
3330.A83	Polish
3330.A85	Russian
3330.A86	Ruthenian

	17th and 18th centuries (1640-1770)
	Individual authors
	Bunyan, John
	Special works
	Pilgrim's progress -- Continued
3330.A9	Criticism
3330.A95	Miscellaneous. Outlines
	Other works
	see class B
	Biography and criticism
3331	General works
3332	Criticism
3333.B7	Burgoyne, General John (Table P-PZ40)
3334.B4	Burke, Edmund (Table P-PZ40)
3334.B7	Burke, Walter (Table P-PZ40)
3334.B8	Burnaby, William (Table P-PZ40)
	Burney, Frances see PR3316.A4
3337.B5	Bushe, Amyas (Table P-PZ40)
3338	Butler, Samuel (Table P-PZ37)
3339.B5	Byrom, John (Table P-PZ40)
3339.C15	Canning, George (Table P-PZ40)
3339.C2	Carew, Thomas (Table P-PZ40)
3339.C23	Carey, Henry (Table P-PZ40)
3339.C245	Carkesse, James, fl. 1652-1679 (Table P-PZ40)
3339.C3	Carpenter, Richard (Table P-PZ40)
3339.C32	Carr, John, 1732-1807 (Table P-PZ40)
3339.C43	Cary, Patrick, fl. 1651 (Table P-PZ40)
3339.C6	Centlivre, Susanna, 1667?-1723 (Table P-PZ40)
3339.C97	Charleton, Walter, 1619-1707 (Table P-PZ40)
3340-3344	Chatterton, Thomas (Table P-PZ35)
3346.C2	Chesterfield, Philip Dormer Stanhope, 4th Earl of (Table P-PZ40)
	For letters to his son and godson see BJ1671+
	Cf. DA501.C5 English history
3346.C3	Chetwood, William (Table P-PZ40)
3346.C6	Chudleigh, Mary Lee, Lady, 1656-1710 (Table P-PZ40)
3346.C8	Churchill, Charles (Table P-PZ40)
3347	Cibber, Colley, 1671-1757 (Table P-PZ37)
3348.C13	Cibber, Theophilus, 1703-1787 (Table P-PZ40)
3348.C2	Clark, Ewan (Table P-PZ40)
3348.C3	Clark, John (Table P-PZ40)
	Clarke, Samuel
	see class B
3348.C65	Cleland, John, 1709-1789 (Table P-PZ40)
3348.C7	Cleveland, John (Table P-PZ40)
3349.C	Coa - Col
3349.C22	Cockburn, Catharine Trotter, 1679-1749 (Table P-PZ40)

	17th and 18th centuries (1640-1770)
	Individual authors
	Coa - Col -- Continued
3349.C3	Cokayne, Sir Aston (Table P-PZ40)
3349.C8	Collier, John (Table P-PZ40)
3349.C85	Collins, An, 17th cent. (Table P-PZ40)
3350-3354	Collins, William (Table P-PZ35)
3356.C5	Collop, John (Table P-PZ40)
3356.C54	Collyer, Mary Mitchell, d. 1763 (Table P-PZ40)
3358	Colman, George (Table P-PZ39)
3359.C27	Colman, Henry (Table P-PZ40)
3359.C29	Colvill, Mr. (Robert), d. 1788 (Table P-PZ40)
3359.C5	Combe, William (Table P-PZ40)
3360-3368	Congreve, William (Table P-PZ33 modified)
	Collected works
3360	By date
3360.D00-.D99	1700-1799
3360.E00-.E99	1800-1899
3360.F00-.F99	1900-1999
3360.G00-.G99	2000-2099
3369.C15	Cooke, Thomas (Table P-PZ40)
3369.C17	Cooper, Mrs. (Elizabeth), fl. 1737 (Table P-PZ40)
3369.C2	Corbet, Richard (Table P-PZ40)
3369.C3	Cotton, Charles (Table P-PZ40)
3369.C7	Coventry, Francis, d. 1759 (Table P-PZ40)
3370-3374	Cowley, Abraham (Table P-PZ35)
3379.C3	Cowley, Hannah (Parkhouse) (Table P-PZ40)
3379.C5	Cowper, Ashley ("Tim Scribble") (Table P-PZ40)
3379.C7	Cowper, Frances Maria (Table P-PZ40)
3380-3384	Cowper, William (Table P-PZ35)
3385.C5	Cradock, Joseph (Table P-PZ40)
3385.C75	Cranley, Thomas, fl. 1635 (Table P-PZ40)
3386	Crashaw, Richard, 1613?-1649 (Table P-PZ37)
3388.C15	Craven, Elizabeth (Berkeley), Baroness Craven, afterwards Margravine of Ansbach (Table P-PZ40)
3388.C2	Crowne, John (Table P-PZ40)
3388.C25	Croxall, Samuel, d. 1752 (Table P-PZ40)
3390-3394	Cumberland, Richard (Table P-PZ35)
3395.D4	Dalrymple, Hugh (Table P-PZ40)
3395.D43	Dalton, John, 1709-1763 (Table P-PZ40)
3395.D54	D'Anvers, Alicia (Table P-PZ40)
3395.D87	Darwall, Mary Whateley, 1738-1825 (Table P-PZ40)
3396	Darwin, Erasmus (Table P-PZ37)
	D'Arblay see PR3316.A4
3397.D6	Davys, Mary, 1674-1731 (Table P-PZ40)
3398.D3	Day, Thomas (Table P-PZ40)
	Defoe, Daniel

	17th and 18th centuries (1640-1770)
	Individual authors
	Defoe, Daniel -- Continued
3400	Works. By date
3401	Selections
3402	Translations
	Separate works
3403	Robinson Crusoe
3403.A1	Texts. By date
3403.A2	Abridgment. School texts, etc.
3403.A3	Adaptations, etc. By author
3403.A5-.Z3	Translations. By language, A-Z

	Under each:
.x	Translation
.x2	Adaptation

| 3403.Z5A-.Z5Z | Criticism |

Class studies of the "Robinsonade" in general or in particular countries, if not dealing largely with Defoe's work, in PN3432

| 3404.A-Z | Other works, A-Z |

Fortunes and misfortunes of the famous Moll Flanders see PR3404.M6+

3404.J6-.J63	Journal of the plague year (Table P-PZ43)
3404.M6-.M63	Moll Flanders (Table P-PZ43)
3405	Apocryphal, spurious works, etc. (Collections only)
	Illustrations

Class at N8215, or with the special artists in NC-NE
Class illustrated editions with other editions
Class portraits, etc., of the author with his biography

	Biography, criticism, etc.
3406.A1-.A19	Periodicals. Societies. Serials
3406.A2-.A3	Dictionaries, indexes, etc.
3406.A31-.A39	Autobiography, journals, memoirs. By title
3406.A4	Letters (Collections). By date
3406.A41-.A49	Letters to and from particular individuals. By correspondent (alphabetically)
3406.A5-Z	General works
	Criticism
3407	General works
3408.A-Z	Special, A-Z

For list of Cutter numbers, see Table P-PZ32 17

3409.D2	Denham, Sir John (Table P-PZ40)
3409.D3	Dennis, John (Table P-PZ40)
3409.D4	Dermody, Thomas (Table P-PZ40)
3409.D5	Digby, Sir Kenelm (Table P-PZ40)
	Doctor Suntax, 1742-1823 see PR3359.C5
3409.D6	Dodd, William (Table P-PZ40)

	17th and 18th centuries (1640-1770)
	Individual authors -- Continued
3409.D7	Dodsley, Robert (Table P-PZ40)
3409.D74	Donaldson, William (Table P-PZ40)
3409.D75	Dorset, Charles Sackville, 6th Earl of, 1643-1706 (Table P-PZ40)
3410-3428	Dryden, John (Table P-PZ32 modified)
	Separate works
3415.A-Z	Dramas, A-Z
	Subarrange each by Table P-PZ43
	Other works
3416.A-.E	By title, A-Esr
	Subarrange each by Table P-PZ43
3417	Essays
3418.E-.P	By title, Est-Pak
	Subarrange each by Table P-PZ43
3419	Palamon and Arcite
	Subarrange by editor
3420.P-Z	Pam-Z
	Subarrange each by Table P-PZ43
3429.D48	Duff, William, 1732-1815 (Table P-PZ40)
3429.D5	Duffett, Thomas (Table P-PZ40)
3429.D6	Duncombe, John, 1729-1786 (Table P-PZ40)
3430.D3	Dunkin, William (Table P-PZ40)
3430.D7	Dunton, John (Table P-PZ40)
3431.D3	D'Urfey, Thomas (Table P-PZ40)
3431.D5	Dyer, John (Table P-PZ38)
3431.E18	Edwards, Thomas (Table P-PZ40)
3431.E19	Egerton, Sarah Fyge (Table P-PZ40)
3431.E2	Elliot, Jane (Table P-PZ40)
3431.E5	Ellwood, Thomas (Table P-PZ40)
3431.E57	Ephelia, fl. 1679 (Table P-PZ40)
3431.E7	Erskine, Ralph (Table P-PZ40)
3432	Etherege, Sir George (Table P-PZ37)
3433.E5	Evelyn, John (Table P-PZ40)
3433.E52	Evelyn, Mary, 1665-1685 (Table P-PZ40)
3433.F3	Falconer, William (Table P-PZ40)
3433.F5	Falkland, Henry Cary, 4th viscount (Table P-PZ40)
3433.F7	Fanshawe, Richard, Sir, 1608-1666 (Table P-PZ40)
3434.F	Fare - Farq
3434.F2	Farewell, James (Table P-PZ40)
3435-3439	Farquhar, George (Table P-PZ35)
3442.F	Farq - Fent
	Faulkland, Henry Cary, 4th viscount see PR3433.F5
3446	Fenton, Elijah (Table P-PZ39)
3448.F3	Fergusson, Robert, 1750-1774 (Table P-PZ38)
3450-3458	Fielding, Henry (Table P-PZ33 modified)

	17th and 18th centuries (1640-1770)
	Individual authors
	Fielding, Henry -- Continued
	Collected works
3450	By date
3450.D00-.D99	1700-1799
3450.E00-.E99	1800-1899
3450.F00-.F99	1900-1999
3450.G00-.G99	2000-2099
3459.F3	Fielding, Sarah (Table P-PZ40)
3460.F	Fin - Fis
3461.F2	Fisher, James (Table P-PZ40)
3461.F3	Flatman, Thomas (Table P-PZ40)
3461.F4	Flecknoe, Richard (Table P-PZ40)
3461.F6	Foote, Samuel, 1720-1777 (Table P-PZ38)
3461.F665	Fowke, Martha, 1689-1736 (Table P-PZ40)
3461.F667	Fowler, Constance Aston, b. ca. 1621 (Table P-PZ40)
3461.F8	Fuller, Thomas (Table P-PZ40)
3461.F9	Fyfe, Alexander (Table P-PZ40)
3463.G4	Galloway, Robert (Table P-PZ40)
3463.G5	Gambold, John (Table P-PZ40)
3465-3469	Garrick, David (Table P-PZ35)
	For the biography of Garrick see PN2598.5
3471.G3	Garth, Sir Samuel (Table P-PZ40)
3473-3474	Gay, John (Table P-PZ36)
3475.G5	Gentleman, Francis (Table P-PZ40)
3475.G9	Gibbes, Phoebe (Table P-PZ40)
3476	Gibbon, Edward (Table P-PZ39)
3477.G4	Gibson, John (Table P-PZ40)
3478.G3	Gildon, Charles (Table P-PZ40)
3478.G5	Glover, Richard (Table P-PZ40)
3478.G7	Godwin, Francis, 1562-1633 (Table P-PZ40)
	Goldsmith, Oliver
	Collected works
3480	By date
3481	By editor
3482	Selections
	Including collected essays and poems
3484.A-Z	Translations. By language, A-Z
	Separate works
3485.A-.D	A - D
3485.B4	The Bee
3485.C5	Citizen of the world
3486	Deserted village
3487.D-.S	D - S
3487.E8	Essays (Collected)
3487.H4	The Hermit

	17th and 18th centuries (1640-1770)
	Individual authors
	Goldsmith, Oliver
	Separate works -- Continued
3488	She stoops to conquer
3489.S-.V	S - V
3489.T7	The Traveller
3490	Vicar of Wakefield
3491.V-Z	V - Z
3492	Dictionaries, indexes, etc.
3493	General works on Goldsmith's life and writings
	Criticism
3494	General works
3498	Language, grammar, style
3499.G5	Grahame, James (Table P-PZ40)
3499.G7	Grainger, James (Table P-PZ40)
3499.G77	Graves, Richard (Table P-PZ40)
3499.G8	Gray, Robert (Table P-PZ40)
	Gray, Thomas
	Collected works
3500.A1	To 1800. By date
	1800-
3500.A2	By date
3500.A5A-.A5Z	By editor, if given
3500.A6-Z	Translations (Collected or selected). By language, A-Z
	Subarrange by translator, if given, or date
3501	Selected works. Selections. By editor, if given, or date
3502.A-Z	Separate works. By title, A-Z
	Subarrange each title by Table P-PZ43
	Biography
3503.A1-.A19	Periodicals. Societies. Serials
3503.A2-.A29	Autobiography, journals, memoirs. By title
	Correspondence
3503.A3	General collections
3503.A4A-.A4Z	Special persons, A-Z
3503.A5-Z	General works
3504	Criticism
3505.G4	Griffin, Benjamin (Table P-PZ40)
3505.G85	Gunning, Susannah Minifie, 1740-1800 (Table P-PZ40)
3505.G86	Guthrie, William (Table P-PZ40)
3505.G94	Gwynn, John, d. 1786 (Table P-PZ40)
3505.H3	Habington, William (Table P-PZ40)
3505.H5	Hales, John (Table P-PZ40)
3506.H2	Halifax, Charles Montagu, Earl of (Table P-PZ40)
3506.H3	Hall, John (Table P-PZ40)
3506.H38	Hamilton, Mary, Lady, 1739-1816 (Table P-PZ40)
3506.H388	Hamilton, William, ca. 1665-1751 (Table P-PZ40)

17th and 18th centuries (1640-1770)
Individual authors -- Continued

3506.H39	Hamilton, William, 1704-1754 (Table P-PZ40)
3506.H47	Hardinge, George, 1743-1816 (Table P-PZ40)
3506.H67	Harvey, Christopher (Table P-PZ40)
3506.H8	Harvey, John (Table P-PZ40)
3506.H86	Hawkesworth, John, 1715?-1773 (Table P-PZ40)
3506.H87	Hawkins, William (Table P-PZ40)
3506.H9	Hayley, William (Table P-PZ40)
3506.H93	Hayward, Amey (Table P-PZ40)
3506.H94	Haywood, Mrs. Eliza (Table P-PZ38)
3507-3508	Herbert, George (Table P-PZ36)
3510-3514	Herrick, Robert (Table P-PZ35)
3515.H145	Heywood, Peter, 1773-1831 (Table P-PZ40)
3515.H16	Hill, Aaron (Table P-PZ40)
3515.H163	Hill, John, 1716?-1775 (Table P-PZ40)
3515.H17	Hoadly, Benjamin (Table P-PZ40)
3515.H2	Holcroft, Thomas (Table P-PZ40)
3515.H5	Hole, Richard (Table P-PZ40)
3516	Home, John (Table P-PZ39)
3517.H118	Hoole, John, 1727-1803 (Table P-PZ40)
3517.H2	Howard, James, fl. 1674 (Table P-PZ40)
3517.H3	Howard, Sir Robert (Table P-PZ40)
3517.H5	Howell, James (Table P-PZ40)
3517.H65	Huddesford, George (Table P-PZ40)
3517.H7	Hughes, John (Table P-PZ40)
3517.H745	Hunter, John, d. 1761 (Table P-PZ40)
3517.H78	Hurd, Richard, Bp. of Worcester, 1720-1808 (Table P-PZ40)
3517.H8	Hurdis, James (Table P-PZ40)
3517.H85	Hutchinson, Lucy, b. 1620 (Table P-PZ40)
3517.I44	Imlay, Gilbert, 1754?-1828? (Table P-PZ40)
3518	Inchbald, Mrs. Elizabeth (Table P-PZ37)
	Ireland, William Henry see PR2950; PR4821.I5
3519.J13	Jacob, Hildebrand, 1693-1739 (Table P-PZ40)
3519.J15	James, Charles, d. 1821 (Table P-PZ40)
3519.J24	Jaques, Francis, fl. 1642 (Table P-PZ40)
3519.J3	Jeffreys, George (Table P-PZ40)
3519.J44	Jenner, Charles, 1736-1774 (Table P-PZ40)
3519.J45	Jenyns, Soame, 1704-1787 (Table P-PZ40)
3519.J47	Jephson, Robert, 1736-1803 (Table P-PZ40)
3519.J5	Jernigham, Edward (Table P-PZ40)
3519.J6	Jodrell, Richard Paul (Table P-PZ40)
3519.J8	Johnson, Charles (Table P-PZ40)
3520-3538	Johnson, Samuel (Table P-PZ32 modified)
3522	Selections
	Including essays and poems

PR

	17th and 18th centuries (1640-1770)
	Individual authors
	Johnson, Samuel -- Continued
3522.5	Miscellaneous essays, literary criticism, etc., by Samuel Johnson
	Separate works
	Diary of a journey into North Wales see DA727
	Idler see PR1365
3526	Irene (Table P-PZ41)
	Journey to the Western Islands of Scotland see DA880.A+
	Lives of poets see PR551+
3527	London (Table P-PZ41)
	Political tracts see DA507
	Rambler see PR1369.R3
3529	Rasselas (Table P-PZ41)
	Taxation no tyranny see E211
3530	Vanity of human wishes (Table P-PZ41)
	Visit to the Hebrides
	see subclass DA
	Voyage to Abyssinia
	see subclass D
3530.5.A-Z	Other, A-Z
	Subarrange each by Table P-PZ43
3539.J22	Johnson, Samuel, 1691-1773 (Table P-PZ40)
3539.J25	Johnstone, Charles, 1719?-1800? (Table P-PZ40)
3539.J66	Jones, William, Sir, 1746-1794 (Table P-PZ40)
3539.K13	Keach, Benjamin (Table P-PZ40)
3539.K15	Keate, George (Table P-PZ40)
3539.K17	Kellet, Alexander (Table P-PZ40)
3539.K2	Kelly, Hugh (Table P-PZ40)
3539.K22	Kelly, John, 1680?-1751 (Table P-PZ40)
3539.K26	Kendrick, W. (William), 1725?-1779 (Table P-PZ40)
3539.K27	Kidgell, John, fl. 1766 (Table P-PZ40)
3539.K3	Killigrew, Anne (Table P-PZ40)
3539.K4	Killigrew, Henry, 1613-1700 (Table P-PZ40)
3539.K5	Killigrew, Thomas, 1612-1683 (Table P-PZ38)
3539.K53	Killigrew, William, Sir, 1601-1695 (Table P-PZ40)
3539.K57	Kimber, Edward, 1719-1769 (Table P-PZ40)
3539.K65	King, Henry, Bp. of Chichester, 1592-1669 (Table P-PZ40)
3539.K7	King, William, 1663-1712 (Table P-PZ40)
3539.K73	King, William, 1685-1763 (Table P-PZ40)
3539.K75	Kirkby, John, 1705-1754 (Table P-PZ40)
3539.K8	Knight, Richard Payne (Table P-PZ40)
3539.L2	Lacy, John (Table P-PZ40)
3539.L3	Langhorne, John (Table P-PZ40)
3539.L4	Lansdowne, George Granville, Earl of (Table P-PZ40)

17th and 18th centuries (1640-1770)
Individual authors -- Continued

3539.L47	Lawrence, Herbert (Table P-PZ40)
3539.L49	Leapor, Mrs. (Mary), 1722-1746 (Table P-PZ40)
3539.L5	Learmont, John (Table P-PZ40)
3539.L6	Lee, Harriet (Table P-PZ40)
3540	Lee, Nathaniel (Table P-PZ39)
3541.L2	Lee, Sophia (Table P-PZ40)
3541.L245	Leland, Thomas, 1722-1785 (Table P-PZ40)
3541.L27	Lennox, Charlotte, ca. 1720-1804 (Table P-PZ38)
3541.L3	L'Estrange, Sir Robert (Table P-PZ40)
3541.L5	Lillo, George (Table P-PZ40)
3541.L55	Lloyd, David (Table P-PZ40)
3541.L6	Lofft, Capel (Table P-PZ40)
3541.L7	Logan, John (Table P-PZ40)
3541.L82	Longueville, Peter, fl. 1727 (Table P-PZ40)
3542.L2	Lovelace, Richard (Table P-PZ40)
3542.L3	Loveling, Benjamin (Table P-PZ40)
3542.L32	Lovell, Robert, 1770?-1796 (Table P-PZ40)
3542.L4	Lower, Sir William (Table P-PZ40)
3542.L43	Lowth, Robert, Bp. of London, 1710-1787 (Table P-PZ40)
3542.L5	Luck, Robert (Table P-PZ40)
3542.L8	Lyttelton, George Lyttelton, 1st baron (Table P-PZ40)
3543.M13	McCarthy, Charlotte, fl. 1745-1768 (Table P-PZ40)
3543.M15	Macdonald, Andrew (Table P-PZ40)
3543.M2	Mackenzie, Henry (Table P-PZ40)
3543.M3	Macklin, Charles (Table P-PZ40)
3543.M5	Macneill, Hector (Table P-PZ40)
3544	Macpherson, James, 1736-1796 ("Ossian") (Table P-PZ37)
3545.M35	Major, Elizabeth (Table P-PZ40)
3545.M4	Mallet, David, 1705?-1765 (Table P-PZ38)
3545.M6	Mandeville, Bernard (Table P-PZ40)
3545.M8	Manley, Delariviere, d. 1724 (Table P-PZ40)
3545.M87	Mante, Thomas, fl. 1772 (Table P-PZ40)
3545.M9	Marmion, Shackerley (Table P-PZ40)
3545.M955	Marshall, Jane, fl. 1765-1788 (Table P-PZ40)
3546	Marvell, Andrew (Table P-PZ37)
3548.M2	Mason, William (Table P-PZ40)
3548.M26	Mathison, Thomas, 1721-1760 (Table P-PZ40)
3548.M4	Mayne, Jasper (Table P-PZ40)
3548.M47	Meades, Anna (Table P-PZ40)
3548.M77	Merry, Robert, 1755-1798 (Table P-PZ40)
3548.M8	Meston, William (Table P-PZ40)
3549.M3	Mickle, William Julius (Table P-PZ40)
3549.M6	Miller, James (Table P-PZ40)
3550-3598	Milton, John (Table P-PZ31 modified)
3552	Selected works. Minor poems, etc.

	17th and 18th centuries (1640-1770)
	Individual authors
	Milton, John -- Continued
3553	Selections. Anthologies
	Prose collections and selections see PR3569
3554.A-Z	Translations. By language, A-Z
	Separate (poetical) works
3555	L'Allegro (and Il Penseroso) (Table P-PZ41)
3556	Il Penserose (separate) (Table P-PZ41)
3557	Comus (Table P-PZ41)
3558	Lycidas (Table P-PZ41)
3559	Ode on the Morning of Christ's nativity (Table P-PZ41)
	Paradise lost (and Paradise regained)
3560	Texts. By date
3561.A-Z	Translations. By language, A-Z
3561.A1	Modern English
	Including literal prose
3562	Criticism
3563	Paradise regained
3564	Translations
3565	Criticism
3566	Samson Agonistes (Table P-PZ41)
3567	Sonnets (Table P-PZ41)
3568.A-Z	Other, A-Z
	Subarrange each by Table P-PZ43
3569	Prose works
3570.A-Z	Separate works, A-Z
	Subarrange each by Table P-PZ43
3571	Works in Latin
3572.A-Z	Works in other languages, A-Z
	e. g.
3572.G7	Greek
3572.I8	Italian
3600.M	Min - Mis
3601.M	Mit - Miz
3602.M	Mo - Mom
3603.M2	Montagu, Elizabeth (Table P-PZ40)
3604	Montagu, Lady Mary Wortley (Table P-PZ39)
3605.M12	Montagu, Walter, 1603?-1677 (Table P-PZ40)
3605.M3	Moore, Edward (Table P-PZ40)
3605.M5	Moore, John (Table P-PZ40)
3605.M6	More, Hannah (Table P-PZ40)
3605.M7	More, Henry (Table P-PZ40)
3605.M8	Morison, David (Table P-PZ40)
3605.M813	Morris, Ralph, fl. 1751- (Table P-PZ40)
3605.M82	Motteux, Peter Anthony (Table P-PZ40)
3605.M83	Mountfort, William (Table P-PZ40)

	17th and 18th centuries (1640-1770)
	Individual authors -- Continued
3605.M85	Mozeen, Thomas, d. 1768 (Table P-PZ40)
3605.M9	Murphy, Arthur (Table P-PZ40)
3605.N2	Newcastle, Margaret (Lucas) Cavendish, Duchess of (Table P-PZ40)
3605.N4	Newcastle, William Cavendish, Duke of (Table P-PZ40)
3605.N7	Newcomb, Rev. Thomas (Table P-PZ40)
3605.N8	Norris, John, 1657-1711 (Table P-PZ40)
3605.N83	North, Dudley North, 3d Baron, 1581-1666 (Table P-PZ40)
3605.N84	North, Dudley North, 4th Baron, 1602-1677 (Table P-PZ40)
3605.N847	Norton, Frances, Lady, 1640-1731 (Table P-PZ40)
3605.O15	Ogilvie, John (Table P-PZ40)
3605.O3	O'Keeffe, John (Table P-PZ40)
3605.O4	Oldham, John (Table P-PZ40)
3605.O5	Oldmixon, John (Table P-PZ40)
3605.O6	Oldys, William (Table P-PZ40)
3607.O3	Orrery, Charles Boyle, 4th Earl of (Table P-PZ40)
3607.O4	Orrery, Roger Boyle, 1st Earl of (Table P-PZ40)
3607.O82	Osborne, Francis, 1593-1659 (Table P-PZ40)
	Ossian, 1736-1796 see PR3544
3610-3614	Otway, Thomas (Table P-PZ35)
3615.O-.P	Otway - Parnell
3615.P5	Paltock, Robert
3615.P74	Parkhurst, Ferdinando
3616	Parnell, Thomas (Table P-PZ39)
3617.P2	Parr, Samuel (Table P-PZ40)
3617.P3	Parry, James (Table P-PZ40)
3617.P7	Peck, Francis (Table P-PZ40)
3617.P76	Pellow, Thomas, b. 1704 (Table P-PZ40)
3617.P78	Penn, James, 1727-1800 (Table P-PZ40)
3617.P8	Penny, Mrs. Anne Christian (Table P-PZ40)
3617.P83	Pennyless, Peter (Table P-PZ40)
3618.P2	Pepys, Samuel (Table P-PZ40)
3619.P2	Philips, Ambrose (Table P-PZ40)
	Philips, Joan, fl. 1679 see PR3431.E57
3619.P3	Philips, John (Table P-PZ40)
3619.P4	Philips, Mrs. Katherine (Table P-PZ40)
3619.P42	Philips, William, d. 1734 (Table P-PZ40)
3619.P43	Phillips, Edward (Table P-PZ40)
	Phillips, Joan, fl. 1679 see PR3431.E57
3619.P442	Pilkington, Laetitia, 1712-1750 (Table P-PZ40)
	Pindar, Peter see PR3765.W7
3619.P5	Piozzi, Mrs. Hester (Thrale) (Table P-PZ40)
3619.P58	Pix, Mary, 1666-1720 (Table P-PZ40)
3619.P67	Polwhele, Elizabeth (Table P-PZ40)
3619.P7	Pomfret, John (Table P-PZ40)

	17th and 18th centuries (1640-1770)
	Individual authors -- Continued
3620-3638	Pope, Alexander (Table P-PZ32 modified)
	Separate works
3625	Dunciad (Table P-PZ41)
3626	Essay on criticism (Table P-PZ41)
3627	Essay on man (Table P-PZ41)
3628	Moral essays (Table P-PZ41)
3629	Rape of the lock (Table P-PZ41)
3630.A-Z	Other special works, A-Z
	Subarrange each by Table P-PZ43
3639.P35	Pordage, Samuel, 1633?-1691? (Table P-PZ40)
3639.P4	Porson, Richard (Table P-PZ40)
3639.P44	Porter, James, 1753-1798 (Table P-PZ40)
3639.P7	Preston, William (Table P-PZ40)
3640-3644	Prior, Matthew (Table P-PZ35)
3646	Prynne, William (Table P-PZ39)
3647.P6	Puckle, James (Table P-PZ40)
3648	Pye, Henry James (Table P-PZ39)
3650-3654	Quarles, Francis (Table P-PZ35)
3655.Q3	Quarles, John (Table P-PZ40)
3656.R15	Radcliffe, Alexander (Table P-PZ40)
	Radcliffe, Mrs. Anne see PR5200+
3657	Ramsay, Allan (Table P-PZ37)
3658.R17	Ravenscroft, Edward (Table P-PZ40)
3658.R2	Rawlins, Thomas (Table P-PZ40)
3658.R5	Reeve, Clara (Table P-PZ40)
	Reynolds, Frederic see PR5221.R3
3658.R62	Reynolds, John, fl. 1621-1650 (Table P-PZ40)
3658.R7	Richards, Nathaniel (Table P-PZ40)
	Richardson, Samuel
3660	Collected works. By date
3661	Collected works. By editor
3662	Selected works. Selections
	Subarrange by editor, if given, or date
3663.A-Z	Translations (Collected or selected). By language, A-Z
3664.A-Z	Separate works. By title
	Subarrange each by Table P-PZ43
3665	Apocryphal, spurious works, etc. (Collections only)
	Illustrations
	Class at N8215, or with the special artists in NC-NE as the case may be
	Class illustrated editions with other editions
	Class portraits, etc., of the author, with his biography
	Biography, criticism, etc.
3666.A1-.A19	Periodicals. Societies. Serials
3666.A2-.A3	Dictionaries, indexes, etc.

	17th and 18th centuries (1640-1770)
	Individual authors
	Richardson, Samuel
	Biography, criticism, etc. -- Continued
3666.A31-.A39	Autobiography, journals, memoirs. By title
3666.A4	Letters (Collections). By date
3666.A41-.A49	Letters to and from particular individuals. By correspondent (alphabetically)
3666.A5-Z	General works
3667	Criticism (General and special)
3668	Richardson - Robertson
3668.R3	Ridley, James (Table P-PZ40)
3668.R5	Roberts, William Hayward (Table P-PZ40)
3669.R18	Robertson, Alexander (Table P-PZ40)
3669.R2	Rochester, John Wilmot, 2d Earl of, 1647-1680 (Table P-PZ38)
3669.R7	Rolt, Richard (Table P-PZ40)
3670.R5	Roscommon, Wentworth Dillon, Earl of (Table P-PZ40)
3671.R3	Ross, Alexander (Table P-PZ40)
3671.R35	Rous, Francis (Table P-PZ40)
3671.R4	Rowe, Elizabeth (Table P-PZ40)
3671.R45	Rowe, John, 1626-1677 (Table P-PZ40)
3671.R5	Rowe, Nicholas (Table P-PZ40)
3671.R55	Rugeley, Rowland (Table P-PZ40)
3671.R6	Russell, Thomas (Table P-PZ40)
3671.R63	Russen, David, fl. 1705 (Table P-PZ40)
3671.R7	Rymer, Thomas (Table P-PZ40)
	Sansom, Martha Fowke, 1689-1736 see PR3461.F665
3671.S2	Savage, Richard (Table P-PZ40)
3671.S3	Scott, John (Table P-PZ40)
3671.S32	Scott, Mary (Table P-PZ40)
3671.S33	Scott, Sarah Robinson, 1723-1795 (Table P-PZ40)
3671.S4	Sedley, Sir Charles (Table P-PZ40)
3671.S6	Settle, Elkanah (Table P-PZ40)
3671.S7	Seward, Anna (Table P-PZ40)
3671.S75	Shadwell, Charles (Table P-PZ40)
3671.S8	Shadwell, Thomas (Table P-PZ38)
	Shaftsbury, Anthony Ashley Cooper, Earl of see B1385+
3675.S	Shaf - Shen
3675.S7	Shaw, Cuthbert (Table P-PZ40)
3675.S73	Shebbeare, John, 1709-1788 (Table P-PZ40)
3677	Shenstone, William
3679.S3	Sheppard, S. (Sanuel) (Table P-PZ40)
3679.S5	Sheridan, Mrs. Frances (Table P-PZ40)
3680-3684	Sheridan, Richard Brinsley (Table P-PZ35)
3687.S	Sher - Sm
3687.S147	Sheridan, Thomas, 1687-1738 (Table P-PZ40)

17th and 18th centuries (1640-1770)
Individual authors
Sher - Sm -- Continued

3687.S16	Shipman, Thomas, 1632-1680 (Table P-PZ40)
3687.S17	Shirley, William (Table P-PZ40)
3687.S24	Shittle-Headed, Sir W. (Table P-PZ40)
3687.S4	Singleton, John, fl. 1767-1776 (Table P-PZ40)
3687.S5	Skene, George (Table P-PZ40)
3687.S6	Skinner, John (Table P-PZ40)
3687.S7	Smart, Christopher (Table P-PZ40)
3687.S75	Smedley, Jonathan, 1671-1729 (Table P-PZ40)
3688.S	Smith, A. - Smith, I.
3688.S4	Smith, Charlotte (Table P-PZ40)
3688.S53	Smith, Elizabeth, of Birmingham (Table P-PZ40)
3689.S	Smith, J. - Smollet
3690-3698	Smollett, Tobias (Table P-PZ33)
3699.S2	Somerville, William (Table P-PZ40)
3699.S3	Southerne, Thomas (Table P-PZ40)
3699.S4	Spence, Joseph (Table P-PZ40)
3699.S7	Sprat, Thomas, Bishop of Rochester (Table P-PZ40)
3699.S8	Stanley, Thomas (Table P-PZ40)
3700-3708	Steele, Sir Richard (Table P-PZ33 modified)
	Collected works
3700	By date
3700.D00-.D99	1700-1799
3700.E00-.E99	1800-1899
3700.F00-.F99	1900-1999
3700.G00-.G99	2000-2099
	Sterne, Laurence
	Collected works
	By date
3710.D00-.D99	1700-1799
3710.E00-.E99	1800-1899
3710.F00-.F99	1900-1999
3710.G00-.G99	2000-2099
3711	By editor
3712	Selected works. Selections
	Subarrange by editor, if given, or date
3713.A-Z	Translations (Collected or selected). By language, A-Z
3714.A-Z	Separate works. By title, A-Z
3715	Apocryphal, spurious works, etc. (Collections only)
	Illustrations
	Class at N8215, or with the special artists in NC-NE as the case may be
	Class illustrated editions with other editions
	Class portraits, etc., of the author, with his biography
3716	Biography and criticism

	17th and 18th centuries (1640-1770)
	Individual authors -- Continued
3717.S	St - Su
3717.S15	Sterry, Peter, 1613-1672 (Table P-PZ40)
3717.S2	Stevens, George Alexander, 1710-1784 (Table P-PZ40)
3717.S57	Strangways, John (Table P-PZ40)
3718	Suckling, Sir John (Table P-PZ39)
3719.S	Su - Sw
3720-3728	Swift, Jonathan (Table P-PZ33 modified)
	Collected works
3720	By date
3720.D00-.D99	1700-1799
3720.E00-.E99	1800-1899
3720.F00-.F99	1900-1999
3720.G00-.G99	2000-2099
3729.S4	Sympson, Joseph (Table P-PZ40)
	Syntax, Dr., 1742-1823 see PR3359.C5
3729.T115	Tate, Nahum (Table P-PZ40)
3729.T12	Tatham, John (Table P-PZ40)
3729.T13	Taylor, Jeremy (Table P-PZ38)
	Cf. B, Religion
3729.T15	Temple, Anne, Countess (Table P-PZ40)
3729.T2	Temple, Sir William (Table P-PZ40)
3729.T4	Thelwall, John (Table P-PZ40)
3729.T5	Theobald, Lewis (Table P-PZ40)
3729.T7	Thistlethwaite, James (Table P-PZ40)
3729.T78	Thompson, Edward, 1738?-1786 (Table P-PZ40)
3730-3734	Thomson, James (Table P-PZ35)
3735.T3	Thornton, Bonnel (Table P-PZ40)
3735.T4	Tickell, Richard (Table P-PZ40)
3735.T5	Tickell, Thomas (Table P-PZ40)
3735.T65	Tone, Theobald Wolfe, 1763-1798 (Table P-PZ40)
3736.T5	Tooke, George (Table P-PZ40)
3736.T516	Tooke, William, 1744-1820 (Table P-PZ40)
3736.T6	Topham, Edward (Table P-PZ40)
3736.T64	Toplady, Augustus Montague (Table P-PZ40)
3736.T7	Traherne, Thomas (Table P-PZ40)
3736.T715	Trapp, Joseph (Table P-PZ40)
3736.T73	Tresham, Henry (Table P-PZ40)
3736.T74	Trimmer, Sarah (Kirby) (Table P-PZ40)
	Trotter, Catharine, 1679-1749 see PR3349.C22
3736.T794	Tutchin, John, 1661?-1707 (Table P-PZ40)
3736.T8	Twining, Thomas (Table P-PZ40)
3736.U6	Urquehart, Sir Thomas (Table P-PZ38)
3736.U8	Uvedale, Thomas (Table P-PZ40)
3737-3738	Vanbrugh, Sir John (Table P-PZ36)
3740-3744	Vaughan, Henry (Table P-PZ35)

17th and 18th centuries (1640-1770)

Individual authors -- Continued

3745.V2	Vaughan, Sir William (Table P-PZ40)
3746.V2	Victor, Benjamin (Table P-PZ40)
3747.W35	Wade, John, fl. 1660-1680 (Table P-PZ40)
3747.W5	Wagstaffe, William (Table P-PZ40)
3748.W2	Wakefield, Gilbert (Table P-PZ40)
3748.W45	Walcott, James (Table P-PZ40)
3748.W5	Waldron, Francis G. (Table P-PZ40)
3750-3754	Waller, Edmund (Table P-PZ35)
3757.W2	Walpole, Horace (Table P-PZ40)
	Cf. DA483.W2 English history
3757.W4	Walsh, William (Table P-PZ40)
3757.W6	Walton, Isaac (Table P-PZ40)
3757.W7	Walburton, William, Bp. of Gloucester, 1698-1779 (Table P-PZ40)
3757.W8	Ward, Edward (Table P-PZ40)
3759.W2	Warton family (Table P-PZ40)
3759.W3	Warton, Joseph, 1722-1800 (Table P-PZ40)
3759.W5	Warton, Thomas, 1688?-1745 (Table P-PZ40)
3761	Warton, Thomas, 1728-1790 (Table P-PZ39)
3762.W3	Washbourne, Thomas (Table P-PZ40)
3763.W2	Watts, Isaac (Table P-PZ40)
	For biography see BX5207.W3
3763.W25	Weamys, Anna, b. ca. 1630 (Table P-PZ40)
3763.W3	Welsted, Leonard, 1688-1747 (Table P-PZ40)
3763.W4	Wesley, Charles (Table P-PZ40)
3763.W5	Wesley, John (Table P-PZ40)
3763.W6	Wesley, Samuel (Table P-PZ40)
3763.W75	Westmorland, Mildmay Fane, Earl of, 1601-1666 (Table P-PZ40)
3763.W9	Whaley, John (Table P-PZ40)
3763.W95	Whincop, Thomas (Table P-PZ40)
(3765.W2)	White, Gilbert
	Natural history of Selborne see QH138.S4
	Biography see QH31.W58
3765.W3	Whitehead, Paul (Table P-PZ40)
3765.W4	Whitehead, William (Table P-PZ40)
3765.W5	Whitelocke, Bulstrode (Table P-PZ40)
3765.W53	Whyte, Samuel (Table P-PZ40)
3765.W5314	Wilde, George, Bp. of Derry (Table P-PZ40)
3765.W5317	Wilkes, John (Table P-PZ40)
3765.W535	Williams, Edward (Table P-PZ40)
	For biography and criticism (General) see PB2297.W45
3765.W54	Williams, Helen Maria (Table P-PZ40)
3765.W55	Wilson, Alexander (Table P-PZ40)
3765.W56	Wilson, John (Table P-PZ40)

	17th and 18th centuries (1640-1770)
	Individual authors -- Continued
3765.W57	Winchilsea, Anne, Countess of (Table P-PZ40)
3765.W6	Wodhull, Michael (Table P-PZ40)
3765.W7	Wolcot, John ("Peter Pindar") (Table P-PZ40)
3767	Wood, Anthony à (Table P-PZ39)
3768.W	Wood - War
3768.W33	Woodfall, Henry Sampson, b. 1768? (Table P-PZ40)
3768.W4	Woolnough, Henry (Table P-PZ40)
	Wotton, Sir Henry see PR2395+
3769.W5	Wotton, William (Table P-PZ40)
3769.W7	Woty, William (Table P-PZ40)
3769.W8	Wright, George (Table P-PZ40)
3770-3778	Wycherley, William (Table P-PZ33)
3779.Y4	Yearsely, Ann (Table P-PZ40)
3780-3784	Young, Edward (Table P-PZ35)
3785.Y-Z	Young - Z
	19th century, 1770/1800-1890/1900
3991	Anonymous works (Table P-PZ28)
	Individual authors
4000.A5	Abrahall, Chandos Hoskyns (Table P-PZ40)
4001.A2	Adams, Sarah Fuller Flower (Table P-PZ40)
4001.A3	Adams, William (Table P-PZ40)
4001.A4	Agg, John (Table P-PZ40)
4001.A45	Aguilar, Grace (Table P-PZ40)
4001.A48	Aïdé, Hamilton (Table P-PZ40)
4001.A5	Aikin, John, 1747-1822 (Table P-PZ40)
4001.A7	Aikin, Lucy, 1781-1864 (Table P-PZ40)
4001.A9	Ainger, Alfred (Table P-PZ40)
4001.A93	Ainslie, Hew, 1792-1878 (Table P-PZ40)
4002-4003	Ainsworth, William Harrison (Table P-PZ36)
4004.A1135	Akerman, Portland Board (Table P-PZ40)
4004.A115	Alcock, Deborah, 1835-1913 (Table P-PZ40)
4004.A119	Alexander, William, 1826-1894 (Table P-PZ40)
4004.A12	Alexander, William, Abp. of Armagh, 1824-1911 (Table P-PZ40)
4004.A15	Alford, Henry (Table P-PZ40)
4004.A2	Allen, Grant (Table P-PZ40)
4004.A5	Allingham, William, 1824-1889 (Table P-PZ38)
4005.A	Ama - Amz
4007.A5	Anderson, Robert (Table P-PZ40)
4007.A56	Anketell, John, b. 1750? (Table P-PZ40)
	Anstey, F. see PR4729.G5
4007.A624	Archdeacon, M. (Matthew), d. 1853 (Table P-PZ40)
4007.A63	Archer, William (Table P-PZ40)
4007.A65	Argyll, John, 9th Duke of (Table P-PZ40)
4007.A68	Arkwright, Richard (Table P-PZ40)

19th century, 1770/1800-1890/1900
Individual authors -- Continued

4007.A695	Armstrong, Tommy, 1848-1919 (Table P-PZ40)
4010-4014	Arnold, Sir Edwin (Table P-PZ35)
4015.A4	Arnold, Frederick (Table P-PZ40)
4020-4024	Arnold, Matthew (Table P-PZ35)
4028.A4	Arnold, Samuel James, 1774-1852 (Table P-PZ40)
	Arnold, Thomas see LF795.R92
4028.A6	Arnold, Thomas, Jr. (Table P-PZ40)
4028.A63	Arnold, William Delafield, 1828-1859 (Table P-PZ40)
4028.A73	Ashby-Sterry, Joseph (Table P-PZ40)
4028.A8	Atherstone, Edwin (Table P-PZ40)
4029.A4	Atkinson, Sarah (Table P-PZ40)
4029.A5	Atkinson, Thomas (Table P-PZ40)
4029.A83	Audley, John (Table P-PZ40)
4030-4038	Austen, Jane (Table P-PZ33)
4039.A98	Austen-Leigh, James Edward, 1798-1874 (Table P-PZ40)
4040-4044	Austin, Alfred (Table P-PZ35)
4046.A5	Axon, William (Table P-PZ40)
4046.A7	Ayton, Richard (Table P-PZ40)
4047-4048	Aytoun, William Edmondstoune (Table P-PZ36)
	Bab see PR4713+
4049.B5	Bage, Robert, 1728-1801 (Table P-PZ40)
4049.B6	Bagehot, Walter (Table P-PZ40)
4050-4054	Bailey, Philip James (Table P-PZ35)
4056	Baillie, Joanna (Table P-PZ39)
4057.B13	Baird, Henry (Table P-PZ40)
4057.B135	Balfour, Arthur James (Table P-PZ40)
4057.B14	Ballantine, James (Table P-PZ40)
4057.B2	Banim, John (Table P-PZ40)
4057.B3	Banim, Michael (Table P-PZ40)
4057.B7	Barbauld, Anna Letitia (Table P-PZ40)
4058-4059	Barham, Richard Harris (Table P-PZ36)
4061-4062	Baring-Gould, Sabine (Table P-PZ36)
4063.B227	Barker, Mary (Table P-PZ40)
	Barlas, John Evelyn, 1860-1914 see PR4613.D418
4063.B3	Barlow, Jane (Table P-PZ40)
4064-4065	Barnes, William (Table P-PZ36)
4069.B38	Barr, Robert, 1850-1912 (Table P-PZ40)
4069.B4	Barre, William (Table P-PZ40)
4069.B5	Barrett, Eaton Stannard (Table P-PZ40)
4069.B64	Barrett, Lennard, Lady, d. 1916 (Table P-PZ40)
4070-4078	Barrie, Sir James Matthew (Table P-PZ33 modified)
	Collected works
4070	By date
4070.E00-.E99	1800-1899
4070.F00-.F99	1900-1999

	19th century, 1770/1800-1890/1900
	Individual authors
	Barrie, Sir James Matthew
	Collected works
	By date -- Continued
4070.G00-.G99	2000-2099
4079.B15	Barry, Thomas, fl. 1800-1802 (Table P-PZ40)
4079.B16	Barry, William Francis, 1849-1930 (Table P-PZ40)
4079.B17	Barrymore, William (Table P-PZ40)
4079.B2	Barton, Bernard (Table P-PZ40)
4079.B5	Bayly, Ada Ellen ("Edna Lyall") (Table P-PZ40)
4079.B6	Bayly, Thomas Haynes (Table P-PZ40)
4080-4088	Beaconsfield, Benjamin Disraeli, 1st Earl of (Table P-PZ33 modified)
	Collected works
4080	By date
4080.E00-.E99	1800-1899
4080.F00-.F99	1900-1999
4080.G00-.G99	2000-2099
4089.B45	Beardsley, Aubrey Vincent, 1872-1898 (Table P-PZ40)
	Beaumont, Averil, 1831-1912 see PR4809.H95
4089.B7	Beck, Thomas (Table P-PZ40)
4089.B75	Becke, Louis, 1855-1913 (Table P-PZ40)
4089.B8	Becket, Andrew (Table P-PZ40)
4091-4092	Beckford, William (Table P-PZ36)
4095.B	Beck - Bedd
4097-4098	Beddoes, Thomas Lovell (Table P-PZ36)
	Bede, Cuthbert, 1827-1889 see PR4161.B53
4099.B12	Beeching, Henry Charles, 1859-1919 (Table P-PZ40)
4099.B15	Bell, Florence E.E. (Oliffe), Lady (Table P-PZ40)
	Earlier known as Mrs. Hugh Bell
	Bennett, Arnold see PR6003.E6
4099.B4	Bennett, William Cox (Table P-PZ40)
4099.B5	Benson, Arthur Christopher (Table P-PZ40)
	Benson, Edward Frederic see PR6003.E66
	Benson, Robert Hugh see PR6003.E7
4099.B8	Beresford, James (Table P-PZ40)
4100-4108	Besant, Sir Walter, and Rice, James (Table P-PZ33)
	Besemers, John Daly, 1822?-1879 see PR4525.D1265
4109.B14	Betham, Mary Matilda, 1776-1852 (Table P-PZ40)
4109.B2	Bethune, Alexander (Table P-PZ40)
4109.B3	Bevington, L. S. (Louisa Sarah), 1845-1895 (Table P-PZ40)
4109.B33	Bewicke, A.E.N. (Table P-PZ40)
4109.B6	Bickersteth, Edward Henry (Table P-PZ40)
4112.B3	Bigg, John Stanyan (Table P-PZ40)
	Binyon, Laurence see PR6003.I75

	19th century, 1770/1800-1890/1900
	Individual authors -- Continued
4112.B7	Bird, James (Table P-PZ40)
4115	Birrell, Augustine (Table P-PZ39)
4117.B	Bir - Bla
4117.B37	Bisset, Robert, 1759-1805 (Table P-PZ40)
4117.B78	Black, Clementine (Table P-PZ40)
4120-4128	Black, William (Table P-PZ33)
4129.B5	Blackie, John Stuart (Table P-PZ40)
4130-4134	Blackmore, Richard Doddridge (Table P-PZ35)
4135.B8	Blackwell, Anna (Table P-PZ40)
4136.B5	Blaikie, John Arthur (Table P-PZ40)
4137.B53	Blair, William b. ca. 1813 (Table P-PZ40)
4140-4148	Blake, William (Table P-PZ33 modified)
	For works primarily of visual arts, see class N
	Collected works
4140	By date
4140.E00-.E99	1800-1899
4140.F00-.F99	1900-1999
4140.G00-.G99	2000-2099
4149.B4	Bland, Edith (Nesbit) (Table P-PZ40)
4149.B43	Bland, Robert, 1779?-1825 (Table P-PZ40)
4149.B5	Blessington, Lady (Table P-PZ40)
	For biography see DA536.B66
4149.B55	Blind, Mathilde (Table P-PZ40)
4149.B57	Bliss, Henry, 1797?-1873 (Table P-PZ40)
4149.B6	Bloomfield, Robert (Table P-PZ40)
4149.B74	Bloundelle-Burton, John,1850-1917 (Table P-PZ40)
4149.B8	Blunt, Wilfrid Scawen (Table P-PZ40)
4149.B957	Boothby, Guy Newell (Table P-PZ40)
4150-4158	Borrow, George (Table P-PZ33 modified)
	Collected works
4150	By date
4150.F00-.F99	1900-1999
4150.G00-.G99	2000-2099
4160.B5	Bosanquet, George William (Table P-PZ40)
4161.B2	Boucicault, Dion (Table P-PZ40)
4161.B3	Bourdillon, Francis William (Table P-PZ40)
4161.B324	Bourne, Arthur Mason (Table P-PZ40)
4161.B4	Bowles, William Lisle (Table P-PZ40)
4161.B42	Bowring, Sir John (Table P-PZ40)
4161.B45	Boyd, Andrew Kennedy Hutchison (Table P-PZ40)
4161.B475	Boyle, Mary Louisa, 1810-1890 (Table P-PZ40)
4161.B49	Bracken, Thomas, 1843-1898 (Table P-PZ40)
	Braddon, M.E. (Mary Elizabeth), 1837-1915 see PR4989.M4
4161.B53	Bradley, Edward, 1827-1889 (Table P-PZ40)

	19th century, 1770/1800-1890/1900
	Individual authors -- Continued
	Bradley, Katherine Harris see PR4699.F5
4161.B564	Brandon, Issac (Table P-PZ40)
4161.B57	Bray, Anna Eliza (Kempe) (Table P-PZ40)
	Breddon, Miss, 1837-1915 see PR4989.M4
4161.B587	Brew, Margaret W. (Table P-PZ40)
4161.B589	Brewer, George, b. 1766 (Table P-PZ40)
4161.B6	Bridges, Robert (Table P-PZ40)
4161.B63	Bridgman, Cunningham V. (Table P-PZ40)
4161.B7	Bristed, Charles Astor (Table P-PZ40)
4161.B74	Bristow, Amelia (Table P-PZ40)
4162-4163	Brontë, Anne (Table P-PZ36)
4165-4169	Brontë, Charlotte (Table P-PZ35)
	Including works on the Brontë family
4172-4173	Brontë, Emily (Table P-PZ36)
4174.B2	Brontë, Patrick, 1777-1861 (Table P-PZ40)
4174.B23	Brontë, Patrick Branwell, 1817-1848
4174.B4	Brooks, Shirley (Table P-PZ40)
4174.B48	Brough, William, 1826-1870 (Table P-PZ40)
4174.B55	Broughton, John Cam Hobhouse, 1st Baron (Table P-PZ40)
4174.B6	Brown, George Douglas (Table P-PZ40)
4175.B2	Brown, John, 1810-1882 (Table P-PZ38)
4175.B35	Brown, Oliver Madox, 1855-1874 (Table P-PZ40)
4175.B5	Brown, Thomas Edward, 1830-1897 (Table P-PZ38)
4180-4198	Browning, Elizabeth Barrett (Table P-PZ32 modified)
	Separate works
4185	Aurora Leigh (Table P-PZ41)
4186	Casa Guidi windows (Table P-PZ41)
4187	Lady Geraldine's courtship (Table P-PZ41)
4188	Poems before Congress (Table P-PZ41)
4189	Sonnets from the Portuguese (Table P-PZ41)
4190.A-Z	Other, A-Z
	Subarrange each by Table P-PZ43
4200-4248	Browning, Robert (Table P-PZ31 modified)
	Separate works
4205	The blot on the 'scutcheon (Table P-PZ41)
4206	Dramatic idyls (Table P-PZ41)
4207	Dramatic lyrics (Table P-PZ41)
4208	Dramatic romances (Table P-PZ41)
4209	Dramatic personae (Table P-PZ41)
4210	In a balcony (Table P-PZ41)
4211	Jocoseria (Table P-PZ41)
4212	King Victor and King Charles (Table P-PZ41)
4213	Luria (Table P-PZ41)
4214	Men and women (Table P-PZ41)

	19th century, 1770/1800-1890/1900
	Individual authors
	Browning, Robert
	Separate works -- Continued
4215	Paracelsus (Table P-PZ41)
4216	Parleyings (Table P-PZ41)
4217	Pauline (Table P-PZ41)
4218	Pippa passes (Table P-PZ41)
4219	Ring and the book (Table P-PZ41)
4220	Sordello (Table P-PZ41)
4221	Strafford (Table P-PZ41)
4222.A-Z	Other, A-Z
	Subarrange each by Table P-PZ43
4250.B	Browning - Bru
4250.B5	Browning, Samuel (Table P-PZ40)
4250.B73	Brunton, Mary, 1778-1818 (Table P-PZ40)
4252.B	Bry - Buch
4252.B56	Bryan, Mary, fl. 1815 (Table P-PZ40)
4252.B7	Brydges, Sir Samuel Egerton (Table P-PZ40)
4252.B8	Buchanan, Andrew (Table P-PZ40)
4260-4264	Buchanan, Robert Williams (Table P-PZ35)
4265.B6	Buckstone, John Baldwin (Table P-PZ40)
4266.B	Bud - Buk
4267.B	Bul - Bum
4267.B56	Bullock, Mrs. (Table P-PZ40)
	Bulwer-Lytton, Edward see PR4900+
4268.B	Bun - Buq
4268.B58	Bunbury, Henry William, 1750-1811 (Table P-PZ40)
4269.B	Bur - Burc
4269.B7	Burbidge, Thomas (Table P-PZ40)
4270.B	Burd - Burf
4270.B3	Burdon, William (Table P-PZ40)
4271.B	Burg - Burk
4271.B3	Burges, Sir James Bland (Table P-PZ40)
4271.B38	Burghclere, Herbert Gardner, Baron, 1846-1921 (Table P-PZ40)
4271.B7	Burk, Edward (Table P-PZ40)
4275.B	Burl - Burna
4275.B7	Burn, David (Table P-PZ40)
4279.B	Burnand - Burns
4279.B5	Burnand, Sir Francis Cowley (Table P-PZ40)
4279.B7	Burney, Sarah Harriet, 1772-1844 (Table P-PZ40)
4279.73	Burnley, James, 1842-1919 (Table P-PZ40)
4280.B	Burns, A.-R.
4280.B6	Burns, John (Table P-PZ40)
	Burns, Robert

	19th century, 1770/1800-1890/1900
	Individual authors
	Burns, Robert -- Continued
4300	Collected works (Collected poems, and poems and prose). By date
	Subarrange by place, A-Z
4301	Prose works
	Including letters, etc.
4302	Selected works. Unedited works. Fragments, etc. By editor
4303	Selections. Anthologies. Extracts. By editor
4304.A-Z	Translations. By language, A-Z
	Subarrange by translator
	Separate works
4306.A-.B	By title, A-B
	Subarrange each by Table P-PZ43
4307.C	By title, C-Cos
	Subarrange each by Table P-PZ43
4307.C6-.C63	Commonplace books (Table P-PZ43)
4308	Cotter's Saturday night (Table P-PZ41)
4309.C-.G	By title, Cot-G
	Subarrange each by Table P-PZ43
4310.H-.J	By title, H-Jok
	Subarrange each by Table P-PZ43
4311	Jolly beggars (Table P-PZ41)
4312.J-.Q	By title, Jol-Q
	Subarrange each by Table P-PZ43
4313.R-.T	By title, R-T
	Subarrange each by Table P-PZ43
4314	Tam O'Shanter (Table P-PZ41)
4321	Doubtful, spurious works
4322	Works edited or annotated by Burns
	Including his "Notes on Scottish song"
4323	Imitations, adaptations
4324	Songs written to music and songs to which music has been composed
	For texts with or without music and music without text, see class M
	Illustrations (Portfolios, etc. without text, illustrations with quotations)
	Class at N8215, or with the special artists in NC-NE as the case may be
	Class illustrated editions with other editions
	Class portraits, etc. of the author with his biography
	Biography, criticism, etc.
4329	Periodicals. Societies. Serials

           19th century, 1770/1800-1890/1900
             Individual authors
              Burns, Robert
               Biography, criticism, etc. -- Continued

4330	Dictionaries, indexes, etc.
	Class here general encyclopedic dictionaries only
	For concordances and dictionaries see PR4345
4330.5	Historical sources and documents of the biography or author
	For sources of literary works see PR4336+
	Autobiographical works
4331.A2	Autobiography. By date
4331.A3-.A39	Journals. Memoirs. By title
4331.A4	Letters (Collections). By date
4331.A41-.A49	Letters to and from particular individuals. By correspondent (alphabetically)
4331.A5-Z	General works
4332	Special periods of the author's life
	Including early life, education, love and marriage, relation to women, relation to men, later life
4333	Relations to contemporaries. Times, etc.
4334	Homes and haunts. Local associations. Landmarks
4335	Anniversaries. Celebrations. Memorial addresses. Iconography. Monuments. Relics. Museums, exhibitions, etc.
	Authorship
	Including manuscripts, sources, etc.
	For textual criticism see PR4343
4336	General works
4337	Chronology of works
	Criticism and interpretation
	History
4337.3	General works
4337.4.A-Z	By region or country, A-Z
4338	General works
4339	Characters
4341	Technique, plot, scenes, time, etc.
4342.A-Z	Treatment and knowledge of special subjects, A-Z
	For list of Cutter numbers, see Table P-PZ31 42
4343	Textual criticism, commentaries, etc.
	Language, style, etc.
4344	General works
4345	Dictionaries. Concordances
4346	Grammar
4347	Versification, meter, rhythm, etc.
4348	Dialect, etc.
4349.B3	Burns, Robert, of Hamilton (Table P-PZ40)

19th century, 1770/1800-1890/1900
Individual authors -- Continued

4349.B5	Burrell, Lady Sophia (Table P-PZ40)
4349.B52	Burton, Sir Richard Francis (Table P-PZ40)
4349.B6	Butler, Edward (Table P-PZ40)
4349.B7	Butler, Samuel, 1835-1902 (Table P-PZ40)
4350-4398	Byron, George Gordon (Table P-PZ31 modified)
	Separate works
4355	Bride of Abydos (Table P-PZ41)
4356	Cain (Table P-PZ41)
4357	Childe Harold's pilgrimage (Table P-PZ41)
4358	Corsair (Table P-PZ41)
4359	Don Juan (Table P-PZ41)
4360	English bards and Scotch reviewers (Table P-PZ41)
4361	Giaour (Table P-PZ41)
4362	Hebrew melodies (Table P-PZ41)
4363	Hours of idleness (Table P-PZ41)
4364	Lara (Table P-PZ41)
4365	Manfred (Table P-PZ41)
4366	Marino Faliero (Table P-PZ41)
4367	Prisoner of Chillon (Table P-PZ41)
4368	Sardanapalus (Table P-PZ41)
4369	Two Foscari (Table P-PZ41)
4370	Vision of Judgment (Table P-PZ41)
4371	Werner (Table P-PZ41)
4372.A-Z	Other, A-Z
	Subarrange each by Table P-PZ43
4399.B3	Byron, Henry James (Table P-PZ40)
4400-4408	Caine, Hall (Table P-PZ33)
4409.C133	Calabrella, E.C., Baroness de (Table P-PZ40)
4409.C14	Calmour, Alfred C. (Table P-PZ40)
4409.C2	Calverley, Charles Stuart (Table P-PZ40)
4409.C23	Calvert, Charles, 1828-1879 (Table P-PZ40)
	Cambridge, Ada see PR4518.C7
4409.C78	Campbell, A. L. V. (Andrew Leonard Voullaire), 1789-1870 (Table P-PZ40)
4410-4414	Campbell, Thomas (Table P-PZ35)
4415.C2	Canton, William (Table P-PZ40)
4415.C7	Carey, Rosa Nauchette, 1840-1909 (Table P-PZ40)
4416-4417	Carleton, William (Table P-PZ36)
4419.C5	Carlyle, Jane Welsh, 1801-1866 (Table P-PZ38)
4420-4438	Carlyle, Thomas (Table P-PZ32 modified)
	Separate works
	Chartism, see subclass DA
	Choice of books, see Z1003+
	Cromwell's letters and speecehes, see subclass DA
	Early kings of Norway, etc., see DL460+

	19th century, 1770/1800-1890/1900
	Individual authors
	Carlyle, Thomas
	Separate works -- Continued
	Essays
4425.A2	Collected. By date
4425.A3	Minor collections. By date
4425.A5-Z	Separate essays and minor collections. By title, A-Z
4426	Heroes and hero worship (Table P-PZ41)
	Inaugural address, University of Edinburgh, 1866;
	Choice of books see Z1003+
	Latter day pamphlets
	see subclass HN
	Past and present
	see subclass HN
4429	Sartor resartus (Table P-PZ41)
	Schiller, Friedrich
	see subclass PT
	Sterling, John see PR5473.S8
	Translations from the German
	see sublcass PT
4430.A-Z	Other works, A-Z
	Subarrange each by Table P-PZ43
4439.C	Carl - Carm
	Carman, Bliss see PR9199.2.C3
4443.C6	Carnavon, Henry, 3rd Earl of (Table P-PZ40)
4451	Carpenter, Edward (Table P-PZ39)
4452.C44	Carr, George Shoobridge, 1837- (Table P-PZ40)
4452.C47	Carr, John, Sir, 1772-1832 (Table P-PZ40)
4452.C5	Carr, Joseph William Comyns (Table P-PZ40)
	Carroll, Lewis, 1832-1898 see PR4611+
4452.C7	Casey, John K. (Table P-PZ40)
4452.C716	Cashman, D.B. (Table P-PZ40)
4452.C8	Cayley, George John (Table P-PZ40)
4453.C17	Chadwick, Sheldon (Table P-PZ40)
4453.C18	Chambers, James (Table P-PZ40)
4453.C2	Chambers, Robert (Table P-PZ40)
4453.C21	Chambers, William (Table P-PZ40)
4453.C225	Charles, Elizabeth (Rundle) (Table P-PZ40)
4453.C28	Cherry, A. (Andrew), 1762-1812 (Table P-PZ40)
4453.C29	Chesney, George Tompkins, 1830-1895 (Table P-PZ40)
4453.C3	Chesson, Nora (Hopper) (Table P-PZ40)
4453.C4	Chesterton, Gilbert Keith (Table P-PZ40)
	Cholmondeley-Pennell, Henry see PR5167.P6
4453.C53	Chorley, Henry Fothergill (Table P-PZ40)
4453.C6	Clare, John (Table P-PZ40)
4453.C65	Claris, John Chalk, 1797?-1866 (Table P-PZ40)

	19th century, 1770/1800-1890/1900
	Individual authors -- Continued
4453.C688	Clarke, A.W. (Table P-PZ40)
4453.C7	Clarke, Charles Cowden (Table P-PZ40)
	Clarke, Marcus see PR9619.2.C53
4453.C8	Clarke, Mary Victoria (Novello) (Mrs. Mary Cowden Clarke) (Table P-PZ40)
4453.C85	Clarke, Stephen (Table P-PZ40)
4453.C86	Clarke, William, 1800-1838 (Table P-PZ40)
4454.C2	Clifford, Mrs. Lucy (Lane) (Table P-PZ40)
4454.C3	Clifford, William Kingdon (Table P-PZ40)
4454.C4	Clive, Caroline, 1801-1873 (Table P-PZ40)
4455-4459	Clough, Arthur Hugh (Table P-PZ35)
4461.C16	Clowes, W. Laird (William Laird), Sir, 1856-1905 (Table P-PZ40)
4461.C28	Cobb, James, 1756-1818 (Table P-PZ40)
4461.C3	Cobbe, Frances Power (Table P-PZ40)
4461.C35	Cobbold, Richard (Table P-PZ40)
4461.C5	Cochrane, James (Table P-PZ40)
4464.C	Col - Coleridge
4464.C65	Cole, O.B. (Table P-PZ40)
4467-4468	Coleridge, Hartley (Table P-PZ36)
4470-4488	Coleridge, Samuel Taylor (Table P-PZ32 modified)
	For Coleridge as philosopher see B1583
	Separate works
4476	Biographia literaria (Table P-PZ41)
4477	Biographia epistolaria (Table P-PZ41)
4478	Poems (Table P-PZ41)
4479	Rime of the ancient mariner (Table P-PZ41)
4480.A-Z	Other, A-Z
	Subarrange each by Table P-PZ43
	Criticism
	Special
4487.A-Z	Other, A-Z
(4487.P5)	Philosophy
	see B1583
4489.C2	Coleridge, Mrs. Sara (Coleridge) (Table P-PZ40)
4489.C23	Collier, John Payne, 1789-1883 (Table P-PZ40)
4489.C247	Collingwood, William Gershom, 1854-1932 (Table P-PZ40)
4489.C5	Collins, Mortimer (Table P-PZ40)
4489.C53	Collins, Richard, Mrs., d. 1862 (Table P-PZ40)
4490-4498	Collins, Wilkie (Table P-PZ33)
	Collins, William Wilkie, 1824-1889 see PR4490+
4499.C5	Collinson, S. (Table P-PZ40)
4501.C3	Colman, George, Jr. (Table P-PZ40)
4501.C35	Colomb, Philip Howard, 1831-1899 (Table P-PZ40)
4501.C4	Colton, Charles Caleb (Table P-PZ40)

	19th century, 1770/1800-1890/1900
	Individual authors -- Continued
	Combe, William see PR3359.C5
4501.C53	Compton, C.G. (Table P-PZ40)
	Conrad, Joseph see PR6005.O4
	Conway, Hugh, 1847-1885 see PR4699.F16
4501.C68	Conybeare, William John, 1815-1857 (Table P-PZ40)
4502	Cook, Eliza (Table P-PZ39)
4503.C12	Cook, Mabel Collins, 1851-1927 (Table P-PZ40)
	Cooper, Edith see PR4699.F5
4503.C2	Cooper, Thomas (Table P-PZ40)
4504-4505	Corelli, Marie (Table P-PZ36)
4506.C48	Cornford, Leslie Cope, 1867- (Table P-PZ40)
	Cornwall, Barry (pseud.) see PR5192
4507.C7	Cottle, Joseph (Table P-PZ40)
4508.C15	Couper, Robert (Table P-PZ40)
4508.C153	Courtenay, John, 1738-1816 (Table P-PZ40)
	Coutts, Francis Burdette Thomas Money see PR4878.L3
(4508.C3)	Couvreur, Mrs. Jessie (Fraser). "Tasma" see PR9619.2.T38
4508.C4	Cox, George William (Table P-PZ40)
4508.C7	Coyne, J. Stirling, 1803-1868 (Table P-PZ40)
4510-4514	Crabbe, George (Table P-PZ35)
4515.C45	Crackanthorpe, Hubert Montague, 1870-1896 (Table P-PZ40)
4515.C7	Craigie, Pearl Mary Teresa Richards, 1867-1906 ("John Oliver Hobbes") (Table P-PZ38)
4516-4517	Craik, Dinah Maria (Mulock) (Table P-PZ36)
4518.C135	Crandolph, Augustus Jacob
4518.C3	Crockett, Samuel Rutherford (Table P-PZ40)
4518.C5	Croker, Crofton (Table P-PZ40)
4518.C53	Croker, John Wilson, 1780-1857 (Table P-PZ40)
4518.C55	Croly, George, 1780-1860 (Table P-PZ40)
4518.C554	Cromie, Robert, 1856-1907 (Table P-PZ40)
4518.C7	Cross, Ada (Cambridge) (Table P-PZ40)
	Cross, Marian Evans, 1819-1880 see PR4650+
4519.C2	Crow, William (Table P-PZ40)
4519.C27	Crowe, Eyre Evans, 1799-1868 (Table P-PZ40)
4519.C4	Cruikshank, George (Table P-PZ40)
4519.C85	Cumberland, George, 1754-1848 (Table P-PZ40)
4520-4524	Cunningham, Allan (Table P-PZ35)
4525.C2	Cunningham, Peter (Table P-PZ40)
4525.C3	Currie, Mary M.L.S. ("Violet Fane") (Table P-PZ40)
4525.C34	Curtiss, T.J. Horsley (Table P-PZ40)
4525.C47	Cusack, George (Table P-PZ40)
4525.C48	Cusack, Mary Francis, 1829-1899 (Table P-PZ40)
4525.C5	Cust, Robert Needham (Table P-PZ40)

	19th century, 1770/1800-1890/1900
	Individual authors -- Continued
4525.D119	Dacre, Charlotte, b. 1782 (Table P-PZ40)
4525.D1243	Dallas, Robert Charles, 1754-1824 (Table P-PZ40)
4525.D1247	Dalton (Table P-PZ40)
4525.D1265	Daly, John, 1822?-1879 (Table P-PZ40)
4525.D13	Dance, Charles, 1794-1863 (Table P-PZ40)
4525.D15	Daniel, George (Table P-PZ40)
4525.D2	Darley, George (Table P-PZ40)
4525.D242	Darling, Peter Middleton, fl. 1810-17 (Table P-PZ40)
4525.D325	Darrell, Edward Price George, 1850?-1921 (Table P-PZ40)
4525.D35	Darusmont, Frances (Wright) (Table P-PZ40)
4525.D5	Davidson, John (Table P-PZ40)
4525.D525	Davies, Charles Maurice, 1828-1910 (Table P-PZ40)
4525.D534	D'Avigdor, Elim Henry, 1841-1895 (Table P-PZ40)
4525.D56	Davis, John, 1774-1854 (Table P-PZ40)
4525.D58	Davis, Thomas Osborne, 1814-1845 (Table P-PZ40)
4526.D	Deb - Del
4527-4528	De la Ramée, Louise (Ouida) (Table P-PZ36)
4529.D17	De Lisle, Percy (Table P-PZ40)
4529.D19	Della (Table P-PZ40)
4529.D3	Dempster, Charlotte Louisa Hawkins (Table P-PZ40)
4530-4538	De Quincey, Thomas (Table P-PZ33 modified)
	Collected works
4530	By date
4530.E00-.E99	1800-1899
4530.F00-.F99	1900-1999
4530.G00-.G99	2000-2099
4539.D	Deq - Det
	e. g.
4539.D5	Derby, 14th earl (Table P-PZ40)
4539.D53	Dering, Edward Heneage, 1827-1892 (Table P-PZ40)
4540	De Tabley, John Byrne Leicester, 3d baron (Table P-PZ39)
4541.D9	De Vere, Sir Aubrey, 2d bart. (Table P-PZ40)
4542-4543	De Vere, Aubrey (Table P-PZ36)
4545.D	De Vere - Dibdin
4549.D3	Dibdin, Charles, 1745-1814 (Table P-PZ40)
4549.D35	Dibdin, Charles, 1768-1833 (Table P-PZ40)
4549.D4	Dibdin, Thomas Frognall, 1776-1847 (Table P-PZ40)
4549.D5	Dibdin, Thomas John, 1771-1841 (Table P-PZ40)
4550-4598	Dickens, Charles (Table P-PZ31 modified)
	Separate works
4555	Barnaby Rudge (Table P-PZ41)
4556	Bleak House (Table P-PZ41)
4557	Christmas books and Christmas stories (Table P-PZ41)
	For special books and stories see PR4572.A+
4558	David Copperfield (Table P-PZ41)

19th century, 1770/1800-1890/1900
Individual authors
Dickens, Charles
Separate works -- Continued

4559	Dombey and son (Table P-PZ41)
4560	Great expectations (Table P-PZ41)
4561	Hard times (Table P-PZ41)
4562	Little Dorrit (Table P-PZ41)
4563	Martin Chuzzlewit (Table P-PZ41)
4564	Mystery of Edwin Drood (Table P-PZ41)
4565	Nicholas Nickleby (Table P-PZ41)
4566	Old curiosity shop (Table P-PZ41)
4567	Oliver Twist (Table P-PZ41)
4568	Our mutual friend (Table P-PZ41)
4569	Pickwick papers (Table P-PZ41)
4570	Sketches by Boz (Table P-PZ41)
4571	Tale of two cities (Table P-PZ41)
4572.A-Z	Other, A-Z
	Subarrange each by Table P-PZ43
4599.D4	Digby, Kenelm Henry (Table P-PZ40)
4599.D42	Dilke, Emilia Francis Strong, Lady, 1840-1904 (Table P-PZ40)
4599.D47	Dillwyn, Amy, 1845-1935 (Table P-PZ40)
4599.D53	Dinwoodie, Peter, 1865-1922 (Table P-PZ40)
	Disraeli, Benjamin see PR4080+
4599.D6	Disraeli, Issac (Table P-PZ40)
4599.D66	Dixon, Richard Watson, 1833-1900 (Table P-PZ40)
4599.D8	Dixon, William Hepworth (Table P-PZ40)
4603-4604	Dobell, Sydney (Table P-PZ36)
4606-4607	Dobson, Austin (Table P-PZ36)
4610.D5	Dodd, James William (Table P-PZ40)
4611-4612	Dodgson, Charles Lutwidge (Lewis Carroll) (Table P-PZ36)
	Dods, Mary Diana see PR4897.L2
4613.D2	Dolben, Digby Mackworth, 1846-1867 (Table P-PZ40)
4613.D32	Domett, Alfred (Table P-PZ40)
	Donovan, Dick, 1843-1934 see PR5101.M363
4613.D36	Doran, John (Table P-PZ40)
4613.D4	Doudney, Sarah, 1843-1926 (Table P-PZ40)
	Douglas, Alfred Bruce, Lord see PR6007.O86
4613.D418	Douglas, Evelyn, 1860-1914 (Table P-PZ40)
4613.D445	Dowden, Edward, 1843-1913 (Table P-PZ40)
4613.D5	Dowson, Ernest (Table P-PZ40)
4620-4624	Doyle, Sir Arthur Conan (Table P-PZ35)
4626.D5	Doyle, Sir Francis Hastings (Table P-PZ40)
4627.D	Dr - Drum
4627.D4	Drake, Daniel (Table P-PZ40)
4628.D2	Drummond, William Hamilton (Table P-PZ40)

	19th century, 1770/1800-1890/1900
	Individual authors -- Continued
	Drummond, William Henry see PR9199.2.D7
4629.D18	Duclaux, Agnes Mary Frances (Robinson) (Table P-PZ40)
	Formerly Mme. James Darmesteter
4629.D2	Dudley, John (Table P-PZ40)
4630-4638	Du Maurier, George (Table P-PZ33)
4639.D2	Dunbar, Robert Nugent (Table P-PZ40)
4639.D3	Dunphie, Charles James (Table P-PZ40)
4639.D84	Dyer, George, 1755-1841 (Table P-PZ40)
4639.E13	Eagles, John, 1783-1855 (Table P-PZ40)
4639.E25	Eastlake, Elizabeth Rigby, Lady, 1809-1893 (Table P-PZ40)
4639.E29	Eden, Emily, 1797-1869 (Table P-PZ40)
4639.E294	Edersheim, Alfred, 1825-1889 (Table P-PZ40)
4639.E3	Edgar, James David (Table P-PZ40)
4640-4648	Edgeworth, Maria (Table P-PZ33 modified)
	Collected works
4640	By date
4640.E00-.E99	1800-1899
4640.F00-.F99	1900-1999
4640.G00-.G99	2000-2099
4649.E26	Edwards, Amelia Ann, Blandford, 1832-1892 (Table P-PZ40)
4649.E45	Egan, Pierce, 1772-1849 (Table P-PZ40)
4649.E47	Egan, Pierce, 1814-1880 (Table P-PZ40)
4649.E5	Egerton-Warburton, R.E. (Table P-PZ40)
4649.E65	Elgar, Alice, Lady (Caroline Alice Roberts) (Table P-PZ40)
4650-4698	Eliot, George, 1819-1880 (Table P-PZ31 modified)
	Separate works
4656	Adam Bede (Table P-PZ41)
4657.A-.D	By title, Ae-Dam
	Subarrange each by Table P-PZ43
4658	Daniel Deronda (Table P-PZ41)
4659.D-.F	By title, Dao-Fek
	Subarrange each by Table P-PZ43
4660	Felix Holt (Table P-PZ41)
4661.F-.M	By title, Fem-Mic
	Subarrange each by Table P-PZ43
4662	Middlemarch (Table P-PZ41)
4663.M	By title, Mie-Mik
	Subarrange each by Table P-PZ43
4664	Mill on the floss (Table P-PZ41)
4665.M-.P	By title, Mim-Pod
	Subarrange each by Table P-PZ43
	Poems
4666.A1	Collected

19th century, 1770/1800-1890/1900

Individual authors

Eliot, George, 1819-1880

Separate works

Poems -- Continued

4666.A6-.Z4	Individual, A-Z
4667.P-.R	By title, Pof-Rol
	Subarrange each by Table P-PZ43
4668	Romola (Table P-PZ41)
4669.R-.S	By title, Ron-Sik
	Subarrange each by Table P-PZ43
4670	Silas Marner (Table P-PZ41)
4672.S-Z	By title, Sim-Z
	Subarrange each by Table P-PZ43
4699.E5	Elliott, Ebenezer (Table P-PZ40)
4699.E56	Elliott, Mary, 1794?-1870 (Table P-PZ40)
4699.E77	Emmett, George (Table P-PZ40)
4699.E78	Erle, T.W. (Table P-PZ40)
4699.E8	Esmond, Henry V. (Table P-PZ40)
	Evans, Marian, 1819-1880 see PR4650+
4699.E835	Evans, Sebastian, 1830-1909 (Table P-PZ40)
4699.E85	Ewing, Mrs. Juliana Horatia (Table P-PZ40)
4699.F11	Faber, Frederick William (Table P-PZ40)
4699.F145	Falconer, Edmund, 1814-1879 (Table P-PZ40)
	Falconer, Lanoe, 1848-1908 see PR6015.A79
4699.F147	Falkner, John Meade, 1858-1932 (Table P-PZ40)
4699.F15	Fane, Julian (Table P-PZ40)
	Fane, Violet, 1843-1905 see PR4525.C3
4699.F16	Fargus, Frederick John, 1847-1885 (Table P-PZ40)
4699.F17	Farjeon, Benjamin Leopold (Table P-PZ40)
4699.F173	Farmer, G.E. (Table P-PZ40)
4699.F175	Farquhar, Ferdinand (Table P-PZ40)
4699.F178	Farrar, Frederic William, 1831-1903 (Table P-PZ40)
4699.F182	Fechter, Charles, 1824-1879 (Table P-PZ40)
4699.F183	Felix, Charles (Table P-PZ40)
4699.F1844	Fenn, George Manville (Table P-PZ40)
4699.F2	Ferguson, Sir Samuel (Table P-PZ40)
4699.F4	Ferrier, Susan (Table P-PZ40)
4699.F45	Fforde, Arthur Brownlow, 1847-1933 (Table P-PZ40)
4699.F5	Field, Michael (Table P-PZ40)
	Pseud. of Katherine Bradley and Edith Cooper
4699.F9	Fitzball, Edward (Table P-PZ40)
4700-4704	Fitzgerald, Edward (Table P-PZ35)
4705.F3	Fitzgerald, Percy (Table P-PZ40)
4705.F312	Fitzgerald, William Thomas, 1759?-1829 (Table P-PZ40)
4705.F35	Forbes, Archibald (Table P-PZ40)
4705.F6	Foster, John (Table P-PZ40)

19th century, 1770/1800-1890/1900
Individual authors -- Continued

4705.F62	Fothergill, Jessie, 1851-1891 (Table P-PZ40)
4705.F63	Fourdrinier, Harriet Elizabeth (Table P-PZ40)
4705.F65	Francillon, Robert Edward (Table P-PZ40)
4705.F8	Frere, John Hookham (Table P-PZ40)
4705.F9	Friswell, James Hain (Table P-PZ40)
4706-4707	Froude, James Anthony (Table P-PZ36)
4708.F7	Fullerton, Lady Georgiana (Table P-PZ40)
4708.F75	Furlong, Thomas, 1794-1827 (Table P-PZ40)
4708.G2	Galt, John (Table P-PZ40)
	Ganconagh see PR5900+
4708.G48	Garnett, Martha Roscoe, 1869-1946 (Table P-PZ40)
4708.G5	Garnett, Richard (Table P-PZ40)
4710-4711	Gaskell, Mrs. Elizabeth (Table P-PZ36)
4712.G126	Gaspey, Thomas, 1788-1871 (Table P-PZ40)
4712.G132	Gatty, Alfred, Mrs., 1809-1873 (Table P-PZ40)
4712.G134	Gent, Thomas, b. 1780 (Table P-PZ40)
4712.G3	Gifford, William (Table P-PZ40)
4712.G6	Gilbert, Ann (Taylor) (Table P-PZ40)
	Including works by Ann and Jane Taylor
	Gilbert, Sir William S. see PR4713+
4713-4714	Gilbert, W.S. (William Schwenck), 1836-1911 (Table P-PZ36)
4715.G5	Gilchrist, Mrs. Anne (Table P-PZ40)
4715.G53	Gilfillan, George (Table P-PZ40)
4715.G55	Gilfillan, Robert (Table P-PZ40)
4716-4717	Gissing, George (Table P-PZ36)
4718.G4	Gladstone, William Ewart (Table P-PZ40)
	Godwin, Mary (Wollstonecraft) see PR5841.W8
4720-4724	Godwin, William, 1756-1836 (Table P-PZ35)
4725.G5	Gore, Catherine (Table P-PZ40)
4725.G7	Gosse, Edmund (Table P-PZ40)
4725.G76	Gould, Frederick James, 1855-1938 (Table P-PZ40)
	Gower, George Leveson see PR4886.L2
4726-4727	Grahame, Kenneth (Table P-PZ36)
4728.G112	Grand, Sarah (Table P-PZ40)
4728.G113	Grant, Ann (McVicar) (Table P-PZ40)
4728.G18	Graves, Charles L. (Table P-PZ40)
4728.G2	Gray, David (Table P-PZ40)
4728.G268	Green, Sarah, ca. 1763-ca. 1825 (Table P-PZ40)
4728.G287	Green, William Child (Table P-PZ40)
4728.G3	Greenwell, Dora (Table P-PZ40)
4728.G35	Greer, Tom (Table P-PZ40)
4728.G4	Greg, Percy (Table P-PZ40)
4728.G5	Gregory, Isabella Augusta, Lady (Table P-PZ40)
4728.G54	Gresley, William, 1801-1876 (Table P-PZ40)

	19th century, 1770/1800-1890/1900
	Individual authors -- Continued
	Grierson, Francis, 1848-1927 see PS3513.R658
4728.G8	Griffin, Gerald (Table P-PZ40)
4728.G83	Griffith, George Chetwynd (Table P-PZ40)
4728.G84	Griffiths, Arthur George Frederick, 1838-1908 (Table P-PZ40)
4729.G24	Grousset, Paschal, 1844-1909 (Table P-PZ40)
4729.G3	Grundy, Sydney (Table P-PZ40)
	Guggenberger, Louisa S. (Louisa Sarah), 1845-1895 see PR4109.B3
4729.G5	Guthrie, Thomas Anstey ("F. Anstey) (Table P-PZ40)
4729.G55	Guyton, Emma Jane Worboise, 1825-1887 (Table P-PZ40)
4731-4732	Haggard, Sir Henry Rider (Table P-PZ36)
4734.H	Hag - Haj
4735.H2	Hake, Thomas Gordon
	Haliburton, Thomas Chandler see PR9199.2.H34
4735.H26	Hall, Anna Maria Fielding, 1800-1881 (Table P-PZ40)
4735.H4	Hallam, Arthur Henry (Table P-PZ40)
4735.H7	Halliday, Andrew (Table P-PZ40)
4737-4738	Hamerton, Philip Gilbert, 1789-1842 (Table P-PZ36)
4739.H164	Hamilton, Elizabeth, 1758-1816 (Table P-PZ40)
4739.H19	Hamilton, Henry, 1853?-1918 (Table P-PZ40)
	Hamilton, Sir William
	see class B
4739.H23	Hamilton, Thomas, 1789-1842 (Table P-PZ40)
4739.H49	Hannay, James, 1827-1873 (Table P-PZ40)
	Hannay, James Owen see PR6015.A48
4739.H7	Hardinge, George (Table P-PZ40)
4739.H77	Hardy, Emma Lavinia Gifford, 1840-1912 (Table P-PZ40)
4739.H774	Hardy, Florence Emily, 1881-1937 (Table P-PZ40)
4740-4758	Hardy, Thomas (Table P-PZ32)
4741	Collected poems
	Separate works
4745	Far from the madding crowd (Table P-PZ41)
4746	Jude the obscure (Table P-PZ41)
4747	Return of the native (Table P-PZ41)
4748	Tess of the d'Urbervilles (Table P-PZ41)
4749	Wessex tales (Table P-PZ41)
4750.A-Z	Other, A-Z
	Subarrange each by Table P-PZ43
4759.H2	Hare, Augustus John Cuthbert (Table P-PZ40)
4759.H258	Harkin, Hugh, 1791-1854 (Table P-PZ40)
	Harkness, Margaret see PR4878.L53
4759.H268	Harley, M. (Table P-PZ40)
4759.H3	Harraden, Beatrice (Table P-PZ40)
4759.H36	Harris, Elizabeth, 1822-1852 (Table P-PZ40)

	19th century, 1770/1800-1890/1900
	Individual authors -- Continued
4759.H37	Harris, Frank (Table P-PZ40)
4759.H386	Harris, John, 1820-1884 (Table P-PZ40)
4759.H4	Harrison, Frederic (Table P-PZ40)
4759.H63	Hartley, John (Table P-PZ40)
4759.H633	Hartley, May Laffan (Table P-PZ40)
4759.H78	Hatton, Joseph (Table P-PZ40)
4759.H8	Havergal, Frances Ridley (Table P-PZ40)
4759.H9	Hawker, Robert Stephen (Table P-PZ40)
4760-4764	Hawkins, Anthony Hope (Table P-PZ35)
4765.H5	Hawtrey, Charles (Table P-PZ40)
4769.H14	Hay, Mary Cecil, 1840?-1886 (Table P-PZ40)
4769.H3	Haynes, James (Table P-PZ40)
4769.H6	Hays, Mary, 1759 or 60-1843 (Table P-PZ40)
4769.H8	Hayward, William Stephens (Table P-PZ40)
4769.H89	Hazleton, Frederick (Table P-PZ40)
4770-4773	Hazlitt, William (Table P-PZ35a)
4777-4778	Hazlitt, William Carew (Table P-PZ36)
4779.H2	Heber, Reginald (Table P-PZ40)
4779.H7	Heinemann, William (Table P-PZ40)
4779.H8	Helme, Elizabeth, d. 1816 (Table P-PZ40)
4779.H9	Helps, Sir Arthur (Table P-PZ40)
4780-4781	Hemans, Mrs. Felicia Dorothea (Table P-PZ36)
	Henley, William Ernest
4783.A1	Works. By date
4783.A2	Selected works. By date
4783.A3	Poetical works. By date
4783.A4	Plays with R.L. Stevenson. By date
4783.A5-.Z4	Separate works
4783.E5-.E53	Essays (Table P-PZ43)
4783.S6-.S63	Song of the sword (and other verses) (Table P-PZ43)
	Views and reviews
	Literature see PN710
	Art see ND27
4784	Biography and criticism
4785.H46	Hennessy, D.C. (Denis C.), d. 1884 (Table P-PZ40)
4785.H5	Henry, James (Table P-PZ40)
4785.H55	Henty, George Alfred (Table P-PZ40)
4785.H6	Hepburn, Thomas Nicoll, 1861- (Table P-PZ40)
4785.H7	Herbert, William, Dean of Manchester (Table P-PZ40)
4785.H72	Herbison, David, 1800-1880 (Table P-PZ40)
4785.H75	Heriot, John, 1760-1833 (Table P-PZ40)
4786.H3	Hersee, William (Table P-PZ40)
4786.H6	Hewlett, Joseph Thomas James, 1800-1847 (Table P-PZ40)
	Hewlett, Maurice

	19th century, 1770/1800-1890/1900
	Individual authors
	Hewlett, Maurice -- Continued
	Collected works
4787.A1	By date
4787.A2	By editor
4787.A23	Selected works
4787.A25-.A28	Translations
4787.A3-Z	Separate works
4788	Biography and criticism
	Hext, Harrington see PR5177
4789.H48	Heygate, William Edward (Table P-PZ40)
	Hichens, Robert see PR6015.I4
4790.H2	Hickey, Emily Henrietta (Table P-PZ40)
4790.H3	Hinkson, Katherine (Tynan) (Table P-PZ40)
4790.H46	Hoare, Edward N. (Table P-PZ40)
4790.H47	Hoare, Prince, 1755-1834 (Table P-PZ40)
	Hobhouse, John Cam see PR4174.B55
4790.H65	Hodgson, Francis, 1781-1852 (Table P-PZ40)
4790.H78	Hoey, Frances Cashel, 1830-1908 (Table P-PZ40)
4790.H8	Hofland, Barbara (Table P-PZ40)
4790.H86	Hogan, Michael, 1832-1899 (Table P-PZ40)
4791-4792	Hogg, James (Table P-PZ36)
4793.H	Hogg - Holl
4793.H4	Hogg, Thomas Jefferson, 1792-1862 (Table P-PZ40)
	Holcroft, Thomas see PR3515.H2
4793.H85	Holl, Henry, 1811-1884 (Table P-PZ40)
4794.H	Holland - Hood
4794.H5	Hone, William (Table P-PZ40)
4795-4799	Hood, Thomas, 1799-1845 (Table P-PZ35)
4800.H2	Hood, Thomas, the younger (Table P-PZ40)
4803.H2	Hook, Theodore Edward (Table P-PZ40)
	Hope, Anthony, 1863-1933 see PR4760+
	Hope, Ascott R. see PR5029.M68
4803.H42	Hope, Thomas (Table P-PZ40)
4803.H44	Hopkins, Gerard Manley, 1844-1889 (Table P-PZ40)
4803.H58	Horne, Herbert Percy, 1864-1916 (Table P-PZ40)
4803.H6	Horne, Richard Henry (Table P-PZ40)
4807-4808	Houghton, Richard Monckton-Milnes, 1st baron (Table P-PZ36)
4809.H15	Housman, A.E. (Alfred Edward), 1859-1936 (Table P-PZ38)
4809.H17	Housman, Clemence (Table P-PZ40)
4809.H18	Housman, Laurence (Table P-PZ40)
4809.H185	Howard, Edward, d. 1841 (Table P-PZ40)
4809.H2	Howitt, Mary (Table P-PZ40)
4809.H3	Howitt, William (Table P-PZ40)

19th century, 1770/1800-1890/1900

Individual authors -- Continued

4809.H8	Hughes, Thomas (Table P-PZ40)
	Hume, Fergus see PR9639.2.H84
4809.H93	Humphreys, Eliza Margaret J. (Gollan) (Table P-PZ40)
4809.H95	Hunt, Alfred William, Mrs. (1831-1912) (Table P-PZ40)
4810-4814	Hunt, Leigh (Table P-PZ35)
	Hunt, Margaret Raine, 1831-1912 see PR4809.H95
4817.H9	Hyde, Douglas (Table P-PZ40)
4818.I	I - Im
4818.I3	Ibbett, William Joseph, b. 1858 (Table P-PZ40)
4818.I55	Image, Selwyn (Table P-PZ40)
4819	Ingelow, Jean (Table P-PZ37)
4821.I3	Ircastrensis (Table P-PZ40)
4821.I5	Ireland, William Henry (Table P-PZ40)
	Cf. PR2950 Shakespearian forgeries
4821.I6	Irving, Laurence (Table P-PZ40)
4821.J2	Jacobs, William Wymark (Table P-PZ40)
4821.J25	Jacox, Francis (Table P-PZ40)
4821.J3	James, Florence Alice (Price), 1857-1929 (Table P-PZ40)
4821.J4	James, George Payne Rainsford (Table P-PZ40)
4821.J45	James, William (Table P-PZ40)
4821.J6	Jameson, Mrs. Anna (Table P-PZ40)
4821.J68	Jamieson, Jane H. (Table P-PZ40)
4821.J8	Jeaffreson, John Cordy (Table P-PZ40)
4822-4823	Jefferies, Richard (Table P-PZ36)
4825.J2	Jeffrey, Francis (Table P-PZ40)
4825.J25	Jerdan, William (Table P-PZ40)
4825.J3	Jerome, Jerome K., 1859-1929 (Table P-PZ38)
4825.J4	Jerrold, Douglas (Table P-PZ40)
4825.J5	Jersey, Margaret Elizabeth Leigh Child-Villiers, Countess of, 1849-1945 (Table P-PZ40)
4825.J7	Jewsbury, Geraldine E. (Table P-PZ40)
4826.J5	Johnson, Lionel Pigot (Table P-PZ40)
4826.J55	Johnston, Ellen, ca. 1835-1873 (Table P-PZ40)
4826.J58	Johnston, Harry Hamilton, Sir, 1858-1927 (Table P-PZ40)
4826.J623	Johnstone, C. I. (Christian Isobel), 1781-1857 (Table P-PZ40)
4826.J7	Jones, Ebenezer (Table P-PZ40)
4826.J75	Jones, Ernest Charles, 1819-1868 (Table P-PZ40)
4827-4828	Jones, Henry Arthur (Table P-PZ36)
4829.J5	Jones, John (Table P-PZ40)
4829.J62	Jones, T. Mason (Table P-PZ40)
4829.K65	Keary, Annie, 1825-1879 (Table P-PZ40)
4830-4838	Keats, John (Table P-PZ33 modified)
	Collected works
4830	By date

	19th century, 1770/1800-1890/1900
	Individual authors
	Keats, John
	Collected works
	By date -- Continued
4830.E00-.E99	1800-1899
4830.F00-.F99	1900-1999
4830.G00-.G99	2000-2099
4839.K15	Keble, John (Table P-PZ40)
4839.K16	Keegan, John, 1816-1849 (Table P-PZ40)
4839.K175	Kelly, Isabella (Table P-PZ40)
4839.K2	Kemble, Frances Anne (Table P-PZ40)
4839.K28	Kenealy, Edward Vaughn (Table P-PZ40)
4839.K3	Kenyon, John (Table P-PZ40)
4839.K365	Kickham, Charles Joseph, ca. 1826-1882 (Table P-PZ40)
4839.K42	King, Charles Gerrard, Mrs., 1810-1885 (Table P-PZ40)
4839.K43	King, Harriet Eleanor Baillie-Hamilton, 1840-1920 (Table P-PZ40)
4839.K9	The Kingsleys (Table P-PZ40)
4840-4844	Kingsley, Charles (Table P-PZ35)
4845.K5	Kingsley, Henry (Table P-PZ40)
4845.K54	Kingston, William Henry Giles, 1814-1880 (Table P-PZ40)
4849.K5	Kipling, Alice (McDonald) (Table P-PZ40)
4850-4858	Kipling, Rudyard (Table P-PZ33 modified)
	Collected works
4850	By date
4850.E00-.E99	1800-1899
4850.F00-.F99	1900-1999
4850.G00-.G99	2000-2099
4851	Collected poems
4859.K4	Knight, Ellis Cornelia, 1757-1837 (Table P-PZ40)
4859.K5	Knowles, James Sheridan (Table P-PZ40)
4859.K7	Kravchinskii, Sergei Mikhailovich, 1852-1895 (Table P-PZ40)
4859.K92	Kynaston, Herbert, 1835-1910 (Table P-PZ40)
4859.L9	Lamb, Lady Caroline Ponsonby, 1785-1828 (Table P-PZ40)
	Lamb, Charles
	Including works of Charles and Mary Lamb
	Works
4860.A2	Poetry and prose. By date
4860.A25	Poetry. By date
4860.A3	Prose. By date
4860.A4	Selections
4860.A6-Z	Translations
4861	Essays of Elia

	19th century, 1770/1800-1890/1900
	Individual authors
	Lamb, Charles -- Continued
4862.A-Z	Other works, A-Z
	Including separate essays
4863	Biography
4864	Criticism
4865.L2	Lamb, Mary (Table P-PZ40)
4865.L33	Lamont, Duncan (Table P-PZ40)
4865.L5	Landon, Letitia Elizabeth ("L.E.L.") (Table P-PZ40)
4865.L8	Landor, Robert Eyres (Table P-PZ40)
4870-4874	Landor, Walter Savage (Table P-PZ35)
4875.L3	Lane, Anna (Eichberg) (Mrs. John Lane) (Table P-PZ40)
4876-4877	Lang, Andrew (Table P-PZ36)
4878.L15	Lang, Leonora Blanche (Mrs. Andrew Lang) (Table P-PZ40)
4878.L17	Latham, John, 1787-1853 (Table P-PZ40)
4878.L18	Lathy, Thomas Pike, 1771-1841 (Table P-PZ40)
4878.L2	La Touche, Maria (Price) (Table P-PZ40)
4878.L3	Latymer, Frances Burdett Thomas Coutts-Nevill, baron (Table P-PZ40)
4878.L53	Law, John, fl. 1891-1921 (Table P-PZ40)
4878.L6	Lawless, Hon. Emily (Table P-PZ40)
4878.L7	Lawrence, George Alfred (Table P-PZ40)
4878.L73	Lawrence, James Henry, 1773-1840 (Table P-PZ40)
4879.L16	Lean, Florence Marryat Church, 1837-1899 (Table P-PZ40)
4879.L2	Lear, Edward (Table P-PZ40)
4879.L3	Lecky, William Edward Hartpole (Table P-PZ40)
	Lee, Harriet and Sophia see PR3541.L2
	Lee, Vernon, 1856-1935 see PR5115.P2
4879.L44	Lee, R., Mrs. 1791-1856 (Table P-PZ40)
	Lee, Sarah, 1791-1856 see PR4879.L44
4879.L53	Lee-Hamilton, Eugene (Table P-PZ40)
4879.L7	Le Fanu, Joseph Sheridan (Table P-PZ40)
4879.L79	Lefroy, Anne Austen. 1793-1872 (Table P-PZ40)
4881-4882	LeGallienne, Richard (Table P-PZ36)
4883.L18	Leigh, Chandos, 1791-1850 (Table P-PZ40)
4883.L2	Leigh, Henry S., 1837-1883 (Table P-PZ40)
4883.L233	Leigh, John, 1813-1887 (Table P-PZ40)
4883.L26	Leighton, Alexander, 1800-1874 (Table P-PZ40)
4883.L3	Leighton, William (Table P-PZ40)
4883.L4	Leith, Disney, Mrs. (Mary Charlotte Julia Gordon Leith) (Table P-PZ40)
4883.L6	Lemon, Mark (Table P-PZ40)
4883.L64	Leonowens, Anna Harriette, 1834-1914 (Table P-PZ40)
4883.L8	Lestocq, W. (William), d. 1920 (Table P-PZ40)
4884-4885	Lever, Charles (Table P-PZ36)

	19th century, 1770/1800-1890/1900
	Individual authors -- Continued
4886.L2	Leveson-Gower, George Granville (Table P-PZ40)
4886.L25	Levy, Amy, 1861-1889 (Table P-PZ40)
4886.L4	Lewes, George Henry (Table P-PZ40)
4886.L8	Lewis, Leopold (Table P-PZ40)
4887-4888	Lewis Matthew Gregory (Table P-PZ36)
4889.L25	Liardet, Frederick (Table P-PZ40)
4889.L28	Lickbarrow, Isabella (Table P-PZ40)
4889.L48	Linskill, Mary (Table P-PZ40)
4889.L5	Linton, Elizabeth (Lynn) (Table P-PZ40)
4889.L6	Linton, William James (Table P-PZ40)
4890.L	Lis - Ll
	Little, Alicia Helen Neva (Bewicke) see PR4109.B33
	Little, Mrs. Archibald see PR4109.B33
4890.L6	Livingston, Peter
4890.L8	Lloyd, Charles
4891.L2	Locker-Lampson, Frederick (Table P-PZ40)
4891.L4	Lockhart, John Gibson (Table P-PZ40)
4891.L6	Long, Catherine Walpole, Lady, d. 1867 (Table P-PZ40)
4891.L62	Longueville, Thomas, 1844-1922 (Table P-PZ40)
4891.L63	Longstaffe, John Lawrance (Table P-PZ40)
	Longworth, Maria Theresa, 1832?-1881 see PR5909.Y45
4891.L65	Loudon, Mrs. (Jane), 1807-1858 (Table P-PZ40)
4892-4893	Lover, Samuel (Table P-PZ36)
4894.L	Lov - Lym
4894.L347	Lucas, Elizabeth S. (Table P-PZ40)
4894.L375	Lumsden, James (Table P-PZ40)
	Lyall, Edna see PR4079.B5
4897.L	Lyn - Lyt
4897.L2	Lyndsay, David (Table P-PZ40)
	Lynn-Linton, Elizabeth see PR4889.L6
4900-4948	Lytton, Edward George Bulwer-Lytton, 1st baron (Table P-PZ31 modified)
4904.5	Miscellaneous prose works
4904.8	Poems and plays. Collected
	Separate works
4905	Caxtons (Table P-PZ41)
4907	Ernest Maltravers (Table P-PZ41)
4908	Eugene Aram (Table P-PZ41)
4909	Godolphin (Table P-PZ41)
4910	Harold (Table P-PZ41)
4911	Kenelm Chillingly (Table P-PZ41)
4912	Last days of Pompeii (Table P-PZ41)
4913	Last of the barons (Table P-PZ41)
4914	Lady of Lyons (Table P-PZ41)
4915	My novel (Table P-PZ41)

	19th century, 1770/1800-1890/1900
	Individual authors
	Lytton, Edward George Bulwer-Lytton, 1st baron
	Separate works -- Continued
4916	Night and morning (Table P-PZ41)
4917	Poems (Table P-PZ41)
4918	Richelieu (Table P-PZ41)
4919	Rienzi (Table P-PZ41)
4920	Strange story (Table P-PZ41)
4921	Zanoni (Table P-PZ41)
4922.A-Z	Other, A-Z
	Subarrange each by Table P-PZ43
4950-4958	Lytton, Edward Robert Bulwer-Lytton, 1st Earl of (Owen Meredith) (Table P-PZ33 modified)
	Collected works
4950	By date
4950.E00-.E99	1800-1899
4950.F00-.F99	1900-1999
4950.G00-.G99	2000-2099
4959.L5	Lytton, Rosina Bulwer-Lytton, Baroness (Table P-PZ40)
4963	Macauley, Thomas Babington, Lord (Table P-PZ39)
	Class here collected works and special literary works
	For biography as a historian see DA3.M3
4964.M5	McCarthy, Justin Huntley (Table P-PZ40)
4965-4969	Macdonald, George (Table P-PZ35)
4970.M2	Macfarlane, James (Table P-PZ40)
4970.M45	McGonagall, William (Table P-PZ40)
4970.M78	Mack, Robert Ellice (Table P-PZ40)
4970.M8	Mackarness, Matilda Anne (Planché) (Table P-PZ40)
4971.M2	Mackay, Charles (Table P-PZ40)
4971.M3	Mackay, Eric (Table P-PZ40)
4971.M37	Mackenzie, Anna Maria (Table P-PZ40)
4971.M6	Mackintosh, Sir James (Table P-PZ40)
4971.M674	Maclaren, Archibald, 1819-1884 (Table P-PZ40)
	Macleod, Fiona, 1855-1905 see PR5350+
4971.M7	Macnish, Robert (Table P-PZ40)
4971.M8	M'Taggart, Mrs. Ann (Table P-PZ40)
4972.M3	Maginn, William (Table P-PZ40)
4972.M33	Mahony, Francis Sylvester ("Father Prout") (Table P-PZ40)
4972.M39	Maitland, Edward, 1824-1897 (Table P-PZ40)
4972.M5	Mallock, William Hurrell (Table P-PZ40)
4973	Mangan, James Clarence (Table P-PZ39)
4974.M148	Mann, Mary E. Rackham (Table P-PZ40)
4974.M15	Manners, J. Hartley (Table P-PZ40)
4974.M2	Manning, Henry Edward, Cardinal (Table P-PZ40)
4974.M33	Mant, Richard, Bp. of Down, Connor, and Dramore, 1776-1848 (Table P-PZ40)

	19th century, 1770/1800-1890/1900
	Individual authors -- Continued
4974.M78	Marks, Richard, 1779?-1840 (Table P-PZ40)
4975-4979	Marryat, Frederick (Table P-PZ35)
4980.M4	Marshall, Emma (Table P-PZ40)
4980.M5	Marshall, George (Table P-PZ40)
4980.M8	Marston, John Westland (Table P-PZ40)
4981-4982	Marston, Philip Bourke (Table P-PZ36)
4984.M28	Martin, Sarah Catherine, 1768-1826 (Table P-PZ40)
4984.M3	Martin, Sir Theodore (Table P-PZ40)
4984.M5	Martineau, Harriet (Table P-PZ40)
4984.M545	Marzials, Theophilus Julius Henry, 1850-1920 (Table P-PZ40)
4984.M6	Mason, James (Table P-PZ40)
4984.M7	Massey, Gerald (Table P-PZ40)
4984.M79	Masson, Charles (Table P-PZ40)
4984.M83	Masters, John White (Table P-PZ40)
4984.M87	Mathew, Frank James, 1865-1924 (Table P-PZ40)
4987.M19	Mathews, Charles James, 1803-1878 (Table P-PZ40)
4987.M2	Mathias, Thomas James (Table P-PZ40)
4987.M7	Maturin, Charles Robert (Table P-PZ40)
4988.M29	Mauduit, Frank (Table P-PZ40)
4988.M3	Maurice, Frederick Denison (Table P-PZ40)
4989.M2	Maxwell, Sir Herbert Eustace (Table P-PZ40)
4989.M4	Maxwell, Mrs. Mary Elizabeth (Braddon) (Table P-PZ40)
4989.M45	Maxwell, William Hamilton, 1792-1850 (Table P-PZ40)
4989.M46	May, Mrs. Georgiana Marion (Craik), 1831-1895 (Table P-PZ40)
4989.M47	Mayhew, Augustus Septimus, 1826-1875 (Table P-PZ40)
4989.M48	Mayhew, Henry, 1812-1887 (Table P-PZ40)
4989.M5	Mayhew, Horace (Table P-PZ40)
4989.M7	Mayo, Isabella (Fyvie) ("Edward Garrett") (Table P-PZ40)
	McFall, Francis Elizabeth see PR4728.G112
4989.M83	Mayson, Walter H., 1835-1904 (Table P-PZ40)
4990.M34	Meade, L.T., 1854-1914 (Table P-PZ40)
4990.M37	Medwin, Thomas, 1788-1869 (Table P-PZ40)
4990.M38	Meeke, Mary, d. 1818 (Table P-PZ40)
5000-5018	Meredith, George (Table P-PZ32 modified)
	Separate works
	Fiction
5005	Collected. By date
5006.A-Z	Separate works, A-Z
	Subarrange each by Table P-PZ43
	Poems
5007	Collected. By date
5008.A-Z	Separate works, A-Z
	Subarrange each by Table P-PZ43

	19th century, 1770/1800-1890/1900
	Individual authors
	Meredith, George
	Separate works -- Continued
5010.A-Z	Other works. By title, A-Z
	Subarrange each by Table P-PZ43
5019.M8	Merivale, Herman Charles (Table P-PZ40)
5020	Merivale, John Herman (Table P-PZ39)
	Merriman, Henry Seton see PR5299.S6
5021.M2	Metcalf, C.J. (Table P-PZ40)
5021.M3	Meynell, Alice Christina Thompson, 1847-1922 (Table P-PZ38)
5021.M4	Meynell, Wilfrid (Table P-PZ40)
5021.M427	Mildmay, Aubrey N. St. John , 1865-1955 (Table P-PZ40)
5021.M45	Miller, Hugh (Table P-PZ40)
5021.M452	Miller, Thomas, 1807-1874 (Table P-PZ40)
5021.M465	Milliken, E. J., 1840?-1897 (Table P-PZ40)
5021.M47	Mills, Charles (Table P-PZ40)
5021.M5	Milman, Henry Hart (Table P-PZ40)
5021.M6	Milner, George (Table P-PZ40)
5022-5023	Mitford Mary Russell (Table P-PZ36)
5029.M35	Mogridge, George (Table P-PZ40)
	Moile, N.T. (Nicolas Thirning), 1797?-1873 see PR4149.B57
5029.M5	Moir, David Macbeth (Table P-PZ40)
5029.M62	Molesworth, Mary Louisa Stewart, 1842-1921 (Table P-PZ40)
5029.M68	Moncrieff, A.R. Hope (Ascott Robert Hope), 1846-1927 (Table P-PZ40)
5029.M7	Moncrieff, William Thomas (Table P-PZ40)
5029.M73	Monkhouse, W. Cosmo (William Cosmo), 1840-1901 (Table P-PZ40)
5029.M78	Monsell, John S. B., 1811-1875 (Table P-PZ40)
5029.M787	Montague, Edward, fl. 1806-1808 (Table P-PZ40)
5029.M8	Montgomery, Alexander (Table P-PZ40)
5030-5034	Montgomery, James (Table P-PZ35)
5036.M5	Montgomery, Robert (Table P-PZ40)
5039.M5	Moore, Dugald (Table P-PZ40)
5039.M58	Moore, George, fl. 1797-1806 (Table P-PZ40)
5040-5044	Moore, George (Table P-PZ35)
5050-5058	Moore, Thomas (Table P-PZ33 modified)
	Collected works
5050	By date
5050.E00-.E99	1800-1899
5050.F00-.F99	1900-1999
5050.G00-.G99	2000-2099
	Moore, Margaret King see PR5101.M343

	19th century, 1770/1800-1890/1900
	Individual authors
5059.M15	Moore, W., fl. 1889 (Table P-PZ40)
5059.M3	Morgan, Sydney (Owenson), Lady (Table P-PZ40)
5059.M37	Morgan, Vaughan (Table P-PZ40)
5059.M4	Morier, James Justinian, 1780?-1849 (Table P-PZ40)
5059.M45	Morley, John Morley, viscount (Table P-PZ40)
5059.M5	Morris, Charles (Table P-PZ40)
5059.M6	Morris, Edward, d. 1815 (Table P-PZ40)
5059.M66	Morris, Isabel (Table P-PZ40)
5060-5064	Morris, Sir Lewis (Table P-PZ35)
	Morris, William
5070	Collected works. By date
5071	Collected works. By editor
5072	Selected works. Selections
	Subarrange by editor, if given, or by date
	Poems
	Collected
5074.A1	Collections (General). By date
5074.A3	Selections. By editor or publisher
5075	Earthly paradise (Table P-PZ41)
5076	Life and death of Jason (Table P-PZ41)
5077	Sigurd the Volsung (Table P-PZ41)
5078.A-Z	Other, A-Z
	Subarrange each by Table P-PZ43
	Prose
5079.A-Z	Tales, A-Z
5080.A-Z	Essays and miscellaneous, A-Z
5081	Translations
	Biography, criticism, etc.
5082.A1-.A5	Periodicals. Societies. Serials
5082.A6-Z	Dictionaries, indexes, etc.
5083.A3-.A39	Autobiography, journals, memoirs. By title
5083.A4	Letters (Collections). By date
5083.A41-.A49	Letters to and from particular individuals. By correspondent (alphabetically)
5083.A5-Z	General works
	Criticism
5084	General works
5085	Textual. Manuscripts, etc.
	Special
5086	Sources
5087.A-Z	Other, A-Z
	For list of Cutter numbers, see Table P-PZ32 17
5088	Language. Grammar. Style
5089.M7	Morrison, Arthur, 1863-1945 (Table P-PZ40)
5089.M72	Morritt, John B.S. (Table P-PZ40)

	19th century, 1770/1800-1890/1900
	Individual authors -- Continued
	Mortimer, Edward, fl. 1806-1808 see PR5029.M787
5094.M5	Mortimer, John (Table P-PZ40)
5097.M3	Morton, John Maddison (Table P-PZ40)
5097.M5	Morton, Thomas (Table P-PZ40)
5101.M3	Motherwell, William (Table P-PZ40)
5101.M327	Mott, Edward Spencer, 1844-1910 (Table P-PZ40)
5101.M34	Moultrie, John (Table P-PZ40)
5101.M343	Mount Cashell, Margaret Jane King Moore, Countess of, 1772-1835 (Table P-PZ40)
5101.M363	Muddock, J. E. (Joyce Emmerson), 1843-1934 (Table P-PZ40)
5101.M39	Munby, Arthur Joseph, 1828-1910 (Table P-PZ40)
5101.M397	Munro, John (Table P-PZ40)
5101.M4	Munro, Neil (Table P-PZ40)
5101.M4214	Murdoch, Alexander G., 1843-1891 (Table P-PZ40)
5101.M43	Murray, Charles Augustus, Sir, 1806-1895 (Table P-PZ40)
5101.M45	Murray, David Christie (Table P-PZ40)
5101.M48	Murray, George, 1819-1865 (Table P-PZ40)
5101.M5	Murray, Robert Fuller (Table P-PZ40)
5101.M6	Myers, Frederic William Henry (Table P-PZ40)
5101.M9	Myrtle, Harriet, 1811?-1876 (Table P-PZ40)
5102.N3	Nairne, Carolina (Oliphant), Baroness (Table P-PZ40)
5102.N6	Nares, Edward (Table P-PZ40)
5103.N2	Neale, John Mason (Table P-PZ40)
5103.N23	Neale, William Johnson, 1812-1893 (Table P-PZ40)
5103.N235	Neaves, Lord, 1800-1876 (Table P-PZ40)
	Nesbit, E. (Edith), 1858-1924 see PR4149.B4
5103.N4	Newbolt, Henry John, Sir, 1862-1938 (Table P-PZ40)
5103.N52	Newman, George, 1835-1911 (Table P-PZ40)
5105-5109	Newman, John Henry, Cardinal (Table P-PZ35)
	Cf. B, Religion
5110.N24	Nichol, John (Table P-PZ40)
5110.N3	Nicoll, Robert (Table P-PZ40)
5110.N4	Nicoll, Sir William Robertson (Table P-PZ40)
5110.N45	Nicolson, Alexander, 1827-1893 (Table P-PZ40)
5110.N7	Noble, Thomas (Table P-PZ40)
5110.N83	Noel, Caroline M. (Table P-PZ40)
5111	Noel, Roden (Table P-PZ39)
	Noonan, Robert, 1870-1911 see PR5671.T85
5112.N27	North, William, d. 1854 (Table P-PZ40)
5112.N5	Norton, Hon. Mrs. Caroline (Sheridan) (Table P-PZ40)
	O'Beirne, Ivan, 1847-1933 see PR4699.F45
5112.O19	O'Brien, William, 1852-1928 (Table P-PZ40)
5112.O5	O'Flaherty, Charles (Table P-PZ40)
5112.O55	O'Grady, Standish. 1846-1928 (Table P-PZ40)

19th century, 1770/1800-1890/1900
Individual authors -- Continued
Old Humphrey, 1787-1854 see PR5029.M35

5112.O8	Oliphant, Laurence (Table P-PZ38)
5113-5114	Oliphant, Mrs. (Margaret), 1828-1897 (Table P-PZ36)
5115.O275	O'Neil, Henry, 1817-1880 (Table P-PZ40)
5115.O3	Opi, Mrs. Amelia (Table P-PZ40)
	O'Rourke, Edmund Falconer, 1814-1879 see PR4699.F145
5115.O34	Orr, James, 1770-1816 (Table P-PZ40)
5115.O4	O'Shaughnessy, Arthur (Table P-PZ38)
5115.O6	Outram, George (Table P-PZ40)
5115.O87	Oxenford, John, 1812-1877 (Table P-PZ40)
5115.P17	Paget, Francis Edward, 1806-1882 (Table P-PZ40)
5115.P2	Paget, Violet ("Vernon Lee") (Table P-PZ40)
5115.P5	Palgrave, Francis Turner (Table P-PZ40)
5115.P73	Palmer, John, Jun. (Table P-PZ40)
5119.P5	Parker, George Williams (Table P-PZ40)
	Parker, Sir Gilbert see PR9199.2.P37
5126.P5	Parker, Louis N. (Table P-PZ40)
5127.P15	Parsons, Mrs. (Eliza), d. 1811 (Table P-PZ40)
5127.P2	Parsons, William (Table P-PZ40)
5130-5138	Pater, Walter (Horatio) (Table P-PZ33 modified)
	Collected works
5130	By date
5130.F00-.F99	1900-1999
5130.G00-.G99	2000-2099
5140-5144	Patmore, Coventry (Table P-PZ35)
5146-5147	Paton, Sir Joseph Noël (Table P-PZ36)
5149.P2	Pattison, Mark (Table P-PZ40)
5150-5158	Payn, James (Table P-PZ33)
5159.P5	Payne, John (Table P-PZ40)
5159.P62	Peacock, Lucy, fl. 1785-1816 (Table P-PZ40)
5160-5164	Peacock, Thomas Love (Table P-PZ35)
5167.P314	Pearce, J.H. (Joseph Henry) (Table P-PZ40)
5167.P35	Pember, Edward Henry, 1833-1911 (Table P-PZ40)
5167.P4	Penn, John (Table P-PZ40)
5167.P6	Pennell, Henry Cholmondeley (Table P-PZ40)
5167.P8	Pennie, John F. (Table P-PZ40)
5168.P3	Pfeiffer, Mrs. Emily (Table P-PZ40)
5169.P697	Phillips, Alfred, Mrs., 1822?-1876 (Table P-PZ40)
5169.P7	Phillips, Charles (Table P-PZ40)
	Phillips, Elizabeth, 1822?-1876 see PR5169.P697
5170-5174	Phillips, Stephen (Table P-PZ35)
5175.P3	Phillips, Watts (Table P-PZ40)
5177	Phillpotts, Eden (Table P-PZ39)
5178.P	Ph - Pi

19th century, 1770/1800-1890/1900

  Individual authors

    Ph - Pi -- Continued

5178.P37	Picken, Joanna Belfrage, 1798-1859 (Table P-PZ40)
5180-5184	Pinero, Sir Arthur Wing (Table P-PZ35)
5185.P	Pin - Piz
5185.P57	Pirkis, Mrs. Catharine Louisa (Table P-PZ40)
5187.P2	Planché, James Robison (Table P-PZ40)
5187.P24	Plarr, Victory Gustave, 1863-1929 (Table P-PZ40)
5187.P3	Plumptre, Edward Hayes (Table P-PZ40)
5187.P5	Polidori, Dr. John William (Table P-PZ40)
5189.P15	Pollock, Sir Frederick (Table P-PZ40)
5189.P17	Pollock, Walter Herries, 1850-1926 (Table P-PZ40)
5189.P2	Pollock, Robert (Table P-PZ40)
5189.P25	Polwhele, Richard (Table P-PZ40)
5189.P4	Porter, Anna Maria (Table P-PZ40)
5189.P5	Porter, Jane (Table P-PZ40)
5189.P7	Praed, Winthrop Mackworth (Table P-PZ40)
5189.P8	Pratt, Samuel Jackson (Table P-PZ40)
5189.P95	Prest, Thomas Peckett, 1810-1879 (Table P-PZ40)
5190.P2	Prichard, Thomas Jeffrey Llewelyn (Table P-PZ40)
5190.P3	Pringle, Thomas (Table P-PZ40)
5190.P7	Probyn, May (Table P-PZ40)
5191	Procter, Adelaide Anne (Table P-PZ39)
5192	Procter, Bryan Waller ("Barry Cornwall") (Table P-PZ39)
	Prout, Father see PR4972.M39
5193.Q67	Quick, Henry, 1792-1857 (Table P-PZ40)
5194-5195	Quiller-Couch, Sir Arthur Thomas (Table P-PZ36)
5197.Q3	Quillinan, Edward (Table P-PZ40)
5200-5204	Radcliffe, Mrs. Ann (Table P-PZ35)
5205.R3	Radecliffe, Noelle (Table P-PZ40)
5205.R53	Raffalovich, André, 1864-1934 (Table P-PZ40)
5209.R2	Rands, William Brighty (Table P-PZ40)
5209.R5	Rathbone, Mrs. Hannah Mary Reynolds, 1798-1878 (Table P-PZ40)
5209.R8	Rawlings, Charles, b. 1805 (Table P-PZ40)
5210-5218	Reade, Charles, 1814-1884 (Table P-PZ33)
5219.R157	Reade, Winwood, 1838-1875 (Table P-PZ40)
5219.R157	Rees, J. Rogers (Table P-PZ40)
5219.R26	Reid, Mayne (Table P-PZ40)
5219.R3	Reid, Robert (Table P-PZ40)
5219.R6	Rennell, James Rennell Rodd, baron (Table P-PZ40)
5220.R	Rep - Rey
5221.R3	Reynolds, Frederick
5221.R35	Reynolds, George William MacArthur, 1814-1879
5221.R5	Reynolds, John Hamilton, 1794-1852
5221.R54	Reynoldson, Thomas H. (Thomas Herbert), 1808?-1888

19th century, 1770/1800-1890/1900

Individual authors -- Continued

Rhone, Lady, 1852-1933 see PR5040+

5223-5224	Rice, James (Table P-PZ36)
	Cf. PR4100+ Works with Sir Walter Besant
5225.R5	Richards, Alfred Bate
5226	Richardson, A-Z
5226.R42	Richardson, James N. (James Nicholson), 1846-1912 (Table P-PZ40)
5227.R26	Richmond, Legh, 1772-1827 (Table P-PZ40)
5227.R3	Rickman, Thomas Clio (Table P-PZ40)
5227.R33	Riddell, Charlotte Eliza Lawson Cown, 1832-1906 (Table P-PZ40)
5227.R34	Riddell, Maria Woodley, 1772?-1808 (Table P-PZ40)
5227.R7	Ritchie, Anne (Thackeray), Lady (Table P-PZ38)
	Roberts, Caroline Alice see PR4649.E65
5232.R15	Roberts, George, b. 1832 (Table P-PZ40)
5232.R19	Roberts, William, 1767-1849 (Table P-PZ40)
5232.R3	Robertson, J. Logie (James Logie), 1846-1922 (Table P-PZ38)
5232.R5	Robertson, Thomas William (Table P-PZ38)
5232.R7	Robertson, William B. (Table P-PZ40)
	Cf. B, Religion
5233.R16	Robinson, Frederick William, 1830-1901 (Table P-PZ40)
5233.R2	Robinson, Henry Crabb (Table P-PZ40)
5233.R27	Robinson, Mrs. Mary (Table P-PZ40)
5233.R3	Robinson, Robert (Table P-PZ40)
5233.R38	Robinson, Thomas R. (Table P-PZ40)
5233.R4	Robinson, William (Table P-PZ40)
5233.R445	Roche, Regina Maria Dalton (Table P-PZ40)
	Rodd, James Rennell see PR5219.R6
5233.R57	Rodwell, G. Herbert (George Herbert), 1800-1852 (Table P-PZ40)
5234-5235	Rogers, Samuel (Table P-PZ36)
5236.R27	Rolfe, Frederick William, 1860-1913 (Table P-PZ40)
5236.R3	Rolleston, Thomas W.H. (Table P-PZ40)
5236.R6	Roscoe, William Caldwell (Table P-PZ40)
5236.R835	Ross, Robert Baldwin, 1869-1918 (Table P-PZ40)
5236.R85	Rosse, Alban (Table P-PZ40)
5236.R9	Rossetti family (Table P-PZ40)
5237-5238	Rossetti, Christina (Table P-PZ36)
5240-5248	Rossetti, Dante Gabriel (Table P-PZ33 modified)
	Collected works
5240	By date
5240.E00-.E99	1800-1899
5240.F00-.F99	1900-1999
5240.G00-.G99	2000-2099

19th century, 1770/1800-1890/1900
Individual authors -- Continued
Rossetti, Gabriele
see subclass PQ

5249.R2	Rossetti, William Michael (Table P-PZ40)
5249.R9	Ruffini, Giovanni (Table P-PZ40)
	Ruskin, John
5250-5251	Collected works
5250.E00-.G99	By date
5250.E00-.E99	1800-1899
5250.F00-.F99	1900-1999
5250.G00-.G99	2000-2099
5251	By editor
5252	Selected works. Selections
	Subarrange by editor, if given, or by date
5253.A-Z	Translations. By language, A-Z
	Separate works
5254	Arrows of the chace
5255	Crown of wild olive
5256	King of the Golden River
5257	On the old road
5258	Poems
5259	Queen of the air
5260	Sesame and lilies
5261.A-Z	Others, A-Z

The following will be found generally in the classes
assigned, but special copies for literary study may be
classed in PR5261
Aratra Petelici see NB1140
Ariadne florentina see NE860
Art of England see N6767+
Eagle's nest see N7445.2
Elements of drawing see NC710
Elements of English prosody see PE1+
Elements of perspective see NC750
Elements of sculpture see NC750
Ethics of the dust see BJ1681+
Fors clavigera
see HD8390
Frondes agrestes see N7445.2
Giotto and his works see ND623.G6
Lectures on architecture and painting see N7445.2
Lectures on art see N7445.2
Letters and advice to young girls see HQ1229
Modern painters see ND1135
Munera pulveris see HB161
Nature of Gothic see NA440+

19th century, 1770/1800-1890/1900
Individual authors
Ruskin, John
Separate works
Others, A-Z -- Continued
Notes on the construction of sheepfolds see B1+
Notes on the Royal Academy see N5054
Notes on Turner see NC242.T9
Poetry of architecture see NA2550
Political economy of art see N7445.2
Pre-Raphaelitism see ND467.5.P7
Proserpina see QK81
Seven lamps of architecture see NA2550
Stones of Venice see NA1121.V4
Time and tide
see HD8390
Two paths see N7445.2
Unto this last see HB161
Verona and other lectures see N7445.2
Illustrations
Class at N8215, or with the special artists in NC-NE as the case may be
Class illustrated editions with other editions
Class portraits, etc., of the author with his biography
Biography, criticism, etc.

5262.A1-.A5	Periodicals. Societies. Serials
5262.A6-Z	Dictionaries, indexes, etc.
5263.A3-.A39	Autobiography, journals, memoirs. By title
5263.A4	Letters (Collections). By date
5263.A41-.A49	Letters to and from particular individuals. By correspondent (alphabetically)
5263.A5-Z	General works
	Criticism
5264	General works
5265	Textual. Manuscripts, etc.
	Special
5266	Sources
5267.A-Z	Other, A-Z
	For list of Cutter numbers, see Table P-PZ32 17
5268	Language. Grammar. Style
5271.R5	Russell, George W.E. (Table P-PZ40)
5271.R8	Russell, William (Table P-PZ40)
5280-5283	Russell, William Clark (Table P-PZ35a)
	Rutherford, Mark, 1831-1913 see PR5795.W7
5285.R5	Rutland, Janetta, Duchess of (Table P-PZ40)
5285.R62	Rutter, J. (Table P-PZ40)

	19th century, 1770/1800-1890/1900
	Individual authors -- Continued
5285.R63	Ruxton, George Frederick Augustus, 1820-1848 (Table P-PZ40)
5289.S	Sa - Sai
5289.S25	Sabine, Charles, 1796-1859 (Table P-PZ40)
5291.S2	St. Aubyn, Mary (Table P-PZ40)
5291.S64	St. Johnston, Alfred, ca. 1858-1891 (Table P-PZ40)
5294-5295	Saintsbury, George (Table P-PZ36)
5299.S2	Sala, George Augustus (Table P-PZ40)
5299.S217	Salt, Henry Stephens, 1851-1939 (Table P-PZ40)
5299.S354	Savage, M.W. (Marmion Wiland), 1803-1872 (Table P-PZ40)
5299.S356	Savery Henry, 1791-1842 (Table P-PZ40)
	Schreiner, Olive see PR9369.2.S37
5299.S44	Schwartz, Jozua M.W. ("Maarten Maartens") (Table P-PZ40)
5299.S5	Scott, Hugh Stowell ("Henry Seton Merriman") (Table P-PZ40)
5299.S6	Scott, Michael (Table P-PZ40)
	Scott, Sir Walter
5300	Collected works (Poetry and prose). By date
	Novels see PR5317+
	Poetical and dramatic works see PR5305+
5301	Miscellaneous prose works
5302	Selected works
5303	Selections and anthologies
5304.A-Z	Translations, A-Z
	Poetical and dramatic works. By date
	Collected works
	Subarrange by date-letters and last two digits of date, e.g. PR5305.E13, The poetical works of Walter Scott, Esq., 1813
5305.E00-.E99	1800-1899
5305.F00-.F99	1900-1999
5305.G00-.G99	2000-2099
5306	Minor collections. Ballads. Lyrics. Select poetical works
5307	Selections. Extracts. Anthologies
	Separate works
5308	Lady of the lake
5309	Lay of the last minstrel
5310	Lord of the isles
5311	Marmion
5312	Rokeby
5313.A-Z	Other, A-Z
	Novels, tales, romances. "Waverley novels"
5315	Collections

	19th century, 1770/1800-1890/1900
	Individual authors
	Scott, Sir Walter
	Novels, tales, romances. "Waverley novels" -- Continued
5316	Selected novels (Collections of three or more)
	Selections, extracts see PR5303
	Separate works
5317	A - I
5318	Ivanhoe
5319	Kenilworth
5320	K - Q
5321	Quentin Durward
5322	Q - Z
5324	Spurious, suppositious works
5326	Adaptations, imitations, paraphrases
5326.A2	Collections
5327	Dramatizations, etc.
	Class here plays founded on Scott's works
5328	Songs and other musical compositions founded in or taken from Scott's works
	Class here texts only
	For music, see class M
5329	Illustrations without text
	For illustrated editions see PR5305+
	Biography and criticism
5330	Periodicals. Societies. Collections
5331	Concordances, dictionaries, indexes, quotations
	Cf. PR5303 Scott's general works
5332	General works
5333	Addresses, essays, lectures
	Biography
	General works see PR5332
5334	Autobiography. Journals. Letters
5335	General minor, miscellaneous details
5336	Love and marriage. Relation to women
5337	Later life. Imprisonment, etc.
5338	Relation to contemporaries. Homes and haunts. Landmarks. Local associations
5339	Anniversaries, celebrations. Exhibitions. Relics. Iconography (Portraits, monuments, etc.)
5340	Authorship
	Criticism
5341	General works
	Characters
5342.A2	General works
5342.A3-.A49	Groups, classes
	e.g. Women

	19th century, 1770/1800-1890/1900
	Individual authors
	Scott, Sir Walter
	Biography and criticism
	Criticism
	Characters -- Continued
5342.A5-Z	Special
5343.A-Z	Special subjects, A-Z
5343.A7	Arts
5343.B52	Bible
5343.C7	Criticism
	Class here works featuring Sir Walter Scott as a critic
5343.H5	History
5343.L26	Landscape
5343.L3	Law
5343.L56	Literature
5343.P52	Picturesque, The
5343.P63	Poetic works
5343.P68	Power (Social sciences)
5343.P82	Publishers
5343.S3	Scotland
5343.T7	Translations
5344	Textual criticism. Commentaries
	Language. Style
5345	General works
5346	Grammar
5347	Versification
5348	Dialect
5349.S2	Scott, William Bell (Table P-PZ40)
5349.S22	Scroggie, George (Table P-PZ40)
5349.S25	Seabridge, Charles (Table P-PZ40)
5349.S4	Selby, Charles (Table P-PZ40)
5349.S426	Serres, Olivia Wilmot, 1772-1834 (Table P-PZ40)
5349.S5	Sewell, Elizabeth M. (Table P-PZ40)
5349.S6	Sewell, Mrs. Mary (Wright) (Table P-PZ40)
5349.S62	Sewell, Mrs. Mary (of Chertsey) (Table P-PZ40)
5349.S65	Sewell, William, 1804-1874 (Table P-PZ40)
5349.S8	Shairp, John Campbell (Table P-PZ40)
5349.S85	Shannon, Edward N., ca. 1795-1860 (Table P-PZ40)
5350-5358	Sharp, William (Fiona McLeod) (Table P-PZ33 modified)
	Collected works
5350	By date
5350.F00-.F99	1900-1999
5350.G00-.G99	2000-2099
5359.S	Sharp, W. - Shaw, G.
	Shaw, George Bernard

	19th century, 1770/1800-1890/1900
	Individual authors
	Shaw, George Bernard -- Continued
5360	Complete works and collected dramas
	Subarrange by date
5361	Selections
	Subarrange by editor or date
5362	Translations
	Separate dramas
5363.A2	The doctor's dilemma, etc.
5363.A25	Misalliance, the dark lady of the sonnets, and Fanny's first play
5363.A3	Plays pleasant and unpleasant
5363.A5	Three plays for Puritans
5363.A8-Z	Individual dramas, A-Z
	Other works
5364	Collected
5365.A-Z	Separate, A-Z
5365.5	Adaptations. Paraphrases
	Biography, criticism, etc.
5366.A1-.A19	Periodicals. Societies. Serials
5366.A2-.A3	Dictionaries, indexes, etc.
5366.A31-.A39	Autobiography, journals, memoirs. By title
5366.A4	Letters (Collections). By date
5366.A41-.A49	Letters to and from particular individuals. By correspondent (alphabetically)
5366.A5-Z	General works
	Criticism
5367	General works
5368.A-Z	Special, A-Z
	For list of Cutter numbers, see Table P-PZ32 17
5369.S	Shaw, G. - Shee, M.
5376	Shee, Sir Martin Archer (Table P-PZ39)
5377.S5	Sheehan, Patrick Augustine (Table P-PZ40)
5379.S2	Sheil, Richard Lalor (Table P-PZ40)
5397-5398	Shelley, Mary Wollstonecraft Godwin, 1797-1851 (Table P-PZ36)
5400-5448	Shelley, Percy Bysshe (Table P-PZ31 modified)
	Collected works. Prose and verse
	Original editions and reprints. By date
5400.E00-.E99	1800-1899
5400.F00-.F99	1900-1999
5400.G00-.G99	2000-2099
5401	Facsimiles of manuscript poems. By date
5402	Poems
5403	Selections. Anthologies

19th century, 1770/1800-1890/1900
Individual authors
Shelley, Percy Bysshe
Collected works -- Continued

5404.A-Z	Translations. By language, A-Z
	Subarrange by translator
5404.8	Prose works
	Separate works
5406	Adonais (Table P-PZ41)
5407	Alastor (Table P-PZ41)
5408	Cenci (Table P-PZ41)
5409	Epipsychidion (Table P-PZ41)
5410	Hellas (Table P-PZ41)
5411	Julian and Maddalo (Table P-PZ41)
5412	Mask of anarchy (Table P-PZ41)
5414	Oedipus tyrannus (Table P-PZ41)
5415	Peter Bell the third (Table P-PZ41)
5416	Prometheus unbound (Table P-PZ41)
5417	Queen Mab (Table P-PZ41)
5418	Revolt of Islam (Table P-PZ41)
5419	Rosalind and Helen (Table P-PZ41)
5420	To a skylark (Table P-PZ41)
5421	Witch of Atlas (Table P-PZ41)
5422.A-Z	Other, A-Z
	Subarrange each by Table P-PZ43
5428.A-Z	Societies. By place, A-Z
5449.S18	Shepherd, Richard Herne (Table P-PZ40)
5449.S4	Sherwood, Mary Martha (Butt) (Table P-PZ40)
5450.S5	Shore, Margaret Emily (Table P-PZ40)
5450.S7	Shorter, Dora (Sigerson) (Table P-PZ40)
5451	Shorthouse, Joseph Henry (Table P-PZ39)
5452.S19	Siddal, Elizabeth (Table P-PZ40)
5452.S25	Sidgwick, Henry (Table P-PZ40)
5452.S27	Simcox, Edith Jemima (Table P-PZ40)
5452.S273	Simcox, George Augustus, 1841-1905 (Table P-PZ40)
5452.S3	Simpson, John Palgrave (Table P-PZ40)
5452.S4	Sims, George R. (Table P-PZ40)
5452.S5	Sinclair, Catherine, 1800-1864 (Table P-PZ40)
5452.S58	Singleton, John, ca. 1793-1877 (Table P-PZ40)
5452.S6	Skelton, Sir John (Table P-PZ40)
5452.S7	Skene, Felicia Mary Frances (Table P-PZ40)
5452.S74	Skipsey, Joseph, 1832-1903 (Table P-PZ40)
5453.S14	Sladen, Douglas B.W. (Table P-PZ40)
5453.S148	Smart, Hawley (Table P-PZ40)
5453.S15	Smedley, Edward (Table P-PZ40)
5453.S2	Smedley, Francis Edward (Table P-PZ40)
5453.S23	Smedley, Menella Bute (Table P-PZ40)

	19th century, 1770/1800-1890/1900
	Individual authors -- Continued
5453.S3	Smethan, James (Table P-PZ40)
5453.S4	Smith, Albert Richard (Table P-PZ40)
5453.S5	Smith, Alexander (Table P-PZ40)
5453.S52	Smith, Catherine (Table P-PZ40)
	Smith, Charlotte see PR3688.S4
	Smith, Elizabeth Thomasina Meade, 1854-1914 see
	PR4990.M34
5453.S684	Smith, Frederick R. (Table P-PZ40)
5453.S7	Smith, Horatio (Table P-PZ40)
5453.S8	Smith, James (and Horatio) (Table P-PZ38)
5454.S	Smith, M. - Smith, S.
5455-5458	Smith, Sydney (Table P-PZ35a)
5459.S18	Smith, Walter C. (Walter Chalmers), 1824-1908 (Table P-
	PZ40)
5459.S3	Smithers, Henry (Table P-PZ40)
5459.S5	Solomon, Simeon (Table P-PZ40)
5459.S6	Sotheby, William (Table P-PZ40)
5459.S69	Southesk, James Carnegie, Earl of, 1827-1905 (Table P-
	PZ40)
5459.S7	Southey, Caroline Anne (Bowles) (Table P-PZ40)
5460-5468	Southey, Robert (Table P-PZ33 modified)
	Collected works
5460	By date
5460.D00-.D99	1700-1799
5460.E00-.E99	1800-1899
5460.F00-.F99	1900-1999
5460.G00-.G99	2000-2099
5469.S	So - Spec
5470.S3	Spedding, James (Table P-PZ40)
5470.S4	Spencer, William Robert (Table P-PZ40)
5470.S57	Spurr, Harry A. (Table P-PZ40)
5470.S65	Stables, Gordon, 1840-1910 (Table P-PZ40)
5470.S7	Stagg, John (Table P-PZ40)
5471-5472	Stanley, Arthur Penrhyn (Table P-PZ36)
5473.S135	Steel, Flora Annie (Table P-PZ40)
5473.S35	Stenbock, Count, 1860-1895 (Table P-PZ40)
5473.S4	Stephen, James Kenneth (Table P-PZ40)
5473.S44	Stephen, Julia Duckworth, 1846-1895 (Table P-PZ40)
5473.S6	Stephen, Sir Leslie, 1832-1904 (Table P-PZ38)
5473.S65	Stephens, George (Table P-PZ40)
5473.S7	Stephens, James Brunton (Table P-PZ40)
5473.S8	Sterling, John, 1806-1844 (Table P-PZ38)
	Stevenson, Robert Louis
5480	Complete works. Novels and stories, collected
	Use date letters as in Table P-PZ31

	19th century, 1770/1800-1890/1900
	Individual authors
	Stevenson, Robert Louis -- Continued
	Miscellaneous prose, essays, etc., collected see PR5488.A+
	Poems and plays, collected see PR5489
5481	Selected works
5482	Selections. Anthologies
5483	Translations
	Separate novels and stories
5484.A-.S	A - S
5484.B18-.B183	Beach of Falesá (Table P-PZ43)
5484.B3-.B33	The Black arrow (Table P-PZ43)
5484.B5-.B53	The Body-snatcher (Table P-PZ43)
5484.B7-.B73	The Bottle imp (Table P-PZ43)
	Catriona see PR5484.D3+
5484.D3-.D33	David Balfour (Table P-PZ43)
	Catriona in English editions
5484.D9-.D93	The Dynamiter (Table P-PZ43)
5484.E3-.E33	The Ebb tide (Stevenson and Osbourne) (Table P-PZ43)
5484.F3-.F33	Fables (Table P-PZ43)
5484.I7-.I73	Island night's entertainments (Table P-PZ43)
5484.K5-.K53	Kidnapped (Table P-PZ43)
5484.L7-.L73	A Lodging for the night (Table P-PZ43)
5484.M2-.M23	The Master of Ballantrae (Table P-PZ43)
5484.M4-.M43	The Merry men, and other tales and fables (Table P-PZ43)
5484.M6-.M63	The Misadventures of John Nicholson (Table P-PZ43)
5484.N5-.N53	New Arabian nights (Table P-PZ43)
5484.N6-.N63	More new Arabian nights (Stevenson and Mrs. Stevenson) (Table P-PZ43)
5484.P57-.P573	Plain John Wiltshire on the situation (Table P-PZ43)
5484.P7-.P73	Prince Otto (Table P-PZ43)
5484.P76-.P763	Providence & the guitar (Table P-PZ43)
5484.S2-.S23	St. Ives (Table P-PZ43)
5484.S5-.S53	The Sire de Maletroit's door (Table P-PZ43)
5484.S7-.S73	The Story of a lie (Table P-PZ43)
5485	Strange case of Dr. Jekyll and Mr. Hyde (Table P-PZ41)
5486	Treasure Island (Table P-PZ41)
5487.T-Z	T - Z
5487.W3-.W33	Weir of Hermiston, an unfinished romance (Table P-PZ43)
5487.W5-.W53	Will o' the mill (Table P-PZ43)

19th century, 1770/1800-1890/1900
  Individual authors
    Stevenson, Robert Louis
      Separate novels and stories
        T - S -- Continued

5487.W7-.W73	The Wrecker (Stevenson and Osbourne) (Table P-PZ43)
5487.W8-.W83	The Wrong box (Table P-PZ43)
5488.A-Z	Other prose works. By title, A-Z
	Subarrange each by Table P-PZ43
	Including collected essays
5489	Poems and plays
5489.A2	Collected works
5489.A3	Selections
	Including collections hiterto unpublished
5489.B2-.B23	Ballads (Table P-PZ43)
5489.C5-.C53	Child's garden of verse (Table P-PZ43)
5489.U7-.U73	Underwoods (Table P-PZ43)
5490.A-Z	Plays. By title, A-Z
	For plays with W.E. Henley see PR4783.A+
	Collected see PR4783.A4
5490.M6-.M63	Monmouth (Table P-PZ43)
5491	Illustrations, etc.
5492.A1-.A3	Societies, etc.
5492.A5-Z	Dictionaries
	General works. Biography
5493.A3	Letters. By date
5493.A35	Vailima letters
5493.A4	Letters to Mrs. Stevenson. By date
5493.A5	Poems about Stevenson
5493.A6	Prose collections about Stevenson
5493.A7-Z	General works
5494	Early years. Education. Home and early haunts. Edinburgh days
5495	Later life. Marriage. Travels. Island home
	Criticism
5496	General works
5497	Special
5498	Language. Style
5499.S1	Stevenson, Mrs. R.L. (Table P-PZ40)
	Fanny (Van de Griff) Osbourne Stevenson
5499.S15	Stewart, John (Table P-PZ40)
5499.S152	Stewart, William Drummond, Sir, 1795 or 6-1871 (Table P-PZ40)
5499.S158	Stirling, Edward, 1807-1894 (Table P-PZ40)
5499.S174	Stocqueler, J.H. (Joachim Hayward), 1800-1885 (Table P-PZ40)

	19th century, 1770/1800-1890/1900
	Individual authors -- Continued
5499.S18	Stoddart, Thomas Tod (Table P-PZ40)
5499.S185	Story, Robert, 1795-1860 (Table P-PZ40)
5499.S19	Stretton, Hesba, 1832-1911 (Table P-PZ40)
5499.S2	Strickland, Agnes (Table P-PZ40)
5499.S242	Sturgis, Howard Overing, 1855-1920 (Table P-PZ40)
5499.S25	Sulivan, Robert (Table P-PZ40)
5499.S27	Summersett, Henry (Table P-PZ40)
5499.S36	Surr, Thomas Skinner, 1770-1847 (Table P-PZ40)
5499.S4	Surtees, Robert Smith (Table P-PZ40)
5499.S5	Swain, Charles (Table P-PZ40)
5499.S52	Swanwick, Anna (Table P-PZ40)
5500-5518	Swinburne, Algernon Charles (Table P-PZ32 modified)
	Individual genres
	Poems
5505	Collected
5506.A-Z	Separate, A-Z
	Subarrange each by Table P-PZ43
	Dramas
5507	Collected
5508.A-Z	Separate, A-Z
	Subarrange each by Table P-PZ43
	Prose works, etc.
5509	Collected
5510.A-Z	Separate, A-Z
	Subarrange each by Table P-PZ43
5519.S45	Symmes, John Cleves, 1780-1829 (Table P-PZ40)
5519.S5	Symmons, Caroline and Charles (Table P-PZ40)
5519.S9	Symonds, John Addington, 1807-1871 (Table P-PZ40)
5520-5523	Symonds, John Addington, 1840-1893 (Table P-PZ35a)
5525-5528	Symons, Arthur, 1865-1945 (Table P-PZ35a)
5530-5534	Synge, John Millington (Table P-PZ35)
5535.S-.T	Synge - Tal
	Tabley, Lord de see PR4540
5535.T55	Talfourd, Francis, 1828-1862 (Table P-PZ40)
5546-5547	Talfourd, Sir Thomas Noon (Table P-PZ36)
5548.T5	Tannahill, Robert (Table P-PZ40)
	"Tasma" see PR4508.C3
	Taylor, Anne see PR4712.G6
5548.T8	Taylor, Sir Henry (Table P-PZ40)
5549.T2	Taylor, Jane (Table P-PZ40)
	Cf. PR4712.G6 Works by Mrs. Ann (Taylor) Gilbert and Jane Taylor
5549.T3	Taylor, John (Table P-PZ40)
5549.T35	Taylor, Mary, 1817-1893 (Table P-PZ40)
5549.T36	Taylor, Meadows (Table P-PZ40)

	19th century, 1770/1800-1890/1900
	Individual authors -- Continued
5549.T4	Taylor, Tom, 1817-1880 (Table P-PZ40)
5549.T5	Taylor, William (Table P-PZ40)
5549.T6	Temple, Frederick, archbishop (Table P-PZ40)
5549.T65	Tennant, William, 1784-1848 (Table P-PZ40)
5550-5598	Tennyson, Alfred Lord (Table P-PZ31 modified)
	Collected works. Poetical works. By date
	Original editions and reprints. By date
5550.E00-.E99	1800-1899
5550.F00-.F99	1900-1999
5550.G00-.G99	2000-2099
5551	Selected works. By date
5552	Suppressed poems
5553	Selections. Anthologies
5554.A-Z	Translations. By language, A-Z
	Separate works and individual poems
5555.A-.E	By title, A-Em
	Subarrange each by Table P-PZ43
5555.D5	Dramatic works (Collected)
5556	Enoch Arden (Table P-PZ41)
5557.E-.I	By title, Eo-Ic
	Subarrange each by Table P-PZ43
	Idylls of the King. The true and the false
5558.A1	Editions. By date
5558.A2	Selections. By date
5558.A3	School editions. By editor
5559.A-Z	Separate parts, A-Z
5559.B2-.B5	Balin and Balan (Table PR8)
	Birth of Arthur see PR5559.C5+
5559.C5-.C8	Coming of Arthur (Table PR8)
	Death of Arthur see PR5559.P2+
5559.E2-.E5	Elaine, Lancelot and Elaine (Table PR8)
5559.E6-.E9	Enid. Marriage of Geriant. Geraint and Enid (Table PR8)
5559.G2-.G5	Gareth and Lynette (Linette, Lineth) (Table PR8)
	Geraint and Enid see PR5559.E6+
5559.G6-.G9	Guinevere (Table PR8)
5559.H5-.H8	Holy Grail (and other poems) (Table PR8)
	Lancelot and Elaine see PR5559.E2+
	Marriage of Geraint see PR5559.E6+
5559.M3-.M6	Merlin and Vivien (Table PR8)
	Nimue see PR5559.M3+
5559.P2-.P5	Passing of Arthur (Table PR8)
5559.P6-.P9	Pelleas and Ettare (Table PR8)
	Vivien see PR5559.M3+
5560	Criticism

	19th century, 1770/1800-1890/1900
	Individual authors
	Tennyson, Alfred, Lord
	Separate works and individual poems -- Continued
5562	In memoriam (Table P-PZ41)
5563.I-.L	By title, Io-Ln
	Subarrange each by Table P-PZ43
5564	Locksley hall (and other poems) (Table P-PZ41)
5565	Locksley hall sixty years after (Table P-PZ41)
5566.L-.M	By title, Lod-Mat
	Subarrange each by Table P-PZ43
5567	Maud (Table P-PZ41)
5568.M-.P	By title, Mav-Pn
	Subarrange each by Table P-PZ43
5569	Poems by two brothers (Table P-PZ41)
	Poems 1830, 1833, 1842 see PR5550.A00+
5570.P	By title, Pof-Prim
	Subarrange each by Table P-PZ43
5571	Princess (Table P-PZ41)
5572.P-Z	By title, Ps-Z
	Subarrange each by Table P-PZ43
5574	Adaptations. Imitations, etc.
5575	Dramatizations. Plays founded on works of Tennyson
	e.g. Enoch Arden
5576	Songs and other works to which music has been
	composed
5577	Illustrations without text of works
	For illustrated editions see PR5550.A00+
5599.T2	Tennyson, Frederick
5600-5648	Thackeray, William Makepeace (Table P-PZ31 modified)
	Separate works
5605.A	By title, A-Ac
	Subarrange each by Table P-PZ43
5606	Adventures of Philip (Table P-PZ41)
5607.A-.B	By title, Ae-Baq
	Subarrange each by Table P-PZ43
5608	Barry Lyndon (Table P-PZ41)
5609.B	By title, Bas-Bn
	Subarrange each by Table P-PZ43
5610	Book of snobs (Table P-PZ41)
5611.B-.H	By title, Bp-Hg
	Subarrange each by Table P-PZ43
5612	History of Henry Esmond (Table P-PZ41)
5613.H-.N	By title, Hit-Nd
	Subarrange each by Table P-PZ43
5614	Newcomes (Table P-PZ41)

	19th century, 1770/1800-1890/1900
	Individual authors
	Thackeray, William Makepeace
	Separate works -- Continued
5615.N-.P	By title, Nf-Pd
	Subarrange each by Table P-PZ43
5616	Pendennis (Table P-PZ41)
5617.P-.V	By title, Pf-Vam
	Subarrange each by Table P-PZ43
5618	Vanity Fair (Table P-PZ41)
5619.V	By title, Vao-Viq
	Subarrange each by Table P-PZ43
5620	Virginians (Table P-PZ41)
5621.V-Z	By title, Vis-Z
	Subarrange each by Table P-PZ43
5649.T35	Theyre-Smith, S. (Spenser) (Table P-PZ40)
5649.T4	Thom, William (Table P-PZ40)
5649.T6	Thomas, Frederick S. (Table P-PZ40)
5650-5651	Thompson, Francis (Table P-PZ36)
5652.T28	Thompson, Jacob (Table P-PZ40)
5652.T5	Thompson, W. Phillips (Table P-PZ40)
5653.T	Thomson, A - Thomson, James
5655-5659	Thomson, James, 1834-1882 (Table P-PZ35)
5670.T5	Thornbury, George W. (Table P-PZ40)
5670.T6	Thornhill, Frederick (Table P-PZ40)
5670.T8	Thurlow, Edward Hovell Thurlow, 2d baron (Table P-PZ40)
5671.T2	Tighe, Mary (Blackford) (Table P-PZ40)
5671.T24	Tobin, John (Table P-PZ40)
5671.T245	Todhunter, John (Table P-PZ40)
	Tomline, F. see PR4713+
5671.T2485	Tomlinson, Charles, 1808-1897 (Table P-PZ40)
5671.T25	Tonna, Charlotte Elizabeth (Table P-PZ40)
5671.T26	Torrens, Henry Whitelock, 1806-1852 (Table P-PZ40)
5671.T4	Traill, Henry Duff (Table P-PZ40)
5671.T5	Trelawny, Edward John (Table P-PZ40)
5671.T6	Trench, Herbert (Table P-PZ40)
5671.T8	Trench, Richard Chenevix, Archbishop (Table P-PZ40)
5671.T85	Tressell, Robert, 1870-1911 (Table P-PZ40)
5674.T5	Trevelyan, Sir George Otto (Table P-PZ40)
5674.T54	Trevelyan, Paulina Jermyn (Jermyn), lady, 1816-1866 (Table P-PZ40)
5680-5688	Trollope, Anthony (Table P-PZ33 modified)
	Collected works
5680	By date
5680.E00-.E99	1800-1899
5680.F00-.F99	1900-1999
5680.G00-.G99	2000-2099

19th century, 1770/1800-1890/1900

Individual authors -- Continued

5699.T3	Trollope, Mrs. Frances, 1780-1863 (Table P-PZ40)
5699.T32	Trollope, Mrs. Frances Eleanor (Table P-PZ40)
5699.T4	Trollope, Thomas Adolphus (Table P-PZ40)
5699.T45	Trotman, John Temple (Table P-PZ40)
5699.T452	Troughton, Adolphus Charles (Table P-PZ40)
5699.T453	Trueba y Cosío, Joaquín Telesforo de, 1799?-1835 (Table P-PZ40)
5699.T46	Tucker, Charlotte Maria ("A.L.O.E.") (Table P-PZ40)
5699.T475	Tuckett, T.R. (Thomas R.), fl. 1814 (Table P-PZ40)
5699.T5	Tupper, Martin Farquhar (Table P-PZ40)
5699.T7	Turner, Charles Tennyson (Table P-PZ40)
5699.T8	Turner, Sharon (Table P-PZ40)
5700.T	Tus - Tz
	Tynan, Katherine see PR4790.H3
5701.U	U
5703.V	V
5703.V425	Venn, Susanna Carnegie
5703.V47	Verney, Frances Parthenope Nightingale, Lady, 1819-1890 (Table P-PZ40)
5703.V53	Vidal, Francis, Mrs. (Table P-PZ40)
5703.V7	Vowell, Richard Longeville (Table P-PZ40)
5705.W	Waa - Wac
5706.W2	Wade, Thomas (Table P-PZ40)
5706.W3	Wainewright, Thomas Griffiths, 1794-1847 (Table P-PZ40)
5706.W35	Waite, Arthur Edward (Table P-PZ40)
5706.W53	Waldron, W. R. (William Richard) (Table P-PZ40)
	Waldstein, Sir Charles see PR5708.W65
5706.W6	Walford, Lucy Bethia, 1845-1915 (Table P-PZ40)
5708.W46	Walker, C. E. (Charles Edward) (Table P-PZ40)
5708.W467	Walker, George, 1772-1847 (Table P-PZ40)
5708.W5	Walker, William Sidney (Table P-PZ40)
5708.W514	Walkes, W. R. (Table P-PZ40)
5708.W56	Wallace, William, 1843-1921 (Table P-PZ40)
5708.W63	Walshe, Elizabeth H., 1835?-1869 (Table P-PZ40)
5708.W65	Walston, Sir Charles (Table P-PZ40)
	Walters, Robert, b. 1832 see PR5232.R15
5710-5718	Ward, Mrs. Mary Augusta (Arnold) ("Mrs. Humphrey Ward") (Table P-PZ33)
5724.W	Ward - Warren
5724.W6	Warner, Richard, 1763-1857 (Table P-PZ40)
5724.W87	Warren, Ernest, 1841-1887 (Table P-PZ40)
5730-5734	Warren, Samuel (Table P-PZ35)
5738.W5	Watson, Henry Brereton Marriott (Table P-PZ40)
5740-5744	Watson, John (Ian Maclaren) (Table P-PZ35)
5748.W5	Watson, Rosamund Marriott (Table P-PZ40)

	19th century, 1770/1800-1890/1900
	Individual authors -- Continued
5750-5754	Watson, William (Table P-PZ35)
5759.W4	Watts, Alaric Alexander (Table P-PZ40)
5760-5764	Watts-Dunton, Theodore (Table P-PZ35)
5765.W3	Waugh, Edwin (Table P-PZ40)
5765.W6	Webbe, Cornelius (Table P-PZ40)
5766.W2	Webster, Mrs. Augusta (Table P-PZ40)
5766.W25	Webster, Benjamin Nottingham (Table P-PZ40)
5766.W46	Wells, Amy Catherine Robbins, d. 1927 (Table P-PZ40)
	Wells, Catherine, 1872-1927 see PR5766.W46
5766.W5	Wells, Charles (Table P-PZ40)
5770-5778	Wells, Herbert George (Table P-PZ33 modified)
	Collected works
5770	By date
5770.F00-.F99	1900-1999
5770.G00-.G99	2000-2099
5779.W3	Weston, Stephen (Table P-PZ40)
(5780-5784)	Weyman, Stanley John, 1855-1928
	see PR6045.E95
5788.W4	Wheelwright, Charles Apthorp (Table P-PZ40)
5789.W3	Whitbread, James W., 1848-1916 (Table P-PZ40)
5789.W4	White, Arnold Henry (Table P-PZ40)
	White, Babington, 1837-1915 see PR4989.M4
5790-5794	White, Henry Kirke (Table P-PZ35)
5795.W	White, H. - Whitez
5795.W45	White, John Pagen, d. 1868 (Table P-PZ40)
5795.W7	White, William Hale ("Mark Rutherford") (Table P-PZ40)
5795.W8	Whitehead, Charles (Table P-PZ40)
5795.W85	Whiteing, Richard, 1840-1928 (Table P-PZ40)
5797.W	Whitf - Whx
5797.W54	Whiting, Sydney, d. 1875 (Table P-PZ40)
5797.W55	Whiting, William, 1825-1878 (Table P-PZ40)
5797.W75	Whitty, Michael James, 1795-1873 (Table P-PZ40)
5799.W	Whya - Whys
5800-5804	Whyte-Melville, George John (Table P-PZ35)
5807.W5	Wicksteed, Gustavus William (Table P-PZ40)
5807.W7	Wiffen, Jeremiah Holmes, 1792-1836 (Table P-PZ40)
5807.W8	Wightwick, George (Table P-PZ40)
5808.W3	Wilberforce, Samuel, Bishop (Table P-PZ40)
5809	Wilde, Jane Francesca (Elgee), Lady (Table P-PZ39)
	Wilde, Oscar
5810	Complete works
5811	Selected works. By date
5812	Selections. Anthologies. By editor
5813.A-Z	Translations. By language, A-Z
	Subarrange by translator

	19th century, 1770/1800-1890/1900
	Individual authors
	Wilde, Oscar -- Continued
5814	Collected poems. By date
5815	Collected dramas. By date
5816	Collected prose works. By date
	Separate works
5818.A7-.A73	Art and decoration (Table P-PZ43)
5818.B2-.B23	Ballad of Reading Gaol (Table P-PZ43)
5818.B4-.B43	Birth of the Infantas (Table P-PZ43)
	Children in prison
	see subclass HV
5818.D3-.D33	De Profundis (Table P-PZ43)
5818.D5-.D53	Decorative art in America, etc. (Table P-PZ43)
5818.D8-.D83	Duchess of Padua (Table P-PZ43)
5818.H2-.H23	Happy prince (Table P-PZ43)
5818.H6-.H63	House of pomegranates (Table P-PZ43)
5818.I2-.I23	Ideal husband (Table P-PZ43)
5818.I4-.I45	Importance of being earnest (Table P-PZ43a)
5818.I7-.I73	Intentions (Table P-PZ43)
5818.L2-.L23	Lady Windermere's fan (Table P-PZ43)
5818.L6-.L63	Lord Arthur Savile's crime (Table P-PZ43)
5818.P2-.P23	Pan and Desespoir (Table P-PZ43)
5819	Picture of Dorian Gray (Table P-PZ41)
	Portrait of Mr. W.H. see PR2935
5820.R2-.R23	Ravenna (Table P-PZ43)
5820.R67-.R673	Roses and rue (Table P-PZ43)
5820.S2-.S23	Salome (Table P-PZ43)
	Soul of man under socialism
	see subclass HX
5820.S6-.S63	Sphinx (Table P-PZ43)
5820.V3-.V33	Vera; or the Nihilists (Table P-PZ43)
5820.W5-.W53	Woman of no importance (Table P-PZ43)
5821	Apocryphal, spurious works, etc. (Collections only)
	Illustrations
	Class at N8215, or with the special artists in NC-NE as the case may be
	Class illustrated editions with other editions
	Class portraits, etc., of the author with his biography
	Biography, criticism, etc.
5822.A2-.A5	Periodicals. Societies. Serials
5822.A6-Z	Dictionaries, indexes, etc.
5823.A3-.A39	Autobiography, journals, memoirs. By title
5823.A4	Letters (Collections). By date
5823.A41-.A49	Letters to and from particular individuals. By correspondent (alphabetically)
5823.A5-Z	General works

19th century, 1770/1800-1890/1900
Individual authors
Wilde, Oscar -- Continued
Criticism

5824	General works
5825	Textual. Manuscripts, etc.
	Special
5826	Sources
5827.A-Z	Other, A-Z
	For list of Cutter numbers, see Table P-PZ32 17
5828	Language. Grammar. Style
5829.W	Wilde - William
5834.W47	Williams, John ("Anthony Pasquin") (Table P-PZ40)
5834.W5	Williams, Rowland (Table P-PZ40)
5834.W53	Williams, Thomas J., 1824-1874 (Table P-PZ40)
5834.W6	Williamson, Charles Norris (Table P-PZ40)
5834.W8	Wills, William Gorman (Table P-PZ40)
5834.W9	Wilson, Caroline (Fry) (Table P-PZ40)
5835-5838	Wilson, John ("Christopher North") (Table P-PZ35a)
5839.W4	Winchilsea and Nottingham, George James, Earl of (Table P-PZ40)
5840.W2	Winkworth, Catherine (Table P-PZ40)
5841.W65	Wise, Thomas James, 1859-1937 (Table P-PZ40)
5841.W7	Wiseman, Nicholas Patrick Stephen, Cardinal (Table P-PZ40)
	Cf. B, Religion
5841.W8	Wollstonecraft, Mary (Table P-PZ40)
5842.W8	Wood, Ellen (Price) (Mrs. Henry Wood) (Table P-PZ40)
5842.W92	Wood, H. Freeman (Table P-PZ40)
5842.W95	Woodruffe, Adelaide (Table P-PZ40)
5842.W97	Woodward, George Ratcliffe, 1848-1934 (Table P-PZ40)
5843.W5	Woolner, Thomas (Table P-PZ40)
	Woolridge, Lestocq Boileau, d. 1920 see PR4883.L8
	Wordsworth, Dorothy, 1771-1855
5849.A1	Collected works. By date.
5849.A3	Selected works. Selections. By date.
5849.A6-.A79	Separate works
5849.A8	Journal
5849.A85	Letters
5849.A9-Z	Biography and criticism
5850-5898	Wordsworth, William (Table P-PZ31 modified)
5851	Prose works
	Separate poetical works
5856	Evening walk (Table P-PZ41)
5858	Excursion (Table P-PZ41)
5859	Home at Grasmere (Table P-PZ41)
5860	Intimations of immortality (Table P-PZ41)

	19th century, 1770/1800-1890/1900
	Individual authors
	Wordsworth, William
	Separate poetical works -- Continued
5862	Memorial of a tour on the continent (Table P-PZ41)
5864	Prelude (Table P-PZ41)
5865	Recluse (Table P-PZ41)
	Cf. PR5858 Excursion
	Cf. PR5859 Home at Grasmere
	Cf. PR5864 Prelude
5866	Sonnets (Table P-PZ41)
5868	White doe of Rylstone (Table P-PZ41)
5869.A-Z	Other, A-Z
	Subarrange each by Table P-PZ43
5870	The Borderers (Drama) (Table P-PZ41)
5871.A-Z	Separate prose works, A-Z
	Subarrange each by Table P-PZ43
5872	Spurious works
5873	Works edited by William Wordsworth
	e.g. Poems and extracts presented to Lady Mary Lowther
5899.W5	Worgan, John Dawes (Table P-PZ40)
5899.W55	Worsley, Philip Stanhope, 1835-1866 (Table P-PZ40)
5899.W65	Wrangham, Francis (Table P-PZ40)
5899.W7	Wrazall, Sir Frederic Charles Lascelles (Table P-PZ40)
5899.W77	Wright, Thomas, 1859-1936 (Table P-PZ40)
5899.W8	Wyatt, Charles Percy (Table P-PZ40)
5899.W9	Wynter, Andrew (Table P-PZ40)
5899.Y3	Yates, Edmund (Table P-PZ40)
	Yeats, William Butler
	Collected works
5900.A1	Comprehensive. By date
5900.A2	By editor
5900.A3	Poems
	Including poetical plays
5900.A4	Plays (Prose or verse)
5900.A5	Miscellaneous. Essays, etc.
	By editor see PR5900.A2
5902	Selected works. Selections
	Subarrange by editor, if given, or date
5903.A-Z	Translations. By language, A-Z
	Subarrange by translator, if given, or date
5904.A-Z	Separate works. By title, A-Z
	Subarrange each by Table P-PZ43
5905	Apocryphal, spurious works, etc. (Collections only)

	19th century, 1770/1800-1890/1900
	Individual authors
	Yeats, William Butler -- Continued
	Illustrations
	Class at N8215, or with the special artists in NC-NE
	Class illustrated editions with other editions
	Class portraits, etc., of the author with his biography
	Biography, criticism, etc.
5906.A1-.A19	Periodicals. Societies. Serials
5906.A2-.A3	Dictionaries, indexes, etc.
5906.A31-.A39	Autobiography, journals, memoirs. By title
5906.A4	Letters (Collections). By date
5906.A41-.A49	Letters to and from particular individuals. By correspondent (alphabetically)
5906.A5-Z	General works
	Criticism
5907	General works
5908.A-Z	Special, A-Z
	For list of Cutter numbers, see Table P-PZ32 17
	For list of Cutter numbers not given below, see Table P-PZ32 17
5908.L33	Language
5908.S8	Style
5909.Y4	Yeldham, Walter (Table P-PZ40)
5909.Y45	Yelverton, Thérèse, Viscountess Avonmore, 1832?-1881 (Table P-PZ40)
5910-5914	Yonge, Charlotte Mary (Table P-PZ35)
5915.Y-Z	Yonge - Zangwill
	Yorke, Stephen, 1840-1891 see PR4889.L48
5920-5924	Zangwill, Israel (Table P-PZ35)
5925.Z	Zangwill - Zz
5990	Miscellaneous minor; uncataloged works
	1900-1960
	Including usually authors beginning to publish about 1890, flourishing after 1900
	For works of fiction cataloged before July 1, 1980, except limited editions and works in the Rare Book Collection see PZ3+
6000	Anonymous works (Table P-PZ28)
	Individual authors
	Subarrange each author by Table P-PZ39 or P-PZ40 unless otherwise specified
6001.A-Z	A
	The author number is determined by the second letter of the name
6001.B38	Abercrombie, Lascelles (Table P-PZ40)
6001.B6	Abrahams, Doris Caroline, 1901- (Table P-PZ40)

	1900-1960
	Individual authors
	A -- Continued
	Adams, Christopher see PR6015.O62
6001.D3	Adcock, Arthur St. John, 1864-1930 (Table P-PZ40)
	Ainsworth, Harriet see PR6005.A225
6001.L4	Aldington, Richard, 1892-1962 (Table P-PZ40)
	Andrews, Cecily Isabel Fairfield, 1892- see PR6045.E8
6001.R77	Armstrong, Terence Ian Fytton, 1912-1970 (Table P-PZ40)
	Arnim, Mary Annette, grafin von see PR6035.U8
6001.R79	Arthur, Frank, 1906- (Table P-PZ40)
6001.S37	Ash, Fenton (Table P-PZ40)
6001.S42	Ashdown, Clifford (Table P-PZ40)
	Ashe, Gordon see PR6005.R517
6001.S44	Ashford, Daisy (Table P-PZ40)
	Ashton, Dorothy Violet, 1889-1956 see PR6045.E53
6001.S5	Ashton, Winifred ("Clemence Dane") (Table P-PZ40)
	Astley, Juliet see PR6023.O35
	Atkins, Frank see PR6001.U27; PR6001.U3
6001.U27	Aubrey, Frank, pseud. (Table P-PZ40)
6001.U3	Aubrey-Fletcher, Henry Lancelot, Sir, bart., 1887-1969 (Table P-PZ40)
6001.U4	Auden, W.H. (Wystan Hugh), 1907-1973 (Table P-PZ40)
6003.A-Z	B
	The author number is determined by the second letter of the name
6003.A2	B B, 1905-1990 (Table P-PZ40)
6003.A4	Bain, Francis William (Table P-PZ40)
6003.A525	Ball, Doris Bell (Collier), 1897- (Table P-PZ40)
(6003.A528)	Banks, Lynne Reid, 1929- see PR6052.A486
6003.A544	Bannerman, Helen, 1862 or 3-1946 (Table P-PZ40)
	Barbellion, W.N.P., 1889-1919 see PR6005.U5
6003.A65	Barber, Margaret Fairless ("Michael Fairless") (Table P-PZ40)
	Barford, Eleanor, 1906- see PR6015.I3
6003.A67	Baring, Maurice (Table P-PZ40)
	Barker, Harley Granville see PR6013.R29
6003.A686	Barnard, Francis Pierrepont, 1854-1931 (Table P-PZ40)
6003.A74	Barnsley, Alan Gabriel, 1916- (Table P-PZ40)
	Barstow, Montagu, Mrs., 1865-1947 see PR6029.R25
6003.A96	Bashford, H.H. (Henry Howarth), Sir, 1880-1961 (Table P-PZ40)
6003.A986	Bax, Arnold, 1883-1953 (Table P-PZ40)
	Beaty, Arthur David see PR6003.E264
6003.E264	Beaty, David (Table P-PZ40)

	1900-1960
	Individual authors
	B -- Continued
6003.E3	Beeding, Francis (Table P-PZ40)
6003.E4	Beerbohm, Max (Table P-PZ40)
6003.E415	Begbie, Harold, 1871-1929 (Table P-PZ40)
6003.E42	Beith, John Hay ("Ian Hay") (Table P-PZ40)
	Bell, Josephine, 1897- see PR6003.A525
	Bell, Neil see PR6037.O843
6003.E45	Belloc, Hilaire (Table P-PZ40)
6003.E6	Bennett, (Enoch) Arnold (Table P-PZ40)
6003.E66	Benson, Edward Frederic (Table P-PZ40)
6003.E7	Benson, Robert Hugh (Table P-PZ40)
6003.E7247	Bentley, E.C., 1875-1956 (Table P-PZ40)
6003.E73	Beresford, John Davys (Table P-PZ40)
	Berkeley, Anthony, 1893-1970 see PR6005.O855
	Bey, Pilaff see PR6007.O88
6003.I73	Binns, Henry Bryan (Table P-PZ40)
6003.I75	Binyon, Laurence (Table P-PZ40)
6003.L24	Blackburn, Douglas, 1857-1929 (Table P-PZ40)
6003.L3	Blackwood, Algernon, 1869-1951 (Table P-PZ40)
	Blair, Eric Arthur, 1903-1950 see PR6029.R8
	Blake, Nicholas see PR6007.A95
6003.L58	Bloom, Ursula (Table P-PZ40)
	Bodington, Nancy, 1912- see PR6037.M57
	Bonett, John, 1906- see PR6005.O79
6003.O613	Borneman, Ernest, 1915- (Table P-PZ40)
6003.O67	Bottomley, Gordon (Table P-PZ40)
	Bradshaw-Isherwood, Christopher William see PR6017.S5
	Brahms, Caryl, 1901- see PR6001.B6
	Bramah, Ernest, 1869?-1942 see PR6037.M425
	Brand, Christianna, 1907- see PR6023.E96
6003.R326	Brazil, Angela, 1868-1947 (Table P-PZ40)
	Bridie, James, 1888-1951 see PR6025.A885
6003.R4	Brooke, Rupert (Table P-PZ40)
6003.R458	Brown, Morna Doris MacTaggart, 1907- (Table P-PZ40)
6003.R484	Brown, Vincent (Table P-PZ40)
	Bruce, Leo, 1903- see PR6005.R673
6003.U13	Buchan, John (Table P-PZ40)
6003.U23	Bullen, Frank Thomas (Table P-PZ40)
6003.U45	Burdekin, Katharine, 1896-1963 (Table P-PZ40)
	Burford, Eleanor, 1906- see PR6015.I3
	Burke, Leda, 1892- see PR6013.A66
	Burnett, I. Compton- (Ivy Compton-), 1884-1969 see PR6005.O3895
	Burney, Anton see PR6015.O62

1900-1960
  Individual authors
    B -- Continued

	Burns, Sheila see PR6003.L58
	Burton, Miles, 1884-1964 see PR6037.T778
6003.U64	Bussy, Dorothy, Strachey (Table P-PZ40)
	Buttle, Myra see PR6031.U7
	Buxton, Anne see PR6025.A943
6005.A-Z	C

The author number is determined by the second letter of the name

6005.A225	Cadell, Elizabeth (Table P-PZ40)
6005.A245	Caird, Mona (Table P-PZ40)
6005.A414	Campbell, Joseph, 1879- (Table P-PZ40)
	Campbell, R.T., 1914- see PR6039.O26
6005.A46	Candler, Edmund, 1874-1926 (Table P-PZ40)
6005.A486	Canning, Victor (Table P-PZ40)
6005.A53	Capes, Bernard (Table P-PZ40)
	Cargoe, Richard, 1911- see PR6031.A93
	Carnac, Carol see PR6023.O66
	Carr, Glyn, 1908- see PR6037.T96
	Carr, Philippa, 1906- see PR6015.I3
6005.A8	Castle, Agnes, d. 1922 (Table P-PZ40)
	Caudwell, Christopher, 1907-1937 see PR6037.P65
6005.A9	Cayzer, Charles William (Table P-PZ40)
	Challans, Mary see PR6035.E55
6005.H25	Chambers, Charles Haddon (Table P-PZ40)
	Chance, Stephen see PR6070.U74
6005.H323	Chapman, Raymond (Table P-PZ40)
6005.H52	Childers, Erskine, 1870-1922 (Table P-PZ40)
6005.H56	Cholmondeley, Mary, 1859-1925 (Table P-PZ40)
6005.H66	Christie, Agatha, 1891-1976 (Table P-PZ40)
6005.L3115	Clark, Alfred Alexander Gordon, 1900- (Table P-PZ40)
6005.L77	Clifford, Sir Hugh Charles, 1866-1941 (Table P-PZ40)
6005.L845	Clouston, Joseph Storer, 1870- (Table P-PZ40)
6005.O15	Cockburn, Claud, 1904- (Table P-PZ40)
	Cockburn, Francis Claud, 1904- see PR6005.O15
6005.O3	Coleridge, Mary Elizabeth (Table P-PZ40)
6005.O33	Coles, Albert John, 1876-1965 (Table P-PZ40)
6005.O368	Colmore, G. (Gertrude), d. 1926 (Table P-PZ40)
6005.O3895	Compton-Burnett, I. (Ivy), 1884-1969 (Table P-PZ40)
	Connor, John Anthony see PR6005.O3935
6005.O3935	Connor, Tony (Table P-PZ40)
6005.O4	Conrad, Joseph (Table P-PZ40)
	Constantine, Murray, 1896-1963 see PR6003.U45
	Cooper, William, 1910- see PR6015.O28
6005.O635	Corfield, Wilmot (Table P-PZ40)

	1900-1960
	Individual authors
	C -- Continued
6005.O69	Cory, Winifred Graham (Table P-PZ40)
6005.O7	Cotton, William Bensley (Table P-PZ40)
6005.O79	Coulson, John (Table P-PZ40)
6005.O82	Cousins, James Henry, 1873-1956 (Table P-PZ40)
6005.O855	Cox, Anthony Berkeley, 1893-1970 (Table P-PZ40)
6005.R517	Creasey, John (Table P-PZ40)
6005.R55	Creswell, H.B. (Table P-PZ40)
6005.R58	Chrichton Smith, Iain (Table P-PZ40)
	Crispin, Edmund see PR6025.O46
6005.R67	Critchett, R.C. ("R.C. Carton") (Table P-PZ40)
6005.R673	Croft-Cooke, Rupert, 1903- (Table P-PZ40)
	Cross, Alan Beverley, 1931- see PR6005.R694
6005.R694	Cross, Beverley, 1931- (Table P-PZ40)
6005.U5	Cummings, Bruce Frederick, 1889-1919 (Table P-PZ40)
	Cunninghame Graham, R.B. (Robert Boutine), 1852-1936 see PR6013.R19
	Curtis, Peter see PR6023.O35
6005.U773	Cust, Henry John Cockayne, 1861-1917 (Table P-PZ40)
6007.A-Z	D
	The author number is determined by the second letter of the name
	Danby, Frank, 1864-1916 see PR6011.R27
	Dane, Clemence see PR6001.S5
6007.A522	D'Arcy, Ella (Table P-PZ40)
	Davey, Jocelyn see PR6035.A64
6007.A7	Davies, Hubert Henry (Table P-PZ40)
6007.A8	Davies, William Henry, 1871-1940 (Table P-PZ40)
	Daviot, Gordon see PR6025.A2547
6007.A95	Day Lewis, C. (Cecil), 1904-1972 (Table P-PZ40)
	De Hartog, Jan, 1914- see PR6015.A674
6007.E3	De LaMare, Walter John (Table P-PZ40)
6007.E33	De La Pasture, Edmée Elizabeth Monica, 1890-1943 (Table P-PZ40)
	Deane, Norman see PR6005.R517
	Delafield, E.M., 1890-1943 see PR6007.E33
6007.E5	DeMorgan, William (Table P-PZ40)
	Devon, John Anthony, 1911- see PR6031.A93
6007.I35	Dickinson, Goldsworthy Lowes (Table P-PZ40)
6007.O35	Dobell, Bertram (Table P-PZ40)
6007.O85	Doughty, Charles Montague, 1843-1926 (Table P-PZ40)
6007.O86	Douglas, Alfred Bruce, Lord, 1870-1945 (Table P-PZ40)
6007.O864	Douglas, Felicity (Table P-PZ40)
	Douglas, George Norman see PR6007.O88
6007.O88	Douglas, Norman, 1868-1952 (Table P-PZ40)

	1900-1960
	Individual authors
	D -- Continued
6007.O8918	Douton, Agnes Maud Mary (Table P-PZ40)
	Doyle, Lynn, 1873-1961 see PR6025.O44
6007.R5	Drinkwater, John (Table P-PZ40)
6007.R718	Drummond, Hamilton, 1857-1935 (Table P-PZ40)
6007.U233	Dudgeon, Robert Ellis, 1820-1904 (Table P-PZ40)
6007.U5	DuMaurier, Guy (Table P-PZ40)
6007.U558	Dunn, George W.M. (Table P-PZ40)
6007.U5615	Dunn, Joseph Allan Elphinstone, 1872-1941 (Table P-PZ40)
6007.U6	Dunsany, Edward John Moreton Drax Plunkett, Baron, 1878-1957 (Table P-PZ40)
6007.U76	Durrell, Lawrence (Table P-PZ40)
6009.A-Z	E
	The author number is determined by the second letter of the name
	Ebert, Arthur Frank, 1906- see PR6001.R79
	Edgar, Josephine see PR6015.O857
6009.D58	Edmiston, Helen Jean Mary, 1913- (Table P-PZ40)
6009.D63	Edmonds, Helen Woods, 1904-1968 (Table P-PZ40)
	Elizabeth, 1866-1941 see PR6035.U8
6009.L8	Ellis, Havelock (Table P-PZ40)
6009.R8	Ervine, St. John Greer (Table P-PZ40)
	Esse, James, 1882-1950 see PR6037.T4
	Essex, Mary see PR6003.L58
	Evans, Margiad, 1909-1958 see PR6045.I544
6011.A-Z	F
	The author number is determined by the second letter of the name
	Falconer, Lanoe, 1848-1908 see PR6015.A79
	Farrell, M.J., 1904- see PR6021.E33
6011.A83	Fawcett, Edward Douglas (Table P-PZ40)
	Ferguson, Helen, 1904-1968 see PR6009.D63
6011.E64	Ferguson, John Alexander, 1873- (Table P-PZ40)
	Ferrars, E.X., 1907- see PR6003.R458
	Fielding, Gabriel, 1916- see PR6003.A74
6011.I49	Findlater, Jane Helen, 1866-1946 (Table P-PZ40)
6011.I494	Findlater, Mary, 1865- (Table P-PZ40)
	Firbank, Arthur Annesley Ronald, 1886-1926 see PR6011.I7
6011.I7	Firbank Ronald, 1866-1926 (Table P-PZ40)
6011.I72	Firth, Violet Mary (Table P-PZ40)
6011.I787	Fitt, Mary, 1897-1959 (Table P-PZ40)
	Fleming, Oliver see PR6025.A2218
6011.L5	Fletcher, Joseph Smith, 1863-1935 (Table P-PZ40)

	1900-1960
	Individual authors
	F -- Continued
	Ford, Elbur, 1906- see PR6015.I3
6011.O53	Ford, Ford Madox, 1873-1939 (Table P-PZ40)
	Fortune, Dion see PR6011.I72
6011.O74	Fowler, Ellen Thorneycroft (Table P-PZ40)
6011.R26	Frankau, Gilbert (Table P-PZ40)
6011.R27	Frankau, Julia, 1864-1916 (Table P-PZ40)
	Frazer, Robert Cain see PR6005.R517
	Freeman, Kathleen, 1897-1959 see PR6011.I787
6011.R43	Freeman, Richard Austin, 1862-1943 (Table P-PZ40)
6011.R45	French, Percy, 1854-1920 (Table P-PZ40)
6013.A-Z	G
	The author number is determined by the second letter of the name
6013.A28	Gale, Norman Rowland (Table P-PZ40)
6013.A5	Galsworthy, John (Table P-PZ40)
6013.A6	Gardiner, Alfred George, 1865-1946 (Table P-PZ40)
6013.A66	Garnett, David 1892- (Table P-PZ40)
	Gawsworth, John, 1912-1970 see PR6001.R77
	Gaye, Carol see PR6037.H3315
	Gibbon, Lewis Grassic, 1901-1935 see PR6025.I833
6013.I29	Gibson, Wilfrid Wilson (Table P-PZ40)
6013.I334	Gilbert, Rosa Mulholland, Lady, 1841-1921 (Table P-PZ40)
6013.I3373	Gilchrist, Murray, 1868-1917 (Table P-PZ40)
6013.I85	Gissing, Algernon, 1860-1937 (Table P-PZ40)
6013.O47	Good, Edward, b. 1885 (Table P-PZ40)
	For Good's Yiddish works see PJ5129.G567
	Gould, Alan see PR6005.A486
6013.R13	Graham, Harry (Table P-PZ40)
6013.R19	Graham, Robert Bontine Cunninghame, 1852-1936 (Table P-PZ40)
	Grand, Sarah see PR4728.G112
6013.R29	Granville-Barker, Harley, 1877-1946 (Table P-PZ40)
	Graves, Charles see PR4728.G18
	Gray, Harriet see PR6035.O554
6013.R367	Gray, John, 1866-1934 (Table P-PZ40)
6013.R416	Green, Henry, 1905-1974 (Table P-PZ40)
6013.R735	Grieve, Christopher Murray, 1892- (Table P-PZ40)
6013.R795	Grossmith, George, 1847-1912 (Table P-PZ40)
6013.W8	Gwynn, Stephen Lucius (Table P-PZ40)
6015.A-Z	H
	The author number is determined by the second letter of the name
	Hall, Adam see PR6039.R518

	1900-1960
	Individual authors
	H -- Continued
	Hall, John, 1886-1943 see PR6015.A33
	Hall, Marguerite Radclyffe see PR6015.A33
6015.A33	Hall, Radclyff (Table P-PZ40)
	Halliday, Michael see PR6005.R517
6015.A44	Hamilton, Cicely Mary (Table P-PZ40)
6015.A46	Hamilton, Cosmo (Table P-PZ40)
	Hammond, Ralph, 1913- see PR6017.N79
	Hammond-Innes, Ralph, 1913- see PR6017.N79
	Hampson, John, 1901- see PR6015.A4673
6015.A4673	Hampson, Simpson, John Frederick Norman, 1901- (Table P-PZ40)
6015.A47	Hankin, St. John (Table P-PZ40)
6015.A48	Hannay, James Owen ("George A. Birmingham") (Table P-PZ40)
	Harding, Peter, M.D. see PR6003.A96
	Hare, Cyril, 1900- see PR6005.L3115
	Harris, John Beynon, 1903-1969 see PR6045.Y64
6015.A6473	Harris-Burland, John Burland, 1870-1926 (Table P-PZ40)
6015.A674	Hartog, Jan de, 1914- (Table P-PZ40)
6015.A77	Hastings, Basil M. (Table P-PZ40)
6015.A79	Hawker, Mary Elizabeth, 1848-1908 (Table P-PZ40)
6015.E244	Heberden, M.V. (Mary Violet), 1906-1965 (Table P-PZ40)
6015.E36	Helston, John (Table P-PZ40)
	Helvick, James, 1904- see PR6005.O15
6015.E7145	Heron-Allen, Edward, 1861-1945 (Table P-PZ40)
6015.I3	Hibbert, Eleanor, 1906- (Table P-PZ40)
6015.I4	Hichens, Robert (Table P-PZ40)
6015.I53	Hilton, James, 1900-1954 (Table P-PZ40)
	Hockaby, Stephens see PR6025.I832
6015.O25	Hodgson, Ralph, 1871-1962 (Table P-PZ40)
6015.O28	Hoff, Harry Summerfield, 1910- (Table P-PZ40)
	Holdsworth, Gladys Bertha, 1890- see PR6037.T453
	Holdsworth, Gladys Bronwyn, 1890- see PR6037.T453
6015.O415	Hollo, Anselm (Table P-PZ40)
	Hollo, Paul Anselm Alexis see PR6015.O415
	Holmes, Gordon, 1863-1928 see PR6039.R23
	Holt, Victoria, 1906- see PR6015.I3
	Hope, Laurence (Violet Nicolson) see PR6027.I37
6015.O619	Hopkin, William Edward, 1862-1951 (Table P-PZ40)
6015.O62	Hopkins, Kenneth (Table P-PZ40)
	Horne, Howard, 1911- see PR6031.A93
6015.O687	Hornung, Ernest William, 1866-1921 (Table P-PZ40)
	Houghton, Claude, 1889- see PR6029.L4
6015.O78	Houghton, Stanley (Table P-PZ40)

	1900-1960
	Individual authors
	H -- Continued
6015.O857	Howard, Mary, 1907- (Table P-PZ40)
	Hudson, Stephen, 1868-1944 see PR6037.C37
6015.U23	Hudson, William Henry, 1841-1922 (Table P-PZ40)
6015.U24	Hueffer, Ford Madox (Table P-PZ40)
6015.U25	Hueffer, Oliver Madox (Table P-PZ40)
6015.U43	Hull, Richard, 1896-1973 (Table P-PZ40)
	Hunt, Kyle see PR6005.R517
6015.U55	Hunt, Violet, 1866-1942 (Table P-PZ40)
6015.U756	Hutchinson, Horace G., 1859-1932 (Table P-PZ40)
6015.Y6	Hyne, Charles John Cutcliffe Wright, 1866-1944 (Table P-PZ40)
6017.A-Z	I
	The author number is determined by the second letter of the name
6017.N79	Innes, Hammond, 1913- (Table P-PZ40)
	Innes, Michael, 1906- see PR6037.T466
	Innes, Ralph Hammond, 1913- see PR6017.N79
6017.R84	Irwin, Margaret (Table P-PZ40)
6017.S5	Isherwood, Christopher, 1904- (Table P-PZ40)
6017.V47	Ives, George, 1867-1941 (Table P-PZ40)
6019.A-Z	J
	The author number is determined by the second letter of the name
6019.A2	Jacks, Lawrence Pearsall, 1860-1955 (Table P-PZ40)
6019.A565	James, Montague Rhodes, 1862-1936 (Table P-PZ40)
6019.A684	Jane, Frederick Thomas, 1865-1910 (Table P-PZ40)
6019.E25	Jeffery, Jeffery E. (Jeffery Eardley), b. 1887 (Table P-PZ40)
6019.O397	Johnston, Denis, 1901- (Table P-PZ40)
6019.O3975	Johnston, Edward, 1872-1944 (Table P-PZ40)
	Johnston, William Denis, 1901- see PR6019.O397
6019.O9	Joyce, James, 1882-1941 (Table P-PZ40 modified)
6019.O9A61-.O9Z458	Separate works
	e. g.
6019.O9F5-.O9F599	Finnegans wake
	The detailed subarrangement provided here is in addition to the normal subarrangement within this span
6019.O9F52	Selections. By date
	Drafts, manuscripts, proofs, etc.

       1900-1960
       Individual authors
        J
         Joyce, James, 1882-1941
          Separate works
           Finnegans wake
            Drafts, manuscripts, proofs, etc. -- Continued
            Individual books. By date
             Subarrange separately published segments of
              individual books by the number of the first
              chapter appearing in the published volume,
              e.g., Finnegans wake, book I, chapters 2-3
              (published in 1978), PR6019.O9F522 1978 ch.
              2

6019.O9F522	Book I
6019.O9F523	Book II
6019.O9F524	Book III
6019.O9F525	Book IV

           The Buffalo notebooks ("Workbooks")

6019.O9F526	Collections. By date

           Individual notebooks
            Numbered according to the categories in Peter
             Spielberg's catalog of the Buffalo collection

6019.O9F527	VI. A (Scribbledehobble notebook). By date
6019.O9F528	VI. B. By date

            Subarranged separately published segments of
             the VI.B notebooks by the number of the
             notebook (or first notebook appearing in the
             published volume), e.g., Buffalo notebooks,
             VI.B.5-VI.B.8 (published in 1978),
             PR6019.O9F528 1978 bk. 5

6019.O9F529	VI. C. By date

            Subarranged separately published segments of
             the VI.B notebooks by the number of the
             notebook (or first notebook appearing in the
             published volume), e.g., Buffalo notebooks,
             VI.B.5-VI.B.8 (published in 1978),
             PR6019.O9F528 1978 bk. 5

6019.O9F53	VI. D. By date

            Subarranged separately published segments of
             the VI.B notebooks by the number of the
             notebook (or first notebook appearing in the
             published volume), e.g., Buffalo notebooks,
             VI.B.5-VI.B.8 (published in 1978),
             PR6019.O9F528 1978 bk. 5

PR

1900-1960
Individual authors
J
Joyce, James, 1882-1941
Separate works -- Continued

6019.O9U4-.O9U79   Ulysses
The detailed subarrangement provided here is in
addition to the normal subarrangement within this
span

6019.O9U42   Selections. By date
Notes, drafts, manuscripts, etc.

6019.O9U422   Complete text. By date

6019.O9U423   Individual episodes
Subarrange collections of individual episodes by
the number of the first episode appearing in
the published volume, e.g. Manuscripts &
typescripts for 17 & 18, PR6019.O9U423 ep.
17

Galley proofs ("Placards")
Subarrange collections of individual episodes by the
number of the first episode appearing in the
published volum, e.g. Manuscripts & typescripts
for 17 & 18, PR6019.O9U423 ep. 17

6019.O9U424   Individual episodes
Subarrange collections of individual episodes by
the number of the first episode appearing in
the published volume, e.g. Manuscripts &
typescripts for 17 & 18, PR6019.O9U423 ep.
17

Page proofs
Subarrange collections of individual episodes by the
number of the first episode appearing in the
published volume, e.g. Manuscripts & typescripts
for 17 & 18, PR6019.O9U423 ep. 17

6019.O9U425   Individual episodes
Subarrange collections of individual episodes by
the number of the first episode appearing in
the published volume, e.g. Manuscripts &
typescripts for 17 & 18, PR6019.O9U423 ep.
17

6021.A-Z   K
The author number is determined by the second letter of the
name
Kallow, Kathleen, 1906- see PR6015.I3
Kavan, Anna, 1904-1968 see PR6009.D63

6021.E33   Keane, Mary Nesta Skrine, 1904- (Table P-PZ40)

6021.I298   Kinross, Albert, 1870-1929 (Table P-PZ40)

	1900-1960
	Individual authors
	K -- Continued
6021.L6	Klickmann, Flora (Table P-PZ40)
6021.N47	Knoblock, Edward, 1874- (Table P-PZ40)
	Knowall, George, 1911-1966 see PR6029.N56
6023.A-Z	L
	The author number is determined by the second letter of the name
	Lawless, Anthony see PR6025.A2218
6023.A93	Lawrence, David Herbert (Table P-PZ40)
(6023.E15)	Leacock, Stephen, 1869-1944 (Table P-PZ40)
	see PR9199.3.L367
6023.E46	Leighton, Marie Connor, d. 1941 (Table P-PZ40)
	Leonard, Charles L. see PR6015.E244
6023.E75	Le Queux, William, 1864-1927 (Table P-PZ40)
6023.E833	Lessing, Doris May, 1919- (Table P-PZ40)
6023.E875	Leverson, Ada (Table P-PZ40)
6023.E9243	Lewis, Arthur, 1854-1951 (Table P-PZ40)
	Lewis, Cecil Day, 1904-1972 see PR6007.A95
6023.E96	Lewis, Mary Christianna Milne (Table P-PZ40)
	Liley, Margaret see PR6017.R84
6023.I58	Lindsay, Caroline Blanche Elizabeth (Fitzroz), Lady (Table P-PZ40)
	Llewellyn, Lloyd Richard David Vivian see PR6023.L47
6023.L47	Llewellyn, Richard (Table P-PZ40)
	Lloyd, Richard David Vivian Llewellyn see PR6023.L47
6023.O15	Locke, Wililam J. (Table P-PZ40)
6023.O35	Lofts, Norah, 1904- (Table P-PZ40)
6023.O66	Lorac, E.C.R., 1894-1958 (Table P-PZ40)
6023.O897	Low, A. Maurice (Alfred Maurice), 1860-1929 (Table P-PZ40)
6023.O95	Lowndes, Marie Adelaide Belloc, 1868-1947 (Table P-PZ40)
6023.U24	Lucas, Edward V. (Table P-PZ40)
6023.Y6	Lyttelton, Edith (Table P-PZ40)
6025.A-Z	M
	The author number is determined by the second letter of the name
	MacCathmhaoil, Seosamh see PR6005.A414
6025.A1684	MacColla, Fionn, 1906-1975 (Table P-PZ40)
	MacDiarmid, Hugh, 1892- see PR6013.R735
6025.A1697	McConnell, James Douglas Rutherford, 1915- (Table P-PZ40)
6025.A22	McDonagh, Thomas (Table P-PZ40)
	MacDonald, Aeneas, 1899- see PR6039.H725
	Macdonald, Filip see PR6025.A2218

1900-1960
Individual authors
M -- Continued

6025.A2218	MacDonald, Philip (Table P-PZ40)
	MacDonald, Thomas Douglas, 1906-1975 see PR6025.A1684
6025.A225	McFee, William (Table P-PZ40)
6025.A245	Machen, Arthur, 1853-1947 (Table P-PZ40)
6025.A2547	Mackintosh, Elizabeth, 1896-1952 (Table P-PZ40)
6025.A28	MacManus, Anna Johnston, 1866-1902 (Table P-PZ40)
6025.A282	MacManus, Seumas, 1869-1960 (Table P-PZ40)
	Mallowan, Agathie Christie, 1891-1976 see PR6005.H66
	Mankowitz, Cyril Wolf see PR6025.A4755
6025.A4755	Mankowitz, Wolf (Table P-PZ40)
	Mann, Deborah see PR6003.L58
	Mannon, Warwick see PR6015.O62
	Manton, Peter see PR6005.R517
6025.A612	Marchmont, Arthur Williams, 1852-1923 (Table P-PZ40)
6025.A629	Marlow, Louis, 1881-1966 (Table P-PZ40)
	Marric, J.J. see PR6005.R517
	Marsh, Paul see PR6015.O62
6025.A65	Marshall, Archibald, 1866-1934 (Table P-PZ40)
	Marshall, Edmund see PR6015.O62
6025.A67	Marshall, Robert, 1863-1910 (Table P-PZ40)
6025.A723	Martin, John, 1892- (Table P-PZ40)
	Martin, John Hansbury see PR6025.A723
	Martin, May W. see PR6073.A4198
	Martin, Richard see PR6005.R517
6025.A77	Masefield, John (Table P-PZ40)
6025.A79	Mason, Alfred E.W. (Table P-PZ40)
6025.A84	Matheson, Annie, 1853-1924 (Table P-PZ40)
6025.A86	Maugham, William Somerset (Table P-PZ40)
6025.A885	Mavor, Osborne Henry, 1888-1951 (Table P-PZ40)
6025.A93	Maxwell, William Babington, 1866-1938 (Table P-PZ40)
6025.A943	Maybury, Anne (Table P-PZ40)
6025.A98	Mayor, F.M. (Flora Macdonald), b. 1872 (Table P-PZ40)
	McCabe, Cameron, 1915- see PR6003.O613
	Mercer, Cecil William, 1885-1960 see PR6047.A73
	Meredith, Arnold see PR6015.O62
6025.E7	Merrick, Leonard, 1864-1939 (Table P-PZ40)
6025.E8	Mew, Charlotte Mary, 1869-1928 (Table P-PZ40)
6025.I3	Middleton, Richard (Table P-PZ40)
6025.I6234	Milligan, Alice, 1866-1953 (Table P-PZ40)
6025.I65	Milne, Alan Alexander (Table P-PZ40)
6025.I75	Minchin, Harry Christopher, 1861-1941 (Table P-PZ40)
6025.I832	Mitchell, Gladys, 1901- (Table P-PZ40)
6025.I833	Mitchell, James Leslie, 1901-1935 (Table P-PZ40)

	1900-1960
	Individual authors
	M -- Continued
6025.I847	Mitchell, Susan L. (Susan Langstaff), 1866-1926 (Table P-PZ40)
	Mole, William, 1917-1961 see PR6047.O6
6025.O4	Montague, Charles Edward, 1867-1928 (Table P-PZ40)
6025.O44	Montgomery, Leslie Alexander, 1873-1961 (Table P-PZ40)
6025.O46	Montgomery, Robert Bruce (Table P-PZ40)
6025.O58	Moore, Thomas Sturge, 1870-1944 (Table P-PZ40)
6025.O7527	Morris, Kenneth, 1879-1937 (Table P-PZ40)
	Morton, Anthony see PR6005.R517
	Morus, Cenydd, 1879-1937 see PR6025.O7527
6025.U675	Munro, Hector Hugh ("Saki") (Table P-PZ40)
6025.U74	Murray, Gilbert, 1866-1957 (Table P-PZ40)
6027.A-Z	N
	The author number is determined by the second letter of the name
	Na Gopaleen, Myles see PR6029.N56
	Nash, Simon see PR6005.H323
6027.E78	Nevinson, Henry W. (Table P-PZ40)
6027.I37	Nicolson, Mrs. Adela Florence (Cory) (Table P-PZ40)
6027.I6	Nister, Ernest (Table P-PZ40)
	Nolan, Brian see PR6029.N56
	Norden, Charles see PR6007.U76
6027.O54	Norway, Nevil Shute, 1899-1960 (Table P-PZ40)
6027.O8	Noyes, Alfred (Table P-PZ40)
6029.A-Z	O
	The author number is determined by the second letter of the name
	O'Brien, Flann, 1911-1966 see PR6029.N56
	O'Byrne, Dermot, 1883-1953 see PR6003.A986
6029.C33	O'Casey, Sean (Table P-PZ40)
	O'Connor, Frank, 1903-1966 see PR6029.D58
6029.D52	O'Donnell, Elliott, 1872-1965 (Table P-PZ40)
6029.D58	O'Donovan, Michael, 1903-1966 (Table P-PZ40)
6029.G4	Ogilvie, Will H., 1869-1963 (Table P-PZ40)
6029.K36	O'Kane, James, 1832-1913 (Table P-PZ40)
6029.K4	O'Kelly, Seumas (Table P-PZ40)
6029.L4	Oldfield, Claude Houghton, 1889- (Table P-PZ40)
	Oldington, Richard, 1892-1962 see PR6001.L4
	Olivia see PR6003.U64
	O'Neill Pearson, Denise Naomi see PR6035.O554
6029.N54	Onions, Oliver, pseud. (Table P-PZ40)
6029.N56	O'Nolan, Brian, 1911-1966 (Table P-PZ40)
6029.P5	Oppenheim, Edward Phillips, 1866-1946 (Table P-PZ40)

	1900-1960
	Individual authors
	O -- Continued
6029.R25	Orczy, Emmuska, baroness (Table P-PZ40)
6029.R45	O'Riordan, Conal O'Connell (Table P-PZ40)
6029.R8	Orwell, George, 1903-1950 (Table P-PZ40)
	O'Sullivan, Seumas, 1879-1958 see PR6037.T19
	Oved, Mosheh, b. 1885 see PR6013.O47
6029.X4	Oxenham, John (Table P-PZ40)
	Oyved, Moysheh, b. 1885 see PR6013.O47
6031.A-Z	P
	The author number is determined by the second letter of the name
6031.A25	Pain, Barry (Table P-PZ40)
6031.A4	Panton, Mrs. Jane Ellen (Table P-PZ40)
6031.A49	Pargeter, Edith, 1913- (Table P-PZ40)
	Payne, Pierre Stephen Robert, 1911 see PR6031.A93
6031.A93	Payne, Robert, 1911- (Table P-PZ40)
	Pearson, Denise Naomi O'Neill see PR6035.O554
6031.E4	Pemberton, Max, Sir, 1863-1950 (Table P-PZ40)
	Pent, Katherine see PR6037.H3315
	Peters, Ellis, 1913- see PR6031.A49
	Pilgrim, David see PR6003.E3
	Plaidy, Jean, 1906- see PR6015.I3
	Plimmer, Charlotte see PR6054.E475
	Plimmer, Denis see PR6054.E475
	Porlock, Martin see PR6025.A2218
6031.O72	Potter, Beatrix, 1866-1943 (Table P-PZ40)
6031.O863	Powerscourt, Sheila Claude Beddington Wingfield, Viscountess of (Table P-PZ40)
6031.O867	Powys, John Cowper, 1872-1963 (Table P-PZ40)
	Including works on the Powys family
6031.R45	Price, Evadne, 1896-1985 (Table P-PZ40)
6031.R76	Prole, Lozania (Bloom, Ursula and Eade, Charles, 1903- as joint authors) (Table P-PZ40)
	Cf. PR6003.L58 Bloom, Ursula
6031.U25	Puddicombe, Anne Adaliza Evans, 1836-1908 (Table P-PZ40)
6031.U7	Purcell, Victor, 1896-1965 (Table P-PZ40)
6033.A-Z	Q
	The author number is determined by the second letter of the name
6033.U43	Quentin, Patrick (Table P-PZ40)
6033.U7	Quinton, John Purcell (Table P-PZ40)
6035.A-Z	R
	The author number is determined by the second letter of the name

	1900-1960
	Individual authors
	R -- Continued
6035.A35	Raile, Arthur Lyon (Table P-PZ40)
	Ranger, Ken see PR6005.R517
6035.A64	Raphael, Chaim (Table P-PZ40)
	Rattray, Simon see PR6039.R518
	Ravindranatha Thakura see PR9499.3.T34
	Reid Banks, Lynne, 1929- see PR6052.A486
	Reilly, William K. see PR6005.R517
6035.E55	Renault, Mary (Table P-PZ40)
	Rhode, John, 1884-1964 see PR6037.T778
6035.H94	Rhys, Ernest, 1859-1946 (Table P-PZ40)
6035.H96	Rhys, Jean (Table P-PZ40)
6035.I34	Richardson, Dorothy Miller, 1873-1957 (Table P-PZ40)
	Riley, Tex see PR6005.R517
	Rivett, Carol see PR6023.O66
	Rivett, Edith Caroline see PR6023.O66
6035.O532	Roberts, Morley, 1857-1942 (Table P-PZ40)
	Robertson, Helen, 1913- see PR6009.D58
6035.O554	Robins, Denise, 1897- (Table P-PZ40)
6035.O56	Robinson, Lennox (Table P-PZ40)
	Rohmer, Sax, 1883-1959 see PR6045.A37
	Roland, Mary see PR6023.E96
6035.O669	Ros, Amanda McKittrick, 1860-1939 (Table P-PZ40)
	Royal-Dawson, Felicity see PR6007.O864
6035.U7	Russell, George William, 1867-1935 ("A.E.") (Table P-PZ40)
6035.U8	Russell, Mary Annette (Table P-PZ40)
	Rutherford, Douglas, 1915- see PR6025.A1697
6037.A-Z	S
	The author number is determined by the second letter of the name
6037.A35	Sackville-West, V. (Victoria), 1892-1936
	Saki see PR6025.U675
	Sampson, Richard Henry, 1896-1973 see PR6015.U43
6037.A96	Sayle, Charles, 1864-1924 (Table P-PZ40)
6037.C37	Schiff, Sydney, 1868-1944 (Table P-PZ40)
6037.C9	Scott, Duncan Campbell (Table P-PZ40)
	Scott, Winifred Mary Watson see PR6045.Y65
6037.E12	Seaman, Sir Owen (Table P-PZ40)
	Serannel, Orpheus, 1912-1970 see PR6001.R77
6037.H29	Shakespear, Olivia, 1864-1938 (Table P-PZ40)
6037.H3315	Shann, Renée (Table P-PZ40)
6037.H333	Sharp, Evelyn, 1869-1955 (Table P-PZ40)
6037.H524	Shiel, Matthew Phipps, 1865-1947 (Table P-PZ40)
	Shute, Nevil see PR6027.O54

1900-1960
 Individual authors
  S -- Continued

6037.I88	Size, Nicholas, 1867-1953 (Table P-PZ40)
6037.L33	Slader, Richard, 1857-1926 (Table P-PZ40)
	Sloane, Sara see PR6003.L58
6037.M35	Smith, C. Fox, d. 1954 (Table P-PZ40)
	Smith, Caesar see PR6039.R518
6037.M425	Smith, Ernest Bramah (Table P-PZ40)
6037.M43	Smith, Florence Margaret, 1902-1971 (Table P-PZ40)
	Smith, Helen Lenna, 1896-1985 see PR6031.R45
	Smith, Iain Crichton see PR6005.R58
6037.M5	Smith, Logan Pearsall, 1865-1946 (Table P-PZ40)
6037.M56	Smith, Pauline (Table P-PZ40)
6037.M57	Smith, Shelley, 1912- (Table P-PZ40)
	Smith, Stevie, 1902-1971 see PR6037.M43
	Somers, Jane see PR6023.E833
6037.O6	Somerville, Edith Anna OEnone, 1858-1949 (Table P-PZ40)
6037.O843	Southwold, Stephen, 1887-1964 (Table P-PZ40)
6037.P65	Sprigg, C. St. John (Christopher St. John), 1907-1937 (Table P-PZ40)
6037.T15	Stacpoole, H. De Vere (Henry De Vere), 1863-1951 (Table P-PZ40)
	Stanton, Paul see PR6003.E264
6037.T19	Starkey, James, 1879-1958 (Table P-PZ40)
6037.T25	Stead, William Force (Table P-PZ40)
6037.T4	Stephens, James (Table P-PZ40)
6037.T453	Stern, G.B (Gladys Bronwyn), 1890- (Table P-PZ40)
	Stern, Gladys Bertha, 1890- see PR6037.T453
	Stern, Gladys Bronwyn, 1890- see PR6037.T453
6037.T466	Stewart, John Innes MacKintosh, 1906- (Table P-PZ40)
6037.T617	Stoker, Bram, 1847-1912 (Table P-PZ40)
6037.T758	Strang, William, 1859-1921 (Table P-PZ40)
6037.T778	Street, Cecil, J.C. (Cecil John Charles), 1884-1964 (Table P-PZ40)
6037.T8	Street, George Slythe (Table P-PZ40)
6037.T875	Stuart, Francis, 1902- (Table P-PZ40)
6037.T95	Stuart, George, 1863-1927 (Table P-PZ40)
	Stuart, Henry Francis Montgomery see PR6037.T875
6037.T96	Styles, Showell, 1908- (Table P-PZ40)
6037.U95	Sutro, Alfred, 1863-1933 (Table P-PZ40)
6037.Y4	Symonds, Emily Morse, d. 1936 (Table P-PZ40)
6039.A-Z	T
	The author number is determined by the second letter of the name

1900-1960
   Individual authors
      S -- Continued

	Tagore, Rabindranath (Ravindranatha Thakura) see PR9499.3.T34
	Tate, Ellalice, 1906- see PR6015.I3
	Tennant, Kylie, 1912- see PR9619.3.T4
	Tey, Josephine, 1896-1952 see PR6025.A2547
	Thompson, China see PR6023.E96
6039.H725	Thomson, George Malcolm, 1899- (Table P-PZ40)
6039.H9	Thurston, Ernest Temple (Table P-PZ40)
6039.H95	Thurston, Mrs. Katherine Cecil (Table P-PZ40)
6039.H975	Thwaite, John, 1873-1941 (Table P-PZ40)
	Tikhonov, Valentin, 1911 see PR6031.A93
6039.O26	Todd, Ruthven, 1914- (Table P-PZ40)
6039.O35	Tomlinson, Henry Major, 1873-1958 (Table P-PZ40)
6039.R23	Tracy, Louis, 1863-1928 (Table P-PZ40)
	Traherne, Michael, 1905-1990 see PR6003.A2
6039.R47	Trevelyan, George Macaulay (Table P-PZ40)
6039.R48	Trevelyan, Robert Calverley (Table P-PZ40)
6039.R518	Trevor, Elleston (Table P-PZ40)
	Trevor, Glen see PR6015.I53
	Troy, Katherine see PR6025.A943
	Troy, Simon see PR6045.A8143
	Tweedsmuir, John Buchan, Baron, 1875-1940 see PR6003.U13
6041.A-Z	U
	The author number is determined by the second letter of the name
6041.P88	Upward, Allen, 1863-1926 (Table P-PZ40)
	Urmson, Janet see PR6037.M56
6041.R84	Urwick, Edward (Table P-PZ40)
6043.A-Z	V
	The author number is determined by the second letter of the name
6043.O78	Voynich, E.L. (Ethel Lillian), 1864-1960 (Table P-PZ40)
6045.A-Z	W
	The author number is determined by the second letter of the name
6045.A2	Waddell, Samuel (Table P-PZ40)
	Wade, Henry, 1887-1969 see PR6001.U3
(6045.A32)	Walkes, W. R. (Table P-PZ40)
	see PR5708.W514
6045.A327	Wallace, Edgar, 1875-1932 (Table P-PZ40)
	Wallace, Richard Horatio Edgar see PR6045.A327
6045.A37	Ward, Arthur Sarsfield, 1883-1959 (Table P-PZ40)
6045.A8143	Warriner, Thurman (Table P-PZ40)

	1900-1960
	Individual authors
	W -- Continued
	Watkins-Pitchford, D. J. (Denys James), 1905-1990 see PR6003.A2
6045.A85	Watson, Edmund Henry Lacon, 1865-1948 (Table P-PZ40)
	Waugh, Arthur Evelyn St. John see PR6045.A97
6045.A97	Waugh, Evelyn, 1903-1966 (Table P-PZ40)
	Webb, Richard Wilson, 1902- see PR6033.U43
6045.E34	Weekes, Charles, 1867-1946 (Table P-PZ40)
6045.E517	Welch, Denton (Table P-PZ40)
	Welch, Maurice Denton see PR6045.E517
	Wellesley, Dorothy, 1889-1956 see PR6045.E53
6045.E53	Wellington, Dorothy Violet Ashton Wellesley, Duchess of (Table P-PZ40)
	Wellington, Dorothy Wellesley, Duchess of, 1889-1956 see PR6045.E53
6045.E8	West, Rebecca, 1892- (Table P-PZ40)
	Westmacott, Mary, 1891-1976 see PR6005.H66
6045.E95	Weyman, Stanley John, 1855-1928 (Table P-PZ40)
	Wheeler, Hugo, 1912- see PR6033.U43
6045.H1536	Whishaw, Frederick (Table P-PZ40)
6045.H156	Whitaker, Malachi, 1895-1975 (Table P-PZ40)
	Whitaker, Marjorie Olive, 1895-1975 see PR6045.H156
6045.H227	Whitechurch, Victor Lorenzo, 1868-1933 (Table P-PZ40)
	Williams, Ella Gwendolen Rees see PR6035.H96
	Wilkinson, Louis Umfreville, 1881-1966 see PR6025.A629
6045.I544	Williams, Peggy Eileen Arabella, 1909-1958 (Table P-PZ40)
	Wingfield, Sheila see PR6031.O863
6045.O65	Woods, Mrts. Margaret L. (Table P-PZ40)
6045.O72	Woolf, Mrs. Virginia (Stephen) (Table P-PZ40)
	Wreford, James see PR9199.3.W375
6045.R45	Wright, Sydney Fowler, 1874-1967 (Table P-PZ40)
6045.Y64	Wyndham, John, 1903-1969 (Table P-PZ40)
6045.Y65	Wynne, Pamela (Table P-PZ40)
6046.A-Z	X
	The author number is determined by the second letter of the name
6047.A-Z	Y
	The author number is determined by the second letter of the name
6047.A73	Yates, Dornford, 1885-1960 (Table P-PZ40)
6047.E3	Yeats, Jack Butler, 1871-1957 (Table P-PZ40)
	York, Jeremy see PR6005.R517

	1900-1960
	Individual authors
	Y -- Continued
	Yorke, Henry Vincent, 1905-1974 see PR6013.R416
	Young, Robert, 1911- see PR6031.A93
6047.O6	Younger, Wiliam Anthony, 1917-1961 (Table P-PZ40)
6049.A-Z	Z
	The author number is determined by the second letter of the name
	1961-2000
	Including usually authors beginning to publish about 1950, flourishing after 1960
	For works of fiction cataloged before July 1, 1980, except limited editions and works in the Rare Book Collection see PZ4
6050	Anonymous works (Table P-PZ28 modified)
6050.A6A-.A6Z	Works by authors indicated by a descriptive phrase. By first word of phrase, A-Z
	Loyal subject of Her Majesty, 1950- see PR6073.I439
	Individual authors
	Subarrange each author by Table P-PZ40 unless otherwise specified
6051.A-Z	A
	The author number is determined by the second letter of the name
6051.I65	Aird, Catherine (Table P-PZ40)
6051.L52	Allbeury, Ted (Table P-PZ40)
	Allen, Barbara see PR6063.A38
	Allen, Conrad, 1940- see PR6063.I3175
6051.L5395	Allen, Michael Derek, 1939- (Table P-PZ40)
	Anders, Rex, 1928-1999 see PR6052.A7175
6051.N62	Annandale, Barbara, 1925- (Table P-PZ40)
	Anthony, Evelyn see PR6069.T428
6051.R46	Ardonne, Marcus (Table P-PZ40)
	Armstrong, Campbell see PR6052.L25
	Ash, Cay Van see PR6072.A55
6051.S45	Ashby, Cliff (Table P-PZ40)
	Ashby, J.C. see PR6051.S45
	Ashfield, Helen see PR6052.E533
	Ashford, Jeffrey see PR6060.E43
	Atkins, Margaret Elizabeth see PR6051.T5
6051.T5	Atkins, Meg Elizabeth (Table P-PZ40)
6052.A-Z	B
	The author number is determined by the second letter of the name
6052.A486	Banks, Lynne Reid, 1929-
	Barber, John Lysberg Nöel see PR6052.A623

	1961-2000
	Individual authors
	B -- Continued
6052.A623	Barber, Nöel (Table P-PZ40)
6052.A7175	Barrett, G. J. (Geoffrey John), 1928-1999 (Table P-PZ40)
	Barwick, James, 1931- see PR6060.A453
	Barwick, Tony, 1931- see PR6060.A453
6052.A764	Bassett, Ronald (Table P-PZ40)
	Bax, Roger, 1908- see PR6073.I56
(6052.E196)	Beaton, M.C.
	see PR6053.H4535
6052.E533	Bennetts, Pamela (Table P-PZ40)
	Berlin, Juanita see PR6053.A8
	Bernard, Jay see PR6069.A94
	Bingham, John, 1908- see PR6053.L283
	Bingham, John Michael Ward, Baron Clanmorris, 1908- see PR6053.L283
6052.L25	Black, Campbell (Table P-PZ40)
6052.L3423	Blackwood, Caroline (Table P-PZ40)
	Blaine, Jeff, 1928-1999 see PR6052.A7175
	Bland, Jennifer see PR6051.N62
	Bordill, Judith see PR6055.C33
	Bowden, Jean see PR6051.N62
	Bowen-Judd, Sara Hutton see PR6073.O63
6052.O919	Boyd, Neil (Table P-PZ40)
	Bradford, Michael, 1939- see PR6051.L5395
	Brennan, John, 1914- see PR6073.E373
	Brett, Michael, 1923- see PR6070.R48
	Britten, Buddy see PR6073.R488
6052.R5893	Brown, Carter, 1923- (Table P-PZ40)
	Bryans, Robert Harbinson, 1928- see PR6058.A617
6052.U638	Burgess, Anthony, 1917- (Table P-PZ40)
	Butler, Richard, 1917 see PR6051.L52
6052.U9	Butterworth, Michael, 1924- (Table P-PZ40)
	Buxton, Anne see PR6025.A943
	Byrne, John Keyes see PR6062.E7
6053.A-Z	C
	The author number is determined by the second letter of the name
6053.A347	Caillou, Alan, 1914-
	Calder-Marshall, Arthur, 1908- see PR6063.A67
	Calvin, Henry see PR6058.A58
	Campbell, J. Ramsey, 1946- see PR6053.A4855
6053.A4855	Campbell, Ramsey, 1946- (Table P-PZ40)
6053.A489	Campsie, Alistair Keith (Table P-PZ40)
	Candy, Edward see PR6064.E83
	Carr, Barbara Comyns, 1909- see PR6053.O452

	1961-2000
	Individual authors
	C -- Continued
	Carr, Barbara Irene Veronica Comyns-, 1909- see PR6053.O452
	Carré, John Le, 1931- see PR6062.E33
	Carter, Bruce, 1922- see PR6058.O82
6053.A8	Casey, Juanita (Table P-PZ40)
6053.A824138	Castle, Brenda (Table P-PZ40)
	Cauldwell, Frank see PR6061.I45
6053.A859	Cave, Emma (Table P-PZ40)
	Chace, Isobel, 1934- see PR6058.U534
	Chaplin, Elizabeth see PR6063.C477
6053.H4535	Chesney, Marion (Table P-PZ40)
	Chetwund-Talbot, Ursula, Lady, 1908-1966 see PR6070.A357
6053.H473	Chevalier, Paul, 1925- (Table P-PZ40)
6053.L283	Clanmorris, John Michael Ward Bingham, Baron, 1908- (Table P-PZ40)
6053.L38	Clayton, Richard (Table P-PZ40)
6053.L42	Cleese, John (Table P-PZ40)
	Clifford, Francis see PR6070.H66
	Columbus, Robert Cimabue Cortez see PR6061.E57
6053.O452	Comyns, Barbara, 1909- (Table P-PZ40)
	Comyns, Barbara, 1912- see PR6053.O452
	Comyns-Carr, Barbara Irene Veronica, 1909- see PR6053.O452
6053.O525	Cookson, Catherine (Table P-PZ40)
6053.O75	Cornwell, Bernard (Table P-PZ40)
	Cornwell, David John Moore, 1931 see PR6062.E33
	Cortez-Columbus, Robert Cimabue see PR6061.E57
6053.O774	Cory, Desmond (Table P-PZ40)
6053.O965	Cowper, Richard, 1926- (Table P-PZ40)
	Crampton, Helen, 1936- see PR6053.H4535
6053.R63	Crossley-Holland, Kevin (Table P-PZ40)
	Crowther, Bruce see PR6057.R29
	Cummins, Mary see PR6073.A72265
	Cunningham, Peter, 1947- see PR6062.A778
	Curry, Avon see PR6051.N62
6054.A-Z	D
	The author number is determined by the second letter of the name
	Darrell, Elizabeth see PR6054.R785
	Davys, Sarah see PR6063.A385
	De Terán, Lisa St. Aubin, 1953- see PR6069.T13
	Dell, Belinda see PR6051.N62
6054.E475	Denis, Charlotte (Table P-PZ40)

	1961-2000
	Individual authors
	D -- Continued
	DeRosa, Peter see PR6052.O919
	Devine, David McDonald see PR6054.E9
6054.E9	Devine, Dominic, 1920- (Table P-PZ40)
	Devine, E.M. see PR6054.E9
	Douglas, Arthur see PR6058.A55456
	Douglas, Barbara see PR6065.E9
6054.R25	Drabble, Margaret, 1939- (Table P-PZ40)
6054.R785	Drummond, Emma, 1931- (Table P-PZ40)
6054.U56	Dunnett, Dorothy (Table P-PZ40)
6055.A-Z	E
	The author number is determined by the second letter of the name
6055.C33	Eccles, Marjorie (Table P-PZ40)
	Edwards, June see PR6056.O6926
6055.G55	Egleton, Clive (Table P-PZ40)
	Ellis, Peter Berresford see PR6070.R366
	Escott, Jonathan see PR6069.C589
6055.V13	Evans, Alan, 1930- (Table P-PZ40)
6055.V3	Evelyn, John Michael, 1916- (Table P-PZ40)
6056.A-Z	F
	The author number is determined by the second letter of the name
	Fairfax, Ann see PR6053.H4535
	Falkirk, Richard, 1929- see PR6062.A47
	Fallon, Martin, 1929- see PR6058.I343
	Fecher, Constance see PR6058.E23
	Ferrand, Georgina see PR6053.A824138
	Finley, Fiona see PR6063.A38
	Forbes, Colin see PR6069.A94
	Forbes, Michael see PR6061.E675
6056.O684	Forrest, David (Table P-PZ40)
	Cf. PR6056.O692 Forrest-Webb, Robert
6056.O692	Forrest-Webb, Robert (Table P-PZ40)
	Cf. PR6056.O684 Forrest, David
6056.O6926	Forrester, Helen (Table P-PZ40)
6056.R285	Franklin, Charles, 1909-1976 (Table P-PZ40)
6056.R286	Fraser, Anthea (Table P-PZ40)
6056.R4	Freeling, Nicolas (Table P-PZ40)
6056.R45	Fremlin, Celia (Table P-PZ40)
6057.A-Z	G
	The author number is determined by the second letter of the name
	Gardner, John, 1926- see PR6057.A63
6057.A63	Gardner, John E. (Table P-PZ40)

	1961-2000
	Individual authors
	G -- Continued
	Gardner, John Edmund see PR6057.A63
	Garland, David, 1940- see PR6063.I3175
	Garve, Andrew, 1908- see PR6073.I56
6057.A728	Gash, Jonathan, b. 1933 (Table P-PZ40)
	Gaunt, Graham see PR6057.A728
	George, Eugene, 1925- see PR6053.H473
6057.I538	Gill, B.M. (Table P-PZ40)
	Gill, Barbara see PR6057.I538
6057.I574	Gillespie, Jane, 1923- (Table P-PZ40)
6057.I88	Givens, Ray (Table P-PZ40)
	Glover-Wright, Geoffrey see PR6073.R488
	Goller, Celia see PR6056.R45
	Gordon, Rex, 1917- see PR6058.O83
6057.O714	Gordon, Richard, 1921- (Table P-PZ40)
	Gort, Sam, 1928-1999 see PR6052.A7175
	Graham, James, 1929- see PR6058.I343
	Graham, Vanessa see PR6056.R286
	Grant, David see PR6070.H56
6057.R29	Grant, James, 1933- (Table P-PZ40)
	Grant, John, b. 1933 see PR6057.A728
	Gray, Malcolm see PR6069.T77
	Gray, Simon see PR6057.R33
6057.R33	Gray, Simon James Holliday (Table P-PZ40)
	Grayson, Richard see PR6057.R55
	Greenaway, Peter Van see PR6072.A65
	Greenwood, John see PR6058.I5
	Greer, Jack, 1928-1999 see PR6052.A7175
6057.R55	Grindal, Richard (Table P-PZ40)
6058.A-Z	H
	The author number is determined by the second letter of the name
	Haggard, William see PR6053.L38
6058.A4385	Hale, Julian Anthony Stuart (Table P-PZ40)
	Halevi, Z'ev ben Shimon see PR6061.E66
	Halliday, Dorothy see PR6054.U56
	Hamilton, Mollie, 1911- see PR6061.A945
6058.A55456	Hammond, Gerald (Table P-PZ40)
6058.A58	Hanley, Clifford (Table P-PZ40)
6058.A617	Harbinson, Robert, 1928- (Table P-PZ40)
	Harper, Kenneth, 1940- see PR6063.I3175
6058.A6886	Harris, John, 1916- (Table P-PZ40)
	Harvey, Marianne see PR6073.I4323
	Hawhimi, Idries Shah, 1924- see PR6069.H28
	Hazeldine, Joan see PR6062.Y477

	1961-2000
	Individual authors
	H -- Continued
6058.E23	Heaven, Constance (Table P-PZ40)
	Hebden, Mark, 1916- see PR6058.A6886
	Hennessy, Max, 1916- see PR6058.A6886
	Hervey, Evelyn, 1926- see PR6061.E26
6058.I343	Higgins, Jack, 1929- (Table P-PZ40)
6058.I448	Hill, Reginald (Table P-PZ40)
6058.I5	Hilton, John Buxton (Table P-PZ40)
	Holland, Kevin Crossley see PR6053.R63
	Holliday, James see PR6057.R33
	Hope, Charlie see PR6063.I3175
6058.O82	Hough, Richard Alexander, 1922- (Table P-PZ40)
6058.O83	Hough, S.B. (Stanley Bennett), 1917- (Table P-PZ40)
	Howard, Colin see PR6069.H375
6058.U534	Hunter, Elizabeth, 1934- (Table P-PZ40)
6058.U54	Hunter, Robin, 1935- (Table P-PZ40)
	Hyde, Jennifer see PR6055.C33
6059.A-Z	I
	The author number is determined by the second letter of the name
	Idries Shah, Sayed, 1924- see PR6069.H28
6060.A-Z	J
	The author number is determined by the second letter of the name
	Jacks, Oliver see PR6068.O98
	Jamal, Mahmood see PR6064.A54
6060.A453	James, Donald, 1931- (Table P-PZ40)
	James, Margaret see PR6052.E533
6060.E43	Jeffries, Roderic, 1926- (Table P-PZ40)
6060.O389	Johnston, Fred, 1951- (Table P-PZ40)
6061.A-Z	K
	The author number is determined by the second letter of the name
6061.A945	Kaye, M.M. (Mary Margaret), 1911- (Table P-PZ40)
6061.E26	Keating, H.R.F. (Henry Reymond Fitzwalter), 1926- (Table P-PZ40)
	Kell, Joseph, 1917- see PR6052.U638
	Kells, Susannah see PR6053.O75
	Kelly, Patrick, 1917- see PR6051.L52
	Kemp, Sarah see PR6052.U9
6061.E57	Kenedy, R.C. (Table P-PZ40)
6061.E66	Kenton, Warren (Table P-PZ40)
6061.E675	Kenyon, Michael (Table P-PZ40)
	Kilbourn, Matt, 1928-1999 see PR6052.A7175
6061.I45	King, Francis Henry (Table P-PZ40)

	1961-2000
	Individual authors
	K -- Continued
	Kirk, Michael, 1928- see PR6061.N6
6061.N6	Knox, Bill, 1928- (Table P-PZ40)
6062.A-Z	L

The author number is determined by the second letter of the name

	Laker, Rosalina see PR6065.E9
6062.A47	Lambert, Derek, 1929- (Table P-PZ40)
	Lands, Neil see PR6058.U54
	Large, Peter Sommerville see PR6069.O43
	Lassalle, Caroline see PR6053.A859
6062.A778	Lauder, Peter (Table P-PZ40)
6062.E33	Le Carré, John, 1931- (Table P-PZ40)
	Lear, Peter see PR6062.O86
	Leighton, Edward, 1928-1999 see PR6052.A7175
6062.E7	Leonard, Hugh, 1926- (Table P-PZ40)
	Leonard, Jason, 1922- see PR6069.C589
6062.L57	Lloyd, Alan, 1927- (Table P-PZ40)
	Long, William Stuart see PR6063.A38
6062.O77	Lorrimer, Claire, 1921- (Table P-PZ40)
6062.O853	Lovell, Marc, 1930- (Table P-PZ40)
6062.O86	Lovesey, Peter (Table P-PZ40)
	Lowell, Caroline see PR6052.L3423
6062.Y477	Lyle, Elizabeth (Table P-PZ40)
	Lyle-Smith, Alan, 1914- see PR6053.A347
6063.A-Z	M

The author number is determined by the second letter of the name

6063.A167	McCutchan, Philip, 1920- (Table P-PZ40)
	Macdonald, Malcolm see PR6068.O827
6063.A1692	MacDonald, Ranald, 1955- (Table P-PZ40)
	Macey, Carn, 1928-1999 see PR6052.A7175
	MacKinnon, Alan see PR6053.A489
6063.A248	MacLean, Alistair, 1922 or 3- (Table P-PZ40)
	MacLeod, Robert, 1928- see PR6061.N6
	MacNeil, Duncan, 1920- see PR6063.A167
6063.A38	Mann, Violet Vivian, 1914- (Table P-PZ40)
6063.A385	Manning, Rosemary (Table P-PZ40)
	Marchant, Catherine see PR6053.O525
	Markov, Georgi Ivanov see PR6069.T15
6063.A67	Marshall, Arthur, 1908- (Table P-PZ40)
	Marshall, Arthur Calder, 1908- see PR6063.A67
	Marston, Edward see PR6063.I3175
6063.A76	Mason, Douglas R. (Table P-PZ40)
	Maybury, Anne see PR6025.A943

PR

1961-2000
 Individual authors
  M -- Continued
   McCarthy, Shaun, 1928- see PR6053.O774
   McCutchan, Philip, 1920- see PR6063.A167
6063.C477 McGown, Jill (Table P-PZ40)
   McIntosh, Kinn Hamilton see PR6051.I65
   McKenzie, Jina see PS3558.A624283
   McShane, Mark, 1930- see PR6062.O853
   Middleton, Stanley see PR6069.I4
6063.I3175 Miles, Keith (Table P-PZ40)
6063.I793 Mitchell, James, 1926- (Table P-PZ40)
   Mont-Royal, Anne-Marie Villefranche, 1899-1980 see
    PR6072.I456
   Mountjoy, Christopher, 1940- see PR6063.I3175
   Montgomery, Derek see PR6069.I4
   Morland, Dick see PR6058.I448
   Murry, Colin, 1926- see PR6053.O965
6064.A-Z N
    The author number is determined by the second letter of the
     name
6064.A54 Nangle, Julian, 1947- (Table P-PZ40)
   Napier, Mary, 1932- see PR6073.R54
   Neillands, Robin Hunter, 1935- see PR6058.U54
6064.E83 Neville, Alison (Table P-PZ40)
   Nicolas, F.R.E. see PR6056.R4
6065.A-Z O
    The author number is determined by the second letter of the
     name
6065.C34 O'Callaghan, Conor, 1968- (Table P-PZ40)
   Ostlere, Richard, 1921- see PR6057.O714
6065.E9 Ovstedal, Barbara (Table P-PZ40)
6066.A-Z P
    The author number is determined by the second letter of the
     name
   Paton Walsh, Gillian, 1937- see PR6066.A84
6066.A84 Paton Walsh, Jill, 1937- (Table P-PZ40)
   Patterson, Harry see PR6058.I343
   Patterson, Henry see PR6058.I343
   Paul, Barbara see PR6065.E9
6066.E496 Penn, John (Table P-PZ40)
   Phillips, David see PR6069.T15
6067.A-Z Q
    The author number is determined by the second letter of the
     name
6067.U347 Quest, Erica (Table P-PZ40)

	1961-2000
	Individual authors -- Continued
6068.A-Z	R
	The author number is determined by the second letter of the name
	Radley, Sheila see PR6068.O846
	Raine, Richard see PR6069.A94
	Ramsay, Jay see PR6053.A4855
	Ramsbottom, Bertie see PR6073.I49
	Rankine, John see PR6063.A76
	Read, Miss, 1913- see PR6069.A42
	Reid Banks, Lynne, 1929- see PR6052.A486
6068.E63	Rendell, Ruth, 1930- (Table P-PZ40)
6068.H4	Rhea, Nicholas (Table P-PZ40)
	Rickard, Cole, 1928-1999 see PR6052.A7175
	Ripley, Jack, 1921- see PR6073.A354
	Robins, Patricia, 1921- see PR6062.O77
	Robinson, Sheila see PR6068.O846
	Ross, Jonathan, 1916- see PR6068.O835
	Ross, Malcolm see PR6068.O827
6068.O827	Ross-Macdonald, Malcolm (Table P-PZ40)
6068.O835	Rossiter, John, 1916- (Table P-PZ40)
6068.O846	Rowan, Hester (Table P-PZ40)
	Royal, Dan, 1928-1999 see PR6052.A7175
6068.O98	Royce, Kenneth (Table P-PZ40)
	Ruell, Patrick see PR6058.I448
6069.A-Z	S
	The author number is determined by the second letter of the name
6069.A42	Saint, Dora Jessie, 1913- (Table P-PZ40)
	Saint Aubin de Terán, Lisa see PR6069.T13
	Salisbury, Carol see PR6052.U9
	Sanders, Brett, 1928-1999 see PR6052.A7175
6069.A94	Sawkins, Raymond H., 1923- (Table P-PZ40)
	Sawyer, John see PR6067.U347
	Sawyer, Nancy see PR6067.U347
6069.C586	Scott, Douglas, 1926- (Table P-PZ40)
6069.C589	Scott, Jack S. (Table P-PZ40)
6069.H28	Shah, Idries, 1924- (Table P-PZ40)
6069.H375	Shaw, Howard (Table P-PZ40)
	Shaw, Jane, 1923- see PR6057.I574
	Sheridan, Jane see PR6073.I553
6069.I4	Simmons, James, 1933- (Table P-PZ40)
	Sinclair, James, 1911-2005 see PR6069.T4467
	Smith, William Scott see PR6069.C586
	Somers, Jane see PR6023.E833
6069.O43	Somerville-Large, Peter (Table P-PZ40)

1961-2000
Individual authors
S -- Continued

6069.T13	St. Aubin de Terán, Lisa, 1953- (Table P-PZ40)
6069.T15	St. George, David (Table P-PZ40)
6069.T177	Stacy, Susannah (Table P-PZ40)
	Stanley, Bennett, 1917- see PR6058.O83
	Staples, Mary Jane see PR6069.T4467
	Staples, Reginald Thomas, 1911-2005 see PR6069.T4467
	Staynes, Jill see PR6069.T177
6069.T428	Stephens, Eve (Table P-PZ40)
	Stern, Max, 1928-1999 see PR6052.A7175
6069.T4467	Stevens, Robert Tyler, 1911-2005 (Table P-PZ40)
	Stoker, Alan, 1930- see PR6055.V13
	Storey, Margaret see PR6069.T177
	Stuart, Alex see PR6063.A38
	Stuart, Anthony, 1940- see PR6058.A4385
6069.T77	Stuart, Ian (Table P-PZ40)
	Stuart, Ian, 1922 or 3- see PR6063.A248
	Stuart, Vivian see PR6063.A38
	Summers, D.B., 1928-1999 see PR6052.A7175
	Summers, Dennis, 1928-1999 see PR6052.A7175
	Swift, Margaret, 1939- see PR6054.R25
6070.A-Z	T
	The author number is determined by the second letter of the name
6070.A357	Talbot, Laura, 1908-1966 (Table P-PZ40)
	Tarrant, John see PR6055.G55
	Thimblethorpe, June Sylvia see PR6070.H73
6070.H56	Thomas, Craig (Table P-PZ40)
6070.H58	Thomas, D.M. (Table P-PZ40)
	Thomas, Donald Michael see PR6070.H58
6070.H66	Thompson, Arthur Leonard Bell (Table P-PZ40)
6070.H689	Thorne, Nicola (Table P-PZ40)
6070.H73	Thorpe, Sylvia (Table P-PZ40)
	Tremaine, Jennie see PR6053.H4535
6070.R366	Tremayne, Peter (Table P-PZ40)
6070.R48	Tripp, Miles (Table P-PZ40)
	Trotman, J.W. and P. see PR6066.E496
6070.U74	Turner, Philip (Table P-PZ40)
	Tyson, Jon Wynne see PR6073.Y73
6071.A-Z	U
	The author number is determined by the second letter of the name
	Underhill, Charles see PR6058.I448
	Underwood, Michael, 1916- see PR6055.V3

	1961-2000
	Individual authors
	U -- Continued
	Usher, Frank Hugh see PR6056.R285
6072.A-Z	V
	The author number is determined by the second letter of the name
6072.A55	Van Ash, Cay (Table P-PZ40)
6072.A65	Van Greenaway, Peter, 1929- (Table P-PZ40)
6072.I456	Villefranche, Anne-Marie, 1899-1980 (Table P-PZ40)
	Volestrangler, Muriel see PR6053.L42
	Voyle, Mary see PR6063.A385
6073.A-Z	W
	The author number is determined by the second letter of the name
	Wade, Bill, 1928-1999 see PR6052.A7175
6073.A354	Wainwright, John William, 1921- (Table P-PZ40)
	Walker, Peter Norman see PR6068.H4
	Wallace, James, 1928-1999 see PR6052.A7175
6073.A4198	Wallace, Jane (Table P-PZ40)
	Walsh, Jill Paton, 1937- see PR6066.A84
6073.A72265	Warmington, Mary Jane (Table P-PZ40)
	Warwick, Anne-Marie Villefranche, 1899-1980 see PR6072.I456
	Webster, Noah, 1928- see PR6061.N6
6073.E373	Welcome, John, 1914- (Table P-PZ40)
6073.H544	Whitehead, E.A. (Table P-PZ40)
	Whitehead, Ted see PR6073.H544
6073.I244	Wichert, Sabine, 1942- (Table P-PZ40)
6073.I4323	Williams, Mary (Table P-PZ40)
6073.I439	Wilson, A.N., 1950- (Table P-PZ40)
	Wilson, John Anthony Burgess, 1917- see PR6052.U638
6073.I49	Windle, Ralph (Table P-PZ40)
6073.I553	Winslow, Pauline Glen (Table P-PZ40)
6073.I56	Winterton, Paul, 1908- (Table P-PZ40)
6073.O63	Woods, Sara (Table P-PZ40)
6073.R488	Wright, Glover (Table P-PZ40)
6073.R54	Wright, Patricia, 1932- (Table P-PZ40)
6073.Y73	Wynne-Tyson, Jon (Table P-PZ40)
6074.A-Z	X
	The author number is determined by the second letter of the name
6075.A-Z	Y
	The author number is determined by the second letter of the name
	Yates, Alan, 1923- see PR6052.R5893
	Yorke, Katherine see PR6070.H689

	1961-2000
	Individual authors -- Continued
6076.A-Z	Z
	The author number is determined by the second letter of the name
	2001-
6100	Anonymous works (Table P-PZ28)
	Individual authors
	Subarrange each author by Table P-PZ40 unless otherwise specified
6101.A-Z	A
	The author number is determined by the second letter of the name
6102.A-Z	B
	The author number is determined by the second letter of the name
	Blackshaw, Brian Edwin, 1932- see PR6103.O69
6103.A-Z	C
	The author number is determined by the second letter of the name
6103.O69	Coppard, Edwin, 1932- (Table P-PZ40)
6104.A-Z	D
	The author number is determined by the second letter of the name
6104.A86	Davies, Freda (Table P-PZ40)
6105.A-Z	E
	The author number is determined by the second letter of the name
6106.A-Z	F
	The author number is determined by the second letter of the name
6107.A-Z	G
	The author number is determined by the second letter of the name
	Griffin, Kate, 1986- see PR6123.E225
6108.A-Z	H
	The author number is determined by the second letter of the name
6109.A-Z	I
	The author number is determined by the second letter of the name
6110.A-Z	J
	The author number is determined by the second letter of the name
6111.A-Z	K
	The author number is determined by the second letter of the name

2001-
Individual authors -- Continued

6112.A-Z	L

The author number is determined by the second letter of the name

6113.A-Z	M

The author number is determined by the second letter of the name

Moray, Keith see PR6119.O675
More, Clay see PR6119.O675

6114.A-Z	N

The author number is determined by the second letter of the name

6115.A-Z	O

The author number is determined by the second letter of the name

6116.A-Z	P

The author number is determined by the second letter of the name

Pirnie, Amy see PR6104.A86

6117.A-Z	Q

The author number is determined by the second letter of the name

6118.A-Z	R

The author number is determined by the second letter of the name

6119.A-Z	S

The author number is determined by the second letter of the name

6119.O675	Souter, Keith M. (Table P-PZ40)
6120.A-Z	T

The author number is determined by the second letter of the name

6121.A-Z	U

The author number is determined by the second letter of the name

6122.A-Z	V

The author number is determined by the second letter of the name

6123.A-Z	W

The author number is determined by the second letter of the name

6123.E225	Webb, Catherine, 1986- (Table P-PZ40)
6124.A-Z	X

The author number is determined by the second letter of the name

2001-
Individual authors -- Continued

6125.A-Z	Y
	The author number is determined by the second letter of the name
6126.A-Z	Z
	The author number is determined by the second letter of the name

English literature: Provincial, local, etc.
Class here literary history, collected biography and collections of the literature of the following: 1) English counties, regions, islands; 2) Scotland, Ireland, Wales; 2) Countries outside of the British Isles
For Celtic literature of Scotland, Ireland, Wales, Isle of Man, Cornwall, etc. (Gaelic, Irish, Welsh, Manx, Cornish) see PB1+
For English provincial and other local dialect literature see PE1701+
For French Canadian literature see PQ3900+
For English literature outside of the British Isles see PR9080+
For American literature (United States) see PS1+
England
Counties, regions, islands, etc.
Subarrange each by Table P-PZ26 unless otherwise specified

8309.A-.C	A - C
8310-8326	Cornwall (Table PR2)
8329.C-.D	C - D
8330-8346	Devonshire (Table PR2)
8349.D-.K	D - K
8350-8366	Kent (Table PR2)
8369.K-.L	K - L
8370-8386	Lancashire (Table PR2)
8389.L-.Y	L - Y
8400-8416	Yorkshire (Table PR2)
8430-8446	Channel Islands (Table PR2)
8450-8466	Man (Table PR2)
8469.A-Z	Other, A-Z
	Places
8470-8486	London (Table PR2)
8489.A-Z	Other, A-Z
	Celtic literature (English)
	History and criticism
8490	General
8491	Poetry
8492	Drama

English literature: Provincial, local, etc.
Celtic literature (English)
History and criticism -- Continued
8493	Prose
(8494)	Folk literature
	see subclass GR
	Collections
8495	General
8496	Poetry
8497	Drama
8498	Prose
(8499)	Folk literature
	see subclass GR
	Scotland
	History and criticism
	Periodicals. Societies. Serials
8500	Periodicals
(8501)	Yearbooks
	see PR8500
8502	Societies
8503	Congresses
8503.5	Museums. Exhibitions
	Collected works (nonserial)
8504	Several authors
8505	Individual authors
8506	Encyclopedias. Dictionaries
	Study and teaching
8508	General works
8509.A-Z	Individual schools. By name, A-Z
	Biography of scholars, teachers, etc.
8509.4	Collective
8509.5.A-Z	Individual, A-Z
	History
	General works
8510	Early works
	Modern treatises
8511	General works
8512	Textbooks
8513	Outlines, syllabi, quizzes, etc.
8514	Addresses, essays, lectures
8517	Awards, prizes (not A-Z)
8518	Relation to history, civilization, culture, etc.
	Relation to other literatures
8519	General works
8520	Translations (as a subject)
8521	Foreign authors (General)
	Treatment of special subject, classes, etc.

English literature: Provincial, local, etc.
Scotland
History and criticism
History
Treatment of special subject, classes, etc. -- Continued

8522.A-Z	Subjects, A-Z
	For list of Cutter numbers, see Table P-PZ20 22.A+
8523.A-Z	Classes, A-Z
	For list of Cutter numbers, see Table P-PZ20 23.A+
8525.A-Z	Individual characters, A-Z
	For list of Cutter numbers, see Table P-PZ20 25.A+
	Biography
8527	Collective
	By period see PR8535+
	Individual
	see numbers for individual authors or works under English literature, e.g. PR1509+ ; PR1803+ ; etc.
8529	Memoirs, letters, etc.
8531	Literary landmarks. Homes and haunts of authors
8533	Women authors. Literary relations of women
8534.A-Z	Other classes of authors, A-Z
	For list of Cutter numbers, see Table P-PZ20 34.A+
	By period
8535	Origins
	Medieval
8538	General works
8539	Addresses, essays, lectures
8540	Special subjects (not A-Z)
	Modern
	Renaissance
8544	General works
8545	Addresses, essays, lectures
8546	Special subjects (not A-Z)
	16th-18th century
8547	General works
8548	Addresses, essays, lectures
8549	Special subjects (not A-Z)
	19th century
8550	General works
8551	Addresses, essays, lectures
8552	Special subjects (not A-Z)
	20th century
8553	General works
8554	Addresses, essays, lectures
8555	Special subjects (not A-Z)
	21st century
8556	General works

English literature: Provincial, local, etc.
Scotland
History and criticism
By period
Modern
21st century -- Continued
8557   Special subjects (not A-Z)
Poetry
8561   General works
Medieval see PR8538+
Modern
8567   16th-18th century
8569   (18th and) 19th century
8571   20th century
8572   21st century
Special forms or subjects
8577   Epic
8579   Lyric
8580   Popular poetry. Ballads, etc.
8581.A-Z   Other, A-Z
For list of Cutter numbers, see Table P-PZ20 81.A+
Drama
8583   General works
8585   Early to 1800
8587   19th century
8589   20th century
8590   21st century
8593.A-Z   Special forms, A-Z
For list of Cutter numbers, see Table P-PZ20 93.A+
8595.A-Z   Special subjects, A-Z
For list of Cutter numbers, see Table P-PZ20 95.A+
Prose. Fiction
8597   General works
8599   Early to 1800
8601   19th century
8603   20th century
8603.2   21st century
8604   Short stories
8607.A-Z   Special topics, A-Z
For list of Cutter numbers, see Table P-PZ20 107.A+
Other forms
8609   Oratory
8610   Diaries
8611   Letters
8613   Essays
8615   Wit and humor
8617   Miscellaneous

English literature: Provincial, local, etc.
  Scotland
    History and criticism -- Continued
      Folk literature
(8621)   General works
                   see subclass GR
(8622)   Collections
                   see subclass GR
         Special
8623.A-Z   Special forms, A-Z
8623.D73   Drama
8624   Chapbooks
8624.A2   Collections
8625   Juvenile literature (General)
               For special genres, see the genre
      Collections
8630   Periodicals
8633   Comprehensive collections
8635   Selections. Anthologies
8636.A-Z   Special classes of authors, A-Z
               For list of Cutter numbers, see Table P-PZ20 136.A+
8636.5.A-Z   Special topics, A-Z
               For list of Cutter numbers, see Table P-PZ20 136.5.A+
8637.A-Z   Translations. By language, A-Z
      By period
8640   Medieval
8641   16th-18th centuries
8643   19th century
8644   20th century
8645   21st century
      Local see PR8691+
      Poetry
8648   Periodicals
8650   Comprehensive collections
8651   Selections. Anthologies
8652   Anthologies of poetry for children
       Special classes of authors
8653   Women
8654.A-Z   Other, A-Z
               For list of Cutter numbers, see Table P-PZ20 154.A+
       By period
8655   Medieval
8656   15th-18th centuries
8657   19th century
8658   20th century
8658.2   21st century
       Special. By form or subject

	English literature: Provincial, local, etc.
	Ireland
	Collections
	Poetry
	Special
	Ballads see PR1181+
8661.A-Z	Other, A-Z
	For list of Cutter numbers, see Table P-PZ20 161.A+
8663.A-Z	Translations. By language, A-Z
	Drama
8664	Comprehensive collections
8665	Selections. Anthologies
8665.5	Stories, plots, etc.
8665.7.A-Z	Special classes of authors, A-Z
	For list of Cutter numbers, see Table P-PZ20 165.7.A+
	By period
8666	To 1800
8667	19th century
8669	20th century
8669.2	21st century
8670.A-Z	Special forms or subjects, A-Z
	For list of Cutter numbers, see Table P-PZ20 170.A+
8671.A-Z	Translations. By language, A-Z
	Prose
8673	General prose collections
8674.A-Z	Special. By form or subject, A-Z
	For list of Cutter numbers, see Table P-PZ20 174.A+
	Fiction
8675	General collections
8676	Short stories
8676.2.A-Z	Special classes of authors, A-Z
	For list of Cutter numbers, see Table P-PZ20 176.2.A+
8676.3	Digests. Synopses, etc.
8676.5.A-Z	Special. By form or subject, A-Z
	For list of Cutter numbers, see Table P-PZ20 176.5.A+
8677.A-Z	Translations. By language, A-Z
8679	Oratory
8680	Diaries
8681	Letters
8683	Essays
8685	Wit and humor
8687	Miscellany
8688.A-Z	Translations. By language, A-Z
(8689)	Folk literature
	see subclass GR
	Local

	English literature: Provincial, local, etc.
	Scotland
	Local -- Continued
8691.A-Z	By region, province, county, etc., A-Z
	Subarrange each by Table P-PZ26
8692.A-Z	By city, A-Z
	Subarrange each by Table P-PZ26
8693.A-Z	Foreign countries, A-Z
	Subarrange each by Table P-PZ26
	Individual authors or works
	see numbers for individual authors or works under English literature, e.g. PR1509+ ; PR1803+ ; etc.
	Ireland
	History and criticism
	Periodicals. Societies. Serials
8700	Periodicals
(8701)	Yearbooks
	see PR8700
8702	Societies
8703	Congresses
8703.5	Museums. Exhibitions
	Collected works (nonserial)
8704	Several authors
8705	Individual authors
8706	Encyclopedias. Dictionaries
	Study and teaching
8708	General works
8709.A-Z	Individual schools. By name, A-Z
	Biography of scholars, teachers, etc.
8709.4	Collective
8709.5.A-Z	Individual, A-Z
	History
	General works
8710	Early works
	Modern treatises
8711	General works
8712	Textbooks
8713	Outlines, syllabi, quizzes, etc.
8714	Addresses, essays, lectures
8717	Awards, prizes (not A-Z)
8718	Relation to history, civilization, culture, etc.
	Relation to other literatures
8719	General works
8720	Translations (as a subject)
8721	Foreign authors (General)
	Treatment of special subject, classes, etc.

	English literature: Provincial, local, etc.
	Ireland
	History and criticism
	History
	Treatment of special subject, classes, etc. -- Continued
8722.A-Z	Subjects, A-Z
	For list of Cutter numbers, see Table P-PZ20 22.A+
8723.A-Z	Classes, A-Z
	For list of Cutter numbers, see Table P-PZ20 23.A+
8725.A-Z	Individual characters, A-Z
	For list of Cutter numbers, see Table P-PZ20 25.A+
	Biography
8727	Collective
	By period see PR8735+
8727.22	Individual
	see numbers for individual authors or works under
	English literature, e.g. PR1509+ ; PR1803+ ; etc.
8729	Memoirs, letters, etc.
8731	Literary landmarks. Homes and haunts of authors
8733	Women authors. Literary relations of women
8734.A-Z	Other classes of authors, A-Z
	For list of Cutter numbers, see Table P-PZ20 34.A+
	By period
8735	Origins
	Medieval
8738	General works
8739	Addresses, essays, lectures
8740	Special subjects (not A-Z)
	Modern
	Renaissance
8744	General works
8745	Addresses, essays, lectures
8746	Special subjects (not A-Z)
	16th-18th century
8747	General works
8748	Addresses, essays, lectures
8749	Special subjects (not A-Z)
	19th century
	Including the Irish literary revival
8750	General works
8751	Addresses, essays, lectures
8752	Special subjects (not A-Z)
	20th century
8753	General works
8754	Addresses, essays, lectures
8755	Special subjects (not A-Z)
	21st century

English literature: Provincial, local, etc.
  Ireland
    History and criticism
    By period
      Modern
        21st century -- Continued

8756	General works
8757	Special subjects (not A-Z)
	Poetry
8761	General works
	Medieval see PR8738+
	Modern
8767	16th-18th century
8769	(18th and) 19th century
8771	20th century
8772	21st century
	Special forms or subjects
8777	Epic
8779	Lyric
8780	Popular poetry. Ballads, etc.
8781.A-Z	Other, A-Z
	For list of Cutter numbers, see Table P-PZ20 81.A+
	Drama
8783	General works
8785	Early to 1800
8787	19th century
8789	20th century
8790	21st century
8793.A-Z	Special forms, A-Z
	For list of Cutter numbers, see Table P-PZ20 93.A+
8795.A-Z	Special subjects, A-Z
	For list of Cutter numbers, see Table P-PZ20 95.A+
	Prose. Fiction
8797	General works
8799	Early to 1800
8801	19th century
8803	20th century
8803.2	21st century
8804	Short stories
8807.A-Z	Special topics, A-Z
	For additional Cutter numbers, see Table P-PZ20 107.A+
8807.I7	Ireland. Irish life in fiction
	Other forms
8809	Oratory
8810	Diaries
8811	Letters
8813	Essays

	English literature: Provincial, local, etc.
	Ireland
	History and criticism
	Other forms -- Continued
8815	Wit and humor
8817	Miscellaneous
	Folk literature
(8821)	General works
	see subclass GR
(8822)	Collections
	see subclass GR
	Special
8823.A-Z	Special forms, A-Z
8823.D73	Drama
8824	Chapbooks
8824.A2	Collections
8825	Juvenile literature (General)
	For special genres, see the genre
	Collections
8830	Periodicals
8833	Comprehensive collections
8835	Selections. Anthologies
8836.A-Z	Special classes of authors, A-Z
	For list of Cutter numbers, see Table P-PZ20 136.A+
8836.5.A-Z	Special topics, A-Z
	For list of Cutter numbers, see Table P-PZ20 136.5.A+
8837.A-Z	Translations. By language, A-Z
	By period
8840	Medieval
8841	16th-18th centuries
8843	19th century
8844	20th century
8845	21st century
	Local see PR8891+
	Poetry
8848	Periodicals
8850	Comprehensive collections
8851	Selections. Anthologies
8852	Anthologies of poetry for children
	Special classes of authors
8853	Women
8854.A-Z	Other, A-Z
	For list of Cutter numbers, see Table P-PZ20 154.A+
	By period
8855	Medieval
8856	15th-18th centuries
8857	19th century

English literature: Provincial, local, etc.
  Ireland
    Collections
      Poetry
        By period -- Continued

8858	20th century
8858.2	21st century
	Special. By form or subject
	Ballads see PR1181+
8861.A-Z	Other, A-Z
	For list of Cutter numbers, see Table P-PZ20 161.A+
8863.A-Z	Translations. By language, A-Z
	Drama
8864	Comprehensive collections
8865	Selections. Anthologies
8865.5	Stories, plots, etc.
8865.7.A-Z	Special classes of authors, A-Z
	For list of Cutter numbers, see Table P-PZ20 165.7.A+
	By period
8866	To 1800
8867	19th century
8869	20th century
8869.2	21st century
8870.A-Z	Special forms or subjects, A-Z
	For list of Cutter numbers, see Table P-PZ20 170.A+
8871.A-Z	Translations. By language, A-Z
	Prose
8873	General prose collections
8874.A-Z	Special. By form or subject, A-Z
	For list of Cutter numbers, see Table P-PZ20 174.A+
	Fiction
8875	General collections
8876	Short stories
8876.2.A-Z	Special classes of authors, A-Z
	For list of Cutter numbers, see Table P-PZ20 176.2.A+
8876.3	Digests. Synopses, etc.
8876.5.A-Z	Special. By form or subject, A-Z
	For list of Cutter numbers, see Table P-PZ20 176.5.A+
8877.A-Z	Translations. By language, A-Z
8879	Oratory
8880	Diaries
8881	Letters
8883	Essays
8885	Wit and humor
8887	Miscellany
8888.A-Z	Translations. By language, A-Z

	English literature: Provincial, local, etc.
	Ireland
	Collections -- Continued
(8889)	Folk literature
	see subclass GR
	Local
8891.A-Z	By region, province, county, etc., A-Z
	Subarrange each by Table P-PZ26
8892.A-Z	By city, A-Z
	Subarrange each by Table P-PZ26
8893.A-Z	Foreign countries, A-Z
	Subarrange each by Table P-PZ26
	Individual authors or works
	see numbers for individual authors or works under English literature, e.g. PR1509+ ; PR1803+ ; etc.
8950-8967	Wales (Table P-PZ23 modified)
(8969.A-Z)	Individual authors or works
	see numbers for individual authors or works under English literature, e.g. PR1509+ ; PR1803+ ; etc.
	English literature outside of Great Britain
	Including present and former British colonies and dependencies except the United States
9080-9088.2	General (Table P-PZ24 modified)
	Including the Commonwealth
(9088.5.A-Z)	This number not used
(9089.A-Z)	This number not used
	Europe
9090	General works. History
9091	Collections
	Individual countries
9095-9095.9	Austria (Table P-PZ25)
9100-9100.9	Belgium (Table P-PZ25)
9105-9105.9	France (Table P-PZ25)
9110-9110.9	Germany (Table P-PZ25)
9115-9115.9	Greece (Table P-PZ25)
	Ireland see PR8700+
9120-9120.9	Italy (Table P-PZ25 modified)
9120.9.A-Z	Individual authors or works, A-Z
	Subarrange individual authors by Table P-PZ40 unless otherwise specified
	Subarrange individual works by Table P-PZ43 unless otherwise specified
	e. g.
9120.9.T82	Tucci, Niccolò, 1908- (Table P-PZ40)
9125-9125.9	Malta (Table P-PZ25)
9130-9130.9	Netherlands (Table P-PZ25 modified)

English literature: Provincial, local, etc.
English literature outside of Great Britain
Europe
Individual countries
Netherlands -- Continued

9130.9.A-Z   Individual authors or works, A-Z

Subarrange individual authors by Table P-PZ40 unless otherwise specified

Subarrange individual works by Table P-PZ43 unless otherwise specified

e. g.

9130.9.B87   Buruma, Ian (Table P-PZ40)
9135-9135.9   Portugal (Table P-PZ25 modified)
9135.9.A-Z   Individual authors or works, A-Z

Subarrange individual authors by Table P-PZ40 unless otherwise specified

Subarrange individual works by Table P-PZ43 unless otherwise specified

e. g.

9135.9.P47   Pessoa, Fernando, 1888-1935 (Table P-PZ40)

Search, Alexander see PR9135.9.P47

Scandinavia

9142-9142.9   Denmark (Table P-PZ25)
9143-9143.9   Iceland (Table P-PZ25)
9144-9144.9   Norway (Table P-PZ25)
9145-9145.9   Sweden (Table P-PZ25 modified)
9145.9.A-Z   Individual authors or works, A-Z

Subarrange individual authors by Table P-PZ40 unless otherwise specified

Subarrange individual works by Table P-PZ43 unless otherwise specified

e. g.

9145.9.M85   Munthe, Axel Martin Frederick, 1857-1949 (Table P-PZ40)
9150-9150.9   Soviet Union (Table P-PZ25)
9155-9155.9   Spain (Table P-PZ25)
9160-9160.9   Switzerland (Table P-PZ25)
9165-9165.9   Turkey (Table P-PZ25)
9170.A-Z   Other, A-Z

Under each country:

.x	*General works. History*
.x2	*Collections*
.x3	*Individual authors*

America

9175   General works. History
9177   Collections

Individual countries

	English literature: Provincial, local, etc. English literature outside of Great Britain America Individual countries -- Continued United States see PS1+
9180-9199.4	Canada (Table P-PZ21 modified) For National Library of Canada classification of Canadian literature see PS8001+ Individual authors or works Subarrange each author by Table P-PZ40 unless otherwise specified
9199.2.A-Z	Through 1900, A-Z e. g.
9199.2.A33	Adam, Graeme Mercer, 1839-1912 (Table P-PZ40)
9199.2.A35	Adams, Levi, d. 1832 (Table P-PZ40)
9199.2.A44	Alline, Henry, 1748-1784 (Table P-PZ40)
9199.2.B87	Burke, Johnny, 1851-1930 (Table P-PZ40)
9199.2.C28	Campbell, William Wilfred, 1858-1918 (Table P-PZ40)
9199.2.C3	Carman, Bliss, 1816-1929 (Table P-PZ40) Connor, Ralph, 1860-1937 see PR9199.2.G6
9199.2.C68	Cotes, Everard, Mrs., 1861-1922 (Table P-PZ40)
9199.2.C7	Crawford, Isabella Valancy, 1850-1887 (Table P-PZ40) Dhu, Oscar, 1865-1923 see PR9199.2.M43
9199.2.D7	Drummond, William Henry, 1854-1907 (Table P-PZ40)
9199.2.F37	Farr, Charles Cobbold, 1850-1914 (Table P-PZ40) Forsyth, Jean see PR9199.2.M42
9199.2.F73	Fréchette, Annie Howells (Table P-PZ40)
9199.2.G58	Goldsmith, Oliver, 1794-1861 (Table P-PZ40)
9199.2.G6	Gordon, Charles William, 1860-1937 (Table P-PZ40)
9199.2.H34	Haliburton, Thomas Chandler (Table P-PZ40)
9199.2.H37	Hart, Julia Catherine Beckwith, 1796-1867 (Table P-PZ40)
9199.2.H4	Heavysege, Charles, 1816-1876 (Table P-PZ40)
9199.2.H56	Holmes, Abraham S. (Table P-PZ40)
9199.2.H6	Howe, Joseph, 1804-1873 (Table P-PZ40)
9199.2.H89	Hugghue, Douglas S., 1816-1891 (Table P-PZ40)
9199.2.H93	Hunter-Duvar, John, 1821-1899 (Table P-PZ40)
9199.2.I75	Iroquoise (Table P-PZ40)
9199.2.J64	Johnson, Emily Pauline, 1861-1913 (Table P-PZ40)
9199.2.L3	Lampman, Archibald, 1861-1899 (Table P-PZ40)

English literature: Provincial, local, etc.
  English literature outside of Great Britain
    America
      Individual countries
        Canada
          Individual authors or works
            Through 1900, A-Z -- Continued

9199.2.L44	Leslie, Mary, 1842-1920 (Table P-PZ40)
9199.2.L66	Longmore, George, b. 1793? (Table P-PZ40)
9199.2.M3	McLachlan, Alexander, 1820-1896 (Table P-PZ40)
9199.2.M33	Mair, Charles, 1838-1927 (Table P-PZ40)
9199.2.M35	Martin, George, 1822-1900 (Table P-PZ40)
9199.2.M36	Mason, George, 1829-1893 (Table P-PZ40)
9199.2.M42	McIlwraith, Jean N. (Jean Newton), 1859-1938 (Table P-PZ40)
9199.2.M43	McKay, Angus, 1865-1923 (Table P-PZ40)
9199.2.M65	Moodie, Susanna Strickland, 1803-1885 (Table P-PZ40)
9199.2.M69	Moynihan, Cornelius, 1862-1915 (Table P-PZ40)
9199.2.N38	Native of New-Brunswick (Table P-PZ40)
9199.2.O35	Odell, Jonathan, 1737-1818 (Table P-PZ40)
9199.2.O37	O'Grady, Standish, fl. 1793-1841 (Table P-PZ40)
9199.2.P37	Parker, Gilbert, Sir, bart., 1862-1932 (Table P-PZ40)
9199.2.R53	Richardson, John, 1796-1852 (Table P-PZ40)
9199.2.R6	Roberts, Charles George Douglas, Sir, 1860-1943 (Table P-PZ40)
9199.2.R64	Robertson, Margaret M. (Margaret Murray), 1821-1897 (Table P-PZ40)
9199.2.S16	Sangster, Charles, 1822-1893 (Table P-PZ40)
9199.2.S57	Slader, Arthur (Table P-PZ40)
9199.2.S73	Strachan, John, 1778-1867 (Table P-PZ40)
9199.2.S93	Sui Sin Far, 1865-1914 (Table P-PZ40)
9199.2.T73	Traill, Catherine Parr Strickland, 1802-1899 (Table P-PZ40)
9199.2.V54	Viets, Roger, 1738-1811 (Table P-PZ40)
9199.2.W66	Wood, Joanne E. (Joanne Ellen), 1867-1927 (Table P-PZ40)
9199.3.A-Z	20th century, A-Z

Subarrange each author by Table P-PZ40 unless otherwise specified
e. g.
Akiwenzie-Damm, Kateri, 1965- see PR9199.3.D24
Amboise, Jacqueline d', 1948- see PR9199.3.D23
Ames, Leslie, 1912- see PR9199.3.R5996

English literature: Provincial, local, etc.
  English literature outside of Great Britain
    America
      Individual countries
        Canada
          Individual authors or works
            20th century, A-Z -- Continued

	Austen-Leigh, Joan see PR9199.3.H85
9199.3.B342	Bailey, Shannon (Table P-PZ40)
	Braithwaite, John Victor Maxwell see PR9199.3.B68
9199.3.B68	Braithwaite, Max (Table P-PZ40)
	Cameron, Anne see PR9199.3.H75
	Chambers, Penny see PR9199.3.K417
9199.3.C553	Cody, H.A. (Hiram Alfred), 1872-1948 (Table P-PZ40)
9199.3.C714	Crozier, Lorna, 1948- (Table P-PZ40)
9199.3.D23	D'Amboise, Jacqueline, 1948- (Table P-PZ40)
9199.3.D24	Damm, Kateri, 1965- (Table P-PZ40)
	Dana, Amber, 1912- see PR9199.3.R5996
	Dana, Richard, 1912- see PR9199.3.R5996
	Dana, Rose, 1912- see PR9199.3.R5996
	Daniels, Jan, 1912- see PR9199.3.R5996
9199.3.D28	Davey, Frank (Table P-PZ40)
	Davey, Frankland Wilmot, 1940- see PR9199.3.D28
9199.3.D3	Davies, Robertson, 1913- (Table P-PZ40)
	Davies, William Robertson, 1913- see PR9199.3.D3
9199.3.D373	Dean, Carole (Table P-PZ40)
	Dorset, Ruth, 1912- see PR9199.3.R5996
(9199.3.D8)	Ducornet, Rikki, 1943- (Table P-PZ40) see PS3554.U279
	Eaton, Winnifred, 1879-1954 see PR9199.3.W3689
	Farrow, John, 1947- see PR9199.3.F455
9199.3.F45	Fennario, David (Table P-PZ40)
9199.3.F455	Ferguson, Trevor, 1947- (Table P-PZ40)
9199.3.F535	Fischman, Sheila (Table P-PZ40)
9199.3.F574	Foster, Marion (Table P-PZ40)
9199.3.G45	Gervais, Charles Henry, 1946- (Table P-PZ40)
	Gervais, Marty, 1946- see PR9199.3.G45
9199.3.G49	Gibson, Margaret, 1948- (Table P-PZ40)
	Gilboard, Margaret Gibson, 1948- see PR9199.3.G49
	Gilmer, Ann, 1912- see PR9199.3.R5996
	Giroux, E.X. see PR9199.3.S49

English literature: Provincial, local, etc.
   English literature outside of Great Britain
      America
         Individual countries
           Canada
              Individual authors or works
                20th century, A-Z -- Continued

9199.3.G688	Grainger, Martin Allerdale, 1874-1941 (Table P-PZ40)
9199.3.H4466	Heming, Arthur, 1871-1940 (Table P-PZ40)
	Heming, Arthur Henry see PR9199.3.H4466
	Herk, Aritha van see PR9199.3.V359
	Holmes, John, 1921- see PR9199.3.S6
9199.3.H75	Hubert, Cam (Table P-PZ40)
9199.3.H85	Hurley, Joan Mason (Table P-PZ40)
9199.3.J6276	Jones, Dennis, 1945- (Table P-PZ40)
	Jones, Robert D., 1945- see PR9199.3.J6276
9199.3.K417	Kemp, Penny (Table P-PZ40)
	Kent, Cromwell, 1926- see PR9199.3.S62
9199.3.L367	Leacock, Stephen Butler, 1869-1944 (Table P-PZ40)
	MacEven, Gwendolyn, 1941- see PR9199.3.M313
9199.3.M313	MacEwen, Gwendolyn, 1941- (Table P-PZ40)
9199.3.M32355	Mackay, Isabel Ecclestone, 1875-1929 (Table P-PZ40)
9199.3.M4237	McClung, Nellie L., 1873-1951 (Table P-PZ40)
	McCormack, Charlotte, 1912- see PR9199.3.R5996
9199.3.M424	McCrae, John, 1872-1918 (Table P-PZ40)
	McLeod, J.B. Thornton see PR9199.3.T48
9199.3.M493	Minni, C.D. (C. Dino), 1942- (Table P-PZ40)
	Minni, Dino, 1942- see PR9199.3.M493
9199.3.M6	Montgomery, Lucy Maud, 1874-1942 (Table P-PZ40)
9199.3.O343	O'Grady, Rohan, 1922- (Table P-PZ40)
	Percy, Bill see PR9199.3.P427
9199.3.P427	Percy, H.R. (Table P-PZ40)
	Percy, Herbert R. see PR9199.3.P427
9199.3.P8	Purdy, Al, 1918- (Table P-PZ40)
	Purdy, Alfred Wellington, 1918- see PR9199.3.P8
	Randolph, Ellen, 1912- see PR9199.3.R5996
9199.3.R47	Richardson, R.L. (Table P-PZ40)
	Rikki, 1943- see PS3554.U279
	Roberts, Daniel, 1912- see PR9199.3.R5996
	Roberts, Ernest Albert Kevin see PR9199.3.R528
9199.3.R528	Roberts, Kevin (Table P-PZ40)

English literature: Provincial, local, etc.
  English literature outside of Great Britain
    America
      Individual countries
        Canada
          Individual authors or works
            20th century, A-Z -- Continued

	Ross, Clarissa, 1912- see PR9199.3.R5996
	Ross, Dana, 1912- see PR9199.3.R5996
	Ross, Marilyn, 1912- see PR9199.3.R5996
9199.3.R5996	Ross, W.E.D. (William Edward Daniel), 1912- (Table P-PZ40)
	Rossiter, Jane, 1912- see PR9199.3.R5996
9199.3.S248	Saunders, Marshall, 1861-1947 (Table P-PZ40)
	Sauvage, Tristan, 1924- see PR9199.3.S29
9199.3.S29	Schwarz, Arturo, 1924- (Table P-PZ40)
9199.3.S33	Scott, Duncan Campbell, 1862-1947 (Table P-PZ40)
9199.3.S45	Service, Robert W. (Robert Wiliam), 1874-1958 (Table P-PZ40)
9199.3.S49	Shannon, Doris (Table P-PZ40)
	Shea, Shirley see PR9199.3.F574
	Sheedy, Edna, 1939- see PR9199.3.D373
	Skinner, June O'Grady, 1922- see PR9199.3.O343
9199.3.S6	Souster, Raymond, 1921- (Table P-PZ40)
9199.3.S62	Sparshott, Francis Edward, 1926- (Table P-PZ40)
	Steele, Tex, 1912- see PR9199.3.R5996
9199.3.S854	Sullivan, Alan, 1868-1947 (Table P-PZ40)
9199.3.T474	Thomson, Edward William, 1849-1924 (Table P-PZ40)
9199.3.T48	Thornton, Joan (Table P-PZ40)
9199.3.V359	Van Herk, Aritha, 1954- (Table P-PZ40)
9199.3.W3689	Watanna, Onoto, 1879-1954 (Table P-PZ40)
9199.3.W375	Watson, James Wreford (Table P-PZ40)
	Wayman, Thomas Ethan, 1945- see PR9199.3.W39
9199.3.W39	Wayman, Tom, 1945- (Table P-PZ40)
	Williams, Rose see PR9199.3.R5996
	Wiper, David William see PR9199.3.F45
9199.4.A-Z	21st century, A-Z
	Subarrange each author by Table P-PZ40 unless otherwise specified
	Latin America
9200-9200.9	Mexico (Table P-PZ25)
9205-9205.82	Caribbean area (Table P-PZ25 modified)
(9205.85.A-Z)	This number not used

	English literature: Provincial, local, etc.
	English literature outside of Great Britain
	America
	Individual countries
	Latin America
	Caribbean area -- Continued
(9205.9.A-Z)	This number not used
	West Indies
9210-9218.2	General (Table P-PZ24 modified)
(9218.5.A-Z)	This number not used
(9219.A-Z)	This number not used
9220-9220.9	Bahamas (Table P-PZ25)
9230-9230.9	Barbados (Table P-PZ25 modified)
9230.9.A-Z	Individual authors or works, A-Z
	Subarrange individual authors by Table P-PZ40
	unless otherwise specified
	Subarrange individual works by Table P-PZ43
	unless otherwise specified
	e. g.
9230.9.B7	Brathwaite, J. Ashton (Table P-PZ40)
	Kwamdela, Odimumba see PR9230.9.B7
9240-9240.9	Cuba (Table P-PZ25)
9250-9250.9	Dominican Republic (Table P-PZ25)
9260-9260.9	Haiti (Table P-PZ25)
9265-9265.9	Jamaica (Table P-PZ25 modified)
9265.9.A-Z	Individual authors or works, A-Z
	Subarrange individual authors by Table P-PZ40
	unless otherwise specified
	Subarrange individual works by Table P-PZ43
	unless otherwise specified
	e. g.
9265.9.D43	Dedi Shakka Gyata (Table P-PZ40)
9265.9.P37	Perkins, Cyrus Francis, b. 1813 (Table P-PZ40)
	Wellington, Melvyn Mykeal see PR9265.9.D43
	Puerto Rico see PS1+
9272-9272.9	Trinidad (Table P-PZ25 modified)
9272.9.A-Z	Individual authors or works, A-Z
	Subarrange individual authors by Table P-PZ40
	unless otherwise specified
	Subarrange individual works by Table P-PZ43
	unless otherwise specified
	e. g.
9272.9.B55	Boissiere, Ralph de, 1907- (Table P-PZ40)
9272.9.D37	Darklight, Senya (Table P-PZ40)
	De Boissiere, Ralph, 1907- see PR9272.9.B55
	O'Connor, Anthony Michael Gerard, 1951- see PR9272.9.D37

English literature: Provincial, local, etc.
   English literature outside of Great Britain
     America
       Individual countries
         Latin America
           West Indies
             Trinidad
               Individual authors, A-Z -- Continued

9272.9.P48	Philip, Maxwell, 1829-1888 (Table P-PZ40)
	Virgin Islands of the United States see PS1+
9275.A-Z	Other, A-Z
9275.A52-.A523	Anquilla (Table PR7)
9275.A58-.A583	Antigua and Barbada (Table PR7)
9275.A72-.A723	Aruba (Table PR7)
9275.B74-.B743	British Virgin Islands (Table PR7)
9275.C39-.C393	Cayman Islands (Table PR7)
9275.D65-.D653	Dominica (Table PR7)
9275.G7-.G73	Grenada (Table PR7)
9275.M65-.M653	Montserrat (Table PR7)
9275.N58-.N583	Netherlands Antilles (Table PR7)
9275.S23-.S233	Saba (Table PR7)
9275.S24-.S243	Saint Croix (Table PR7)
9275.S26-.S263	Saint Kitts and Nevis (Table PR7)
9275.S27-.S273	Saint Lucia (Table PR7)
9275.S28-.S283	Saint Martin (Table PR7)
9275.S29-.S293	Saint Vincent (Table PR7)
	Central America
9280-9280.9	Belize (Table P-PZ25)
9283-9283.9	Costa Rica (Table P-PZ25)
9286-9286.9	Guatemala (Table P-PZ25)
9289-9289.9	Honduras (Table P-PZ25)
9292-9292.9	Nicaragua (Table P-PZ25)
9295-9295.9	Panama (Table P-PZ25 modified)
9295.9.A-Z	Individual authors, A-Z
	e. g.
9295.9.K67	Koster, R.M., 1934- (Table P-PZ40)
9298-9298.9	El Salvador (Table P-PZ25)
	South America
9300-9300.9	Argentina (Table P-PZ25)
9303-9303.9	Bolivia (Table P-PZ25)
9306-9306.9	Brazil (Table P-PZ25)
9309-9309.9	Chile (Table P-PZ25)
9312-9312.9	Colombia (Table P-PZ25)
9315-9315.9	Ecuador (Table P-PZ25)
9318-9318.9	French Guiana (Table P-PZ25)
9320-9320.9	Guyana (Table P-PZ25 modified)

	English literature: Provincial, local, etc.
	English literature outside of Great Britain
	America
	Individual countries
	Latin America
	South America
	Guyana -- Continued
9320.9.A-Z	Individual authors, A-Z
	Subarrange each author by Table P-PZ40 unless otherwise specified
	e. g.
	Arlen, Leslie see PR9320.9.N5
	Cade, Robin see PR9320.9.N5
	Grange, Peter see PR9320.9.N5
	Gray, Caroline see PR9320.9.N5
	Harris, Theodore Wilson see PR9320.9.H3
9320.9.H3	Harris, Wilson (Table P-PZ40)
	Logan, Mark see PR9320.9.N5
	Nicholson, Christina see PR9320.9.N5
9320.9.N5	Nicole, Christopher (Table P-PZ40)
	York, Alison see PR9320.9.N5
	York, Andrew see PR9320.9.N5
9323-9323.9	Paraguay (Table P-PZ25)
9325-9325.9	Peru (Table P-PZ25)
9328-9328.9	Suriname (Dutch Guiana) (Table P-PZ25)
9331-9331.9	Uruguay (Table P-PZ25)
9333-9333.9	Venezuela (Table P-PZ25)
	Africa
9340-9348.2	General (Table P-PZ24 modified)
(9348.5.A-Z)	This number not used
(9349.A-Z)	This number not used
	Individual countries
9350-9369.4	South Africa (Table P-PZ21 modified)
	Individual authors
9369.2.A-Z	Through 1900, A-Z
	Subarrange each author by Table P-PZ40 unless otherwise specified
	e. g.
9369.2.C64	Colenso, Frances Ellen, 1849-1887 (Table P-PZ40)
9369.2.S37	Schreiner, Olive, 1855-1920 (Table P-PZ40)
	Wylde, Atherton, 1849-1887 see PR9369.2.C64
	Zandile, 1849-1887 see PR9369.2.C64
9369.3.A-Z	20th century, A-Z
	Subarrange each author by Table P-PZ40 unless otherwise specified
	e. g.

English literature: Provincial, local, etc.
English literature outside of Great Britain
Africa
Individual countries
South Africa
Individual authors
20th century, A-Z -- Continued
Jordan, Lee see PR9369.3.S3

9369.3.S3	Scholefield, Alan (Table P-PZ40)
9369.3.S35	Scully, William Charles (Table P-PZ40)
9369.4.A-Z	21st century, A-Z

Subarrange each author by Table P-PZ40 unless
otherwise specified
e. g.

9369.4.S35	Schimmel, Gail (Table P-PZ40)

Van Onselen, Gail see PR9369.4.S35

9372-9372.9	Cameroon. Cameroun (Table P-PZ25)
9375-9375.9	Egypt (Table P-PZ25)
9378-9378.9	Gambia (Table P-PZ25)
9379-9379.9	Ghana (Table P-PZ25 modified)
9379.9.A-Z	Individual authors or works, A-Z

Subarrange individual authors by Table P-PZ40 unless
otherwise specified
Subarrange individual works by Table P-PZ43 unless
otherwise specified
e.g.

9379.9.O76	Oppong, Peggy (Table P-PZ40)

Safo, Margaret see PR9379.9.O76

9381-9381.9	Kenya (Table P-PZ25 modified)
9381.9.A-Z	Individual authors or works, A-Z

Subarrange individual authors by Table P-PZ40 unless
otherwise specified
Subarrange individual works by Table P-PZ43 unless
otherwise specified
e. g.

9381.9.D42	De Silva, Hazel (Table P-PZ40)

Mugot, Hazel see PR9381.9.D42

9384-9384.9	Liberia (Table P-PZ25 modified)
9384.9.A-Z	Individual authors or works, A-Z

Subarrange individual authors by Table P-PZ40 unless
otherwise specified
Subarrange individual works by Table P-PZ43 unless
otherwise specified
e.g.

9384.9.W35	Walters, Joseph J. (Joseph Jeffrey), d. 1894 (Table P-PZ40)
9385-9385.9	Malawi (Table P-PZ25)

English literature: Provincial, local, etc.
   English literature outside of Great Britain
      Africa
         Individual countries -- Continued

9387-9387.9	Nigeria (Table P-PZ25 modified)
9387.9.A-Z	Individual authors or works, A-Z

             Subarrange individual authors by Table P-PZ40 unless
               otherwise specified
             Subarrange individual works by Table P-PZ43 unless
               otherwise specified
             e. g.

9387.9.I34	Ighavini, Dickson, 1949- (Table P-PZ40)
	Krugga, Leslie P., 1949- see PR9387.9.I34
	Launko, Okinba see PR9387.9.O85
9387.9.O85	Osofisan, Femi (Table P-PZ40)
9390-9390.9	Zimbabwe (Table P-PZ25 modified)
9390.9.A-Z	Individual authors or works, A-Z

             Subarrange individual authors by Table P-PZ40 unless
               otherwise specified
             Subarrange individual works by Table P-PZ43 unless
               otherwise specified
             e. g.

9390.9.C74	Cripps, Arthur Shearly, 1869-1952 (Table P-PZ40)
9393-9393.9	Sierra Leone (Table P-PZ25)
9396-9396.9	Somalia (Table P-PZ25)
9399-9399.9	Tanzania (Table P-PZ25)
9402-9402.9	Uganda (Table P-PZ25)
9405-9405.9	Zambia (Table P-PZ25)
	Zimbabwe see PR9390+
9408.A-Z	Other, A-Z
9408.A5-.A53	Angola (Table PR7)
9408.B68-.B683	Botswana (Table PR7)
9408.B92-.B923	Burkina Faso (Table PR7)
9408.E65-.E653	Eritrea (Table PR7)
9408.E8-.E83	Ethiopia (Table PR7)
9408.L4-.L43	Lesotho (Table PR7)
9408.M25-.M253	Mali (Table PR7)
(9408.M3-.M33)	Mauritius
	see PR9680.M3+
9408.M67-.M673	Morocco (Table PR7)
9408.N36-.N363	Namibia (South-West Africa) (Table PR7)
9408.R8-.R83	Rwanda (Table PR7)
9408.S8-.S83	Sudan (Table PR7)
9408.S9-.S93	Swaziland (Table PR7)
	Asia. The Orient
9410-9418.2	General (Table P-PZ24 modified)
(9418.5.A-Z)	This number not used

English literature: Provincial, local, etc.
English literature outside of Great Britain
Asia. The Orient
General -- Continued

(9419.A-Z)	This number not used
	Individual countries
9420-9420.9	Bangladesh (Table P-PZ25)
9424-9424.9	Bhutan (Table P-PZ25)
9430-9430.9	Burma. Myanmar (Table P-PZ25)
9440-9440.9	Sri Lanka (Table P-PZ25)
9450-9450.9	China (Table P-PZ25)
9460-9460.9	Cyprus (Table P-PZ25)
9470-9470.9	Taiwan (Table P-PZ25)
9480-9499.4	India (Table P-PZ21 modified)
	Individual authors
9499.2.A-Z	Through 1900, A-Z
	Subarrange each author by Table P-PZ40 unless otherwise specified
	e. g.
9499.2.C53	Chatterji, Bankim Chandra, 1838-1894 (Table P-PZ40)
9499.2.D38	Day, Lal Behari, 1826-1894 (Table P-PZ40)
9499.2.D47	Derozio, Henry, 1807-1831 (Table P-PZ40)
9499.2.D88	Dutt, Toru, 1856-1877 (Table P-PZ40)
9499.2.M33	Madhaviah, A., 1872-1925 (Table P-PZ40)
9499.2.S85	Sunity Devee, Maharani of Cooch Behar, b. 1864 (Table P-PZ40)
9499.3.A-Z	20th century, A-Z
	Subarrange each author by Table P-PZ40 unless otherwise specified
	e.g.
9499.3.D352	Das, Manmath Nath (Table P-PZ40)
9499.3.G52	Ghose, Aurobindo, 1872-1950 (Table P-PZ40)
9499.3.G53	Ghose, Manmohan, 1869-1924 (Table P-PZ40)
	Murugesan, Murugaiyan Sivanandam Paramaswam, 1939- see PR9499.3.V33
9499.3.T34	Tagore, Sir Rabindranath, 1861-1941 (Table P-PZ40)
9499.3.V33	Vaiyavan (Table P-PZ40)
9500-9500.9	Indonesia (Table P-PZ25)
9507-9507.9	Iran (Table P-PZ25)
9510-9510.9	Israel (Table P-PZ25 modified)
9510.9.A-Z	Individual authors or works, A-Z
	Subarrange individual authors by Table P-PZ40 unless otherwise specified
	Subarrange individual works by Table P-PZ43 unless otherwise specified

PR

English literature: Provincial, local, etc.
English literature outside of Great Britain
Asia. The Orient
Individual countries
Israel
Individual authors, A-Z -- Continued

9510.9.B3	Bar-Zohar, Michael, 1938- (Table P-PZ40)
	Barak, Michael, 1938- see PR9510.9.B3
	Hastings, Michael, 1938 Jan. 30- see PR9510.9.B3
9515-9515.9	Japan (Table P-PZ25)
9520-9520.9	Korea (Table P-PZ25 modified)
9520.9.A-Z	Individual authors or works, A-Z
	Subarrange individual authors by Table P-PZ40 unless otherwise specified
	Subarrange individual works by Table P-PZ43 unless otherwise specified
9520.9.K52	Kim, Kyu-sik, 1881-1950 (Table P-PZ40)
9520.9.S64	Solis Mayora, Eduardo, 1928- (Table P-PZ40)
9530-9530.9	Malaysia (Table P-PZ25 modified)
9530.9.A-Z	Individual authors or works, A-Z
	Subarrange individual authors by Table P-PZ40 unless otherwise specified
	Subarrange individual works by Table P-PZ43 unless otherwise specified
	Min, Dato James Wong Kim, 1922- see PR9530.9.W59
9530.9.W59	Wong, James Kim Min, Dato, 1922- (Table P-PZ40)
	Wong, Kim Min, Dato, 1922- see PR9530.9.W59
	Myanmar see PR9430+
9540-9540.9	Pakistan (Table P-PZ25)
9550-9550.9	Philippines (Table P-PZ25 modified)
9550.9.A-Z	Individual authors or works, A-Z
	Subarrange individual authors by Table P-PZ40 unless otherwise specified
	Subarrange individual works by Table P-PZ43 unless otherwise specified
9550.9.J6	Joaquin, Nick (Table P-PZ40)
	Quijano de Manila see PR9550.9.J6
	Soviet Union see PR9150+
9560-9560.9	Vietnam (Table P-PZ25)
9570.A-Z	Other, A-Z
9570.A3-.A33	Afghanistan (Table PR7)
9570.B34-.B343	Bahrain (Table PR7)
9570.I72-.I723	Iraq (Table PR7)
9570.J65-.J653	Jordan (Table PR7)
9570.L4-.L43	Lebanon (Table PR7)
9570.N4-.N43	Nepal (Table PR7)

English literature: Provincial, local, etc.
English literature outside of Great Britain
Asia. The Orient
Individual countries
Other, A-Z -- Continued

9570.S5-.S53	Singapore (Table PR7)
9570.S64-.S642	South Asia (Table P-PZ26)
9570.S644-.S6442	Southeast Asia (Table P-PZ26)
9570.T5-.T53	Thailand (Table PR7)
9570.T87-.T873	Turkey (Table PR7)
9570.U54-.U543	United Arab Emirates (Table PR7)
9570.Y4-.Y43	Yemen (Table PR7)
9600-9619.4	Australia (Table P-PZ21 modified)
	Individual authors
9619.2.A-Z	Through 1900, A-Z

Subarrange each author by Table P-PZ40 unless
otherwise specified
e. g.

9619.2.A85	Astley, William, 1855-1911 (Table P-PZ40)
9619.2.A88	Atkinson, Louisa, 1834-1872 (Table P-PZ40)
9619.2.B32	Baynton, Barbara (Table P-PZ40)
9619.2.B43	Becke, Louis, 1855-1913 (Table P-PZ40)
	Boldrewood, Rolf, 1826- see PR9619.2.B74
9619.2.B73	Bright, Mary Chavelita Dunne (Table P-PZ40)
9619.2.B74	Browne, Thomas Alexander, 1826-1915 (Table P-PZ40)
9619.2.C34	Cambridge, Ada, 1844-1926 (Table P-PZ40)
9619.2.C36	Carleton, Caroline, 1820-1874 (Table P-PZ40)
9619.2.C38	Cawthorne, W.A. (William Alexander) (Table P-PZ40)
9619.2.C53	Clarke, Marcus Andrew Hislop, 1846-1881 (Table P-PZ40)
9619.2.C57	Cooper, Walter, 1842-1880 (Table P-PZ40)
	Couvreur, Jessie, 1848-1897 see PR9619.2.T38
9619.2.F38	Favenc, Ernest, 1846-1908 (Table P-PZ40)
9619.2.F67	Fortune, Mary, b. 1833 (Table P-PZ40)
9619.2.F87	Furphy, Joseph, 1843-1912 (Table P-PZ40)
9619.2.G5	Gilmore, Mary Cameron, Dame, 1865-1962 (Table P-PZ40)
9619.2.G68	Gordon, Adam Lindsay, 1833-1870 (Table P-PZ40)
9619.2.H24	Halloran, Henry, 1811-1893 (Table P-PZ40)
9619.2.H27	Harpur, Charles, 1813-1868 (Table P-PZ40)
9619.2.H3	Harris, Alexander, 1805-1874 (Table P-PZ40)
9619.2.H45	Hennessey, John David, 1847-1935 (Table P-PZ40)
9619.2.J67	Jose, Arthur W. (Arthur Wilberforce), 1863-l934 (Table P-PZ40)
9619.2.K4	Kendall, Henry, 1839-1882 (Table P-PZ40)
9619.2.K54	Knox, James, d. 1865 (Table P-PZ40)

English literature: Provincial, local, etc.
  English literature outside of Great Britain
    Australia
      Individual authors
        Through 1900, A-Z -- Continued

9619.2.L26	Lang, John, 1817-1864 (Table P-PZ40)
9619.2.L3	Lawson, Henry Archibald Hertzberg, 1867-1922 (Table P-PZ40)
9619.2.L34	Lawson, Louisa, 1848-1920 (Table P-PZ40)
9619.2.L46	Le Maitre, S. (Samuel), 1815-1876 (Table P-PZ40)
9619.2.M35	MacLean, Donald Findlay, 1874-1937 (Table P-PZ40)
9619.2.M355	MacNamara, Francis, 1811-ca. 1868 (Table P-PZ40)
9619.2.M385	Martin, Catherine, 1848-1937 (Table P-PZ40)
9619.2.M47	Meredith, Louisa Anne Twamley, 1812-1895 (Table P-PZ40)
9619.2.M53	Midgley, Alfred, 1849-1930 (Table P-PZ40)
9619.2.N387	Neilson, John, 1844-1922 (Table P-PZ40)
9619.2.P7	Praed, Mrs. Campbell (Rosa Caroline), 1851-1935 (Table P-PZ40)
9619.2.R63	Robinson, Michael Massey, 1744-1826 (Table P-PZ40)
9619.2.R64	Rogers, J. (Table P-PZ40)
9619.2.S69	Spence, Catherine Helen, 1825-1910 (Table P-PZ40)
9619.2.S737	Stenhouse, Nicol Drysdale, 1806-1873 (Table P-PZ40)
9619.2.S76	Sterndale, Handley Bathurst, 1829-1878 (Table P-PZ40)
9619.2.S83	Swan, N. Walter (Nathaniel Walter), 1834-1884 (Table P-PZ40)
9619.2.T38	Tasma, 1848-1897 (Table P-PZ40)
9619.2.T48	Thompson, Charles, 1807-1883 (Table P-PZ40)
9619.2.W34	Walch, Garnett, 1843-1913 (Table P-PZ40)
9619.3.A-Z	20th century, A-Z

Subarrange each author by Table P-PZ40 unless
  otherwise specified
e. g.

9619.3.A1A-.A1Z	Anonymous works. By title, A-Z
9619.3.B26	Bailey, Bert (Table P-PZ40)
	Barnard, Marjorie Faith, 1897- see PR9619.3.E418
9619.3.B453	Bedford, Randolph, 1868-1941 (Table P-PZ40)
9619.3.B68	Brennan, Christopher John, 1870-1932 (Table P-PZ40)
	Brent of Bin Bin see PR9619.3.F68
	Cameron, Ian see PR9619.3.P3
9619.3.C644	Cox, Erle (Table P-PZ40)
	Coyle, William see PR9619.3.K46
	Davies, John Evan Weston see PR9619.3.M3

English literature: Provincial, local, etc.
　English literature outside of Great Britain
　　Australia
　　　Individual authors
　　　　20th century, A-Z -- Continued

	Davis, Arthur Hoey, 1868- see PR9619.3.R7
	Eldershaw, Flora Sydney Patricia, 1897- see PR9619.3.E418
9619.3.E418	Eldershaw, M. Barnard, pseud. (Table P-PZ40)
	Everage, Edna, Dame see PR9619.3.H785
9619.3.F68	Franklin, Miles, 1879-1954 (Table P-PZ40)
	Franklin, Stella Marie Miles Lampe see PR9619.3.F68
	Franklyn, Ross see PR9619.3.H32
9619.3.G33	Garran, Robert, Sir, 1867-1957 (Table P-PZ40)
	Gordon, Donald, 1924- see PR9619.3.P3
	Gordon, Judith, 1936- see PR9619.3.R6
	Green, Judith see PR9619.3.R6
9619.3.H29	Halls, Geraldine (Table P-PZ40)
9619.3.H32	Hardy, Frank J. (Table P-PZ40)
9619.3.H4	Hewett, Dorothy (Table P-PZ40)
9619.3.H785	Humphries, Barry (Table P-PZ40)
	Jacobs, Anna see PR9619.3.J245
9619.3.J245	Jacobs, Sherry-Anne, 1941- (Table P-PZ40)
	Jay, Charlotte, 1919- see PR9619.3.H29
	Jay, Shannah see PR9619.3.J245
	Johnson, Colin, 1938- see PR9619.3.N32
9619.3.K46	Keneally, Thomas (Table P-PZ40)
9619.3.L3516	Lancaster, G.B., 1874-1945 (Table P-PZ40)
9619.3.L352	Lane, William, 1861-1917 (Table P-PZ40)
	Lilley, Dorothy see PR9619.3.H4
9619.3.L5	Lindsay, Norman, 1879-1969 (Table P-PZ40)
	Lyttleton, Edith J., 1874- see PR9619.3.L3516
	Marshall, James Vance, 1924- see PR9619.3.P3
9619.3.M3	Mather, Berkely (Table P-PZ40)
9619.3.M3232	McDougall, J.K. (John Keith), 1867-1957 (Table P-PZ40)
	Miller, John, 1861-1917 see PR9619.3.L352
	Mudrooroo, 1938- see PR9619.3.N32
9619.3.M74	Murdoch, Sir Walter, 1874-1970 (Table P-PZ40)
	Murray, Gilbert, 1866-1957 see PR6025.U74
9619.3.N32	Narogin, Mudrooroo, 1938- (Table P-PZ40)
9619.3.N4	Neilson, John Shaw, 1872-1942 (Table P-PZ40)
9619.3.O3	O'Dowd, Bernard, 1866-1953 (Table P-PZ40)
9619.3.P28	Paterson, Andrew Barton, 1864-1941 (Table P-PZ40)
9619.3.P3	Payne, Donald Gordon, 1924- (Table P-PZ40)
9619.3.P72	Pratt, William Nathaniel, 1847-1933 (Table P-PZ40)

English literature: Provincial, local, etc.

English literature outside of Great Britain

Australia

Individual authors

20th century, A-Z -- Continued

9619.3.P75	Prichard, Katharine Susannah, 1884-1969 (Table P-PZ40)
9619.3.R5	Richardson, Henry Handel, pseud. (Table P-PZ40)
	Robertson, Ethel Florence Lindesay Richardson see PR9619.3.R5
9619.3.R6	Rodriguez, Judith, 1936- (Table P-PZ40)
9619.3.R7	Rudd, Steele, 1868-1935 (Table P-PZ40)
9619.3.S835	Stone, Louis, 1871-1935 (Table P-PZ40)
	Stow, Julian Randolph, 1935- see PR9619.3.S84
9619.3.S84	Stow, Randolph, 1935- (Table P-PZ40)
9619.3.T4	Tennant, Kylie, 1912- (Table P-PZ40)
9619.3.T86	Turner, Ethel Sybil, 1872-1958 (Table P-PZ40)
9619.3.W285	Wallace, Robert, 1938- (Table P-PZ40)
	Wallace-Crabbe, R. Goanna, 1938- see PR9619.3.W285
	Wallace-Crabbe, Robin, 1938- see PR9619.3.W285
9619.4.A-Z	21st century, A-Z
	Subarrange each author by Table P-PZ40 unless otherwise specified
9619.4.A1A-.A1Z	Anonymous works. By title, A-Z
9620-9639.4	New Zealand (Table P-PZ21 modified)
	Individual authors
9639.2.A-Z	Through 1900, A-Z
	Subarrange each author by Table P-PZ40 unless otherwise specified
	e. g.
9639.2.H84	Hume, Fergus, 1859-1932 (Table P-PZ40)
9639.2.P93	Pyke, Vincent, 1827-1894 (Table P-PZ40)
9639.2.R54	Richmond, Mary Elizabeth, b. 1853 (Table P-PZ40)
9639.3.A-Z	20th century, A-Z
	Subarrange each author by Table P-PZ40 unless otherwise specified
	e. g.
9639.3.A1A-.A1Z	Anonymous works. By title, A-Z
9639.3.B43	Bethell, Ursula, 1874-1945 (Table P-PZ40)
9639.3.E38	Eden, Dorothy, 1912- (Table P-PZ40)
9639.3.E83	Escott, Margaret, 1908- (Table P-PZ40)
	Hayes, Evelyn, 1874-1925 see PR9639.3.B43
	Hooper, Hedley Colwill see PR9639.3.H65
9639.3.H65	Hooper, Peter (Table P-PZ40)
9639.3.M258	Mansfield, Katherine, 1888-1923 (Table P-PZ40)
9639.3.M264	Mantell, Laurie (Table P-PZ40)

English literature: Provincial, local, etc.
English literature outside of Great Britain
New Zealand
Individual authors
20th century, A-Z -- Continued
Mantell, Lorraine see PR9639.3.M264
Marsh, Edith Ngaio see PR9639.3.M27

9639.3.M27	Marsh, Ngaio, 1899- (Table P-PZ40)
	Packer, Lewis, 1935- see PR9639.3.P3
9639.3.P3	Packer, Richard, 1935- (Table P-PZ40)
	Paradise, Mary, 1912- see PR9639.3.E38
9639.3.R476	Riddle, Marian Campbell, 1852-1922 (Table P-PZ40)
9639.3.W49	Wilkinson, Iris Guiver, 1906-1939 (Table P-PZ40)
	Pacific islands
9645	History and criticism
9645.5	Collections
9650-9650.9	Fiji (Table P-PZ25)
	Guam see PS1+
	Hawaii see PS1+
9655-9655.9	Papua New Guinea (Table P-PZ25)
9660-9660.9	Tonga (Friendly Islands) (Table P-PZ25)
9665-9665.9	Samoa (Table P-PZ25)
	American Samoa see PS1+
9670.A-Z	Other, A-Z
9670.C6-.C63	Cook Islands (Table PR7)
9670.K57-.K573	Kiribati (Table PR7)
9670.M37-.M373	Marshall Islands (Table PR7)
9670.M63-.M633	Micronesia (Federated States) (Table PR7)
9670.N49-.N493	New Hebrides (Table PR7)
9670.P3-.P33	Palau (Table PR7)
9670.P65-.P653	Polynesia (Table PR7)
9670.S6-.S63	Solomon Islands (Table PR7)
9680.A-Z	Isolated islands, A-Z
9680.B4-.B43	Bermuda (Table PR7)
9680.M25-.M253	Maldives (Table PR7)
9680.M3-.M33	Mauritius (Table PR7)
9680.S45-.S453	Seychelles (Table PR7)

	American literature
1	Periodicals
(3)	Yearbooks
	see PS1
5	Societies
7	Congresses
	Collections
15	Series. Monographs by different authors
	For collected essays, studies, etc., of individual authors see PS121
21	Dictionaries. Encyclopedias
25	Theory and principles of the study of American literature
	History of American literary history
27	General works
29.A-Z	Biography of historians of American literature, A-Z
31	Philosophy, relations, etc.
	Study and teaching
41	General
42	General special
44	By period
47.A-Z	By place, A-Z
49.A-Z	By school, A-Z
51	Literary research
	Criticism
55	Treatises
58	Addresses, essays, lectures
62	History
65.A-Z	Special topics, A-Z
	By period
	Colonial period
71	Treatises. Theory. History
72	Specimens. Selections
	19th century
74	Treatises. Theory. History
75	Specimens. Selections
	20th century
78	Treatises. Theory. History
79	Specimens. Selections
	21st century
80	Treatises. Theory. History
81	Specimens. Selections
	History of American literature
	Periodicals see PS1
	By language
	English
85	Early through 1860
	Recent

History of American literature
  By language
    English
      Recent -- Continued

88	Treatises
92	Compends
94	Outlines, syllabi, tables, charts, etc.
96	Children's books. Stories of American literature

     French

102	Treatises. Compends

     German

106	Treatises. Compends
111.A-Z	Other languages, A-Z
	e. g.
111.I5	Italian
121	Collected essays, studies, etc., of individual authors
124	Individual addresses, essays, lectures, etc.

    Awards, prizes

125	General works
125.5.A-Z	Special, A-Z

    Biography, memoirs, letters, etc.
      Collected biography

126	Early through 1800
128	1801-1900
129	1901-
135	Collected memoirs, letters, etc.

      Memoirs of individual authors
        see the author

137	Iconography: Portraits, monuments, etc.
138	Miscellany: Satire, humor, etc.

    Literary landmarks. Homes and haunts of authors, etc.

141	General
144.A-Z	By place, A-Z

    Special classes of authors
      Women authors
         For women of specific occupations, ethnic groups, etc.
           see PS153.A+

147	General
149	Through 1860
151	1860-
152	Women and literature. Feminine influence
153.A-Z	Other classes of authors, A-Z
	African Americans see PS153.N5
153.A73	Arab Americans
153.A75	Armenian Americans
153.A84	Asian-Americans
	Blacks see PS153.N5

History of American literature
   Special classes of authors
      Other classes of authors, A-Z -- Continued

153.B83	Buddhists
153.C27	Caribbean Americans
153.C3	Catholic authors
153.C45	Chinese Americans
153.C6	Clergy
153.C67	Cowboys
153.C83	Cuban Americans
153.E37	East European Americans
	Friends see PS153.Q34
153.G38	Gays
153.H56	Hispanic Americans
153.H65	Homeless persons
153.I52	Indians, American
153.I78	Irish-Americans
153.I8	Italians
153.J34	Japanese-American authors
153.J4	Jewish
153.K67	Korean American authors
153.L42	Lebanese American authors
153.L46	Lesbians
153.M3	Men
153.M35	Mennonites
153.M4	Mexican-Americans

          Including works about Mexican-American (Chicano)
            authors writing in English or mixed English-Spanish

153.M56	Minorities
153.M66	Mormons
153.N5	Negroes. African Americans. Blacks
153.N57	Newspaper carriers
153.P48	People with disabilities
153.P64	Polish Americans
153.P74	Prisoners
153.P83	Puerto Ricans
153.P87	Puritans
153.Q34	Quakers. Friends
153.S28	Scots. Scottish Americans
153.S39	Sexual minorities (General)

          Cf. PS153.G38 Gays
          Cf. PS153.L46 Lesbians

153.S45	Shaker authors
153.S58	Slovene Americans
153.S68	South Asian Americans
153.V54	Vietnamese Americans
155	Anonymous literature

	History of American literature -- Continued
	Relation to other literatures and countries
157	General
159.A-Z	By country or language, A-Z
	Prefer the country
	e. g.
159.S7	Spain
	Translations of American literature
160	General works
161.A-Z	By language, A-Z
	Collections see PS514+; PS619.A+
	Treatment of special subjects
	For treatment of special subjects by a specific class of author see PS147+
163	Nature
166	Religion
169.A-Z	Other, A-Z
169.A33	Adam (Biblical figure)
169.A42	AIDS (Disease)
169.A47	Allegory
169.A49	American Dream
169.A54	Animals
169.A66	Apocalyptic literature
169.A88	Art
169.A9	Arthurian romances
169.A95	Autobiography
169.B36	Baseball
169.B5	Belief and doubt
169.B54	Benevolence
	Bigotry see PS169.T6
169.B85	Burr, Aaron
169.C35	Cancer
169.C355	Cannibalism
169.C36	Captivity narratives
169.C37	Carnivals
169.C57	Cities and towns
169.C65	Communities
169.C67	Conservatism
169.C75	Crowds
	Determinism see PS169.F68
	Doubt see PS169.B5
169.E25	Ecology. Environment
169.E48	Emotions
169.E53	End of the world
	Environment see PS169.E25
169.E63	Epic
169.E83	Ethics

History of American literature
Treatment of special subjects
Other, A-Z -- Continued
Evil see PS169.G66
169.E94	Experience
169.F34	Failure (Psychology)
169.F35	Family
169.F56	Fly fishing
169.F64	Folklore
169.F68	Free will and determinism
169.F69	Friendship
169.F7	Frontier and pioneer life
169.G37	Gardens
169.G45	Gender
169.G47	Geography
169.G66	Good and evil
169.G75	Grotesque
169.H4	Heroes
169.H5	History. Patriotism
169.H65	Homosexuality
169.H97	Hysteria
169.I45	Imperialism
169.I47	Imprisonment
169.I5	Incest
169.I53	Individualism
	Intolerance see PS169.T6
169.K45	Knowledge, Theory of
169.L35	Landscape
169.L36	Language and languages
169.L37	Law
169.L5	Liberty
169.L56	Liminality
169.L67	Love
169.L95	Lynching
169.M35	Manners and customs
169.M4	Mexico
169.M56	Mines and mineral resources
169.M63	Mock-heroic literature
169.M85	Multilingualism
169.M88	Myth
169.N35	National characteristics
169.N38	Naturalism
169.N65	Nonviolence
169.O73	Oracles
169.P35	Passing (Identity)
169.P36	Patriarchy
	Patriotism see PS169.H5

History of American literature
Treatment of special subjects
Other, A-Z -- Continued

	Pioneer life see PS169.F7
169.P55	Play
169.P63	Popular culture
169.P64	Popular literature
169.P68	Pragmatism
169.P7	Prairies
169.P76	Prodigal son (Parable)
169.P79	Psychic trauma
169.R28	Racism
169.R32	Raleigh's Roanoke colonies, 1584-1590
169.R43	Realism
169.R45	Regionalism
169.R47	Repetition
169.R58	Rivers
169.R6	Romanticism
169.S23	Sacrifice
169.S413	Science
169.S42	Sea
169.S423	Secrecy
169.S425	Self
169.S43	Separation
169.S45	Setting (Literature)
169.S454	Sex
169.S456	Sexual perversion
169.S46	Shame
169.S57	Social problems
169.S62	Sports
169.S83	Subconsciousness
169.S84	The sublime
169.S843	Success
169.S85	Suicide
169.S9	Symbolism
169.S93	Sympathy
169.T37	Teacher-student relationships
169.T4	Technology
169.T44	Temperance
169.T5	Time
169.T6	Toleration and bigotry
169.T74	Travel
169.T78	Truthfulness and falsehood
169.U85	Utopias
169.W27	War
169.W3	Washington, George
169.W34	Water

	History of American literature
	Treatment of special subjects
	Other, A-Z -- Continued
169.W4	The West
169.W55	Wilderness areas
173.A-Z	Treatment of special classes, A-Z
173.A26	Acadians
	African Americans see PS173.N4
173.A35	Aged men. Older men
173.A85	Athletes
	Blacks see PS173.N4
173.B74	Brothers and Sisters
173.B87	Businessmen
173.C63	Coal miners
173.D65	Domestics
173.D88	Dutch Americans
173.E8	Ethnic minorities
	Fur traders see PS173.T73
173.H85	Hunters
173.I6	Indians
173.I75	Irish Americans
173.J4	Jews
173.M36	Men
173.M39	Mexican Americans
173.M68	Mothers
	Mountain men see PS173.T73
173.N4	Negroes. African Americans. Blacks
173.N46	Newspaper carriers
173.N85	Nuns
	Older men see PS173.A35
173.O75	Orphans
173.P7	Provincial types
173.R33	Racially mixed people
173.R87	Rural poor
	Sisters and brothers see PS173.B74
173.T73	Trappers. Fur traders. Mountain men
173.W45	White collar workers
173.W46	Whites
173.W6	Women
	By period
	17th-18th centuries
185	General works
186	General special
	Special periods
191	17th century
193	18th century
195.A-Z	Special topics, A-Z

History of American literature
  By period
    17th-18th centuries
      Special topics, A-Z -- Continued
195.C35   Capitalism
195.I56   Insurance
195.L35   Landscape
195.N35   National characteristics
195.P76   Providence and government of God
195.R55   Rivers
    19th century
201   General works
      Special periods
208   1801-1850
211   1850-1870
214   1870-1900
217.A-Z   Special topics, A-Z
                   Abolitionism see PS217.S55
217.A25   Accidents
217.A32   Addicts
217.A35   Aesthetics
217.A43   Alchemy
217.A45   Alienation
217.A46   Allegory
217.A56   Antarctica
217.A72   Arabs
217.A73   Architecture
217.B55   Blacks
217.B63   Body, Human
217.B65   Bohemianism
217.B75   Brother Jonathan
217.B85   Bunyan, John
217.C34   Canada
217.C36   Captivity narratives
217.C46   Chance
217.C48   Chivalry
217.C5748   Cities and towns
217.C58   Civil War, 1861-1865
217.C64   Collaborative authorship
217.C66   Conjoined twins
217.C85   Culture
217.D43   Death
217.D53   Dialect literature
217.D57   Discoveries
217.D75   Drinking customs
217.E35   Economics
217.E47   Emotions

History of American literature
By period
19th century
Special topics, A-Z -- Continued

217.E68	Equality
217.E75	Ethnology
217.E87	Europe
217.F35	Family
217.F67	Forests
217.G46	Geography
217.G75	Grief
217.H54	Hieroglyphics
217.H57	History
217.H65	Homosexuality
	Human body see PS217.B63
217.H8	Humanism
217.I32	Ice
217.I35	Identity (Psychology)
217.I47	Imperialism
217.I49	Indians
217.I52	Intimacy
217.L37	Law
217.L44	Leisure
217.L47	Letter writing
217.L57	Lists
217.M35	Mary, Blessed Virgin, Saint
217.M37	Masculinity
217.M44	Medicine
217.M47	Mesmerism
217.M57	Miscegenation
217.M58	Mississippi River
217.M62	Modernism
217.M65	Mothers
217.M67	Mourning customs
217.M85	Multilingualism
217.M93	Myth
217.N38	National characteristics
217.N42	Naturalism
217.O33	Occultism
217.P43	Personalism
217.P45	Philosophy
217.P48	Physicians
217.P54	Pluralism (Social sciences)
217.P64	Politics
217.P67	Poverty
217.P85	Puns and punning
217.R4	Realism

History of American literature
By period
19th century
Special topics, A-Z -- Continued

217.R44	Regionalism
217.R6	Romanticism
217.S34	Science
217.S4	Sea
217.S44	Self
217.S46	Senses and sensation
217.S5	Skepticism
217.S55	Slavery
	Including abolitionism
217.S58	Social change
217.S6	Social problems
217.S62	Socialization
217.S65	Spiritualism
217.S92	Subconsciousness
217.S95	Swamps
217.T43	Technology
217.T48	Theodicy
217.T56	Time
217.T7	Transcendentalism
217.T75	Travel
217.T79	Tricksters
217.U8	Utopias
217.W5	Witchcraft
217.W64	Women
	Work see PS217.W66
217.W66	Working class. Work
	20th century
221	General works
	Special periods
223	1900-1945
225	1945-
228.A-Z	Special topics, A-Z
228.A35	Adoption
	Cf. PS228.I69 Interracial adoption
228.A47	Aesthetics
228.A52	Agriculture
228.A57	Airplanes
228.A58	Alcoholism
228.A6	Alienation (Social psychology)
228.A65	Apocalyptic literature
228.A74	Architecture
228.A77	Art
228.A83	Athletes

History of American literature
  By period
    20th century
      Special topics, A-Z -- Continued

228.A87	Authors and publishers
228.A88	Authorship (as a theme)
228.A95	Automobiles
	Beat generation see PS228.B6
228.B47	Bergson, Henri
228.B6	Bohemianism. Beat generation
228.C34	Calvinism
228.C5	Christianity
228.C53	Cities and towns
228.C54	City life
228.C58	Cold War
228.C59	The comic
228.C596	Communication
228.C6	Communism
228.C63	Confession
228.C65	Consumption (Economics)
228.C68	Counterfeits and counterfeiting
228.C96	Cynicism
228.D43	Death
228.D57	Diseases
228.D74	Drinking of alcoholic beverages
228.E53	Electric signs
228.E55	Emigration and immigration
228.E76	Erotic literature
228.E85	Eugenics
228.E9	Existentialism
228.F35	Fantastic literature
228.F38	Fathers and sons
228.F43	Federal Writers' Project
228.F45	Feminism
228.F48	Fetishism
228.F64	Folklore
228.G38	Gay culture
228.G4	Germany
228.G45	Glamour
228.H57	History
228.H58	Hitler, Adolf
228.H65	Homelessness
228.I6	Imperialism
228.I66	Imprisonment
228.I68	Incest
228.I69	Interracial adoption
228.J39	Jazz

History of American literature
  By period
    20th century
      Special topics, A-Z -- Continued

228.L33	Labor. Working class
228.L36	Landscape
228.L39	Law
228.L47	Lesbianism
228.L58	Little presses
228.M37	Masculinity
228.M57	Miscegenation
228.M63	Modernism
228.M66	Mothers. Mothers and daughters
228.M9	Mythology
228.N38	National characteristics
228.N39	Nature
228.N65	Noise
228.N83	Nuclear warfare
228.O96	Outer space
228.P35	Passing (Identity)
228.P43	Peace
228.P48	Photography
228.P55	Pluralism (Social sciences)
228.P57	Poliomyelitis
228.P6	Politics
228.P67	Popular literature
228.P675	Portuguese
228.P68	Postmodernism
228.P69	Pragmatism
228.P7	Primitive societies
228.P72	Primitivism
228.P73	Protest
228.P74	Psychoanalysis
228.R32	Race
228.R34	Radicalism
228.R36	Rape
228.R38	Realism
228.R4	Regionalism
228.S36	Self
228.S42	Sex
228.S57	Skin
228.S63	Social classes
228.S65	Spirituality
228.S83	Suicide
228.S85	Suspicion
228.S9	Symbolism
228.T42	Technology

	History of American literature
	By period
	20th century
	Special topics, A-Z -- Continued
	Towns see PS228.C53
228.T73	Travel
228.V5	Vietnam War, 1961-1975
228.W37	War
228.W65	Women
	Working class see PS228.L33
	21st century
229	General works
231.A-Z	Special topics, A-Z
231.R34	Racially mixed people
231.S47	September 11 Terrorist Attacks, 2001
	Special regions, states, etc.
	North
241	General works
243	New England
251	Middle states
253.A-.W	Special states, A-W
253.C8	Connecticut
253.D3	Delaware
253.D6	District of Columbia
253.M2	Maine
253.M4	Massachusetts
253.N4	New Hampshire
253.N5	New Jersey
253.N7	New York
253.P4	Pennsylvania
253.R4	Rhode Island
253.V4	Vermont
255.A-Z	Special cities, A-Z
	e. g.
255.B6	Boston
255.N5	New York
255.P5	Philadelphia
	South
261	General works
263	South Atlantic
264	Gulf states
265	Ozark Mountains Region
266.A-.W	Special states, A-W
266.A5	Alabama
266.A8	Arkansas
266.F6	Florida
266.G4	Georgia

PS

History of American literature
  Special regions, states, etc.
    South
      Special states, A-W -- Continued

266.K4	Kentucky
266.L8	Louisiana
266.M3	Maryland
266.M7	Mississippi
266.N8	North Carolina
266.S6	South Carolina
266.T2	Tennessee
266.T4	Texas
266.V5	Virginia
266.W4	West Virginia
267.A-Z	Special cities, A-Z

    West and Central

271	General
273	Middle West
274	Great Plains
275	Mississippi Valley
277	Southwest
279	Rocky Mountain states
281	Pacific states
282	Northwest
283.A-.W	Special states, A-W
283.A4	Alaska
283.A6	Arizona
283.C2	California
283.C6	Colorado
283.H3	Hawaii
283.I2	Idaho
283.I3	Illinois
283.I6	Indiana
283.I8	Iowa
283.K2	Kansas
283.M5	Michigan
283.M6	Minnesota
283.M8	Missouri
283.M9	Montana
283.N2	Nebraska
283.N3	Nevada
283.N6	New Mexico
283.N9	North Dakota
283.O3	Ohio
283.O5	Oklahoma
283.O7	Oregon
283.S8	South Dakota

History of American literature
    Special regions, states, etc.
        West and Central
            Special states, A-W -- Continued

283.U8	Utah
283.W2	Washington
283.W6	Wisconsin
283.W8	Wyoming
285.A-Z	Special cities, A-Z
286.A-Z	Other special regions, A-Z
286.A6	Appalachian region
286.O3	Ohio Valley

    Special forms
        Poetry
            Cf. PS476+ Folk literature

301	Periodicals. Societies. Serials
303	Treatises
305	Addresses, essays, lectures
	Study and teaching. Outlines, syllabi, etc.
306	General works
	Audiovisual aids
306.5.A1-.Z8	General works
306.5.Z9	Catalogs of audiovisual materials
	Special classes of authors see PS147+
309.A-Z	Special forms of poetry, A-Z
309.B55	Blues lyrics
309.C48	Children's poetry
309.D53	Didactic poetry
309.D73	Dramatic monologues
309.E4	Elegies
309.E64	Epic poetry
309.F35	Fantastic poetry
309.F7	Free verse
309.H85	Humorous poetry
309.L8	Lyrics
309.N37	Narrative poetry
309.O25	Occasional verse
309.O33	Odes
309.P37	Pastoral poetry
309.P67	Prose poems
309.P7	Protest poetry
309.S6	Sonnets
309.S75	Sound poetry
309.Y69	Young adult poetry
310.A-Z	Special topics, A-Z
	African Americans see PS310.N4
310.A34	Aged. Older people

History of American literature
  Special forms
    Poetry
      Special topics, A-Z -- Continued

310.A4	AIDS (Disease)
310.A44	Alienation
310.A49	Animals
310.A55	Anti-war poetry
310.A57	Apocalypse
310.A76	Art
310.A83	Athletics
310.B43	Beat generation
	Blacks see PS310.N4
310.B83	Buddhism
310.C48	Childbirth
310.C5	Children
310.C54	Chinese
310.C58	Cities and towns
310.C6	Cold War
310.C62	Colonies
310.C63	Colors
310.C65	Confession
310.C67	Contemplation
310.C73	Creation
310.D35	Dandies
310.D42	Death
310.D74	Dreams
310.E6	Epiphany
310.E8	Evolution
310.F3	Farm life
310.F45	Feminism
310.H57	History
310.H64	Holocaust, Jewish (1939-1945)
310.H66	Homosexuality
310.I5	Imagism
310.I52	Indians
310.I57	Intimacy
310.J39	Jazz
310.L3	Landscape
310.L33	Language and languages
310.L65	Love
310.M37	Metamorphosis
310.M4	Metaphor
310.M57	Modernism
310.M6	Monuments
310.M65	Motion picture actors. Motion pictures
310.M76	Museums

	History of American literature
	Special forms
	Poetry
	Special topics, A-Z -- Continued
310.M8	Music
310.M96	Myth
310.N3	Nature
310.N4	Negroes. African Americans. Blacks
310.N66	Nothingness
310.N83	Nuclear warfare
310.O33	Occultism
	Older people see PS310.A34
310.O73	Order (Philosophy)
310.P3	Patriotism
310.P46	Philosophy
310.P48	Photography
310.P6	Politics
310.P63	Postmodernism
310.P66	Pragmatism
310.P67	Prairies
310.P68	Primitivism
310.P7	Printing
310.P75	Privacy
	Quaker authors see PS153.Q34
310.R34	Race
310.R4	Religion
310.R45	Repetition
310.R66	Romanticism
310.S33	Science
310.S34	Self
310.S44	Sex. Sex role
310.S7	Social problems
310.S85	Subjectivity
310.S87	The Sublime
310.S9	Symbolism
310.T47	Threat (Psychology)
310.T56	Time
310.U85	Utopias
310.V54	Vietnam War, 1961-1975
310.V57	Vision
310.W34	Walking
	Women authors see PS147+
310.W67	Working class
310.W679	World War I
310.W68	World War II
310.Y68	You (The English word)
	By period

History of American literature
 Special forms
  Poetry
   By period -- Continued

312	17th-18th centuries. Colonial period
314	Revolutionary period
	19th century
316	General works
319	Early through 1860
321	Later
323	Later 19th and early 20th centuries
	20th century
323.5	General
324	Through 1960
325	1961-2000
326	21st century
	Drama
330	Dictionaries. Encyclopedias
332	Treatises
334	Addresses, essays, lectures
335	Study and teaching. Outlines, syllabi, etc.
	Special classes of authors see PS147+
336.A-Z	Special forms, A-Z
336.C7	Comedy
336.D5	Didactic
336.M44	Melodrama
336.M65	Monologues. Monodramas
336.O54	One-act plays
336.P3	Passion plays
336.R33	Radio plays
336.T45	Television plays
336.T7	Tragedy
336.T73	Travel
336.V4	Verse drama
338.A-Z	Special topics, A-Z
	African Americans see PS338.N4
338.A74	Asian Americans
	Blacks see PS338.N4
338.C42	Celtic influences
338.C43	Characters and characteristics
338.C47	Chinese Americans
338.E94	Eugenics
338.F35	Family
338.F48	Feminism
338.F6	Foreigners
338.F76	Frontier and pioneer life
338.H56	History

History of American literature
  Special forms
    Drama
      Special topics, A-Z -- Continued

338.H66	Homosexuality
338.I49	Immigrants
338.I53	Indians
338.J4	Jews
338.L6	Loneliness
338.L65	Love
338.M37	Masculinity
338.M44	Memory
338.M46	Men
338.M63	Modernism
338.M65	Mormons
	Motion picture industry see PS338.M67
338.M67	Motion pictures. Motion picture industry
338.N38	Naturalism
338.N4	Negroes. African Americans. Blacks
338.N84	Nuclear warfare
338.O74	Oriental influences
338.O87	Outsiders
338.P4	People with disabilities
	Pioneer life see PS338.F76
338.P6	Politics
338.P67	Postmodernism
338.P74	Pregnancy
338.P76	Prostitutes
338.R42	Realism
338.S6	Small towns
338.S63	Social problems
338.S64	Soldiers
338.S74	Steel industry and trade
338.T43	Technology
338.T45	Temperance
338.V56	Violence
338.W45	Whites
338.W6	Women
338.W65	Work
338.W67	World War II

      By period

341	17th-18th centuries. Colonial period
	19th century
343	Early through 1860
345	Later
	20th century
350	General

	History of American literature
	Special forms
	Drama
	By period
	20th century -- Continued
351	Through 1960
352	1961-2000
353	21st century
	Prose
360	Periodicals. Societies. Serials
362	Treatises
364	Addresses, essays, lectures
	Special classes of authors see PS147+
366.A-Z	Special topics, A-Z
366.A35	African Americans. Blacks
366.A44	Alienation (Social psychology)
366.A74	Asian Americans
366.A88	Autobiography
	Blacks see PS366.A35
366.C4	Characters and characteristics
	Con artists see PS366.S95
366.C67	Country life
366.E58	Environment
366.F76	Frontier and pioneer life
366.J47	Jeremiads
366.J68	Journalism. Press
366.M49	Mexican Americans
366.M55	Minimalism
366.N36	Natural history. Nature
	Negroes see PS366.A35
366.P37	Passing (Identity)
	Press see PS366.J68
366.P75	Prisoners
366.R44	Reportage literature
366.S35	Sentimentalism
366.S4	Sexual deviation
366.S62	Social problems
366.S95	Swindlers and swindling
366.T44	Teenage girls
366.T73	Travel
366.V53	Vietnam War, 1961-1975
366.W58	Wisdom
	By period
367	Early
368	19th century
369	20th century
369.2	21st century

	History of American literature
	Special forms
	Prose -- Continued
	Prose fiction
370	Periodicals. Societies. Serials
371	General works
373	Digests, synopses, etc.
374.A-Z	Special forms and topics, A-Z
374.A24	Abortion
374.A28	Absurd (Philosophy)
374.A3	Adolescence
374.A34	Adultery
374.A35	Adventure stories
374.A37	Aeronautics
	African Americans see PS374.N4
374.A38	Aggressiveness
374.A39	AIDS (Disease)
374.A42	Alcoholism
374.A44	Alienation (Social psychology)
374.A45	Allegory
374.A54	Animals
374.A57	Antiheroes
374.A58	Antinomianism
	Antinuclear movement see PS374.N82
374.A65	Apocalypse
374.A73	Arab-Israeli conflict
374.A75	Archetype (Psychology)
374.A76	Art
374.A78	Arthurian romances
374.A85	Athletes
374.A87	Atomic bomb
374.A88	Autobiographical fiction
374.A94	Automobiles
374.B34	Bachelors
374.B37	Baseball stories
374.B45	Best sellers
374.B55	Bildungsromans
374.B57	Birth control
374.B63	Black English
	Blacks see PS374.N4
374.B64	Body, Human
374.B67	Books and reading
374.B69	Boys
374.B87	Business
374.C34	Cannibalism
374.C36	Capitalism
374.C39	Chance

History of American literature
  Special forms
    Prose
      Prose fiction
        Special forms and topics, A-Z -- Continued

374.C4	Chaotic behavior in systems
374.C43	Characters and characteristics
374.C44	Chicago (Ill.)
374.C45	Children
374.C454	Children's stories
374.C46	Chinese Americans
374.C48	Christian fiction
374.C49	Citizenship
374.C5	City life
374.C53	Civil War, 1861-1865
374.C55	Clergy
	Cloning, Human see PS374.H83
374.C56	Closure
374.C565	Clothing and dress
374.C57	Cold War
	Colleges see PS374.U52
374.C58	Colonies
374.C586	Communities. Community life
374.C59	Conservatism
374.C594	Conspiracies
374.C6	Corruption in politics
374.C68	Counterculture
374.C9	Cybernetics
	Darkness see PS374.L47
374.D29	Daughters
374.D34	Death
374.D35	Demonology. Demoniac possession
374.D36	Depressions
374.D38	Desire
374.D4	Detective and mystery stories
374.D43	Dialogue
374.D45	Difference (Psychology)
374.D5	Dime novels
374.D55	Divorce
374.D57	Domestic fiction
374.D96	Dystopias
374.E4	Economic conditions
374.E65	Epistolary fiction
374.E75	Erotic stories
374.E8	Escape
374.E83	Eschatology
374.E86	Ethics

History of American literature
  Special forms
    Prose
      Prose fiction
        Special forms and topics, A-Z -- Continued

374.E87	Evangelicalism
374.E88	Evolution
374.E9	Existentialism
374.E95	Experimental fiction
374.F24	Failure
374.F26	Fall of man
374.F265	Family violence
374.F27	Fantastic fiction
374.F3	Farm life
374.F35	Fathers
374.F45	Feminism
374.F5	Florida
374.F62	Folklore
374.F63	Food
374.F64	Foreign influences
374.F7	French Canadians
374.F73	Frontier
374.F83	Fugitives from justice
374.F86	Future
374.G35	Gangs
374.G36	Gangsters
374.G45	Ghost stories
374.G55	Girls
374.G63	God
374.G68	Gothic revival
374.G73	Greek Americans
374.G75	Grief
374.G78	Grotesque
374.H27	Hagar (Biblical character)
374.H33	Haunted houses
374.H35	Hawthorne, Nathaniel
374.H47	Heroines
374.H5	Historical fiction
374.H55	Hollywood (Calif.)
374.H56	Holocaust, Jewish (1939-1945)
374.H6	Homicide
374.H63	Homosexuality
374.H67	Horror tales
374.H69	Housewives
374.H83	Human cloning
374.H86	Humorous stories
374.I42	Identity (Psychology)

History of American literature
  Special forms
    Prose
      Prose fiction
        Special forms and topics, A-Z -- Continued

374.I45	Illinois
374.I48	Immigrants
374.I485	Impostors and imposture
374.I49	Indians, American
374.I5	Initiations
374.I53	Inner cities
374.I54	Internationalism
374.I56	Intertextuality
374.I7	Irish
374.I8	Isolation
374.J38	Jazz
374.J48	Jews
374.J68	Journalism
374.K55	Knowledge, Theory of
374.L28	Landscape
374.L34	Law
374.L42	Liberalism
374.L47	Light and darkness
374.L52	Lists
	Lockouts see PS374.S8
374.L56	Loneliness
374.L57	Los Angeles (Calif.)
374.L6	Love
374.M28	Magic realism
374.M32	Mannerism
374.M33	Manners and customs
374.M34	Maps
374.M35	Marriage
374.M37	Masculinity
374.M38	Mass media
374.M39	Material culture
374.M415	Maturation (Psychology)
374.M42	Meaning (Philosophy)
374.M433	Medicine
374.M437	Menstruation
374.M44	Mental illness. Mentally ill
374.M45	Mental disabilities, People with
374.M47	Mentoring
374.M474	Middle class
374.M4837	Mexican Americans
374.M49	Middle age
374.M492	Middle Ages

History of American literature
    Special forms
        Prose
            Prose fiction
                Special forms and topics, A-Z -- Continued

374.M5	Militarism
374.M52	Millennialism
374.M53	Miscegenation
374.M535	Modernism
374.M54	Money
374.M543	Monism
374.M544	Monsters
374.M547	Mothers
374.M55	Motion pictures
	Cf. PN1997.85 Film and video adaptations
374.M6	Mountain life
374.M84	Mulattoes
	Mystery stories see PS374.D4
374.M88	Myth
374.N28	Narcotics
374.N285	Narration (Rhetoric)
374.N29	Naturalism
374.N3	Nature
374.N4	Negroes. African Americans. Blacks
374.N42	Neighborhood
374.N43	New York (N.Y.)
374.N435	New York (State)
374.N45	Newspapers
374.N57	Noble savage
374.N6	Nonfiction novel
374.N65	Nonverbal communication
374.N82	Nuclear warfare. Antinuclear movement
374.O28	Occult fiction. Paranormal fiction
374.O34	Offices
374.O43	Old age
374.O94	Outsiders
374.P35	Paranoia
	Paranormal fiction see PS374.O28
	People with disabilities see PS374.P44
374.P43	Photography
374.P44	Physical disabilities, People with
374.P45	Physics
374.P47	Picaresque literature
374.P5	Pioneers
374.P57	Police
374.P6	Political fiction
374.P625	Pollution

PS

History of American literature
Special forms
Prose
Prose fiction
Special forms and topics, A-Z -- Continued

374.P63	Popular literature
374.P635	Postcolonialism
374.P64	Postmodernism
374.P644	Power (Social sciences)
374.P646	Princesses
374.P647	Privacy
374.P65	Proletariat
374.P67	Prostitutes
374.P69	Psychic trauma
374.P7	Psychological fiction
374.P8	Puritans
374.Q35	Quakers
374.Q47	Quests
374.Q54	Quilting
374.R32	Race
374.R34	Racism
374.R344	Railroad stories
374.R35	Rape
374.R37	Realism
374.R39	Regeneration
374.R4	Regionalism
374.R47	Religion
374.R48	Repression (Psychology)
374.R49	Rescues
374.R5	Return motif
374.R6	Romanticism
374.R67	Rosenberg, Julius and Ethel
374.R87	Rural conditions
374.S15	San Francisco (Calif.)
374.S2	Satire
374.S3	Scandinavians
374.S33	Science
374.S35	Science fiction
374.S38	Scots
374.S4	Sea stories
374.S42	Seduction
374.S44	Self
374.S444	Sensitivity
374.S445	September 11 Terrorist Attacks, 2001
374.S446	Serialized fiction
374.S45	Settings
374.S46	Sex role

History of American literature
  Special forms
    Prose
      Prose fiction
        Special forms and topics, A-Z -- Continued

374.S48	Shamanism
374.S5	Short stories
374.S53	Sidekicks
374.S54	Silence
374.S56	Skin
374.S58	Slavery and slaves
374.S67	Social change
374.S68	Social classes
374.S7	Social problems
374.S714	Social psychology
374.S72	Social values
374.S725	Southampton Insurrection, 1831
374.S73	Space and time
374.S735	Speech
374.S74	Spinsters
374.S76	Sports
374.S766	Steampunk fiction
374.S77	Stereotype (Psychology)
374.S78	Streetcars
374.S8	Strikes and lockouts
374.S82	Suburban life
374.S83	Supernatural
374.S85	Survival
374.S87	Suspense fiction
374.S95	Symbolism
374.S96	Symmetry
374.S97	Sympathy
374.T43	Teachers
374.T434	Technology
374.T44	Television
374.T48	Textual criticism
374.T55	Time
374.T66	The tragic
374.T7	Tricksters
374.T78	Truthfulness. Truth
374.U5	United States
374.U52	Universities and colleges
374.U73	Urban fiction
374.U8	Utopias
374.V35	Vampires
374.V53	Victims
374.V55	Vietnam War, 1961-1975

History of American literature
  Special forms
    Prose
      Prose fiction
        Special forms and topics, A-Z -- Continued

374.V56	Vigilantes
374.V58	Violence
374.W34	Wall Street
374.W35	War stories
374.W355	Washington (D.C.)
374.W36	Waste (Economics)
374.W38	Wealth
374.W39	Weddings
374.W4	The West
374.W45	White women
374.W57	Witchcraft
374.W6	Women
374.W64	Work. Working class
374.W65	World War I
374.W66	World War II
374.Y57	Young adult fiction
374.Y6	Youth

        By period

375	Early
377	19th century
379	20th century
380	21st century

    Oratory

400	General works

      By period

406	Early
407	19th century
408	20th century
408.2	21st century
409	Diaries

    Letters

410	General works

      By period

416	Early
417	19th century
418	20th century
419	21st century

    Essays

420	General works

      By period

426	Early
427	19th century

PS

	History of American literature
	Special forms
	Essays
	By period -- Continued
428	20th century
429	21st century
	Wit and humor. Satire
	For collections see PN6157
430	General works
	By period
436	Early
437	19th century
438	20th century
439	21st century
441	Miscellany. Curiosa. Eccentric literature
	Folk literature
	For general works on folk literature, see GR105+
	Cf. PZ8.1 Juvenile literature (Folklore, legends, romance)
(451)	General works
(461.A-Z)	Special topics, A-Z
	Chapbooks
472	History and criticism
475.A-Z	Special works, A-Z
	e. g.
475.F3	Dr. Faustus
	Poetry. Ballads (Broadsides, etc.)
476	History and criticism
	Collections
477	General works
477.5.A-Z	Special. By form or subject, A-Z
477.5.B37	Bawdy songs
477.5.C45	Children's poetry
477.5.C67	Cowboys
477.5.T6	Toasts
477.5.W37	War songs
478	Special ballads, etc.
490	Juvenile literature (General)
	For special genres, see the genre
	For special subjects, see the subject
	Collections of American literature
501	Periodicals. Societies. Serials
504	General works
	Collections before 1800 see PS530+
507	Selections. Anthologies, etc.
	Cf. PN6075+ Selections for daily reading
508.A-Z	Special classes of authors, A-Z

Collections of American literature
Special classes of authors, A-Z -- Continued

508.A42	Adult child abuse victims
508.A43	Afghan Americans
	African Americans see PS508.N3
508.A44	Aged. Older people
	Anorexia nervosa patients see PS508.E37
508.A67	Arab American authors
508.A7	Armenian authors
508.A8	Asian-American authors
	Blacks see PS508.N3
508.B66	Bookstore employees
508.B74	Breast cancer patients
	Bulimia patients see PS508.E37
508.C27	Caribbean American authors
508.C5	Children
508.C54	Christians
508.C6	College students
508.C83	Cuban Americans
508.C93	Czech American authors
508.D43	Deaf authors
508.E37	Eating disorders patients
	Including anorexia nervosa patients and bulimia patients
508.F53	Filipino American authors
508.F55	Finnish American authors
508.F66	Folklorists
508.F74	French-American authors
508.G36	Gang members
508.G39	Gays
508.H33	Haitian Americans
508.H57	Hispanic Americans
508.H63	Hmong Americans
508.H65	Homeless persons
508.I45	Immigrants
508.I5	Indian authors
508.I69	Iranian American authors
508.I72	Irish-American authors
508.I73	Italian Americans
508.J36	Japanese-American authors
508.J4	Jewish authors
508.K67	Korean Americans
508.L43	Learning disabled
508.L47	Lesbians
508.M35	Medical personnel
508.M37	Mentally ill

Collections of American literature
Special classes of authors, A-Z -- Continued

508.M4	Mexican-American authors
	Including works by Mexican-American (Chicano) authors writing in English or mixed English-Spanish
508.M54	Minority authors
508.M67	Mormon authors
508.N3	Negroes. African Americans. Blacks
508.N38	New literates
508.N39	Newspaper carriers
508.N4	Newspaper contributors
508.N67	Norwegian-American authors
508.N87	Nurses
	Older people see PS508.A44
	Oriental authors see PS508.A8
508.P56	People with disabilities
508.P58	Physicians
508.P7	Prisoners
508.P84	Puerto Rican authors
508.P87	Puritan authors
508.S43	Secondary school students
508.S48	Sexual abuse victims
508.S49	Sexual minorities
508.S6	Soldiers
508.S67	South Asian American authors
508.S83	Stevedores
508.T44	Teenagers
508.T73	Transsexuals
508.V45	Veterans
508.V54	Vietnamese American authors
508.W44	West Indian American authors
508.W5	Whalers
508.W7	Women
508.W73	Working class
508.Y68	Youth
509.A-Z	Special topics (Prose and verse), A-Z
	For collections on special topics by a specific class of author see PS508.A+
509.A25	Accounting
509.A27	Addiction
509.A28	Adoption
509.A29	Adultery
509.A3	Adventure stories
	African Americans see PS509.N4
509.A37	Aging
509.A4	Agriculture
509.A43	AIDS (Disease)

Collections of American literature
    Special topics (Prose and verse), A-Z -- Continued

509.A5	Animals
	Antinuclear movement see PS509.A85
509.A73	Archetype (Psychology)
509.A76	Art
509.A85	Atomic weapons and disarmament
509.A89	Automobile driving. Automobile travel. Automobiles
509.B36	Barbie dolls
509.B37	Baseball
509.B38	Beaches
509.B39	Beatles (Musical group)
509.B5	Birds
	Blacks see PS509.N4
509.B55	Blessing
509.B63	Boats and boating
509.B66	Books and reading
509.B665	Boston (Mass.)
509.B68	Bridges
509.B7	Brooks, Gwendolyn
509.B83	Buddhism
509.C37	Cats
509.C47	Chance
509.C48	Change (Psychology)
509.C5154	Childbirth
509.C518	Childlessness
509.C519	Children and politics
509.C52	Children with disabilities
509.C525	Chocolate
509.C53	Choice (Psychology)
509.C55	Christian literature
509.C56	Christmas
509.C57	City and town life
509.C58	Civilization
	Cocaine see PS509.C587
509.C587	Cocaine habit. Cocaine
509.C59	Computers
509.C593	Condoms
509.C594	Connecticut River
509.C595	Cooking
509.C598	Country life
509.C6	Courage
509.C65	Coyote (Legendary character)
509.C7	Crime. Criminals
509.C82	Cuba
509.D4	Death
509.D44	Deep diving

Collections of American literature
  Special topics (Prose and verse), A-Z -- Continued
    Disarmament see PS509.A85

509.D5	Dissenters
509.D6	Dogs
509.D73	Dreams
509.D75	Drinking customs
509.E3	Ecology, Human
509.E36	Education
509.E54	Encouragement
509.E7	Erotic literature
509.F27	Family
509.F3	Fantasy
509.F34	Fathers and sons
509.F44	Feminism
509.F46	Ferries
509.F5	Fishing
509.F56	Flight
509.F6	Football
509.F63	Fourth of July
509.F64	Fox hunting
509.F67	Frogs
509.F7	Frontier and pioneer life
509.G39	Gardening
509.G5	Ghosts
509.G57	Girls
509.G68	Grail
509.G7	Grandparents
509.H28	Hair
509.H29	Halloween
509.H3	Hand
509.H5	Historical and patriotic
509.H55	Holidays
509.H57	Homosexuality
509.H59	Horror
509.H67	Horses
509.H7	Hosiery, Nylon
509.H78	Hudson River
509.H85	Hunting
509.H87	Hurricane Katrina, 2005
509.I5	Indians
509.I53	Infants
509.I57	Intergenerational relations
509.I578	Interpersonal relations
509.I58	Interplanetary voyages
509.I68	Irish. Ireland
509.I7	Iron and steel workers

Collections of American literature
Special topics (Prose and verse), A-Z -- Continued

509.I73	Italy
509.J33	Jazz
509.J8	Justice
509.K67	Korean War, 1950-1953
509.L3	Landscape
509.L47	Lesbianism
509.L54	Life change events
509.L68	Love
509.L94	Lynching
509.M45	Memorial Day
509.M46	Men
509.M47	Mentally ill
509.M477	Mexico
509.M48	Middle East
509.M5	Minorities
509.M58	Monroe, Marilyn
509.M59	Mormons
509.M6	Mother
509.M65	Motion pictures
509.M67	Motorcycles. Motorcycling. Motorcyclists
509.M83	Murder
509.M87	Myth
509.N3	Nature
509.N4	Negroes. African Americans. Blacks
509.N5	New York City
509.N54	Night
	Nuclear disarmament see PS509.A85
	Nuclear warfare see PS509.A85
	Nylon hosiery see PS509.H7
	Ocean see PS509.S34
509.P28	Paris (France)
	Patriotism see PS509.H5
509.P32	Peace
	People with disabilities see PS509.P58
509.P43	Perception (Philosophy)
509.P45	Personality disorders
509.P58	Physical disabilities, People with
	Pioneer life see PS509.F7
509.P59	Play
509.P6	Poe, Edgar Allan
509.P62	Poker
509.P63	Poor children
509.P64	Popular culture
509.P65	Porches
509.P67	Pregnancy

Collections of American literature
    Special topics (Prose and verse), A-Z -- Continued

509.P675	Presley, Elvis
509.P68	Prince William Sound Region (Alaska)
509.P83	Public libraries
509.Q55	Quilting
509.R3	Railroads
509.R57	River life. Rivers
509.R6	Rome (City)
509.R85	Running
509.S2	Sales personnel
509.S24	Sasquatch
509.S3	Science
509.S34	Sea. Ocean
509.S35	Seashore
509.S36	Seasons
509.S38	September 11 Terrorist Attacks, 2001
509.S42	Sisters
509.S436	Slavery
509.S44	Sleep
509.S46	Social classes
509.S47	Social life and customs
509.S5	Social problems
509.S62	Spiritual life
509.S65	Sports
509.S8	Students
509.S85	Success
509.S87	Summer
509.S88	Surfing
509.T37	Technology
509.T39	Tennis
509.T57	Titanic (Steamship)
509.T63	Tobacco
	Town life see PS509.C57
509.T85	Twenty-first century
509.U45	Unemployed
509.U52	United States
509.V53	Vietnam War, 1961-1975
509.W3	War
509.W44	Weddings
509.W47	The West
509.W55	Wilderness
509.W57	Witchcraft
509.W6	Women
509.W62	Women and animals
509.W63	Women athletes
509.W66	World War II

Collections of American literature
    Special topics (Prose and verse), A-Z -- Continued

509.X24	X, Malcolm
509.Y44	Yellowstone National Park
(511)	Translations from foreign languages (including translations with texts)
	see PN6019+

    Translations of American literature into foreign languages

514	Polyglot
516	French
517	German
519	Italian
525.A-Z	Other, A-Z

    By period
      17th-18th centuries. Colonial

530	Contemporary works
531	Works published since 1800
533	Revolutionary period
535	19th century

      20th century

535.5	General
536	Through 1960
536.2	1961-2000
536.3	21st century

    By region
      Including collections of poetry or prose or both

537	Atlantic Coast of North America. Middle Atlantic States
	Including Atlantic States (Maine to Florida); Middle States; Appalachian Mountains (General)
	For Middle States alone see PS545

      North

538	General works
541	New England
545	Middle States
548.A-.W	By state, A-W
	For list of states see PS253.A+
549.A-Z	By city, A-Z
	e. g.
549.B6	Boston
549.N5	New York
549.P5	Philadelphia

      South

551	General works
553	South Atlantic states
554	Appalachian Mountains, Southern
555	Gulf states
556	Ozark Mountain region

Collections of American literature
　By region
　　South -- Continued
558.A-.W　　　　　By state, A-W
　　　　　　　　　　　For list of states see PS266.A+
559.A-Z　　　　　　By city, A-Z
　　　　　　　　　West and Central
561　　　　　　　　General works
562　　　　　　　　Great Lakes Region
563　　　　　　　　Middle West
564　　　　　　　　Great Plains
565　　　　　　　　Mississippi Valley
566　　　　　　　　Southwest
567　　　　　　　　Rocky Mountain states
569　　　　　　　　Pacific states
570　　　　　　　　Northwest
571.A-.W　　　　　By state, A-W
　　　　　　　　　　　For list of states see PS283.A+
572.A-Z　　　　　　By city, A-Z
574.A-.W　　　　Islands, A-Z
574.A45　　　　　　American Samoa
574.N67　　　　　　Northern Marianas
574.V5　　　　　　Virgin Islands of the United States
　　　　　　　　　　Including Saint Croix, Saint Thomas, and Saint John
　　　　　　　Poetry
580　　　　　　　Periodicals. Societies. Serials
　　　　　　　　Collections published before 1801 see PS601
583　　　　　　　Collections published 1801-1960
584　　　　　　　Collections published 1961-
586　　　　　　　Selections, anthologies, "birthday books," etc.
　　　　　　　　　　For selections from a single author, see the author, e.g.
　　　　　　　　　　　　PS1603, Emerson
　　　　　　　　　Cf. PR1176 English literature
586.3　　　　　　Anthologies of poetry for children
586.5　　　　　　Digests, synopses, etc.
586.8　　　　　　Concordances, dictionaries, indexes, etc.
587　　　　　　　Collections of leaflets and pamphlets not separately
　　　　　　　　　　cataloged
　　　　　　　　Special
589　　　　　　　Women poets
590　　　　　　　Men poets
591.A-Z　　　　　Special groups of authors, A-Z
591.A32　　　　　　Adult child abuse victims
591.A34　　　　　　Adult children of alcoholics
　　　　　　　　　African American authors see PS591.N4
591.A35　　　　　　Aged authors. Older authors
591.A58　　　　　　Anthropologists

Collections of American literature
  Poetry
    Special
      Special groups of authors, A-Z -- Continued

591.A7	Arab American authors
591.A75	Armenian authors
591.A76	Asian-American authors
	Black authors see PS591.N4
591.C27	Cancer patients
591.C3	Catholic authors
	Children see PS591.S3
591.C48	Chinese American authors
591.C65	College students
591.D4	Deaf authors
591.D57	Disabled authors
591.D58	Divers
591.G38	Gay authors
591.G74	Greek American authors
591.H33	Haitian American authors
591.H54	High school students
591.H58	Hispanic American authors
591.I54	Incest victims
591.I55	Indians
591.I69	Irish-American authors
591.I73	Italian American authors
591.J4	Jewish authors
591.K67	Korean American authors
591.L47	Lesbians
591.M43	Mennonite authors
591.M45	Mental patients
591.M49	Mexican Americans
	Including works by Mexican-American (Chicano) authors writing in English or mixed English-Spanish
591.M5445	Minority authors
591.M6	Mormon authors
591.N4	Negroes. African Americans. Blacks
591.N8	Nurses
	Older authors see PS591.A35
	Physically disabled authors see PS591.D57
591.P48	Physicians
591.P63	Poets laureate
591.P64	Polish-American authors
591.P7	Prisoners
591.P8	Puerto Rican authors
591.S3	School children
591.S5	Shaker authors
591.S57	Social workers

Collections of American literature
Poetry
Special
Special groups of authors, A-Z -- Continued

591.S575	Socially disabled people
591.S6	Soldiers
591.S68	South Asian American authors
591.T4	Teachers
591.T45	Teenagers
591.V4	Veterans
591.W65	Working class
593.A-Z	By form
593.C43	Charms
593.C63	Concrete poetry
593.D6	Double dactyls
	Epilogues see PS593.P7
593.E63	Epistolary poetry
	Folk songs see PS593.L8
593.F68	Found poetry
593.F7	Fugitive verse. Newspaper poetry
593.G44	Ghazals
593.H3	Haiku
	Limericks see PN6231.L5
593.L8	Lyrics. Songs
593.N2	Narrative poetry
	Newspaper poetry see PS593.F7
593.O33	Odes
593.P37	Pastoral poetry
593.P7	Prologues and epilogues
593.P75	Prose poems
593.P77	Protest poetry
593.S46	Senryu
593.S5	Songbooks (Popular)
	Songs see PS593.L8
593.S6	Sonnets
593.S67	Sound poetry
593.V4	Vers de société
593.V47	Visual poetry
593.W3	Waka
595.A-Z	By subject, A-Z
595.A22	Abu-Jamal, Mumia
595.A25	Adoption
595.A26	Aeronautics
	African American rimes and songs see PS595.N3
595.A32	African American women
595.A33	Age groups
595.A34	Aged women. Older women

Collections of American literature
  Poetry
    Special
      By subject, A-Z -- Continued

595.A36	AIDS (Disease)
595.A39	Alcoholism
595.A4	Alienation (Social psychology)
595.A42	Alzheimer's disease
595.A43	America
595.A47	Angels
595.A48	Anger
595.A5	Animals
	Animals, Extinct see PS595.E93
595.A55	Anniversaries
595.A58	Antiquities
595.A75	Arts
595.A84	Atomic power
595.A86	Authors
595.A87	Automobiles
595.A89	Autumn
	Babies, Death of see PS595.I54
595.B25	Baby boom generation
595.B33	Baseball
595.B334	Basketball
595.B336	Baths
595.B34	Bears
595.B37	Bells
595.B4	Berryman, John
595.B48	Biography
595.B54	Birds
595.B57	Birthdays
	Black rimes and songs see PS595.N3
595.B6	Blues (Music)
595.B65	Books and reading
595.B73	Breast cancer
595.B76	Brothers and sisters
595.B83	Buddhist poetry
595.C2	Cape Cod
595.C37	Care of the sick
595.C38	Cats
595.C42	Cerebrovascular disease patients
595.C45	Children
595.C47	Christian poetry
595.C48	Christmas
595.C53	Circus
595.C54	City and town life
595.C55	Civil War, 1861-1865

Collections of American literature
   Poetry
      Special
         By subject, A-Z -- Continued

595.C557	Columbine High School (Littleton, Colo.)
595.C56	Communication
595.C565	Conduct of life
595.C567	Conservatism
595.C57	Courage
595.C6	Cowboy verse
595.C75	Crime
	Daughters and fathers see PS595.F387
	Daughters and mothers see PS595.M65
595.D42	Death
	Cf. PS595.I54 Death of infants
595.D45	Denver, John
595.D46	Desserts
595.D5	Dickinson, Emily
	Dinosaurs see PS595.E93
	District of Columbia see PS595.W37
595.D58	Divorce
595.D63	Dogs
595.D76	Dreams
595.E34	Easter
595.E38	Education
595.E54	Emigration and immigration
595.E56	Emotions
595.E76	Erotic
595.E93	Extinct animals
595.F32	Fairy poetry
595.F34	Family
595.F36	Fantasy
595.F38	Farm life
595.F386	Father and child
595.F387	Fathers and daughters
595.F39	Fathers and sons
595.F45	Feminism
595.F56	Financial crises
595.F57	Fire
595.F59	Flight
595.F6	Flowers
595.F65	Food
595.F7	Forests. Trees
595.F74	Friendship
595.G33	Gardens
595.G38	Generosity
595.G4	Geography

Collections of American literature
Poetry
Special
By subject, A-Z -- Continued

595.G44	Ghosts
595.G47	Girls
595.G49	Glenn, John, 1921-
595.G54	Goddesses
595.G57	Good and evil
595.G6	Goudy, Frederic William
595.G73	Grandmothers
595.G75	Grandparents
595.G77	Greece
595.H34	Hair
595.H35	Halloween
595.H37	Hanukkah
595.H5	Historical. Patriotic
595.H6	Holidays
595.H62	Holmes, Sherlock (Fictitious character)
595.H64	Holocaust, Jewish (1939-1945)
595.H645	Home
595.H65	Homosexuality
595.H67	Horses
595.H69	Housekeeping
595.H76	Human rights
595.H8	Humorous verse
595.H87	Hurricane Katrina, 2005
595.I46	Imagination
	Immigration see PS595.E54
595.I53	Incarnation
595.I54	Infants, Death of
595.I56	Insects
595.I57	Interplanetary voyages
595.I63	Iraq War, 2003-2011
595.I67	Ireland
595.I7	Irish-American
595.J34	Jazz
595.J64	John Paul II, Pope
595.K35	Kansas
595.K67	Korean War, 1950-1953
595.L46	Lesbianism
(595.L5)	Little, Malcolm
	see PS595.X24
595.L57	Loss (Psychology)
595.L6	Love
595.L95	Lynching
595.M23	Machinery

Collections of American literature
Poetry
Special
By subject, A-Z -- Continued

595.M24	Magic
595.M25	Maine
595.M3	Marriage
595.M36	Mathematics
595.M43	Medicine
595.M46	Men
595.M5	Mines and mineral resources. Miners. Mine accidents
595.M55	Missions
595.M58	Modjeska, Helena, 1840-1909
595.M62	Monsters
595.M63	Months
595.M635	Moon
595.M64	Mother and child
595.M65	Mothers and daughters
595.M66	Mothers and sons
595.M67	Motion
595.M68	Motion pictures
595.M683	Murder
595.M684	Music
595.M69	Mysticism
595.M74	Mythology
595.N18	Narcotic addicts
595.N22	Nature
595.N3	Negro (African American, Black) rimes and songs
595.N35	Neopaganism
595.N4	New Year
595.N45	New York (N.Y.)
595.N54	Night
595.O23	Obama, Barack
595.O47	Oklahoma City Federal Building Bombing, 1995
595.O5	Old age
	Older women see PS595.A34
595.O87	Outer space
	Patriotic see PS595.H5
595.P37	Parent and child. Parenting
595.P43	Peace
595.P44	Peace Corps (U.S.)
	People wit disabilities see PS595.P58
595.P46	Persian Gulf War, 1991
595.P55	Photography
595.P58	Physical disabilities, People with
595.P6	Play
	Pilgrims see PS595.P8

Collections of American literature
Poetry
Special
By subject, A-Z -- Continued

595.P62	Poetics
595.P63	Poetry as a topic
595.P632	Police
595.P634	Politics
595.P64	Pollution
595.P65	Popular culture
595.P66	Potatoes
595.P72	Presley, Elvis
	Pope John Paul II see PS595.J64
595.P75	Pro-life movement
595.P8	Puritans. Pilgrims
595.Q47	Questions and answers
595.Q48	Quilting
595.R3	Rabbits
595.R32	Race relations
595.R325	Railroads
595.R33	Rain and rainfall
595.R35	Raleigh's Roanoke colonies, 1584-1590
595.R37	Ranch life
	Reading see PS595.B65
595.R4	Religious poetry
595.R47	Retirement
595.R52	Rivers
595.R57	Rock music
595.R6	Rocky Mountain region
595.S34	Schools
595.S348	Science
595.S35	Science fiction
595.S39	The sea
595.S42	Seasons
595.S45	Self-actualization (Psychology)
595.S47	September 11 Terrorist Attacks, 2001 in literature
595.S55	Single people
595.S57	Sisters
595.S65	Slavery
595.S68	Snow
	Social justice see PS595.S75
595.S75	Social problems. Social justice
595.S754	Social psychology
595.S757	Sociology
595.S76	Sodomy
595.S764	Solitude
	Sons and fathers see PS595.F39

Collections of American literature
  Poetry
    Special
      By subject, A-Z -- Continued

595.S767	Spam (Trademark)
595.S768	Spanish Civil War
595.S77	Spiders
595.S78	Sports
595.S79	Spring
595.S82	Success
595.S83	Sufi poetry
595.S85	Summer
595.S87	Sun
595.S94	Supernatural
595.S96	Swine
595.T4	Tea
595.T43	Teddy bears
595.T53	Thanksgiving Day
595.T57	Three Stooges
595.T62	Time
595.T65	Tomatoes
595.T73	Traffic congestion
595.T75	Travel
	Trees see PS595.F7
595.T78	Tsunamis
595.T84	Twentieth century
595.U5	United States
595.V5	Vietnam War, 1961-1975
595.V55	Violence
595.W36	War
595.W37	Washington, D.C.
595.W374	Water
595.W38	Weather
595.W39	The West
595.W395	Whales
595.W398	Whistler, James A. McNeill, 1834-1903
595.W4	White Mountains
595.W45	Winds
595.W5	Winter
595.W59	Women
595.W63	World War I
595.W64	World War II
595.X24	X, Malcolm
595.Z66	Zoo animals
	By period
601	17th-18th centuries. Colonial period
604	Revolutionary period

	Collections of American literature
	Poetry
	By period -- Continued
	19th century
607	General
609	Early through 1860
611	Later
612	Late 19th and early 20th centuries
	20th century
613	General
614	Through 1960
615	1961-2000
617	21st century
	Translations of American poetry
619.A2	Polyglot
619.A5-Z	By language, A-Z
	Drama
623	General
625	Selections, anthologies, etc.
625.5	Anthologies of plays for children and youth
626	Stories, plots, etc.
627.A-Z	Special forms and topics, A-Z
627.A32	Advent
	African Americans see PS627.N4
627.A35	Aged. Aging. Older people
627.A53	AIDS (Disease)
627.B56	Biography
	Blacks see PS627.N4
627.B87	Business
627.C54	Chinese Americans
627.C57	Christmas
627.C62	Coal miners
627.C65	Comedy
627.D42	Death
627.E37	Easter
627.F6	Folk drama. Folklore
627.H55	Historical plays. Patriotic plays
627.H65	Holidays
627.H67	Homosexuality
627.H87	Hurricane Katrina, 2005
627.L46	Lent
627.L48	Lesbians
627.L95	Lynching
627.M42	Medicine
627.M44	Melodrama
627.M5	Minorities
627.M63	Monologues

Collections of American literature
Drama
Special forms and topics, A-Z -- Continued

627.N4	Negroes. African Americans. Blacks
627.N84	Nudism
	Older people see PS627.A35
627.O53	One-act plays
	Patriotic plays see PS627.H55
627.P65	Political plays
627.P74	Presley, Elvis
627.R33	Radio plays
627.R4	Religious drama
627.S38	Science
627.S39	Science fiction plays
627.S4	Sea plays
627.S63	Social problems
627.S7439	Suffragists
627.V47	Verse drama
627.V53	Vietnam War, 1961-1975
627.W37	War stories
627.W66	Women
628.A-Z	Special classes of authors, A-Z
	African American authors see PS628.N4
628.A85	Asian American authors
	Black authors see PS628.N4
628.C55	Children. Youth
628.C82	Cuban American authors
628.H57	Hispanic American authors
628.I53	Indian authors
628.J47	Jewish authors
628.M34	Methodist authors
628.M4	Mexican American authors

Including works by Mexican-American (Chicano) authors
writing in English or mixed English-Spanish

628.M44	Middle Eastern American authors
628.N4	Negro (African American, Black) authors
628.P46	People with disabilities
628.P67	Portuguese American authors
628.P84	Puerto Rican authors
628.W6	Women authors
	By period
631	Early through 1800
632	19th century
634	20th century
634.2	21st century
634.5.A-Z	Translations of American drama. By language, A-Z
	e. g.

	Collections of American literature
	Drama
	Translations of American drama. By language, A-Z --
	Continued
634.5.S7	Spanish
(635)	Minor material of individual authors
	see the author
	Prose (General)
	For prose fiction cataloged before July, 1980 see PZ1+
642	Periodicals. Societies. Serials
643	General
645	Selections, anthologies, etc.
647.A-Z	Special classes of authors, A-Z
647.A35	African Americans. Blacks
647.A72	Arab Americans
647.A74	Armenian Americans
647.A75	Asian Americans
	Blacks see PS647.A35
(647.C3)	Carrier boys
	see PS647.N47
647.C4	Catholics
647.C42	Children
647.C6	College students
647.E85	Ethnic minorities
647.G39	Gays
647.H58	Hispanic American
647.I5	Indians, American
647.I74	Irish Americans
647.I82	Italian Americans
647.J4	Jews
647.K67	Korean Americans
647.L47	Letter carriers
647.M49	Mexican Americans
	Including works by Mexican-American (Chicano) authors
	writing in English or mixed English-Spanish
647.M67	Mormons
647.M8	Mutes
	Negroes see PS647.A35
647.N47	Newspaper carriers
647.O9	Ozark Mountain people
647.P7	Prisoners
647.Q34	Quakers
647.R63	Rock musicians
647.S4	School children
647.T43	Teachers
647.W6	Women
647.Y68	Youth

Collections of American literature

Prose (General) -- Continued

648.A-Z	Special forms and topics, A-Z
648.A29	Abortion
648.A32	Abused women
648.A34	Adolescence
648.A35	Adultery
648.A36	Adventure stories
648.A365	Aeronautics
648.A37	Aging
648.A39	AIDS (Disease)
648.A42	Alcoholics
648.A45	Amish
648.A48	Angels
648.A5	Animals
648.A78	Arthurian romances
648.A82	Athletes
648.A85	Automobiles
648.B37	Baseball
648.B49	Basketball
648.B53	Beowulf (Legendary character)
648.B57	Bisexuality
648.B67	Boxing
648.B84	Buddhism
648.B87	Bureaucracy
648.B89	Business
648.C3	California
648.C35	Camps
648.C38	Cats
648.C415	Chick lit
	Child and parent see PS648.P33
648.C42	Children
648.C43	Christian fiction
648.C45	Christmas stories
648.C48	Circus
648.C5	City and town life
648.C53	Civil rights movement
648.C54	Civil War, 1861-1865
648.C59	Cocaine abuse
648.C64	College stories
648.C65	Computers
648.C66	Confession stories
648.C7	Crime stories
648.C85	Cults
648.D27	Dancing
	Daughters and fathers see PS648.F36
648.D35	Dean, James

Collections of American literature
Prose (General)
Special forms and topics, A-Z -- Continued

648.D4	Detective and mystery stories
648.D43	Developing countries
648.D53	Didactic fiction
648.D55	Dime novels
648.D56	Dinosaurs
648.D58	Divorce
648.D64	Dogs
648.D73	Dragons
648.E3	Ecology, Human
648.E33	Education
648.E48	Elves
648.E7	Erotic stories
648.E95	Exceptional children
648.F24	Faith
648.F27	Family
648.F3	Fantastic fiction
648.F34	Farm life
648.F36	Fathers and daughters
648.F4	Feminism
648.F43	Fetishism
648.F57	Fishing
648.F65	Football
648.F68	Fourth of July celebrations
648.F72	Friendship
648.F74	Frontier and pioneer life
648.F87	Future life
648.G37	Gardens
648.G48	Ghost stories
648.G64	Golf stories
648.G72	Grandmothers
648.G73	Grandparents
648.G74	Greed
648.H22	Halloween
648.H23	Handicapped. People with disabilities
648.H3	Hawaii
648.H4	Heroes
648.H54	Holidays
648.H55	Home
648.H57	Homosexuality
648.H6	Horror tales
648.H64	Horses
648.H84	Humorous stories
648.H86	Hunting stories
648.I53	Indians of North America

Collections of American literature
Prose (General)
Special forms and topics, A-Z -- Continued

648.J29	Japan
648.J33	Jazz musicians
648.J4	Jews
648.J87	Juvenile delinquency
648.K55	Knitting
648.L3	Law and lawyers
648.L47	Lesbianism
648.L53	Life on other planets
648.L6	Love
648.M25	Magic
648.M28	Marriage
648.M3	Mars (Planet)
648.M33	Mathematicians
648.M36	Medicine
648.M365	Men
648.M37	Mennonites
648.M38	Mental illness
648.M4	Mexican Americans
648.M42	Mexico
648.M46	Mississippi River
648.M53	Monroe, Marilyn
648.M54	Monsters
648.M57	Mormons
648.M59	Mothers
648.M6	Motion picture industry
648.M63	Motorcycling
	Mystery stories see PS648.D4
648.N3	Naturalism
648.N32	Nature
648.N38	New England
648.N39	New York (N.Y.)
648.N4	Newspaper prose
648.N47	Night
648.N64	Noir fiction
648.N83	Nuclear warfare
648.N85	Nuns
648.N87	Nurses
648.O33	Occultism
	Outdoor life see PS648.O88
648.O88	Outdoor recreation. Outdoor life
648.O93	Overweight persons
648.P27	Pacific Ocean
648.P33	Parent and child
648.P36	Paris (France)

Collections of American literature
Prose (General)
Special forms and topics, A-Z -- Continued

648.P45	Pennsylvania
	People with disabilities see PS648.H23
648.P6	Politics
648.P65	Presley, Elvis, 1935-1977
648.P67	Priests
648.P7	Prostitution
648.P75	Psychological fiction
648.P77	Psychotherapy
648.Q56	Quilting
648.R3	Railroad stories
648.R4	Reconstruction (Post-Civil War period)
648.R43	Rejection (Psychology)
648.R44	Religious fiction
648.R48	Revenge
648.R63	Rock music
648.R85	Rural youth
648.S24	Sadomasochism
648.S3	Science fiction
648.S36	Scotland
648.S4	Sea stories
648.S47	Sex
648.S5	Short stories
648.S53	Single women
648.S54	Sisters
648.S55	Slavery
648.S58	Social problems
648.S6	Soldiers
648.S78	Sports
648.S85	Spy stories
648.S86	Steampunk fiction
648.S88	Suspense fiction
648.T37	Tattooing
648.T45	Templars
648.T55	Time travel
	Town life see PS648.C5
648.T73	Travel
648.U64	Unicorns
648.U65	United States Highway 66
648.U85	Utopias
648.V35	Vampires
648.V5	Vietnam War, 1961-1975
648.V66	Voodooism
	Voyages and travels see PS648.T73
648.W3	Walking

Collections of American literature
  Prose (General)
    Special forms and topics, A-Z -- Continued

648.W34	War stories
648.W37	Werewolves
648.W4	Western stories
648.W5	Witchcraft
648.W58	Wolf children
648.W6	Women
648.W63	Work
648.W65	World War II
648.Y68	Young adults
648.Z64	Zombiism

    By period

651	Early through 1800
	19th century
653	General
655	Early through 1860
658	Recent
659	20th century
659.2	21st century
659.5.A-Z	Translations of American prose fiction. By language, A-Z

  Oratory

660	Early through 1800
661	1801-
662	General works
662.Z9A-.Z9Z	Individual authors, A-Z
663.A-Z	Special, A-Z
	African American see PS663.N4
	Black see PS663.N4
663.C6	Collegiate
663.C74	Commencement
663.M55	Minority authors
663.N4	Negro. African American. Black
663.P5	Phi Beta Kappa
663.S6	Southern
663.W65	Women authors
664.A-.W	Special states, A-W

    By period

666	17th-18th centuries
667	19th century
668	20th century
668.2	21st century
669	Diaries
	Letters
670	Early through 1800
671	1801-

	Collections of American literature
	Letters -- Continued
672	General works
673.A-Z	Special authors, A-Z
673.C5	Children's letters
673.L7	Love letters
	By period
676	17th-18th centuries
677	19th century
678	20th century
678.2	21st century
	Essays
680	Early through 1800
681	1801-
682	General works
683.A-Z	Special classes of authors, A-Z
683.A35	African American authors. Black authors
	Black authors see PS683.A35
683.C6	College students
683.I83	Italian American authors
683.M49	Mexican American authors
	Negro authors see PS683.A35
683.T45	Teenagers
683.W65	Women
684.A-Z	Special. By topics, A-Z
684.B76	Brothers and sisters
684.C57	Christmas
	Sisters and brothers see PS684.B76
	By period
686	17th-18th centuries
687	19th century
688	20th century
689	21st century
	Individual authors
	Colonial period (17th and 18th centuries)
700	Anonymous works (Table P-PZ28)
701.A3	Adams, John, 1704-1740 (Table P-PZ40)
701.A4	Adams, John (President) (Table P-PZ40)
701.A5	Adams, Samuel (Table P-PZ40)
702	Allston, Washington (Table P-PZ39)
703.A2	Alsop, George (Table P-PZ40)
703.A5	Alsop, Richard (Table P-PZ40)
703.A6	Ames, Nathaniel (Table P-PZ40)
703.A7	Arnold, Josias Lyndon (Table P-PZ40)
703.B3	Bacon, James (Table P-PZ40)
703.B34	Bancroft, Edward, 1744-1821 (Table P-PZ40)
704-705	Barlow, Joel (Table P-PZ36)

Individual authors
Colonial period (17th and 18th centuries) -- Continued

706.B5	Bartlett, Joseph (Table P-PZ40)
707.B2	Barton, Andrew (Table P-PZ40)
707.B4	Belknap, Jeremy, 1744-1798 (Table P-PZ40)
707.B5	Beverly, Robert (Table P-PZ40)
707.B7	Blair, James (Table P-PZ40)
708.B3	Bleecker, Ann Eliza (Table P-PZ40)
708.B5	Breckenridge, Hugh Henry (Table P-PZ40)
708.B7	Bradford, William (Table P-PZ40)
711-712	Bradstreet, Anne (Table P-PZ36)
715.B43	Bradstreet, Bruce (Table P-PZ40)
	Brown, Charles Brockden see PS1130+
715.B6	Brown, William Hill, 1765-1793 (Table P-PZ40)
719	Bruce, David (Table P-PZ39)
721.B3	Bulkeley, Peter (Table P-PZ40)
721.B35	Burke, John, d. 1808 (Table P-PZ40)
721.B5	Byles, Mather (Table P-PZ40)
723-724	Byrd, William (Table P-PZ36)
726.C2	Calef, Robert (Table P-PZ40)
726.C4	Callender, John (Table P-PZ40)
727.C3	Carey, Mathew (Table P-PZ40)
727.C6	Chalkley, Thomas (Table P-PZ40)
727.C8	Chapin, Peletiah (Table P-PZ40)
728.C3	Chauncy, Charles (Table P-PZ40)
728.C4	Church, Benjamin, 1734-1776 (Table P-PZ40)
728.C5	Clap, Roger (Table P-PZ40)
728.C7	Cliffton, William (Table P-PZ40)
728.C75	Cobby, John (Table P-PZ40)
731-732	Cook, Ebenezer (Table P-PZ36)
733.C4	Coombe, Thomas (Table P-PZ40)
734-735	Cotton, John (Table P-PZ36)
736.C32	Cotton, Rowland (Table P-PZ40)
736.C6	Cox, John (Table P-PZ40)
737.C42	Cradock, Thomas, 1718-1770 (Table P-PZ40)
737.C5	Crevecoeur, St. John de (Table P-PZ40)
737.D17	Darby, William, fl. 1665 (Table P-PZ40)
737.D27	Decalves, Alonso, pseud. (Table P-PZ40)
737.D3	Denton, Daniel (Table P-PZ40)
737.D35	Digges, Thomas Attwood, 1742-1821 (Table P-PZ40)
737.D5	Douglass, William (Table P-PZ40)
737.D7	Dummer, Jeremiah (Table P-PZ40)
739	Dwight, Timothy (Table P-PZ39)
741-742	Edwards, Jonathan (Table P-PZ36)
	Cf. B870+ Philosophy
744.E3	Eliot, John (Table P-PZ40)
744.E6	Evans, Nathaniel (Table P-PZ40)

Individual authors
Colonial period (17th and 18th centuries) -- Continued
744.F5   Folger, Peter (Table P-PZ40)
744.F7   Foster, Hannah (Webster) (Table P-PZ40)
                Franklin, Benjamin
                    Cf. B880+ Philosophy
                Collected works see E302.F82
                Literary works
                    Including works consisting of his life written by himself,
                        together with essays (Humorous, moral, and literary)
                        and similar selections
745.A2   By date
745.A3   By editor
745.A6-Z   Translations. By language, A-Z
746   Anthologies. Sayings. Thoughts, etc.
                   Separate works
                       Autobiography (without the "Essays") see E302.6.F7+
                       "Essays" (without the "Life written by himself")
748.A2   By date
748.A5-Z   By editor, A-Z
749   Poor Richard's almanac
749.A2   Collection of original issues
                        Facsimiles. Collections
749.A3   General
749.A4   Separate issues
749.A5   Reprints. By date
749.A6   Selections
749.A7   Adaptations, imitations, spurious issues, etc.
750.A-Z   Other works, A-Z
                       Dissertation on liberty and necessity see BJ1460+
                       Experiments and observations on electricity see QC517
                       Historical review of Pennsylvania see F152
                       Interest of Great Britain considered see E199
                       Observations on the causes and cure of smoky
                            chimneys see TH2284
                       Physical and meteorological observations see QC859
                       Way to health see E302.6.F7+
751   Literary biography. Franklin as a man of letters
                       General biography see E302.F82
752   Criticism
755-759   Freneau, Philip Morin, 1752-1832 (Table P-PZ35)
760.G3   Gardiner, John Sylvester John (Table P-PZ40)
761   Godfrey, Thomas (Table P-PZ39)
763.G5   Gookin, Daniel (Table P-PZ40)
763.G7   Green, Joseph (Table P-PZ40)
763.H35   Hamilton, Alexander, 1712-1756 (Table P-PZ40)

	Individual authors
	Colonial period (17th and 18th centuries) -- Continued
766	Hamilton, Alexander, 1757-1804 (Table P-PZ39)
	Cf. E302.H2+ Collected works
	Cf. E302.6.H2 Biography
767.H15	Hammon, Jupiter (Table P-PZ40)
767.H2	Hammond, John (Table P-PZ40)
768.H5	Higginson, Francis (Table P-PZ40)
768.H57	Hitchcock, Enos (Table P-PZ40)
769.H3	Honeywood, St. John (Table P-PZ40)
771-772	Hooker, Thomas (Table P-PZ36)
773.H7	Hopkins, Lemuel (Table P-PZ40)
775-776	Hopkinson, Francis (Table P-PZ36)
778.H4	Hubbard, William (Table P-PZ40)
778.H5	Humphreys, David (Table P-PZ40)
778.H7	Hutchinson, Thomas (Table P-PZ40)
781-782	Jay, John (Table P-PZ36)
785-789	Jefferson, Thomas (Table P-PZ35)
	Cf. B885 Philosophy
791.J3	Johnson, Edward (Table P-PZ40)
791.J44	Johnson, Thomas, 1760-1820? (Table P-PZ40)
791.J5	Jones, Hugh (Table P-PZ40)
791.J7	Josselyn, John (Table P-PZ40)
791.K5	Knight, Sarah Kemble (Table P-PZ40)
791.L2	Lathrop, Barnabas (Table P-PZ40)
	Lawson, John see F257
791.L25	Lee, Richard (Table P-PZ40)
791.L4	Livingston, William (Table P-PZ40)
791.L6	Logan, James (Table P-PZ40)
791.L7	Low, Samuel, b. 1765 (Table P-PZ40)
	Lucas, Eliza see PS824.P7
793.M3	Mack, Alexander (Table P-PZ40)
795-799	Madison, James (Table P-PZ35)
801.M5	Mansfield, Joseph, 1771-1830 (Table P-PZ40)
801.M7	Markoe, Peter (Table P-PZ40)
802	Mason, John (Table P-PZ39)
804	Mason - Mather
804.M3	Mason, Mrs. (Table P-PZ40)
805	Mather, Cotton (Table P-PZ39)
	Cf. B876.M2+ Philosophy
	Cf. F67 Biography
806.M6	Mather, Increase (Table P-PZ40)
	Cf. F67 Biography
806.M8	Maylem, John (Table P-PZ40)
807.M55	Mitchell, Isaac, 1759?-1812 (Table P-PZ40)
808.M3	Morrell, William (Table P-PZ40)
808.M5	Morton, Nathaniel (Table P-PZ40)

Individual authors
  Colonial period (17th and 18th centuries) -- Continued

808.M7	Morton, Sarah Wentworth (Apthorp) (Table P-PZ40)
808.M75	Munford, Robert, d. 1784 (Table P-PZ40)
808.M78	Munford, William, 1775-1825 (Table P-PZ40)
808.M79	Murdock, John, 1748-1834 (Table P-PZ40)
808.M8	Murray, Judith Sargent, 1751-1820 (Table P-PZ40)
811.N3	Niles, Nathaniel (Table P-PZ40)
811.N5	Norton, John, 1606-1663 (Table P-PZ40)
811.N6	Norton, John, 1651-1716 (Table P-PZ40)
811.N8	Noyes, Nicholas (Table P-PZ40)
813.O2	Oakes, Urian (Table P-PZ40)
813.O4	Odell, Jonathan (Table P-PZ40)
813.O6	Otis, James (Table P-PZ40)
815-819	Paine, Thomas (Table P-PZ35)
	Cf. JC177+ Political theory
820.P2	Parke, John, 1754-1789 (Table P-PZ40)
	Lyric works of Horace see PA6394.A5+
821	Penn, William (Table P-PZ39)
822.P5	Pepper, Henry (Table P-PZ40)
823	Percy, George (Table P-PZ39)
824.P67	Pinchard, Mrs. (Table P-PZ40)
824.P7	Pinckney, Eliza (Lucas) (Table P-PZ40)
	Cf. F272 Biography
824.P8	Porter, Sarah, fl. 1793- (Table P-PZ40)
825	Pory, John (Table P-PZ39)
826	Prime, Benjamin Young, 1733-1791 (Table P-PZ39)
827	Prince, Thomas (Table P-PZ39)
828.Q5	Quincy, Josiah, 1744-1775 (Table P-PZ40)
829.R2	Ralph, James (Table P-PZ40)
829.R3	Relf, Samuel, 1776-1823 (Table P-PZ40)
829.R4	Rich, R. (Table P-PZ40)
829.R5	Richards, George, 1755?-1814 (Table P-PZ40)
829.R6	Rogers, Robert (Table P-PZ40)
829.R8	Rose, Aguila (Table P-PZ40)
829.R9	Rumford, Sir Benjamin Thompson, count (Table P-PZ40)
	Sandys, George see PR2338
	Saunders, Richard see PS745+
836.S3	Scull, Nicholas (Table P-PZ40)
836.S45	Searson, John (Table P-PZ40)
836.S5	Seccomb, John (Table P-PZ40)
836.S7	Sewall, Jonathan Mitchell (Table P-PZ40)
837-838	Sewall, Samuel (Table P-PZ36)
839.S4	Sherburne, Henry, 1741-1825 (Table P-PZ40)
839.S5	Smith, Elihu Hubbard (Table P-PZ40)
839.S7	Smith, John (Table P-PZ40)
	Cf. F229 Biography

Individual authors

Colonial period (17th and 18th centuries) -- Continued

841.S2	Smith, William, 1727-1803 (Table P-PZ40)
841.S3	Smith, William, 1728-1793 (Table P-PZ40)
841.S44	Snowden, Richard, 1753-1825 (Table P-PZ40)
843.S5	Stansbury, Joseph (Table P-PZ40)
843.S74	Steere, Richard, 1643-1721 (Table P-PZ40)
843.S84	Stiles, Ezra, 1727-1795 (Table P-PZ40)
845-846	Stith, William (Table P-PZ36)
847.S4	Stockton, Annis Boudinot, 1736-1801 (Table P-PZ40)
847.S5	Story, Isaac (Table P-PZ40)
848-849	Strachey, William (Table P-PZ36)
850.S8	Swanwich, John, 1740-1798 (Table P-PZ40)
850.T2	Taylor, Edward, 1642-1729 (Table P-PZ40)
850.T3	Thomas, Gabriel (Table P-PZ40)
	Thompson, Benjamin see PS829.R9
850.T45	Tompson, Benjamin, 1642-1714 (Table P-PZ40)
850.T5	Touchstone, Geoffrey, d. 1801 (Table P-PZ40)
852-853	Trumbull, John (Table P-PZ36)
855.T2	Tucker, St. George (Table P-PZ40)
855.T7	Tyler, Royall (Table P-PZ40)
855.V34	Vaill, Joseph, 1751-1838 (Table P-PZ40)
857.W3	Wadsworth, Benjamin (Table P-PZ40)
858.W2	Ward, Nathaniel (Table P-PZ40)
858.W8	Warren, Mercy Otis, 1728-1814 (Table P-PZ38)
860-864	Washington, George (Table P-PZ35)
	Cf. E312+ Biography
866.W5	Wheatley, Phillis (Table P-PZ40)
867-868	Whitaker, Alexander (Table P-PZ36)
869	Whitaker - Wigglesworth
871-872	Wigglesworth, Michael (Table P-PZ36)
874	Williams, Roger (Table P-PZ39)
875.W3	Williams, William, 1727-1791 (Table P-PZ40)
	Wilson, Alexander see PR3765.W55
875.W7	Winchester, Elhanan (Table P-PZ40)
875.W74	Winkfield, Unca Eliza, pseud. (Table P-PZ40)
877-878	Winthrop, John (Table P-PZ36)
881.W5	Wise, John (Table P-PZ40)
885-886	Witherspoon, John (Table P-PZ36)
888.W7	Wolcott, Roger (Table P-PZ40)
889.W5	Wood, William (Table P-PZ40)
891-892	Woolman, John (Table P-PZ36)
893.W7	Worcester, Francis (Table P-PZ40)

19th century

991	Anonymous works (Table P-PZ28)
1000.A3	Abbey, Henry (Table P-PZ40)
1000.A5	Abbott, Charles Conrad (Table P-PZ40)

	Individual authors
	19th century -- Continued
1000.A8	Abbott, Jacob (Table P-PZ40)
1001-1002	Abbott, John Stevens Cabot (Table P-PZ36)
1003.A2	Acton, John (Table P-PZ40)
1003.A3	Adams, A.P. (Table P-PZ40)
1003.A35	Adams, Abigail (Smith) (Table P-PZ40)
1003.A4	Adams, Catharine A. Van Buren (Table P-PZ40)
1003.A45	Adams, Charles Follen ("Yawcob Strauss") (Table P-PZ40)
1003.A5	Adams, Charles Francis (Table P-PZ40)
1003.A6	Adams, E.F. (Table P-PZ40)
1004.A3	Adams, G.Z. (Table P-PZ40)
1004.A35	Adams, George (Table P-PZ40)
1004.A37	Adams, Hannah (Table P-PZ40)
1004.A4	Adams, Henry (Table P-PZ40)
1004.A45	Adams, Henry W. (Table P-PZ40)
1004.A5	Adams, Herbert (Table P-PZ40)
1004.A6	Adams, John Jay (Table P-PZ40)
1005	Adams, John Quincy (Table P-PZ39)
1006.A3	Adams, Miss L.B. (Table P-PZ40)
1006.A32	Adams, Mary (Table P-PZ40)
1006.A33	Adams, Mary (Mathews) (Table P-PZ40)
1006.A4	Adams, Oscar Fay (Table P-PZ40)
1006.A5	Adams, William Taylor, 1822-1897 (Table P-PZ40)
1006.A6	Ade, George (Table P-PZ40)
1006.A615	Adee, David Graham, 1837-1901 (Table P-PZ40)
	Adeler, Max see PS1299.C166
1006.A64	Aermont, Paul, pseud. (Table P-PZ40)
1006.A75	Aiken, George L., 1830-1876 (Table P-PZ40)
1007.A5	Albee, John (Table P-PZ40)
1010-1013	Alcott, Amos Bronson (Table P-PZ35a)
	Including works on the Alcott family
	For Alcott's philosophy see B908.A5+
1015-1018	Alcott, Louisa May (Table P-PZ35a)
1019.A2	Alcott, May (Mrs. Abigail May Nieriker) (Table P-PZ40)
1019.A5	Alden, Isabella (Macdonald) ("Pansy") (Table P-PZ40)
1019.A53	Alden, Joseph, 1807-1885 (Table P-PZ40)
1019.A7	Aldrich, Anne Reeve (Table P-PZ40)
	Aldrich, Thomas Bailey
1020	Collected works (Prose and poetry; collected poems)
1021	Collected prose works
1022	Selected works. Selections
	Subarrange by editor, if given, or date
1024	Poems
1024.B2	Ballad of Babie Bell
1024.B4	Bells
1024.C5	Cloth of gold

	Individual authors
	19th century
	Aldrich, Thomas Bailey
	Poems -- Continued
1024.C6	Course of true love
1024.F5	Flower and thorn
1024.F7	Friar Jerome's beautiful book
1024.J8	Judith and Holofernes
1024.M3	Mercedes and later lyrics
1024.P2	Pampinea
1024.S4	Sister's tragedy
1024.U6	Unguarded gates
1024.W7	Wyndham Towers
1025	Prose works
	From Ponkapog to Pesth see D919
1025.M2	Marjorie Daw and other stories
1025.O4	An old town by the sea
1025.P6	Ponkapog papers
1025.P7	Prudence Palfrey
1025.Q8	Queen of Sheba
1025.S6	Stillwater tragedy
1025.S8	Story of a bad boy
1025.T8	Two bites at a cherry, with other tales
	Biography, criticism, etc.
1026.A1-.A19	Periodicals. Societies. Serials
1026.A2-.A3	Dictionaries, indexes, etc.
1026.A31-.A39	Autobiography, journals, memoirs. By title
1026.A4	Letters (Collections). By date
1026.A41-.A49	Letters to and from particular individuals. By correspondent (alhpabetically)
	Criticism
1027	General works
1028.A-Z	Special, A-Z
	For list Cutter numbers, see Table P-PZ32 17
1029.A17	Alexander, Francesca (Table P-PZ40)
1029.A3	Alger, Horatio (Table P-PZ40)
1029.A5	Allen, Benjamin (Table P-PZ40)
1029.A7	Allen, Elizabeth Akers (Table P-PZ40)
1029.A75	Allen, Fred Raphael (Table P-PZ40)
1030-1038	Allen, James Lane (Table P-PZ33)
1039.A242	Allen, Junius Mordecai (Table P-PZ40)
1039.A25	Allen, William (President of Bowdoin College) (Table P-PZ40)
1039.A265	Allibone, Samuel Austin (Table P-PZ40)
1039.A29	Altgeld, Emma F. (Table P-PZ40)
1039.A32	Ames, Mary (Clemmer) (Table P-PZ40)
1039.A33	Ames, Nathan (Table P-PZ40)

Individual authors
19th century -- Continued

1039.A34	Amory, Thomas Coffin (Table P-PZ40)
1039.A36	Amsbary, Wallace Bruce (Table P-PZ40)
1039.A365	Anagnos, Julia Romana (Howe) (Table P-PZ40)
1039.A39	Andrews, Jane (Table P-PZ40)
1039.A5	Appleton, Thomas Gold (Table P-PZ40)
1039.A7	Arnold, George (Table P-PZ40)
1039.A77	Arthur, Timothy Shay, 1809-1885 (Table P-PZ40)
	Ashton, Warren T., 1822-1897 see PS1006.A5
1039.A87	Astor, John Jacob, 1864-1912 (Table P-PZ40)
1040-1043	Atherton, Gertrude (Horn) (Table P-PZ35a)
1044	Ath - Atz
1044.A38	Atkinson, John Hampton, 1868-1953 (Table P-PZ40)
1049.A	Au - Auss
1049.A5	Auringer, Obadiah Cyrus (Table P-PZ40)
1050-1053	Austin, Jane (Goodwin) (Table P-PZ35a)
1054.A16	Austin, John Osborne, 1849-1918 (Table P-PZ40)
1054.A17	Austin, William (Table P-PZ40)
1054.B3	Bacheller, Irving (Table P-PZ40)
1054.B54	Bacon, Alice Mabel, 1858-1918 (Table P-PZ40)
1054.B57	Bacon, Delia (Table P-PZ40)
1054.B6	Bacon, Ezekiel (Table P-PZ40)
1054.B62	Bacon, Josephine Dodge (Daskam) (Table P-PZ40)
1054.B64	Bacon, William Thompson (Table P-PZ40)
1056.B	Bad - Bag
1057	Bagby, George William (Table P-PZ39)
1059.B	Bah - Bam
1059.B14	Bailey, Margaret Jewett, 1812?-1882 (Table P-PZ40)
1059.B2	Baker, George Augustus (Table P-PZ40)
1059.B4	Baker, William Mumford (Table P-PZ40)
1059.B418	Balch, Elisabeth, 1843-1890 (Table P-PZ40)
1059.B48	Baldwin, James, 1841-1925 (Table P-PZ40)
1059.B6	Balestier, Wolcott (Table P-PZ40)
1059.B86	Bamford, Mary E. (Mary Ellen) (Table P-PZ40)
1060.B	Ban - Bancq
1061	Bancroft, George (Table P-PZ39)
1063.B2	Bancroft, Hubert Howe (Table P-PZ40)
1063.B8	Bandelier, Adolph Francis Alphonse, 1840-1914 (Table P-PZ40)
1064.B3	Bangs, John Kendrick (Table P-PZ40)
1064.B5	Banks, Charles Eugene (Table P-PZ40)
1064.B557	Banning, William L. (Table P-PZ40)
1065.B4	Barbe, Waitman (Table P-PZ40)
1065.B83	Barker, James Nelson (Table P-PZ40)
1065.B9	Barlow, Warren S. (Table P-PZ40)
1066.B3	Barnard, Charles (Table P-PZ40)

Individual authors
19th century -- Continued

1066.B337	Barnard, Edna Anna, 1829-1887 (Table P-PZ40)
1066.B34	Barnard, Elizabeth (Table P-PZ40)
1066.B8	Barnes, Almont (Table P-PZ40)
1067.B15	Barnes, G.H. (Table P-PZ40)
1068.B2	Barnitz, Albert T.S. (Table P-PZ40)
1068.B6	Barnum, Frances Courtenay (Baylor) (Table P-PZ40)
1070-1073	Barr, Amelia Edith (Huddleston) (Table P-PZ35a)
1074.B12	Barr, James, 1862-1923 (Table P-PZ40)
1074.B124	Barr, John Gorman, 1823-1858 (Table P-PZ40)
1074.B3	Barron, Elwyn Alfred (Table P-PZ40)
1074.B7	Bartley, James Avis (Table P-PZ40)
1074.B75	Bartol, Cyrus Augustus (Table P-PZ40)
1074.B8	Barton, Ardelia Maria (Cotton) (Table P-PZ40)
1074.B88	Barton, William Eleazar (Table P-PZ40)
1075.B	Bas - Bat
1076	Bates, Arlo (Table P-PZ39)
	Bates, Charlotte Fiske see PS2729.R4
1077.B4	Bates, Katharine Lee (Table P-PZ40)
1077.B6	Bates, Margret Holmes (Ernsperger) (Table P-PZ40)
1078.B	Bau - Baw
1079.B	Bax - Bayl
	Baylor, Frances Courtenay see PS1068.B6
1081.B	Baym - Baz
1082.B	Bea - Beb
1082.B46	Beal, Nathan Stone Reed, b. 1827 or 8
1083.B	Bec - Beecher, G.
1084.B2	Beecher, Henry Ward (Table P-PZ40)
1084.B3	Beecher, Lyman (Table P-PZ40)
1084.B6	Beers, Henry Augustin (Table P-PZ40)
1085.B	Bela - Bell
1085.B23	Belasco, David (Table P-PZ40)
1085.B3	Belisle, D.W. (David W.) (Table P-PZ40)
1085.B63	Bell, Lillian L. (Mrs. A.H. Bogue) (Table P-PZ40)
1085.B92	Bellamy, Charles Joseph, 1852-1910 (Table P-PZ40)
1086-1087	Bellamy, Edward (Table P-PZ36)
1088.B3	Bellamy, Elizabeth Whitfield (Table P-PZ40)
1088.B6	Benedict, Frank Lee (Table P-PZ40)
1090-1093	Benjamin, Park (Table P-PZ35a)
1094.B2	Benjamin, Samuel Green Wheeler (Table P-PZ40)
1094.B45	Bennett, Emerson, 1822-1905 (Table P-PZ40)
1094.B9	Bensel, James Berry (Table P-PZ40)
1094.B94	Benson, W.H. (William Henry) (Table P-PZ40)
1095.B4	Benton, Thomas Hart (Table P-PZ40)
	Cf. E337.8.A+ Collected works
	Cf. E340.B4 Biography

Individual authors
19th century -- Continued

1096.B15	Beschke, William (Table P-PZ40)
1096.B3	Bethune, George Washington (Table P-PZ40)
1096.B34	Bettersworth, Alexander Pitts (Table P-PZ40)
1097	Bierce, Ambrose (Table P-PZ39)
1098.B	Big - Bim
1099.54	Bird, Robert Montgomery (Table P-PZ40)
1100	Bishop, William Henry (Table P-PZ39)
1101.B	Bis - Black
1101.B8	Black, Alexander (Table P-PZ40)
1102.B	Blacka - Blam
1102.B6	Blaine, James Gillespie (Table P-PZ40)
	Cf. E660.B6+ Collected works
	Cf. E664.B6 Biography
1102.B8	Blake, James Vila (Table P-PZ40)
1102.B86	Blake, Lillie Devereux, 1835-1913 (Table P-PZ40)
1102.B9	Blake, Mary Elizabeth (McGrath) (Table P-PZ40)
1103.B46	Blanden, Charles Granger (Table P-PZ40)
1103.B8	Bloede, Gertrude ("Stuart Sterne") (Table P-PZ40)
1103.B85	Blood, Henry Ames (Table P-PZ40)
1104.B	Boa - Bok
	Bogue, Lillian (Bell) see PS1085.B63
	Boisgilbert, Edmund see PS1545.D55
1104.B45	Bodman, Manoah, 1765-1830
1105-1106	Boker, George Henry (Table P-PZ36)
1107.B2	Bolles, Frank (Table P-PZ40)
1107.B7	Bolton, Charles Knowles (Table P-PZ40)
1107.B8	Bolton, Sarah (Knowles) (Table P-PZ40)
1108.B	Bom - Bond
1109.B3	Boner, John Henry (Table P-PZ40)
	Bonner, Sherwood, 1849-1883 see PS2357+
1110.B	Bos - Botta
1110.B48	Bostwick, F. M.
1111	Botta, Anna Charlotte (Lynch) (Table P-PZ39)
1112.B	Bott - Bouton
1112.B835	Bouton, John Bell, 1830-1902 (Table P-PZ40)
1113.B35	Bouvet, Marguerite, 1865-1915 (Table P-PZ40)
1113.B6	Bovee, Christian Nestell (Table P-PZ40)
1113.B8	Bowen, Herbert Wolcott (Table P-PZ40)
	Bowen, Susan Petigru, 1824-1875 see PS2179.K36
1114.B	Bower - Boyesen
1115-1118	Boyesen, Hjalmar Hjorth (Table P-PZ35a)
1119.B	Boyesen - Bq
1119.B38	Boynton, Warren (Table P-PZ40)
1120.B414	Bradford, Joseph, 1843-1886 (Table P-PZ40)
1120.B45	Bradlee, Caleb Davis (Table P-PZ40)

Individual authors
19th century -- Continued

1120.B459	Bradley, Eliza, b. 1783 (Table P-PZ40)
1120.B47	Bradley, Mary Emily (Neely) (Table P-PZ40)
1120.B5	Brady, Cyrus Townsend (Table P-PZ40)
1120.B8	Brainard, John Gardiner Calkins (Table P-PZ40)
1121.B	Bram - Braz
1121.B5	Branch, William Jr. (Table P-PZ40)
1122.B	Bre - Brh
1123.B2	Bridges, Robert ("Droch") (Table P-PZ40)
1123.B25	Bridgman, Marcus Fayette (Table P-PZ40)
1123.B44	Brine, Mary D. (Table P-PZ40)
	Bronco Bill, 1836-1920 see PS1757.G4
1123.B83	Brooks, Charles Timothy (Table P-PZ40)
1123.B835	Brooks, Elbridge S. (Table P-PZ40)
1123.B86	Brooks, Maris (Gowen) (Table P-PZ40)
1123.B89	Brooks, Noah (Table P-PZ40)
1123.B9	Brooks, Phillips (Table P-PZ40)
1123.B93	Brooks, Sarah Warner (Table P-PZ40)
1124.B276	Brothers Cobb (Table P-PZ40)
	Cf. PS1356.C46 Cyrus Cobb
	Cf. PS1356.C464 Darius Cobb
1124.B3	Brotherton, Alice William (Table P-PZ40)
1124.B6	Brougham, John (Table P-PZ40)
1125-1128	Brown, Alice (Table P-PZ35a)
1129.B6	Brown, Carrie (Table P-PZ40)
1130-1138	Brown, Charles Brockden (Table P-PZ33)
1139.B32	Brown, Helen E. (Table P-PZ40)
1139.B5	Brown, Joseph Brownlee (Table P-PZ40)
1139.B53	Brown, Joseph M., 1851-1932 (Table P-PZ40)
1139.B69	Brown, Solomon G., 1829?-1906 (Table P-PZ40)
1139.B76	Brown, Theron, 1832-1914 (Table P-PZ40)
1139.B9	Brown, William Wells, 1815-1884 (Table P-PZ40)
1140-1143	Brown, Charles Farrar ("Artemus Ward") (Table P-PZ35a)
	Cf. PN6161 Wit and humor
1144.B3	Browne, Frances Elizabeth (Table P-PZ40)
1145.B3	Browne, John Ross (Table P-PZ40)
1145.B35	Browne, Martha Griffith, d. 1906 (Table P-PZ40)
1145.B46	Brownell, (Mrs.) Gertrude (Hall), 1863- (Table P-PZ40)
1145.B5	Brownell, Henry Howard (Table P-PZ40)
1145.B6	Brownell, William Crary (Table P-PZ40)
1145.B7	Brownson, Orestes Augustus (Table P-PZ40)
1146.B5	Bruce, Wallace (Table P-PZ40)
1147.B2	Bruner, Albert Milton (Table P-PZ40)
1148.B5	Bryan, Daniel (Table P-PZ40)
1148.B8	Bryan, William Jennings (Table P-PZ40)
1149.B48	Bryant, Charles S., 1808-1885 (Table P-PZ40)

Individual authors
19th century -- Continued

1149.B5	Bryant, John D. (Table P-PZ40)
1150-1198	Bryant, William Cullen (Table P-PZ31 modified)

Individual genres
Poetical works

1155	Among the trees (Table P-PZ41)
1156	Death of the flowers (Table P-PZ41)
1158	Flood of years (Table P-PZ41)
1159	Forest hymn (Table P-PZ41)
1160	Fringed gentian (Table P-PZ41)
1161	Little people of the snow (Table P-PZ41)
1163	Sella (Table P-PZ41)
1164	Song of the sower (Table P-PZ41)
1165	Story of the fountain (Table P-PZ41)
1166	Thanatopsis (Table P-PZ41)
1167	To a waterfowl (Table P-PZ41)
1169.A-Z	Other, A-Z
	Subarrange each by Table P-PZ43
1170	Translations by Bryant
	Prose works
1171	Collected works
1172.A-Z	Separate works, A-Z
	Subarrange each by Table P-PZ43
1199.B265	Buckman, H.H. (Table P-PZ40)
1199.B355	Bullard, Laura Curtis (Table P-PZ40)
1199.B5	Bunce, Oliver Bell (Table P-PZ40)
	Bunner, Henry Cuyler
1200	Works
1200.A2	Collected. By date
1200.A3	By editor
1200.A4	Selected works. By editor
1200.A5A-.A5Z	Translations. By language
1200.Z5	Selections. Anthologies
	Poetry and drama
1201.A3	Collected poems
1201.A5	Collected drama
1201.A6-Z	Separate works
	Prose
1202.A3	Collected. By date
1202.A5-Z	Special works
	Class here first editions
1203	Biography and criticism
1204.B5	Burch, Adelle (Table P-PZ40)
1204.B8	Burdett, Charles (Table P-PZ40)
1205	Burdette, Robert Jones (Table P-PZ39)
	Cf. PN6161 Wit and humor

	Individual authors
	19th century -- Continued
1206.B6	Burgess, Adelaide Maria (Table P-PZ40)
1207.B4	Burleigh, William Henry (Table P-PZ40)
1210-1218	Burnett, Frances (Hodgson) (Table P-PZ33)
1219.B4	Burnham, Clara Louise (Table P-PZ40)
1219.B7	Burritt, Elihu (Table P-PZ40)
1220-1228	Burroughs, John (Table P-PZ33 modified)
	Class here collections and literary criticism only
	For special works, see class Q
	Collected works
1220	By date
1220.E00-.E99	1800-1899
1220.F00-.F99	1900-1999
1220.G00-.G99	2000-2099
1229.B6	Burton, Richard (Table P-PZ40)
1229.B62	Burton, Robert Wilton, 1848-1917 (Table P-PZ40)
1234.B	Bus - Busz
1234.B5	Busch, William, b. 1836 (Table P-PZ40)
1235.B28	Butler, James, 1755?-1842 (Table P-PZ40)
1235.B5	Butler, William Allen (Table P-PZ40)
1235.B7	Butterworth, Hezekiah (Table P-PZ40)
1236.B	By - Bynm
1237	Bynner, Edwin Lasseter (Table P-PZ39)
1238.B	Bynner - Bz
1238.B5	Byrn, Marcus Lafayette (Table P-PZ40)
1238.B55	Byrne, Charles Alfred (Table P-PZ40)
1239.C	Ca - Cab
1240-1248	Cable, George Washington (Table P-PZ33)
1249.C	Cable - Cak
1249.C2	Cabot, James Eliot (Table P-PZ40)
1250.C	Cala - Calk
1251.C	Call - Camp
1251.C3	Call, I. (Table P-PZ40)
1251.C36	Callahan, S. Alice, b. 1868 (Table P-PZ40)
1251.C7	Calvert, George Henry (Table P-PZ40)
1252.C	Campa - Caq
1252.C25	Campbell, Bartley T. (Table P-PZ40)
1252.C33	Campbell, Helen (Stuart) (Table P-PZ40)
1252.C4	Campbell, John Preston (Table P-PZ40)
1253.C	Car - Card
1254.C	Care - Carl
1254.C9	Carleton, Henry Guy, 1856-1910 (Table P-PZ40)
1255-1258	Carleton, Will (Table P-PZ35a)
1259.C	Carleton - Carq
1259.C6	Carpenter, Henry Howard
1260.C	Carr - Carrz

	Individual authors
	19th century
	Carr - -- Continued
1260.C65	Carryl, Charles E. (Charles Edward) (Table P-PZ40)
1260.C7	Carryl, Guy Wetmore (Table P-PZ40)
1261.C	Cars - Carter, R.
1262.C	Carter, S. - Carx
1262.C6	Carus, Paul
1263-1266	Cary, Alice (Table P-PZ35a)
	Including works by Alice and Phoebe Cary and biographies of the two
1267	Cary, Phoebe (Table P-PZ39)
1268.C	Cary - Casr
1268.C2	Cary, Richard L. (Table P-PZ40)
1268.C38	Case, Lydia Hinman, 1850-1915 (Table P-PZ40)
1269.C	Cass - Cath
1270-1273	Catherwood, Mary (Hartwell) (Table P-PZ35a)
1274.C7	Caverly, Robert B. (Table P-PZ40)
1275-1278	Cawein, Madison Julius (Table P-PZ35a)
1279.C3	Chadwick, John White (Table P-PZ40)
1279.C896	Chambers, Julius (Table P-PZ40)
1280-1288	Chambers, Robert William (Table P-PZ33)
1289.C	Cham - Chan
1290-1291	Channing, William Ellery (Table P-PZ36)
1292.C3	Chapman, John Jay (Table P-PZ40)
1292.C5	Cheney, John Vance (Table P-PZ40)
1292.C518	Cheney, Walter Thomas (Table P-PZ40)
1292.C54	Chesebro', Caroline, 1825-1873 (Table P-PZ40)
1292.C59	Chesnut, Mary Boykin Miller, 1823-1886 (Table P-PZ40)
1292.C6	Chestnutt, Charles Waddell, 1858-1932 (Table P-PZ40)
1292.C85	Child, Francis James (Table P-PZ40)
1293	Child, Lydia Maria (Francis) (Table P-PZ39)
1294.C27	Chipman, De Witt C. (Table P-PZ40)
1294.C4	Chivers, Thomas Holley (Table P-PZ40)
	Choate, Lowell see PS1999.H414
1294.C6	Choate, Rufus (Table P-PZ40)
	Cf. E337.8.A+ Collected works
	Cf. E340.C4 Biography
1294.C63	Chopin, Kate O'Flaherty, 1851-1904 (Table P-PZ38)
1295-1298	Churchill, Winston (Table P-PZ35a)
1299.C1654	Clark, B. (Table P-PZ40)
1299.C166	Clark, Charles Heber, 1841-1915 (Table P-PZ40)
1299.C168	Clark, Franklin Chase (Table P-PZ40)
1299.C3	Clark, Willis Gaylord (Table P-PZ40)
1299.C5	Clarke, James Freeman (Table P-PZ40)
	Cf. B908.C6+ Philosophy
1299.C58	Clarke, McDonald (Table P-PZ40)

Individual authors

19th century -- Continued

1299.C6	Clarke, Mary Bayard, 1854-1886 (Table P-PZ40)
1299.C725	Clay, Henry (Table P-PZ40)
	Cf. E337.8.C55 Collected works
	Cf. E340.C6 Biography
1299.C87	Cleary, Kate M. (Table P-PZ40)
1300-1348	Clemens, Samuel Langhorne ("Mark Twain") (Table P-PZ31 modified)

Separate works

1305	Adventures of Huckleberry Finn (Table P-PZ41)
1306	Adventures of Tom Sawyer (Table P-PZ41)
1307	American claimant (Table P-PZ41)
1308	Connecticut yankee in King Arthur's court (Table P-PZ41)
1309	Extracts from Adam's diary (Table P-PZ41)
1310	Following the equator (Table P-PZ41)
1311	Gilded age (Table P-PZ41)
1312	Innocents abroad (Table P-PZ41)
1313	Joan of Arc (Table P-PZ41)
1314	Life on the Mississippi (Table P-PZ41)
1315	Million pound bank note (Table P-PZ41)
1316	Prince and the pauper (Table P-PZ41)
1317	Pudd'nhead Wilson (Table P-PZ41)
1318	Roughing it (Table P-PZ41)
1319	Sketches old and new (Table P-PZ41)
1320	Tom Sawyer abroad (Table P-PZ41)
1321	Tramp abroad (Table P-PZ41)
1322.A-Z	Other, A-Z
	Subarrange each by Table P-PZ43
1351.C2	Cleveland, Grover (Table P-PZ40)
	Cf. E697 Biography
	Cf. J82.C5+ Speeches and messages as President
1351.C4	Cleveland, Rose Elizabeth (Table P-PZ40)
1351.C6	Clinton, DeWitt (Table P-PZ40)
	Cf. E337.8.A+ Collected works
	Cf. E340.C65 Biography
1355	Clymer, Ella (Dietz) (Table P-PZ39)
1356.C	Cly - Coe
1356.C23	Coastes, Laning (Table P-PZ40)
1356.C46	Cobb, Cyrus (Table P-PZ40)
	Cf. PS1124.B276 Brothers Cobb
1356.C464	Cobb, Darius, 1834-1919 (Table P-PZ40)
	Cf. PS1124.B276 Brothers Cobb
1356.C57	Cobb, Sylvanus, 1823-1887 (Table P-PZ40)
1356.C58	Cobbe, William Rosser, d. 1907 (Table P-PZ40)
1357.C	Cof - Cok

Individual authors
19th century
Cof - Cok -- Continued

1357.C35	Coffin, Charles Carleton (Table P-PZ40)
1357.C48	Coffin, Robert Stevenson (Table P-PZ40)
1358.C	Col - Coler
1359.C	Coles - Conv
1359.C2	Coles, Abraham (Table P-PZ40)
1359.C5	Collier, Thomas Stephens (Table P-PZ40)
1359.C53	Collingwood, Herbert W. (Herbert Winslow), 1857-1927 (Table P-PZ40)
1359.C563	Collins, Julia C., d. 1865 (Table P-PZ40)
1359.C565	Collins, Mercy Hutchinson Jones, 1822-1898 (Table P-PZ40)
1359.C6	Collyer, Robert (Table P-PZ40)
1359.C7	Cone, Helen Gray (Table P-PZ40)
1361	Conway, John Donlon (Table P-PZ39)
1362.C3	Conway, Katherine Eleanor (Table P-PZ40)
1366-1367	Conway, Moncure, Daniel (Table P-PZ36)
1368.C	Conway, W - Conz
1368.C4	Conway, William B. (Table P-PZ40)
1368.C44	Conwell, Russell Herman (Table P-PZ40)
1378.C	Coo - Cooke, J.
1380-1383	Cook, John Esten (Table P-PZ35a)
1385-1388	Cooke, Philip Pendleton (Table P-PZ35a)
1390-1393	Cooke, Rose (Terry) (Table P-PZ35a)
1397.C	Cooke - Coold
1397.C5	Coolbrith, Ina Donna
1398.C	Coole - Coolz
1398.C36	Coolidge, Cassius M. (Table P-PZ40)
	Coolidge, Susan see PS3358.W6
1399.C	Coom - Coop
1400-1448	Cooper, James Fenimore (Table P-PZ31 modified)
	Separate works
1405.A4	Afloat and ashore (Table P-PZ43)
1405.A8	Autobiography of a pocketbook handkerchief (Table P-PZ43)
	Borderers see PS1418.W7
1405.B7	Bravo (Table P-PZ43)
1405.C4	Chainbearer (Table P-PZ43)
1405.C7	Crater, or Vulcan's peak (Table P-PZ43)
1406	Deerslayer (Table P-PZ41)
1406.5	Elinor Myllys (Table P-PZ41)
	Eve Effingham see PS1407.H7
1407.H2	Headsman (Table P-PZ43)
1407.H4	Heidenmauer (Table P-PZ43)
1407.H7	Home as found (Table P-PZ43)

Individual authors
19th century
Cooper, James Fenimore
Separate works -- Continued

1407.H8	Homeward bound (Table P-PZ43)
1407.J3	Jack Tier (Table P-PZ43)
1408	Last of the Mohicans (Table P-PZ41)
1409.L4	Lionel Lincoln (Table P-PZ43)
1409.M3	Mercedes of Castile (Table P-PZ43)
1409.M5	Miles Wallingford (Table P-PZ43)
1409.M7	Monikins (Table P-PZ43)
1409.N3	Ned Myers (Table P-PZ43)
1409.O2	Oak openings (Table P-PZ43)
1410	Pathfinder (Table P-PZ41)
1412	Pilot (Table P-PZ41)
1414	Pioneers (Table P-PZ41)
1416	Prairie (Table P-PZ41)
1417.P6	Precaution (Table P-PZ43)
1417.R3	Red Rover (Table P-PZ43)
1417.R5	Redskins (Table P-PZ43)
1417.S3	Satanstoe (Table P-PZ43)
1417.S5	Sea lions (Table P-PZ43)
1417.S7	Spy (Table P-PZ43)
1418.T5	Two admirals (Table P-PZ43)
1418.W3	Water witch (Table P-PZ43)
1418.W5	Ways of the hour (Table P-PZ43)
1418.W7	Wept of the Wish-ton-wish (Table P-PZ43)
1419.W3	Wing-and-wing (Table P-PZ43)
1419.W7	Wyandotte (Table P-PZ43)
1421.A7-Z	Other, A-Z
	Subarrange each by Table P-PZ43
	Cornish, Kate see PS1449.C47
1449.C378	Coryell, John Russell, 1851-1924 (Table P-PZ40)
1449.C415	Cotton, A.J. (Alfred Johnson), 1800-1858 (Table P-PZ40)
1449.C47	Courtland, Kil (Table P-PZ40)
1449.C5	Cowen, Frank (Table P-PZ40)
1449.C5	Cowen, Frank (Table P-PZ40)
1449.C6	Coxe, Arthur Cleveland (Table P-PZ40)
1449.C65	Cozzens, Frederic S. (Table P-PZ40)
1449.C673	Crafts, Hannah (Table P-PZ40)
1449.C73	Crakes, Sylvester (Table P-PZ40)
1449.C8	Cranch, Christopherr Pearse (Table P-PZ40)
1449.C85	Crane, Stephen (Table P-PZ40)
1453-1457	Crawford, Francis Marion (Table P-PZ35a)
1469.C3	Crawford, John Wallace ("Capt. Jack Crawford") (Table P-PZ40)
1469.C536	Creamer, Hannah Gardner (Table P-PZ40)

Individual authors
19th century -- Continued

1470.C	Cri - Cro
1471-1472	Croly, Jane (Cunningham) ("Jennie June") (Table P-PZ36)
1473.C3	Crosby, Frederick K. (Table P-PZ40)
1473.C6	Croswell, William (Table P-PZ40)
	Crothers, Samuel McChord see PS3505.R9
1473.C86	Cuckow, J.G. (Table P-PZ40)
1474.C	Cul - Cur
1474.C483	Cummings, Ariel Ivers, 1823-1863 (Table P-PZ40)
1474.C5	Cummins, Maria S. (Table P-PZ40)
1475-1476	Curtis, George Ticknor (Table P-PZ36)
1480-1498	Curtis, George William (Table P-PZ32 modified)
	Separate works
1485	From the easy chair (Table P-PZ41)
	The Howadji in Syria see DS94
	Literary and social essays see PR121
	Lotus-eating see E166
	Nile notes of a Howadji see DT54
1486	Potiphar papers (Table P-PZ41)
1487	Prue and I (Table P-PZ41)
1488	Speeches, addresses, etc. (Table P-PZ41)
1489	Trumps (Table P-PZ41)
	The wanderer in Syria see DS107
1490.A-Z	Other, A-Z
	Subarrange each by Table P-PZ43
	Curtis, Laura J. see PS1199.B355
1499.C27	Curtis, Newton Mallory (Table P-PZ40)
1499.C45	Cutler, Elbridge Jefferson (Table P-PZ40)
1499.D4	Dabney, Richard (Table P-PZ40)
1499.D63	Dail, C.C. (Table P-PZ40)
1499.D83	Dall, Caroline Wells Healey, 1822-1912 (Table P-PZ40)
1499.D84	Dalton, Joseph Grinnell, 1828- (Table P-PZ40)
1499.D85	Daly, Augustin (Table P-PZ40)
1499.D96	Dana, Katharine Floyd, 1835-1886 (Table P-PZ40)
1501-1502	Dana, Richard Henry, 1787-1879 (Table P-PZ36)
1505-1506	Dana, Richard Henry, Jr., 1815-1882 (Table P-PZ36)
1507.D	Dana - Dandridge
1508-1509	Dandridge, Danske (Bedinger) (Table P-PZ36)
1510.D	Dand - Daq
	Daniels, Ione G. see PS2048.I67
1513.D	Dar - Davie
1513.D62	Darrow, Clarence Seward, 1857-1938 (Table P-PZ40)
	Dart, 1863-1919 see PS2430.M59
	Daskam, Josephine Dodge see PS1054.B62
1513.D8	Davidson, Lucretia Maria (Table P-PZ40)
1513.D9	Davidson, Margaret Miller (Table P-PZ40)

Individual authors

19th century -- Continued

1514.D	Davie - Davis, Me.
1514.D95	Davis, Mary Elizabeth (Moragne) (Table P-PZ40)
1516.D2	Davis, Miles Avery (Table P-PZ40)
1516.D25	Davis, Mollie Evelyn Moore, 1844-1909 (Table P-PZ40)
1517	Davis, Rebecca (Harding) (Table P-PZ39)
1519.D42	Davis, Reuben, 1813-1890 (Table P-PZ40)
1519.D5	Davis, Richard Bingham (Table P-PZ40)
1520-1523	Davis, Richard Harding (Table P-PZ35a)
1524.D	Davis, R - Dax
1525.D24	Day, Martha, 1813-1833 (Table P-PZ40)
1525.D3	Day, Richard Edwin (Table P-PZ40)
1525.D35	De Quille, Dan, 1829-1898 (Table P-PZ40)
1525.D434	De Cleyre, Voltairine, 1866-1912 (Table P-PZ40)
1525.D4344	Decon, Thomas William (Table P-PZ40)
1525.D46	Deering, Nathaniel (Table P-PZ40)
1525.D5	DeForest, John William (Table P-PZ40)
1525.D7	DeKay, Charles (Table P-PZ40)
1525.D8	DeKroyft, Sarah Helen (Aldrich) (Table P-PZ40)
1530-1533	DeLand, Margaret Wade (Campbell) (Table P-PZ35a)
1534.D13	Demos, 1819-1861 (Table P-PZ40)
1534.D2	DeMille, Henry C. (Table P-PZ40)
1534.D3	DeMille, James (Table P-PZ40)
1534.D4	Deming, Philander (Table P-PZ40)
1534.D413	Demos, 1819-1861 (Table P-PZ40)
1534.D6	Dennie, Joseph (Table P-PZ40)
1535	Derby, George Horatio ("John Phoenix") (Table P-PZ39)
1536.D47	Detter, Thomas, b. ca. 1826 (Table P-PZ40)
1536.D5	DeVere, Mary Ainge ("Madeline Bridges") (Table P-PZ40)
1537.D	DeWint - Dickinson
1537.D6	Diaz, Abby (Morton)
1537.D64	Dibble, F.D. (Frank Dalos)
	Dibble, Frank Dalos see PS1537.D64
1538	Dickinson, Anna Elizabeth (Table P-PZ39)
1539.D5	Dickinson, Charles M. (Table P-PZ40)
1541	Dickinson, Emily (Table P-PZ39)
1542.D3	Dickinson, Mary (Lowe) (Table P-PZ40)
1542.D492	Diffenderffer, Henry (Table P-PZ40)
1543.D	Din - Dodge
1543.D17	Dinmore, Richard (Table P-PZ40)
1543.D2	Dinsmoor, Robert (Table P-PZ40)
1543.D5	Dodd, Anna Bowman (Blake) (Table P-PZ40)
1544	Dodge, Mary Abigail ("Gail Hamilton") (Table P-PZ39)
1545.D15	Dodge, Mary Barker (Table P-PZ40)
1545.D2	Dodge, Mary (Mapes) (Table P-PZ40)
	Doesticks, Q.K. Philander, 1831-1875 see PS3039.T6

	19th century
	Individual authors
1545.D25	Doggett, John Marshall (Table P-PZ40)
1545.D27	Doggett, Solon (Table P-PZ40)
1545.D3	Dole, Nathan Haskell (Table P-PZ40)
1545.D4	Donahoe, Daniel Joseph (Table P-PZ40)
1545.D45	Donaldson, Samuel (Table P-PZ40)
1545.D5	Donnelly, Eleanor Cecilia (Table P-PZ40)
1545.D55	Donnelly, Ignatius, 1831-1901 (Table P-PZ40)
1545.D83	Dooner, Pierton W.. 1844-1907? (Table P-PZ40)
1546.D	Dop - Dorr
1546.D5	Dorgan, John Aylmer
1547-1548	Dorr, Julia Carolina (Ripley) (Table P-PZ36)
1549.D	Dorr - Drake, J.
1549.D3	Dorsey, Anna Hanson McKenney, 1815-1896 (Table P-PZ40)
1549.D53	Doten, Elizabeth, 1827-1913 (Table P-PZ40)
	Doten, Lizzie see PS1549.D53
1549.D614	Douglas, Amanda Minnie, 1831-1916 (Table P-PZ40)
1549.D96	Drake, David, ca. 1800-ca. 1870 (Table P-PZ40)
1550-1553	Drake, Joseph Rodman (Table P-PZ35a)
1554.D	Drake, J. - Dt.
1555.D	Du - Dunbar
1555.D385	Dugan, James (Table P-PZ40)
1555.D4	Duganne, Augustine Joseph Hickey (Table P-PZ40)
1555.D44	Dugger, Shepherd Monroe, 1854-19438 (Table P-PZ40)
1555.D6	Duhring, Julia (Table P-PZ40)
1555.D64	Dumont, Julia L. (Julia Louisa), 1794-1857 (Table P-PZ40)
1556-1557	Dunbar, Paul Lawrence (Table P-PZ36)
1558.D	Dunbar - Dunlap
1558.D5	Duniway, Abigail Scott, 1834-1915 (Table P-PZ40)
1560-1561	Dunlap, William (Table P-PZ36)
1562.D	Dunlap - Dv
1562.D3	Dupuy, Eliza Ann (Table P-PZ40)
1562.D5	Durivage, Francis Alexander (Table P-PZ40)
1562.D66	Dutton, Warren, 1774-1857 (Table P-PZ38)
1562.D67	Duval, John C. (John Crittenden, 1816-1897 (Table P-PZ38)
1562.D7	Duyckinck, Evert Augustus (Table P-PZ38)
1564.D	Dw - Dx
1566.D	Dy - Dz
1567.E	E - Edf
1567.E22	Eastman, Charles Gamage (Table P-PZ40)
1567.E225	Eastman, Elaine (Goodale) (Table P-PZ40)
1567.E7	Eddy, Mary Morso (Baker) Glover (Table P-PZ40)
1567.E74	Edelen, Susan Mary, b. 1833 (Table P-PZ40)

	Individual authors
	19th century -- Continued
1568.E	Edg - Edv
1569.E6	Edwards, George Wharton (Table P-PZ40)
1570	Edwards, Harry Stillwell (Table P-PZ39)
1574.E	Edwards - Egan
1575-1576	Egan, Maurice Francis (Table P-PZ36)
1577.E	Egan - Eggleston
1580-1583	Eggleston, Edward (Table P-PZ35a)
1584.E2	Eggleston, George Cary (Table P-PZ40)
1585	Eliot, Charles William (Table P-PZ39)
	Cf. LB875.E43+ General educational writings
	Cf. LD2148 Biography
1586.E	Eliot - Elliott
1587-1588	Elliott, Maud (Howe) (Table P-PZ36)
1589.E	Elliott - Ellr
1589.E28	Elliott, Sarah Barnwell, 1848-1928 (Table P-PZ40)
1589.E3	Ellis, Edward Sylvester, 1840-1916 (Table P-PZ40)
1591.E	Ells - Ellz
1593.E	Elm - Elz
1598.E	Em - Emd
1598.E5	Embury, Emma Catherine Manley, 1806-1863 (Table P-PZ40)
	Emersie, John see PS2489.O74
1599.E5	Emerson, Edward Waldo (Table P-PZ40)
1599.E7	Emerson, Edwin (Table P-PZ40)
1600-1648	Emerson, Ralph Waldo (Table P-PZ31 modified)
	Prose works
1605	Collected works
	Separate works
1606	Conduct of life (Table P-PZ41)
1607	English traits (Table P-PZ41)
1608	Essays, first and second series
	Separate
1609	Character (Table P-PZ41)
1610	Friendship (Table P-PZ41)
1611	History (Table P-PZ41)
1612	Love (Table P-PZ41)
1613	Nature (Table P-PZ41)
1614	Self-reliance (Table P-PZ41)
1615.A-Z	Other, A-Z
1615.C6	Compensation (Table P-PZ43)
1615.E7	Experience (Table P-PZ43)
1615.H4	Heroism (Table P-PZ43)
1615.I6	Intellect (Table P-PZ43)
1615.M2	Manners (Table P-PZ43)
1615.O94	Over-soul (Table P-PZ43)

Individual authors
  19th century
    Emerson, Ralph Waldo
      Prose works
        Separate works
          Essays, first and second series
            Separate
              Other, A-Z -- Continued

1615.P6	Prudence (Table P-PZ43)
1615.S6	Spiritual laws (Table P-PZ43)

           Other prose works

1616	Lectures and biographical sketches (Table P-PZ41)
1617	Letters and social aims (Table P-PZ41)
1618	Miscellanies (Table P-PZ41)
1619	Natural history of the intellect (Table P-PZ41)
1620	Nature, addresses, and letters (Table P-PZ41)
1621	Representative men (Table P-PZ41)
1622	Society and solitude (Table P-PZ41)

           Other
            Individual works, A-Z

1623.A-Z	Individual works, A-Z
	Subarrange each by Table P-PZ43
	Including parts of works in PS1616-PS1622

        Poems

1624.A1	Collected. By date
1624.A5-Z	Separate, A-Z
	Subarrange each by Table P-PZ43
1649.E	Emerson - Eml
1650.E	Emm - Emz
1650.E7	Emmons, Richard
1651.E	En - English
1652-1653	English, Thomas Dunn (Table P-PZ36)
1654.E55	Everett, David (Table P-PZ40)
1654.E6	Everett, Edward (Table P-PZ40)
	F.X.L., 1846-1920 see PS3066.T
1654.F3	Fairchild, Summer L. (Table P-PZ40)
1654.F34	Fairman, Henry Clay (Table P-PZ40)
1654.F77	Farrar, Mrs. (Table P-PZ40)
1654.F8	Farrar, Eliza Ware Rotch, 1791-1870 (Table P-PZ40)
1655-1658	Fawcett, Edgar (Table P-PZ35a)
1659.F3	Fay, Theodore Sedgwick (Table P-PZ40)
1659.F5	Fenner, Cornelius George (Table P-PZ0)
1659.F6	Fenollosa, Ernest Francisco (Table P-PZ40)
1661-1662	Fenollosa, Mary (McNeil) ("Sidney McCall") (Table P-PZ36)
	Fern, Fanny, 1811-1872 see PS2523.P9
1664.F2	Fessenden, Thomas Green (Table P-PZ40)
1665-1668	Field, Eugene (Table P-PZ35a)
1669.F2	Field, Kate (Table P-PZ40)

	Individual authors
	19th century -- Continued
1669.F3	Field, Roswell (Table P-PZ40)
1669.F5	Fields, Annie (Adams) (Mrs. James T. Fields) (Table P-PZ40)
1670-1671	Fields, James T. (Table P-PZ36)
1672.F5	Finch, Francis Miles (Table P-PZ40)
1673	Fiske, John (Table P-PZ39)
	Cf. B945.F4+ Philosophy
	Cf. E175.5.A+ Biography
1674.F	Fiske - Fitch
1675-1678	Fitch, Clyde (Table P-PZ35a)
1679.F2	Flagg, Edmund, 1815-1890 (Table P-PZ40)
1679.F4	Flash, Henry Lynden (Table P-PZ40)
1679.F6	Fletcher, Julia Constance ("George Fleming") (Table P-PZ40)
1679.F7	Flint, Timothy (Table P-PZ40)
1681.F	Flo - Fn
1681.F4	Flower, Benjamin Orange
1683.F	Fo - Foos
1683.F4	Follen, Eliza Lee (Cabot) (Table P-PZ40)
1685-1688	Foote, Mary (Hallock) (Table P-PZ35a)
1689.F	Foote - Ford
1689.F8	Ford, James Lauren, 1854-1928
1690-1693	Ford, Paul Leicester (Table P-PZ35a)
1694.F	Ford - Fox
	Forester, Fanny see PS2156.J3
1694.F14	Fortune, Timothy (Table P-PZ40)
1694.F2	Foss, Sam Walter (Table P-PZ40)
1694.F5	Foster, Stephen Collins (Table P-PZ40)
1694.F8	Foulke, William Dudley (Table P-PZ40)
1694.F82	Fowle, Charles H., 1852- (Table P-PZ40)
1700-1703	Fox, John, Jr. (Table P-PZ35a)
1704.F	Fox - Frederic
1705-1708	Frederic, Harold (Table P-PZ35a)
1709.F	Frederic - Freeman
1710-1713	Freeman, Mary Eleanor Wilkins, 1852-1930 (Table P-PZ35a)
1714.F	Freeman - French
1715-1718	French, Alice ("Octave Thanet") (Table P-PZ35a)
1719.F	French - Frer
1719.F38	French, Joseph Lewis, 1858-1936 (Table P-PZ40)
1719.F6	French, L. Virginia (Smith) (Table P-PZ40)
1720.F	Fres - Frh
1721.F	Fri - Frn
1722.F	Fro - Frx
1722.F5	Frothingham, Nathaniel Langdon (Table P-PZ40)

	Individual authors
	19th century
	Fro - -- Continued

1722.F8	Frothingham, Octavius Brooks (Table P-PZ40)
1723.F	Fry - Ft
1724.F	Fu - Fulld
1725-1728	Fuller, Henry Blake (Table P-PZ35a)
1729.F16	Fuller, Jane Jay (Table P-PZ40)
	Fuller, Margaret see PS2500+
1729.G5	Gallagher, William Davis (Table P-PZ40)
1729.G57	Ganilh, Anthony (Table P-PZ40)
1729.G74	Gardener, Helen Hamilton, 1858-1925 (Table P-PZ40)
1729.G8	Gardner, Celia E. (Table P-PZ40)
1730-1733	Garland, Hamlin (Table P-PZ35a)
1734.G2	Garrison, Wendell Phillips (Table P-PZ40)
1734.G257	Garver, Will L., b. 1867 (Table P-PZ40)
1734.G3	Gates, Ellen Maria (Huntington) (Table P-PZ40)
1734.G774	Gay, Eva, fl. 1889 (Table P-PZ40)
1735-1738	Gayarre, Charles Etienne Arthur (Table P-PZ35a)
1739.G48	Gibbs, D. Cecil (Table P-PZ40)
1739.G49	Gibbs, Oliver (Table P-PZ40)
1739.G9	Gilder, Jeannette Leonard (Table P-PZ40)
1740-1743	Gilder, Richard Watson (Table P-PZ35a)
1744.G2	Gillette, William (Table P-PZ40)
1744.G5	Gilman, Caroline (Howard) (Table P-PZ40)
1744.G57	Gilman, Charlotte (Perkins) Stetson (Table P-PZ40)
1744.G6	Gilman, Samuel (Table P-PZ40)
1744.G68	Gilmore, James Roberts (Table P-PZ40)
1744.G77	Gladden, Washington (Table P-PZ40)
	Glasgow, Ellen see PS3513.L34
1749.G2	Glass, John W. (Table P-PZ40)
1749.G345	Glennon, Michael J., b. 1855 (Table P-PZ40)
1749.G5	Goddard, Martha LeBaron (Table P-PZ40)
1750-1751	Godkin, Edwin Lawrence (Table P-PZ36)
	Cf. PN4874.A+ Biography
1752.G5	Godwin, Parke (Table P-PZ40)
1753.G	Good - Goodrich
1753.G3	Goodale, Dora Reed (Table P-PZ40)
	Goodale, Elaine (Mrs. Charles A. Eastman) see PS1567.E225
1754-1755	Goodrich, Samuel Griswold ("Peter Parley") (Table P-PZ36)
1757.G	Goods - Got
1757.G4	Gordon, Hanford Lennox (Table P-PZ40)
1757.G64	Gorman, Henrie Clay Ligon (Table P-PZ40)
1758.G	Gou - Gov
1758.G25	Gould, Edward Sherman (Table P-PZ40)

Individual authors
 19th century
  Gou - -- Continued

1758.G4	Gould, Hannah Flagg (Table P-PZ40)
1758.G83	Goulding, Francis Robert (Table P-PZ40)
1759.G	Gow - Grans
1759.G53	Graham, A.J. (Andrew J.) (Table P-PZ40)
1760-1763	Grant, Robert (Table P-PZ35a)
1764.G238	Grayson, William John (Table P-PZ40)
	Green, Anna Katharine see PS2730+
1764.G27	Greene, Aella (Table P-PZ40)
1764.G275	Greene, Asa, 1789-1838 (Table P-PZ40)
1764.G29	Greene, Sarah Pratt (McLean) (Table P-PZ40)
1764.G67	Griffith, Mary, d. 1877 (Table P-PZ40)
1764.G774	Grinnell, George Bird, 1849-1938 (Table P-PZ40)
1764.G8	Griswold, Hattie (Tyng) (Table P-PZ40)
1764.G82	Griswold, Rufus Wilmot (Table P-PZ40)
1764.G95	Guild, Curtis (Table P-PZ40)
1765-1768	Guiney, Louise Imogene (Table P-PZ35a)
1769.G25	Gunsaulus, Frank Wakely (Table P-PZ40)
	Guthrie, William Norman see PS3513.U88
1769.H5	Habberton, John (Table P-PZ40)
1769.H7	Hageman, Samuel Miller (Table P-PZ40)
1769.H73	Hagen, John Cole (Table P-PZ40)
1769.H76	Hager, Levi Lewis (Table P-PZ40)
1770-1773	Hale, Edward Everett (Table P-PZ35a)
1774.H13	Hale, Lucretia Peabody (Table P-PZ40)
1774.H2	Hale, Sarah Josepha (Buell) (Table P-PZ40)
1774.H25	Hale, Susan (Table P-PZ40)
1774.H455	Hall, Baynard Rush, 1798-1863 (Table P-PZ40)
	Hall, Gertrude see PS1145.B46
1779.H16	Hall, James, 1793-1868 (Table P-PZ40)
1779.H33	Hall, Louisa Jane (Park) (Table P-PZ40)
1779.H4	Hall, Thomas Winthrop ("Tom Hall") (Table P-PZ40)
1780-1783	Halleck, Fitz-Greene (Table P-PZ35a)
1784.H2	Halpine, Charles Graham (Table P-PZ40)
1784.H24	Halsey, Harlan Page, 1839?-1898 (Table P-PZ40)
1784.H25	Halstead, Murat (Table P-PZ40)
1784.H3	Halsted, Leonora B. (Table P-PZ40)
1784.H6	Harbaugh, Thomas Chalmers (Table P-PZ40)
1785-1788	Harben, William Nathaniel (Table P-PZ35a)
1790-1793	Hardy, Arthur Sherburne (Table P-PZ35a)
1794.H2	Hardy, E. Trueblood (Edward Trueblood) (Table P-PZ40)
1795-1798	Harland, Henry ("Sidney Luska") (Table P-PZ35a)
	Harland, Marion see PS3005+
1799.H	Harlow - Harper
1799.H24	Harlow, William Burt, b. 1856 (Table P-PZ40)

Individual authors
19th century
Harlow -- Harper -- Continued

1799.H7	Harper, Frances Ellen Watkins (Table P-PZ40)
1799.H73	Harrigan, Edward, 1845-1911 (Table P-PZ40)
1800-1818	Harris, Joel Chandler (Table P-PZ32 modified)
	Separate works
1805.A-.N	A-Nif
	Subarrange each by Table P-PZ43
	Georgia from the invasion of DeSoto see F286
	Life of Henry W. Grady see E664.G73
1806	Nights with Uncle Remus (Table P-PZ41)
1807.N-.U	Nih-Unb
	Subarrange each by Table P-PZ43
	Stories of Georgia see F286
1808	Uncle Remus and his friends (Table P-PZ41)
1809	Uncle Remus, his songs and sayings (Table P-PZ41)
1810.U-Z	Und-Z
	Subarrange each by Table P-PZ43
1819.H5	Harris, Miriam Coles (Table P-PZ40)
1819.H6	Harris, Thomas Lake (Table P-PZ40)
1819.H7	Harrison, Constance (Cary) (Mrs. Burton Harrison) (Table P-PZ40)
1819.H97	Hart, Joseph C., d. 1855 (Table P-PZ40)
	Harte, Bret
	Collected works
	By date
1820.E00-.E99	1800-1899
1820.F00-.F99	1900-1999
1820.G00-.G99	2000-2099
1821	By editor
1822	Selected works. Selections
	Subarrange by editor, if given, or by date
1823.A-Z	Translations. By language, A-Z
	Prose
	Including dramatic works
1824	Collected works
	Separate works
1825	Col. Starbottle's client (Table P-PZ41)
1826	First family of Tasajara (Table P-PZ41)
1827	Luck of Roaring Camp (Table P-PZ41)
1828	Tales of the Argonauts (Table P-PZ41)
1829.A-Z	Other, A-Z
	Subarrange each by Table P-PZ43
	Poems
1830	Collected works

	Individual authors
	19th century
	Harte, Bret
	Poem
1831.A-Z	Separate works, A-Z
	Subarrange each by Table P-PZ43
	Illustrations
	Class at N8215, or with the special artists in NC-NE as the case may be
	Class illustrated editions with other editions
	Class portraits, etc., of the author with his biography
	Biography, criticism, etc.
1832.A1-.A5	Periodicals. Societies. Serials
1832.A6-Z	Dictionaries, indexes, etc.
1833.A3-.A39	Autobiography, journals, memoirs. By title
1833.A4	Letters (Collections). By date
1833.A41-.A49	Letters to and from particular individuals. By correspondent (alphabetically)
1833.A5-Z	General works
	Criticism
1834	General works
1835	Textual. Manuscripts, etc.
	Special
1836	Sources
1837.A-Z	Other, A-Z
	For list of Cutter numbers, see Table P-PZ32 17
1838	Language. Grammar. Style
1839.H	Harte - Haru
1839.H43	Hartmann, Franz, d. 1912 (Table P-PZ40)
1840.H	Harv - Harz
1841.H	Has - Hasz
1842.H	Hat - Hau
1843.H	Hav - Havz
1844.H	Haw - Haws
1845-1848	Hawthorne, Julian (Table P-PZ35a)
1850-1898	Hawthorne, Nathaniel (Table P-PZ31 modified)
	Separate works
1855	Blithedale romance (Table P-PZ41)
1856	Dr. Grimshawe's secret (Table P-PZ41)
1858	Grandfather's chair (Table P-PZ41)
1861	House of seven gables (Table P-PZ41)
1862	Marble faun (Table P-PZ41)
1863	Mosses from an old manse (Table P-PZ41)
1864	Our old home (Table P-PZ41)
1865	Passages from the American notebooks (Table P-PZ41)
1866	Passages from the English notebooks (Table P-PZ41)

	Individual authors
	19th century
	Hawthorne, Nathaniel
	Separate works -- Continued
1867	Passages from the French and Italian notebooks (Table P-PZ41)
1868	Scarlet letter (Table P-PZ41)
1869	Tanglewood tales (Table P-PZ41)
1870	Twice-told tales (Table P-PZ41)
	Wonder-book see PZ8.1
1872.A-Z	Other, A-Z
	Subarrange each by Table P-PZ43
1900-1903	Hay, John (Table P-PZ35a)
	Hayes, John Russell see PS3515.A94
1905-1908	Hayne, Paul Hamilton (Table P-PZ35a)
1909.H	Hayne - Hayv
1910.H	Hayw - Hayz
1911.H	Haza - Hazd
1912.H	Haze - Hazz
1912.H45	Hazelton, Harry (Table P-PZ40)
1913.H	Hea - Heaq
1915-1918	Hearn, Lafcadio (Table P-PZ35a)
	Henry, O. see PS2649.P5
1919.H4	Hentz, Caroline Lee (Whiting) (Table P-PZ40)
1919.H6	Herbert, Henry William ("Frank Forester") (Table P-PZ40)
1919.H75	Herne, James A., 1839-1901 (Table P-PZ40)
1920-1923	Herrick, Robert (Table P-PZ35a)
1924.H58	Hext, Julia A. (Table P-PZ40)
1924.H64	Heywood, Joseph Converse (Table P-PZ40)
1925-1928	Higginson, Thomas Wentworth (Table P-PZ35a)
1929.H2	Hildreth, Charles Lotin (Table P-PZ40)
1929.H6	Hill, George (Table P-PZ40)
1929.H652	Hill, Theophilus H. (Theophilus Hunter), 1836-1901 (Table P-PZ40)
1929.H69	Hillis, Newell Dwight (Table P-PZ40)
1929.H78	Hinman, Wilbur F. (Wilbur Fisk), d. 1905 (Table P-PZ40)
1929.H83	Hitchcock, David (Table P-PZ40)
1929.H8394	Hoadley, J.C. (John Chipman), 1818-1886 (Table P-PZ40)
1930-1938	Hoffman, Charles Fenno (Table P-PZ33)
1939.H6	Holden, Warren (Table P-PZ40)
1940-1948	Holland, Josiah Gilbert (Table P-PZ33 modified)
	Complete works. Collected prose works
1940	By date
1940.E00-.E99	1800-1899
1940.F00-.F99	1900-1999
1940.G00-.G99	2000-2099
1941	Collected poems

	Individual authors
	19th century -- Continued
1949.H5	Holley, Marietta (Table P-PZ40)
1949.H587	Holman, Jesse Lynch, 1784-1842 (Table P-PZ40)
1949.H59	Holman, Myra T. (Table P-PZ40)
1949.H6	Holmes, Alice A. (Table P-PZ40)
1949.H7	Holmes, Georgiana (Klingle) ("George Klingle") (Table P-PZ40)
1949.H742	Holmes, Hamilton (Table P-PZ40)
1949.H8	Holmes, Mary Jane (Hawes) (Table P-PZ40)
1950-1998	Holmes, Oliver Wendell (Table P-PZ31 modified)
	Individual genres
	Poems
1955	Collected works
1956	Early poems
	Separate works
1957	Last leaf (Table P-PZ41)
1958	One horse shay (Table P-PZ41)
1959.A-Z	Other, A-Z
	Subarrange each by Table P-PZ43
	Prose
	Fiction
1959.5	Collected works
	Separate works
1960	Elsie Venner (Table P-PZ41)
1961	Guardian angel (Table P-PZ41)
1962	A mortal antipathy (Table P-PZ41)
	Other works
1964	Autocrat of the breakfast table (Table P-PZ41)
	Our hundred days in Europe see DA625
1968	Over the tea-cups (Table P-PZ41)
1969	Pages from an old volume of life (Table P-PZ41)
1970	Poet at the breakfast table (Table P-PZ41)
1971	Professor at the breakfast table (Table P-PZ41)
1972.A-Z	Other, A-Z
	Subarrange each by Table P-PZ43
1999.H1	Holmes, Oliver Wendell, 1841- (Table P-PZ40)
1999.H25	Hooper, Johnson Jones (Table P-PZ40)
1999.H3	Hooper, Lucy Hamilton (Jones) (Table P-PZ40)
1999.H4	Hope, James Barron (Table P-PZ40)
1999.H414	Hopkins, Alice K. (Alice Kimball), b. 1839 (Table P-PZ40)
1999.H4226	Hopkins, Pauline Elizabeth (Table P-PZ40)
1999.H425	Hopkins, Seward W. (Table P-PZ40)
1999.H43	Hopper, Edward (Table P-PZ40)
1999.H439	Horner, J. (Table P-PZ40)
	Hornor-Snelling, Lee, 1863-1919 see PS2430.M59
1999.H473	Horton, George Moses, 1798?-1880 (Table P-PZ40)

PS

	Individual authors
	19th century -- Continued
1999.H52	Hosmer, Frederick L. (Table P-PZ40)
1999.H53	Hosmer, James Kendall (Table P-PZ40)
1999.H54	Hosmer, William Howe Cuyler (Table P-PZ40)
1999.H6	Houghton, George Washington Wright (Table P-PZ40)
2005-2008	Hovey, Richard (Table P-PZ35a)
2010.H	Hovey - Howard
2010.H45	Howard, Adah M. (Table P-PZ40)
	Howard, Blanche Willis see PS3009.T7
2014.H12	Howard, Bronson (Table P-PZ40)
2014.H2	Howarth, Ellen Clementine (Doran) (Table P-PZ40)
2014.H5	Howe, Edgar Watson (Table P-PZ40)
2015-2018	Howe, Julia (Ward) (Table P-PZ35a)
2019.H7	Howell, John Edward (Table P-PZ40)
2020-2038	Howells, William Dean (Table P-PZ32 modified)
	Individual genres
	Novels
2025.A2	Collected
2025.A3-Z	Separate. By title, A-Z
	Plays
2026	Collected
2027.A-Z	Separate, A-Z
	Other prose works
2028	Collected
2029.A-Z	Separate, A-Z
	Poems
2030	Collected
2030.5.A-Z	Separate, A-Z
2039.H2	Howland, Marie
2039.H6	Hoyt, Ralph (Table P-PZ40)
2040-2043	Hubbard, Elbert (Table P-PZ35a)
2044.H24	Hubner, Charles William, 1835-1929 (Table P-PZ40)
2044.H28	Hudson, James Thomas, 1860-1929 (Table P-PZ40)
	Hudson, Mary (Clemmer) see PS1039.A32
2044.H4	Huneker, James Gibbons (Table P-PZ40)
2044.H4307	Huntington, George, 1835-1916 (Table P-PZ40)
2044.H4442	Huntington, Jedediah Vincent, 1815-1862 (Table P-PZ40)
2044.H5	Hutton, Laurence (Table P-PZ40)
2044.H67	Hyde, Cornelius Willet Gillam, 1838-1920 (Table P-PZ40)
2044.H8	Hylton, John Dunbar (Table P-PZ40)
2044.I2	Iliowizi, Henry (Table P-PZ40)
2044.I22	Illsley, Charles P. (Table P-PZ40)
2044.I3	Ingalls, John James (Table P-PZ40)
	Cf. E664.I4 Biography
2044.I5	Ingersoll, Charles Jared (Table P-PZ40)
2045-2046	Ingersoll, Robert Green (Table P-PZ36)

	Individual authors
	19th century -- Continued
2048.I52	Ingraham, Joseph Holt (Table P-PZ40)
2048.I67	Iogo, Veen (Table P-PZ40)
2049.I	Ir - Irving
2050-2098	Irving, Washington (Table P-PZ31 modified)
	Separate works
	Adventures of Captain Bonneville see F592
2056	Alhambra (Table PS1)
	Astoria see F880
	Biography and poetical remains of Margaret Davidson
	see PS1513.D9
2057	Bracebridge Hall (Table PS1)
	Chronicle of the conquest of Granada see DP121+
2060	Crayon miscellany (Table PS1)
2062	Legends of the conquest of Spain (Table PS1)
	History of New York by Diedrich Knickerbocker see
	F122
	Life and voyages of Columbus see E111
	Life of Oliver Goldsmith see PR3493
	Life of Washington see E312
	Mohamet and his successors see BP75
2063	Reviews and miscellanies (Table PS1)
2064	Salmagundi (Irving and Paulding) (Table PS1)
2066	Sketchbook (Table PS1)
2067	Legend of Sleepy Hollow (Table PS1)
2068	Rip Van Winkle (Table PS1)
2069.A-Z	Other, A-Z
	Subarrange each by Table P-PZ43
	e. g.
2069.C4-.C43	Christmas papers: "Christmas in England," "Old
	Christmas" (Table P-PZ43)
2070	Tales of traveller (Table PS1)
	Tour on the prairies see F697
	Voyages of the companions of Columbus see E123
2071	Wolfert's roost (Table PS1)
2072.A-Z	Other, A-Z
	Subarrange each by Table P-PZ43
2099.I5	Irving, William (Table P-PZ40)
2101.I	Is - Iu
2102.I	Iv - Ivz
2103.I	Iw - Iz
2104.J	J - Jackson
2105-2108	Jackson, Helen Hunt (Table P-PZ35a)
2109.J4	James, Charles (Table P-PZ40)
2110-2128	James, Henry (Table P-PZ32 modified)
2111	Collected plays

PS

	Individual authors
	19th century
	James, Henry -- Continued
	Separate plays see PS2120.A+
	Novels and tales
	Collected works see PS2110+
2116.A-Z	Separate works. By title, A-Z
	Subarrange each by Table P-PZ43
2120.A-Z	Other works (Essays, etc.). By title, A-Z
	Subarrange each by Table P-PZ43
2129.J2	Janvier, Francis de Haes (Table P-PZ40)
2129.J3	Janvier, Margaret Thomson ("Margaret Vandegrift") (Table P-PZ40)
2129.J5	Janvier, Thomas Allibone (Table P-PZ40)
2129.J7	Jeffrey, Rosa Vertner (Griffith) (Table P-PZ40)
2129.J8	Jennison, Lucy White (Table P-PZ40)
2129.J95	Jessup, Alexander (Table P-PZ40)
2130-2133	Jewett, Sarah Orne (Table P-PZ35a)
2134.J	Jewett - Johnson, L.
2134.J2	Jewett, Sophie (Table P-PZ40)
2134.J515	Johnson, A.E., Mrs. (Table P-PZ40)
2134.J516	Johnson, A.E. (Amelia E.), b. 1859 (Table P-PZ40)
2135.J	Johnson, M. - Johnson, R.
2135.J37	Johnson, Richard S. (Table P-PZ40)
2135.J4	Johnson, Robert Underwood (Table P-PZ40)
2135.J7	Johnson, Rossiter (Table P-PZ40)
2136.J	Johnson, S. - Johnson, Z.
2136.J5	Johnson, Virginia Wales (Table P-PZ40)
2137.J	Johnston, A. - Johnston, M.
2140-2143	Johnston, Mary (Table P-PZ35a)
2145-2148	Johnston, Richard Malcolm (Table P-PZ35a)
2149.J8	Johnston, William Preston (Table P-PZ40)
2150.J2	Jones, Alice Ilgenfritz, 1846-1905 (Table P-PZ40)
2150.J3	Jones, Amanda Theodosia (Table P-PZ40)
2150.J78	Jones, Hamilton Chamberlain, 1798-1868 (Table P-PZ40)
2151.J	Jones, J. - Jones, Z.
2151.J28	Jones, J. McHenry (Table P-PZ40)
2151.J42	Jones, John Beauchamp, 1810-1866 (Table P-PZ40)
2152.J	Jordan - Joyce
2152.J4	Jordan, David Starr (Table P-PZ40)
2153.J4	Joyce, John Alexander (Table P-PZ40)
2153.J65	Judah, Samuel Benjamin Herbert, b. 1799 (Table P-PZ40)
2155	Judd, Sylvester (Table P-PZ39)
2156.J3	Judson, Emily Chubbuck, 1817-1854 (Table P-PZ40)
2157-2158	Keenan, Henry Francis (Table P-PZ36)
2159.K13	Kelley, Emma Dunham (Table P-PZ40)
2159.K2	Kelley, William Valentine (Table P-PZ40)

	Individual authors
	19th century -- Continued
2159.K3	Kellogg, Elijah (Table P-PZ40)
2160-2163	Kennedy, John Pendleton (Table P-PZ35a)
2164.K3	Kenyon, James Benjamin (Table P-PZ40)
2164.K6	Ketchum, Annie (Chambers) (Table P-PZ40)
2165-2168	Key, Francis Scott (Table P-PZ35a)
2169.K4	Kimball, Harriet McEwen (Table P-PZ40)
2169.K6	Kimball, Richard Burleigh (Table P-PZ40)
2169.K8	King, Benjamin Franklin, Jr. ("Ben King") (Table P-PZ40)
2170-2173	King, Charles (Table P-PZ35a)
2174.K3	King, Clarence, 1842-1901 (Table P-PZ40)
2174.K5	King, Edward (Table P-PZ40)
2175-2178	King, Grace Elizabeth (Table P-PZ35a)
2179.K36	King, Susan Petigru, 1824-1875 (Table P-PZ40)
2179.K4	Kingsley, Florence Morse, 1859-1937 (Table P-PZ40)
2179.K5	Kinney, Coates (Table P-PZ40)
2182-2183	Kinney, Elizabeth Clementine (Dodge) (Table P-PZ36)
2186.K5	Kip, Leonard (Table P-PZ40)
2187-2188	Kirk, Ellen Warner (Olney) (Table P-PZ36)
2189.K	Kirk - Kirkland
2189.K4	Kirk, Hyland Clare, 1846-1917 (Table P-PZ40)
2191-2192	Kirkland, Caroline Matilda (Stansbury) (Table P-PZ36)
2194-2195	Kirkland, Joseph (Table P-PZ36)
2196.K	Kirkland - Knn
	Klingle, George see PS1949.H7
2197.K11	Knott, William Wilson (Table P-PZ40)
	Knowles, Frederic Lawrence see PS3521.N75
2197.K4	Knox, Thomas Wallace (Table P-PZ40)
2197.K6	Koopman, Harry Lyman (Table P-PZ40)
2198.L	Lai - Lal
2199.L3	Lamar, Mirabeau Buonaparte (Table P-PZ40)
2199.L5	Landon, Melville D. ("Eli Perkins") (Table P-PZ40)
	Cf. PN6161 Wit and humor
2199.L54	Lane, Mary E. Bradley (Table P-PZ40)
2199.L75	Langille, J.H. (James Hibbert) (Table P-PZ40)
2199.L8	Lanier, Clifford (Table P-PZ40)
2200-2218	Lanier, Sidney (Table P-PZ32 modified)
	Individual genres
	Poems
2205	Collected works
2206.A-Z	Separate works. By title, A-Z
	Subarrange each by Table P-PZ43
	Prose works
2207	Collected works
	Separate works
	Bob see QL676

	Individual authors
	19th century
	Lanier, sidney
	Individual genres
	Prose works
	Separate works
	The English novel see PR826
	Florida see F311
	Music and poetry see ML60.L24
2209	Retrospects and prospects (Table P-PZ41)
	Science of English verse see PE1505
	Shakespeare and his forerunners see PR2956
	Tiger-lilies see PZ3
2219.L4	Lanigan, George Thomas (Table P-PZ40)
2219.L47	Lanman, Charles (Table P-PZ40)
2220-2223	Larcom, Lucy (Table P-PZ35a)
2225-2226	Lathrop, George Parsons (Table P-PZ36)
2227.L	Lathrop, G. - Lathrop, R.
2230-2231	Lathrop, Rose (Hawthorne) (Table P-PZ36)
2232.L3	Latimer, Henry Randolph (Table P-PZ40)
2233-2234	Lazarus, Emma (Table P-PZ36)
2235.L5	Learned, Walter (Table P-PZ40)
2235.L7	Leavitt, John McDowell (Table P-PZ40)
2236	Lae - Legaré
2236.L267	Lee, Eliza Buckminster, 1794-1864 (Table P-PZ40)
2236.L273	Lee, Hannah Farnham Sawyer, 1780-1865 (Table P-PZ40)
2236.L32	Lee, Minnie Mary, 1826-1903 (Table P-PZ40)
2237-2238	Legaré, Hugh Swinton (Table P-PZ36)
2239.L3	Leggett, William (Table P-PZ40)
2239.L5	Leighton, William (Table P-PZ40)
2240-2243	Leland, Charles Godfrey ("Hans Breitman") (Table P-PZ35a)
2244.L	Leland - Leu
2244.L5	Leslie, Eliza (Table P-PZ40)
2245.L	Lev - Lewir
2246.L2	Lewis, Alonzo (Table P-PZ40)
2246.L3	Lewis, Charles Bertrand ("M. Quad") (Table P-PZ40)
2246.L35	Lewis, Estella Anna Blanche (Robinson) (Table P-PZ40)
2246.L369	Libbey, Laura Jean, 1862-1924 (Table P-PZ40)
2246.L47	Lillie, Lucy Cecil (White), 1855- (Table P-PZ40)
	Lincoln, Abraham see E457
2246.L7	Linn, John Blair (Table P-PZ40)
2246.L8	Lippard, George (Table P-PZ40)
2247	Lippincott, Sarah Jane (Clarke) ("Grace Greenwood") (Table P-PZ39)
2248.L2	Lippmann, Julie Mathilde (Table P-PZ40)

	Individual authors
	19th century -- Continued
2248.L3	Litchfield, Grace Denio (Table P-PZ40)
2248.L6	Lloyd, David Demarest (Table P-PZ40)
	Lloyd, John Uri see PS3523.L64
2248.L8	Lock, David Ross ("Petroleum V. Nasby") (Table P-PZ40)
	Cf. PN6161 Wit and humor
2248.L835	Locke, Richard Adams, 1800-1871 (Table P-PZ40)
2248.L85	Lockhart, Arthur John ("Pastor Felix") (Table P-PZ40)
2248.L9	Lockwood, Ralph Ingersoll (Table P-PZ40)
2249.L4	Lodge, Henry Cabot (Table P-PZ40)
	Cf. E660.L75+ Collected works
	Cf. E664.L7 Biography
2249.L5	Lofland, John (Table P-PZ40)
2249.L6	Logan, Algernon Sydney (Table P-PZ40)
2249.L62	Logan, Olive Logan, 1839-1909 (Table P-PZ40)
2249.L85	Long, John Davis, 1838-1915 (Table P-PZ40)
2250-2298	Longfellow, Henry Wadsworth (Table P-PZ31 modified)
	Separate works
2255	Ballads and other poems (Table P-PZ41)
2256	Belfry of Bruges and other poems (Table P-PZ41)
2257	Birds of passage (Table P-PZ41)
2258	Christus (Table P-PZ41)
2259	The divine tragedy (Table P-PZ41)
2260	The golden legend (Table P-PZ41)
2261	The New England tragedies (Table P-PZ41)
2262	Courtship of Miles Standish, etc. (Table P-PZ41)
2263	Evangeline, etc. (Table P-PZ41)
2264	Hanging of the crane, etc. (Table P-PZ41)
2265	Poems on slavery (Table P-PZ41)
2266	The seaside and the fireside (Table P-PZ41)
2267	The song of Hiawatha, etc. (Table P-PZ41)
2268	The Spanish student (Table P-PZ41)
2269	Tales of a wayside inn (Table P-PZ41)
2270	Voices of the night (Table P-PZ41)
2271.A-Z	Other poetical works, A-Z
	Subarrange each by Table P-PZ43
	Prose
2272	Collected works
	Other
2273.A-Z	Separate works, A-Z
	Subarrange each by Table P-PZ43
2299.L2	Longfellow, Samuel (Table P-PZ40)
2299.L4	Longstreet, Augustus Baldwin (Table P-PZ40)
2299.L6	Lord, William Wilberforce (Table P-PZ40)
2299.L8	Loring, Frederick Wadsworth (Table P-PZ40)
2299.L98	Lowe, Martha Ann (Perry) (Table P-PZ40)

	Individual authors
	19th century -- Continued
2300-2348	Lowell, James Russell (Table P-PZ31 modified)
	Individual genres
	Poems
2305	Collected works
	Separate works
2306	Biglow papers (Table P-PZ41)
2307	The courtin' (Table P-PZ41)
2308	Early poems (Table P-PZ41)
2309	Fable for critics (Table P-PZ41)
2310	Last poems (Table P-PZ41)
2311	Under the old elm (Table P-PZ41)
2312	Vision of Sir Launfel (Table P-PZ41)
2314.A-Z	Other, A-Z
	Subarrange each by Table P-PZ43
	Prose
2315	Collected works
	Separate works
2316	Among my books (Table P-PZ41)
2317	Early prose works (Table P-PZ41)
2318	Fireside travels (Table P-PZ41)
2319	Latest literary essays (Table P-PZ41)
2320	My study windows (Table P-PZ41)
2322.A-Z	Other, A-Z
	Subarrange each by Table P-PZ43
2349.L2	Lowell, Maria (White) (Table P-PZ40)
2349.L4	Lowell, Robert Traill Spence (Table P-PZ40)
2349.L6	Lucas, Daniel Bedinger (Table P-PZ40)
2350.L	Lud - Luec
2350.L5	Ludlow, Fitz Hugh (Table P-PZ40)
2351.L2	Lueders (Lüders), Charles Henry (Table P-PZ40)
2351.L35	Lum, Dyer D. (Dyer Daniel), 1840-1893 (Table P-PZ40)
2351.L4	Lunt, George (Table P-PZ40)
	Luska, Sidney, 1861-1905 see PS1795+
2351.L6	Lytle, William Haines (Table P-PZ40)
2353-2354	Mabie, Hamilton Wright (Table P-PZ36)
2355.M1555	MacAlpine, Avery (Table P-PZ40)
2355.M168	McCall, John Cadwalader, 1793-1846 (Table P-PZ40)
2355.M2	McClelland, Mary Greenway (Table P-PZ40)
2355.M6	McCord, Louisa Susannah (Cheves) (Table P-PZ40)
2356.M	McCubbin - McDowell
2356.M5	McDermott, George Lawrence (Table P-PZ40)
2357-2358	McDowell, Katherine Sherwood Bonner, 1849-1883 (Table P-PZ36)
2359.M14	McGaffey, Ernest (Table P-PZ40)
2359.M1494	McGuire, M. Heber (Table P-PZ40)

	Individual authors
	19th century -- Continued
2359.M16	McHenry, James (Table P-PZ40)
2359.M176	McIntosh, Burr, 1862-1942 (Table P-PZ40)
2359.M48	McKellar, Thomas (Table P-PZ40)
2359.M587	Macnie, John (Table P-PZ40)
2359.M635	Macy, Arthur (Table P-PZ40)
2359.M6448	Magruder, Julia, 1854-1907 (Table P-PZ40)
2359.M648	Major, Charles (Table P-PZ40)
2359.M652	Makeever, John L. (Table P-PZ40)
2359.M66	Maline, Walter (Table P-PZ40)
2359.M69	Mann, Horace (Table P-PZ40)
2359.M6914	Mann, Mary Tyler Peabody, 1806-1887 (Table P-PZ40)
2359.M7	Mansfield, Lewis W. (Table P-PZ40)
2360-2363	Markham, Edwin. (Table P-PZ35a)
2364.M8	Martin, Edward Sandford (Table P-PZ40)
2365	Marvin, Frederic Rowland (Table P-PZ39)
2366.M	Marvin - Marz
2367.M	Mas - Masz
2367.M3	Mason, Caroline Atherton (Briggs) (Table P-PZ40)
2367.M6	Masson, Thomas Lansing (Table P-PZ40)
2368.M	Mat - Mats
2368.M3	Mathews, Albert ("Paul Siogvolk") (Table P-PZ40)
2368.M4	Mathews, Cornelius (Table P-PZ40)
	Mathews, Theodore Dehone, 1819-1861 see PS1534.D413
2368.M8	Mathews, William (Table P-PZ40)
2369.M	Matt - Mattg
2370-2373	Matthews, Brander (Table P-PZ35a)
2374.M	Matthews - Maw
2374.M18	Matthews, Brinsley, 1849-1920 (Table P-PZ40)
2374.M9	Maturin, Edward (Table P-PZ40)
2374.M94	Maurice, Richards S. (Table P-PZ40)
2375.M	Max - Maxz
2376.M	May - Maz
2376.M56	Mayer, Nathan, 1838-1912 (Table P-PZ40)
2376.M57	Mayer, O.B., 1818-1891 (Table P-PZ40)
2376.M7	Mayo, William Starbuck (Table P-PZ40)
2377.M	Mea - Meaz
2377.M52	Mead, Lucia True Ames, 1856-1936 (Table P-PZ40)
2378.M	Meb - Mek
2378.M27	Meeker, Nathan Cook, 1814-1879 (Table P-PZ40)
2379.M2	Mellen, Grenville (Table P-PZ40)
2380-2388	Melville, Herman (Table P-PZ33 modified)
	Collected works
2380	By date
2380.E00-.E99	1800-1899

	Individual authors
	19th century
	Melville, Herman
	Collected works
	By date -- Continued
2380.F00-.F99	1900-1999
2380.G00-.G99	2000-2099
2389.M2	Menard, John Willis, 1838-1893 (Table P-PZ40)
2389.M24	Menken, Adah Isaacs, 1835-1868 (Table P-PZ40)
2389.M287	Merrill, James Milford, 1847- (Table P-PZ40)
2389.M3	Messenger, Lillian Rozell (Table P-PZ40)
2389.M5	Meyer, John Joseph, 1873- (Table P-PZ40)
2390.M	Mi - Mifflin
2391-2392	Mifflin, Lloyd (Table P-PZ36)
2393.M	Mifflin - Millard
2393.M6	Miles, George Henry (Table P-PZ40)
2394.M	Miller, A. - Miller, James
2394.M14	Miller, Alex M. (Table P-PZ40)
2395-2398	Miller, Joaquin (Table P-PZ35a)
2399.M755	Milne, Robert Duncan, 1844-1899 (Table P-PZ40)
2400-2408	Mitchell, Donald Grant ("Ik Marvel") (Table P-PZ33)
2409.M2	Mitchell, John Ames (Table P-PZ40)
2409.M4	Mitchell, Langdon Elwyn (Table P-PZ40)
2410-2418	Mitchell, Silas Weir (Table P-PZ33 modified)
	Collected works
2410	By date
2410.E00-.E99	1800-1899
2410.F00-.F99	1900-1999
2410.G00-.G99	2000-2099
2411	Collected poems
2419.M3	Mitchell, Walter (Table P-PZ40)
2420-2423	Monroe, Harriet (Table P-PZ35a)
2424.M	Monroe - Moody
2425-2428	Moody, William Vaughn (Table P-PZ35a)
2429.M4	Moore, Charles Leonard (Table P-PZ40)
2429.M5	Moore, Clement Clarke (Table P-PZ40)
2429.M8	Moore, John Trotwood (Table P-PZ40)
2430.M	Moore - More
2430.M3	Moore, Mrs. Julia A. (Davis) (Table P-PZ40)
2430.M59	Moqué, Mrs. Alice Lee Horner, 1863-1919 (Table P-PZ40)
2431-2432	More, Paul Elmer (Table P-PZ36)
2433.M	More - Morris
2433.M5	Morris, George Pope (Table P-PZ40)
2434.M264	Morrison, R.M. (Roderick M.), d, 1849 (Table P-PZ40)
2434.M4	Morse, James Herbert (Table P-PZ40)
2434.M43	Morse, Salmi, 1826-1884 (Table P-PZ40)

Individual authors
19th century -- Continued

2434.M627	Morton, S.S. (Susan S.) (Table P-PZ40)
2435-2436	Motley, John Lothrop (Table P-PZ36)
2437.M	Motley - Moulton
2440-2443	Moulton, Louise (Chandler) (Table P-PZ35a)
2444.M	Moulton - Moz
2447.M	Mu - Muk
2447.M5	Muir, John (Table P-PZ40)
2448.M	Mul -Mum
2449.M	Mun - Mur
2449.M26	Mundo, Oto (Table P-PZ40)
2449.M4	Munger, Theodore Thornton (Table P-PZ40)
2449.M54	Monroe, Kirk, 1850-1930 (Table P-PZ40)
2449.M83	Murdock, William C. (Table P-PZ40)
2450-2458	Murfree, Mary Noailles ("Charles Egbert Craddock") (Table P-PZ33)
2459.M43	Murray, W.H.H. (William Henry Harrison), 1840-1904 (Table P-PZ40)
2459.M7	Myers, Peter Hamilton, 1812-1878 (Table P-PZ40)
2459.N2	Nadal, Ehrman Syme (Table P-PZ40)
2459.N28	Neal, John (Table P-PZ40)
2459.N2814	Neal, Joseph Clay, 1807-1847 (Table P-PZ40)
2459.N3	Nesmith, James E. (Table P-PZ40)
	Nevada, Ned see PS3068.T34
2459.N3485	Newcomb, Simon (Table P-PZ40)
2459.N4	Newell, Robert Henry ("Orpheus C. Kerr") (Table P-PZ40)
	Cf. PN6161 Wit and humor
2459.N49	Newman, Eugene William ("Savoyard") (Table P-PZ40)
2459.N565	Nichols, Mary Sargeant Gove, 1810-1884 (Table P-PZ40)
2459.N6	Nichols, Starr Hoyt (Table P-PZ40)
2464.N	Nicholson - Nid
2466.N	Nie - Nik
2467.N	Nil - Niw
2468.N	Nix - Niz
2468.N18	Nix, Robert, 1854-1910 (Table P-PZ40)
2469.N	Noa - Norris
2469.N15	Noah, Mordecai Manuel, 1785-1851 (Table P-PZ40)
2470-2473	Norris, Frank (Table P-PZ35a)
2474.N	Norris - Norton
2475-2478	Norton, Charles Eliot (Table P-PZ35a)
2479.N	Norton - Nt
2480.N	Nu - Nye
2481-2482	Nye, Edgar Wilson ("Bill Nye") (Table P-PZ36)
	Cf. PN6161 Wit and humor
2483.N	Nye - Nz
2484.O	O - O'Brien, F.

Individual authors
19th century
O - O'Brien, F. -- Continued

2484.O4	Oberholtzer, Sara Louisa (Vickers) (Table P-PZ40)
2484.O47	O'Brien, Dillon, 1817-1992 (Table P-PZ40)
2485	O'Brien, Fitz-James (Table P-PZ39)
2486.O	O'Brien, F. - O'Hara, T.
2486.O5	O'Connor, William Douglas (Table P-PZ40)
2486.O56	Odiorne, Thomas, 1769-1851 (Table P-PZ40)
2487-2488	O'Hara, Theodore (Table P-PZ36)
2489.O	O'Hara, T. - O'Reilly, J.
	Oliver, John, 1863-1919 see PS2430.M59
	Oliver, N.T. see PS3068.T34
2489.O49	Olmstead, Edwards Keeler (Table P-PZ40)
2489.O63	O'Neill, James, b. 1860 (Table P-PZ40)
2489.O74	Oppenheim, Ansel, Mrs. d. 1915 (Table P-PZ40)
	Optic, Oliver, 1822-1897 see PS1006.A5
2490-2493	O'Reilly, John Boyle (Table P-PZ35a)
2494.O	O'Reilly - Osborne
2494.O19	Ormar, James Allan (Table P-PZ40)
2494.O4	Osborn, Laughton (Table P-PZ40)
2495	Osborne, Lloyd (Table P-PZ39)
2496.O	Osbourne - Osgood, F.
2497	Osgood, Frances Sargent (Locke) (Table P-PZ39)
2498.O	Osgood, F. - Osgz
2499.O	Osh - Oss
2500-2508	Ossoli, Sarah Margaret (Fuller) (Table P-PZ33)
2509.O-.P	Ossoli - Page
2509.O46	Ottolengui, Rodrigues, 1861?-1937 (Table P-PZ40)
	Our Nig, 1808-ca. 1870 see PS3334.W39
2509.O8	Owen, Robert Dale (Table P-PZ40)
	Packard, Clarissa see PS1744.G5
2510-2518	Page, Thomas Nelson (Table P-PZ33 modified)
	Collected works
2510	By date
2510.E00-.E99	1800-1899
2510.F00-.F99	1900-1999
2510.G00-.G99	2000-2099
2519.P2	Paine, Robert Treat (Table P-PZ40)
2519.P4	Palmer, John Williamson (Table P-PZ40)
2519.P6	Palmer, Ray (Table P-PZ40)
2520.P	Pam - Parkman
2520.P33	Parish, George, Jr.
2520.P4	Parker, Benjamin Strattan
	Parkes, Elizabeth (Robins) see PS2719.R4
2521-2522	Parkman, Francis (Table P-PZ36)
	Cf. E175.5.A+ Biography

Individual authors
    19th century -- Continued

2523.P8	Parsons, Thomas William (Table P-PZ40)
2523.P9	Parton, Sarah Payson (Willis) ("Fanny Fern") (Table P-PZ40)
2524.P	Pat - Paulding
2524.P49	Patten, J.A. (Table P-PZ40)
2525-2528	Paulding, James Kirke (Table P-PZ35a)
2530-2533	Payne, John Howard (Table P-PZ35a)
2534.P	Payne - Peab
2534.P5	Payne, Will (Table P-PZ40)
2539.P14	Peacock, Thomas Brower (Table P-PZ40)
2539.P214	Pearson, Charles H. (Table P-PZ40)
2539.P275	Peck, George Washington, 1817-1859 (Table P-PZ40)
2539.P28	Peck, George Wilbur (Table P-PZ40)
	Cf. PN6161 Wit and humor
2539.P3	Peck, Harry Thurston (Table P-PZ40)
2539.P4	Peck, Samuel Minturn (Table P-PZ40)
2539.P5	Peck, William Henry (Table P-PZ40)
2539.P7	Pellew, George (Table P-PZ40)
2540-2543	Percival, James Gates (Table P-PZ35a)
2544.P	Percival - Perq
2545.P4	Perry, Bliss (Table P-PZ40)
2545.P5	Perry, George (Table P-PZ40)
2545.P7	Perry, Lilla Cabot (Table P-PZ40)
2550-2553	Perry, Nora (Table P-PZ35a)
2554.P396	Peterson, Charles Jacobs, 1819-1887 (Table P-PZ40)
2554.P4	Peterson, Henry (Table P-PZ40)
	Petigru, Susan DuPont, 1824-1875 see PS2179.K36
2555.P	Pett - Petth
2556.P	Petti - Phelps, D.
2557.P	Phelps, E. - Phelps, R.
2557.P4	Phelps, Elizabeth Stuart, 1815-1852 (Table P-PZ40)
	Phelps, Elizabeth Stuart, 1844-1911 see PS3140+
2558.P	Phelps, S. - Phh
2559.P	Phi - Phillips, I.
	Phillips, David Graham see PS3531.H5
2565.P	Phillips, J. - Phillips, W.
2566-2567	Phillips, Wendell (Table P-PZ36)
2576.P4	Piatt, Donn (Table P-PZ40)
2578-2579	Piatt, John James (Table P-PZ36)
2581-2582	Piatt, Sarah Morgan (Bryan) (Table P-PZ36)
2583.P	Piatt - Pic
2583.P44	Pickens, Lucy Petaway Holcombe (Table P-PZ40)
2584.P2	Pidgin, Charles Felton (Table P-PZ40)
2584.P55	Pierce, Squier Littell, 1832-1918 (Table P-PZ40)
2584.P7	Pierpont, John (Table P-PZ40)

	Individual authors
	19th century -- Continued
2585-2586	Pike, Albert (Table P-PZ36)
2587.P5	Pike, Mary Hayden (Green) ("Mary Langdon") (Table P-PZ40)
2588.P	Pil - Pim
2588.P5	Pilgrim, James (Table P-PZ40)
2589.P	Pin - Pind
2590.P	Pine - Pinkney
2590.P57	Pinkney, Amelia (Table P-PZ40)
2591-2592	Pinkney, Edward Coote (Table P-PZ36)
2593.P	Pinkney - Poe
2593.P3	Pise, Charles Constantine, 1801-1866 (Table P-PZ40)
2593.P347	Plato, Ann (Table P-PZ40)
2600-2648	Poe, Edgar Allan (Table P-PZ31 modified)
	Individual genres
	Poems
2605	Collected works
	Separate works
2606	Annabel Lee (Table P-PZ41)
2607	Bells (Table P-PZ41)
2608	Lenore (Table P-PZ41)
2609	Raven (Table P-PZ41)
2610.A-Z	Other, A-Z
	Subarrange each by Table P-PZ43
2611.A-Z	Dramatic works, A-Z
	Subarrange each by Table P-PZ43
	e. g.
2611.P7-.P73	Politian (Table P-PZ43)
	Prose works
	Fiction
2612	Collected works
	Separate works
2613	Black cat (Table P-PZ41)
2614	Fall of the house of usher (Table P-PZ41)
2615	Gold bug (Table P-PZ41)
2616	Ligeia (Table P-PZ41)
2617	Murders in the Rue Morgue (Table P-PZ41)
2618.A-Z	Other, A-Z
	Subarrange each by Table P-PZ43
	Critical and miscellaneous
2619	Collected works
	Separate works
2620	Eureka (Table P-PZ41)
2622.A-Z	Other, A-Z
	Subarrange each by Table P-PZ43
2649.P	Poe - Poz

Individual authors
19th century
Poe - Poz -- Continued

2649.P4	Pool, Maria Louise (Table P-PZ40)
2649.P422	Pope, Gustaveus W. (Table P-PZ40)
2649.P44	Porter, David Dixon, 1813-1891 (Table P-PZ40)
2649.P5	Porter, William Sydney ("O. Henry") (Table P-PZ40)
2649.P55	Posey, Alexander Lawrence, 1873-1908 (Table P-PZ40)
2649.P78	Pounds, Jessie Brown, 1861-1921 (Table P-PZ40)
2649.P813	Power, Susan Anna, 1813-1877 (Table P-PZ40)
2649.P82	Powers, Horatio Nelson (Table P-PZ40)
2651.P	Pra - Prem
2653-2654	Prentice, George Denison (Table P-PZ36)
2655.P5	Prentiss, Elizabeth (Payson) (Table P-PZ40)
2656-2657	Prescott, William Hickling (Table P-PZ36)
2659.P46	Preston, Annie A. (Table P-PZ40)
2659.P5	Preston, Harriet Waters (Table P-PZ40)
2660-2663	Preston, Margaret (Junkin) (Table P-PZ35a)
2664.P15	Preuss, Henry Clay (Table P-PZ40)
2664.P3	Prime, Samuel Irenaeus (Table P-PZ40)
2664.P4	Prime, William Cowper (Table P-PZ40)
2664.P82	Pringle, Elizabeth W. Allston (Elizabeth Waties Allston), 1845-1921 (Table P-PZ40)
2665-2668	Proctor, Edna Dean (Table P-PZ35a)
2669.P3	Proudfit, David Law (Table P-PZ40)
2669.P545	Purvis, T.T. (Table P-PZ40)
	Putnam, Arthur Lee see PS1029.A3
2669.P6	Putnam, Mary Traill Spence (Lowell) (Table P-PZ40)
2670-2671	Pyle, Howard (Table P-PZ36)
2672.Q34	Quigley, Hugh, 1819-1883 (Table P-PZ40)
2672.Q5	Quincy, Edmund (Table P-PZ40)
2672.Q7	Quincy, Josiah, 1772-1864 (Table P-PZ40)
2672.Q8	Quincy, Josiah Phillips, 1829- (Table P-PZ40)
2673.R	Ra - Randall
2673.R15	Ralph, Julian, 1853-1903
2674	Randall, James Ryder (Table P-PZ39)
2675.R2	Randall, John Witt (Table P-PZ40)
2675.R4	Randolph, Anson Davies Fitz (Table P-PZ40)
2675.R47	Randolph, Sarah Nicholas, 1839-1892 (Table P-PZ40)
2675.R56	Rankin, George Castle, 1860-1882 (Table P-PZ40)
2675.R6	Rankin, Jeremiah Eames (Table P-PZ40)
2676.R	Rap - Raymond, G.
	Rattlehead, David, 1826-1903 see PS1238.B5
2676.R8	Ray, William (Table P-PZ40)
2677-2678	Raymond, George Lansing (Table P-PZ36)
2679.R3	Rayner, Isidor (Table P-PZ40)
2679.R55	Read, Martha (Table P-PZ40)

Individual authors

19th century -- Continued

2679.R6	Read, Opie Percival (Table P-PZ40)
2680-2688	Read, Thomas Buchanan (Table P-PZ33 modified)
	Collected works
2680	By date
2680.E00-.E99	1800-1899
2680.F00-.F99	1900-1999
2680.G00-.G99	2000-2099
2690-2691	Realf, Richard (Table P-PZ36)
2692.R33	Redd, Mrs. Rebecca Fergus (Table P-PZ40)
2693-2694	Reese, Lizette Woodworth (Table P-PZ36)
2695.R	Reese - Repplier
2695.R36	Reid, Charles Sloan (Table P-PZ40)
	Reid, Christian see PS3066.T
2695.R72	Remington, Frederic, 1861-1909 (Table P-PZ40)
2696-2697	Repplier, Agnes (Table P-PZ36)
2698.R2	Requier, Augustus Julian (Table P-PZ40)
2698.R3	Rexford, Eben Eugene (Table P-PZ40)
2698.R43	Rhodes, William Henry, 1822-1876 (Table P-PZ40)
2698.R5	Rice, Harvey (Table P-PZ40)
2698.R8	Richards, Laura Elizabeth (Howe) (Table P-PZ40)
2699.R2	Richardson, Albert Deane (Table P-PZ40)
2699.R42	Richardson, Warren (Table P-PZ40)
2699.R48	Richmond, James Cook, 1808-1866 (Table P-PZ40)
2699.R54	Ricketson, Daniel (Table P-PZ40)
2699.R6	Riddle, Albert Gallatin (Table P-PZ40)
2699.R7	Rideing, William Henry (Table P-PZ40)
2700-2708	Riley, James Whitcomb (Table P-PZ33 modified)
	Collected works
2700	By date
2700.E00-.E99	1800-1899
2700.F00-.F99	1900-1999
2700.G00-.G99	2000-2099
2710-2713	Ripley, George (Table P-PZ35a)
2714.R	Ripley - Ritchie
2716-2717	Ritchie, Anna Cora (Ogden) Mowatt (Table P-PZ36)
2718.R	Ritchie - Robd
2718.R47	Rivers, George R.R. (George Robert Russell) d. 1900 (Table P-PZ40)
2718.R49	Rivers, William J. (William James), 1822-1909 (Table P-PZ40)
2719.R	Robe - Roche
2719.R38	Robertson, Morgan, 1861-1915 (Table P-PZ40)
2719.R4	Robins, Elizabeth ("C.E. Raimond") (Mrs. G.R. Parkes) (Table P-PZ40)
2719.R5	Robinson, Annie Douglas (Green) (Table P-PZ40)

Individual authors
 19th century
  Robe - Roche -- Continued

2719.R526	Robinson, Edward A. (Table P-PZ40)
2719.R544	Robinson, Harry Perry, Sir, 1859- (Table P-PZ40)
2719.R68	Robinson, Rowland Evans, 1833-1900 (Table P-PZ40)
2719.R7	Robinson, Tracy (Table P-PZ40)
2719.R85	Rocchietti, Joseph (Table P-PZ40)
2721-2722	Roche, James Jeffrey (Table P-PZ36)
2723.R	Roche - Rocz
2723.R5	Rochford, John A., 1833?-1896 (Table P-PZ40)
2723.R63	Rockwell, M. Emilia (Mary Emilia), b. 1835 or 6 (Table P-PZ40)
2724.R	Rod - Roe
2725-2728	Roe, Edward Payson (Table P-PZ35a)
2729.R15	Roe, Edward Reynolds (Table P-PZ40)
2729.R4	Roge, Charlotte Fiske (Bates) (Table P-PZ40)
2730-2733	Rohlfs, Anna Katharine (Green) (Table P-PZ35a)
2734.R3	Rollins, Alice (Wellington) (Table P-PZ40)
2734.R5	Roosevelt, Theodore (Table P-PZ40)
	Cf. E660.R7+ Collected works
2734.R7	Rosenfeld, Sydney (Table P-PZ40)
2734.R8	Ross, Clinton (Table P-PZ40)
2735.R	Ross, E. - Rowk
2735.R55	Rowe, George Clinton, 1853-1903 (Table P-PZ40)
2736.R	Rowl - Runm
2736.R3	Rowson, Susanna (Haswell) (Table P-PZ40)
2736.R315	Royall, Anne (Newport), 1769-1854 (Table P-PZ40)
2736.R32	Royle, Edwin Milton (Table P-PZ40)
2736.R44	Ruffner, Henry, 1790-1861 (Table P-PZ40)
2736.R53	Ruiz de Burton, Amparo, b. 1832 (Table P-PZ40)
2737.R	Runn - Russel
2737.R6	Rush, James (Table P-PZ40)
2737.R63	Rush, Rebecca, b. 1779 (Table P-PZ40)
2738.R	Russell, A. - Russell, I.
2738.R3	Russell, Addison Peale (Table P-PZ40)
2740-2743	Russell, Irwin (Table P-PZ35a)
2744.R	Russell, I. - Ryan, A.J.
2745-2748	Ryan, Abram Joseph (Table P-PZ35a)
2749.R-.S	Ryan - Saltus
2749.S37	Sadlier, Mary Anne Madden, 1820-1903 (Table P-PZ40)
2749.S42	Saervold, Ola Johan, 1868-1937 (Table P-PZ40)
2750-2753	Saltus, Edgar Evertson (Table P-PZ35a)
2755-2756	Saltus, Francis Saltus (Table P-PZ36)
2758-2759	Sanborn, Franklin Benjamin (Table P-PZ36)
2760.S	Sanborn, F. - Sanborn, K.

	Individual authors
	19th century -- Continued
2761	Sanborn, Katherine Abbott ("Kate Sanborn") (Table P-PZ39)
2762.S	Sanborn, K. - Sanbt
2763.S	Sanbu - Sandr
2764.S	Sands - Sangster, M.
2764.S4	Sands, Robert Charles (Table P-PZ40)
2765-2768	Sangster, Margaret Elizabeth (Munson) (Table P-PZ35a)
2769	Sansay, Leonora, b. 1781 (Table P-PZ39)
2770-2773	Santayana, George (Table P-PZ35a)
2774.S	Santmyer - Sarga
2775-2778	Sargent, Epes (Table P-PZ35a)
2779.S15	Sargent Lucius Manlius (Table P-PZ40)
2779.S187	Satterlee, Henry Yates, 1843-1908 (Table P-PZ40)
2779.S2	Saunders, Frederick (Table P-PZ40)
2779.S25	Savage, John (Table P-PZ40)
2779.S3	Savage, Minot Judson (Table P-PZ40)
2779.S4	Savage, Philip Henry (Table P-PZ40)
2779.S5	Savage, Richard Henry (Table P-PZ40)
2779.S57	Savage, Timothy (Table P-PZ40)
2779.S7	Sawyer, Eugene T. (Table P-PZ40)
2779.S73	Sawyer, Lemuel, 1777-1852 (Table P-PZ40)
2780-2788	Saxe, John Godfrey (Table P-PZ33 modified)
	Collected works
2780	By date
2780.E00-.E99	1800-1899
2780.F00-.F99	1900-1999
2780.G00-.G99	2000-2099
2789.S	Saxe, J.G. - Scollard, C.
2790-2793	Scollard, Clinton (Table P-PZ35a)
2794.S5	Scudder, Eliza (Table P-PZ40)
2795-2796	Scudder, Horace Elisha (Table P-PZ36)
2797.S3	Searing, Laura Catharine (Redden) (Table P-PZ40)
2797.S5	Sears, Edmund Hamilton (Table P-PZ40)
2797.S7	Seawell, Molly Elliot (Table P-PZ40)
2798	Sedgwick, Catharine Maria (Table P-PZ39)
2799.S	Sedgwick, C. - Sel
2800.S	Sem - Seton
2801-2802	Seton, Ernest Thompson (Table P-PZ36)
2803.S	Seton - Sev
2804.S2	Sewall, Harriet (Winslow) (Table P-PZ40)
2804.S4	Shaler, Nathaniel Southgate (Table P-PZ40)
2804.S6	Shanly, Charles Dawson (Table P-PZ40)
2804.S677	Sharon, Thomas (Table P-PZ40)
2805-2808	Shaw, Henry Wheeler ("Josh Billings") (Table P-PZ35a)
	Cf. PN6161 Wit and humor

	Individual authors
	19th century -- Continued
2809.S	Shaw - Sher
2809.S48	Shaw, W.J. (Table P-PZ40)
2810-2813	Sherman, Frank Dempster (Table P-PZ35a)
2814.S3	Sherwood, Mary Elizabeth (Wilson) (Table P-PZ40)
2815-2818	Shillaber, Benjamin Penhallow ("Mrs. Partington") (Table P-PZ35a)
2819.S	Shillaber, B. - Shim
2820.S	Shin - Shinn, C.
2821-2822	Shinn, Charles Edward (Table P-PZ36)
2824-2825	Shinn, Milicent Washburn (Table P-PZ36)
2826.S	Shinn, M. - Shn
2827.S	Sho - Shors
2828.S	Short - Shr
2829.S	Shu - Sig
2829.S3	Shurtleff, Ernest Warburton (Table P-PZ40)
2829.S87	Signaigo, Joseph Augustine, 1835-1876 (Table P-PZ40)
2830-2833	Sigourney, Lydia Howard (Huntley) (Table P-PZ35a)
2835-2838	Sill, Edward Rowland (Table P-PZ35a modified)
2835.A2	Collected poems. By date
2835.A4	Collected prose. By date
2839.S	Sill, E.R. - Simms, W.G.
2839.S29	Simmons, Henry Martyn, 1841-1905 (Table P-PZ40)
2839.S52	Simms, Jeptha Roat, 1807-1883 (Table P-PZ40)
	Simms, William Gilmore
	Collected works
2840	Complete works. By date
2841	Complete poems (Complete collections)
2842	Collected drama
2843	Selections
2844.A-Z	Translations. By language, A-Z
	Separate works
2845.A-Z	Poems, A-Z
	e. g.
2845.A7	Areytos
2845.A8	Atalantis
2845.C3	Cassique of Accabee
2845.C6	City of the silent
2845.D6	Donna Florida
2845.G6	Grouped thoughts
2845.L7	Lyrical and other poems
2845.P6	Poems: Descriptive, dramatic, etc.
2845.S3	Sabbath lyrics
2845.S6	Southern passages and pictures
2845.V5	Vision of Cortes, etc.

	Individual authors
	19th century
	Simms, William Gilmore
	Separate works -- Continued
2846.A-Z	Dramas, A-Z
	e. g.
2846.M5	Michael Bonham
2846.N6	Norman Maurice
	Romances, etc.
2847	Border romances
2848.A-Z	Special, A-Z
2848.A7	As good as a comedy
2848.B2	Beauchampe
2848.B4	Book of my lady
2848.B6	Border beagles
2848.C2	Carl Werner
2848.C3	Cassique of Kiawah
2848.C5	Castle Dismal
2848.C6	Charlemont
2848.C7	Confession
2848.C8	Count Julian
2848.D2	Dassel of Darien
2848.E8	Eutaw
2848.F6	Forayers
2848.G4	Golden Christmas
2848.G8	Guy Rivers
2848.H3	Helen Halsey
2848.J6	Joscelyn
2848.K2	Katherine Walton
2848.K5	Kinsmen
	Published later as The scout
2848.L4	Lily and the totem
2848.M2	Marie de Berniers
	Maroon see PS2848.M2
2848.M6	Martin Faber
2848.M7	Mellichampe
2848.P2	Partisan
2848.P4	Pelayo
2848.R5	Richard Hurdis
	Scout see PS2848.K5
2848.S7	Southward ho
2848.S8	Sword and the distaff
2848.V2	Vasconselos
2848.W4	Wigwam and the cabin
	Woodcraft see PS2848.S8
2848.Y5	Yemassee

	Individual authors
	19th century
	Simms, William Gilmore
	Separate works -- Continued
2850.A-Z	Other works, A-Z
	e. g.
	For works of American history, see class E-F
2850.E3	Egeria
2852	Dictionaries, indexes, etc.
2853	General works on Simms' life and writings
	Criticism
2854	General works
2858	Language. Grammar. Style
2859.S125	Simon, Barbara Allan (Table P-PZ40)
2859.S186	Sliver, W.A. (Table P-PZ40)
2859.S2	Slosson, Annie (Trumbell) (Table P-PZ40)
2859.S5	Smith, Charles Henry ("Bill Arp") (Table P-PZ40)
	Cf. PN6161 Wit and humor
2859.S8	Smith, Elizabeth Oakes (Prince) (Table P-PZ40)
(2859.S82)	Smith, Elizabeth Thomasina Meade, 1854-1914
	see PR4990.M34
2860-2868	Smith, Francis Hopkinson (Table P-PZ33 modified)
	Collected works
2860	By date
2860.E00-.E99	1800-1899
2860.F00-.F99	1900-1999
2860.G00-.G99	2000-2099
2869.S2686	Smith, Mrs. M.B. (Table P-PZ40)
2869.S3	Smith, May (Riley) (Table P-PZ40)
2869.S7	Smith, Richard Penn (Table P-PZ40)
2870-2873	Smith, Samuel Francis (Table P-PZ35a)
2874.S	Smith, Samuel - Smith, Saq
2875.S	Smith, Sar - Smith, Seb
2876-2877	Smith, Seba ("Major Jack Downing") (Table P-PZ36)
2878.S	Smith, S. - Smz
2878.S33	Smith, W. L. G. (William L. G.), 1814-1878 (Table P-PZ40)
2878.S35	Smith, William Ferguson, 1845-1912 (Table P-PZ40)
2879.S	Sna - Snider
2879.S27	Snelling, Anna L. (Table P-PZ40)
2879.S3	Snelling, William Joseph, 1804-1848 (Table P-PZ40)
2880-2883	Snider, Denton Jaques (Table P-PZ35a)
2884.S	Snider - Snow
	Snodgrass, Quintus Curtius see PS1300+
2885.S	Snow - Snz
2885.S17	Snow, Chauncey Edgar (Table P-PZ40)
2885.S22	Snow, Eliza R. (Eliza Roxey), 1804-1887 (Table P-PZ40)

	Individual authors
	19th century -- Continued
2886.S	So - Soq
2887.S	Sor - Sot
2888.S	Sou - Soutg
2889.S	South - Southv
2890-2893	Southworth, Emma D.E. (Nevitte) (Table P-PZ35a)
2894.S	Southworth, E.D.E. - Spofford, H.P.
2894.S33	Spalding, Susan Marr (Table P-PZ40)
2894.S34	Sparkle, Sallie (Table P-PZ40)
2894.S46	Spaulding, Solomon, 1761-1816 (Table P-PZ40)
2894.S54	Speight, Thomas Wilkinson, 1830-1915 (Table P-PZ40)
2894.S57	Spencer, Bella Zilfa, 1840-1867 (Table P-PZ40)
2895-2898	Spofford, Harriet Prescott (Table P-PZ35a)
2900.S	Sprague, A. - Sprague, Z.
2901.S	Sprague - Sta
2901.S42	Sproat, P.W. (Table P-PZ40)
2902.S	Sta - Stand
2903.S	Standish, A. - Standish, Z.
2904.S	Standish, Z. - Stanton, F.L.
2905-2906	Stanton, Frank Lebby (Table P-PZ36)
2907.S	Stanton, F. - Staq
2908.S	Star - Staz
	Starr, Julian see PS1029.A3
2909.S	Ste - Stedman, E.
2910-2918	Stedman, Edmund Clarence (Table P-PZ33 modified)
	Collected works
2910	By date
2910.E00-.E99	1800-1899
2910.F00-.F99	1900-1999
2910.G00-.G99	2000-2099
2919.S3	Stephens, Anna Sophia (Winterbotham) (Table P-PZ40)
2919.S52	Stephens, Robert Neilson (Table P-PZ40)
2919.S8	Stillman, William James (Table P-PZ40)
2920-2923	Stimsom, Frederic Jesup ("J.S. of Dale") (Table P-PZ35a)
2924.S4	Stimson, John Ward (Table P-PZ40)
2925-2928	Stockton, Frank Richard (Table P-PZ35a)
2930-2931	Stoddard, Charles Warren (Table P-PZ36)
2934.S	Stoddard, C. - Stoddard, R.
2934.S3	Stoddard, Elizabeth Drew (Barstow) (Table P-PZ40)
2934.S5	Stoddard, John Lawson (Table P-PZ40)
2935-2939	Stoddard, Richard Henry (Table P-PZ35)
2941-2942	Stoddard, William Osborn (Table P-PZ36)
2943.S	Stoddard, W. - Stone
2943.S2	Stokes, Ellwood H. (Table P-PZ40)
2943.S3	Stone, Cara Elizabeth (Hanscom) Whiton- (Table P-PZ40)

	Individual authors
	19th century -- Continued
2944.S	Stoner - Story
2944.S5	Storrs, Richard Salter (Table P-PZ40)
2944.S7	Story, Joseph (Table P-PZ40)
2945-2948	Story, William Wetmore (Table P-PZ35a)
2949.S	Story, W.W. - Stowe, H.E.
2950-2958	Stowe, Harriet Elizabeth (Beecher) (Table P-PZ33 modified)
	Collected works
2950	By date
2950.E00-.E99	1800-1899
2950.F00-.F99	1900-1999
2950.G00-.G99	2000-2099
	Separate works. By title, A-Z
	Subarrange each title by Table P-PZ43 unless otherwise specified
	Uncle Tom's Cabin
2954.U5 date	Texts. By date
2954.U5A-.U5Z	Translations. By language, A-Z
2954.U6	Criticism
2959.S23	Stowers, Walter H., 1859- (Table P-PZ40)
2959.S5	Street, Alfred Billings (Table P-PZ40)
2960-2961	Stuart, Ruth (McEnery) (Table P-PZ36)
2962.S7	Sturgis, Julian (Table P-PZ40)
2963	Sullivan, Thomas Russell (Table P-PZ39)
2964.S23	Sumner, Charles Pinckney (Table P-PZ40)
2964.S79	Swift, Lindsay (Table P-PZ40)
2964.S8	Swing, David (Table P-PZ40)
2964.S87	Sylvester, Herbert Milton (Table P-PZ40)
2964.S9	Symonds, William Law (Table P-PZ40)
2965-2968	Tabb, John Bannister (Table P-PZ35a)
2969.T45	Talcott, Hannah Elizabeth (Bradbury) Goodwin (Table P-PZ40)
2969.T5	Talmage, Thomas DeWitt (Table P-PZ40)
2969.T6	Tappan, William Bingham (Table P-PZ40)
2970-2973	Tarkington, Booth (Table P-PZ35a)
2978.T	Tarkington - Taylor
2980-2998	Taylor, Bayard (Table P-PZ32 modified)
	Individual genres
	Poems
2985	Collected works
2986.A-Z	Separate works, A-Z
	Subarrange each by Table P-PZ43
	Prose fiction
2987	Collected works

	Individual authors
	19th century
	Taylor, Bayard
	Individual genres
	Prose fiction -- Continued
2988.A-Z	Separate works, A-Z
	Subarrange each by Table P-PZ43
	Other works (Dramas, etc.)
2989	Collected works
2990.A-Z	Separate works, A-Z
	Subarrange each by Table P-PZ43
	Travels
	Collected works see PS2989
	Separate works
	see class D
2999.T	Taylor - Tel
2999.T2	Taylor, Benjamin Franklin
3000.T	Tem - Terhune
3000.T5	Tenney, Tabitha, 1762-1837
3005-3008	Terhune, Mary Virginia (Hawes) ("Marion Harland") (Table P-PZ35a)
3009.T7	Teuffel, Blanche Willis (Howard) von (Table P-PZ40)
	Thanet, Octave see PS1715+
3010-3013	Thaxter, Celia (Laighton) (Table P-PZ35a)
3014.T3	Thayer, Ernest Lawrence, 1863-1940 (Table P-PZ40)
3015-3016	Thayer, William Roscoe (Table P-PZ36)
3019.T	Thayer - Thomas
3020-3023	Thomas, Augustus (Table P-PZ35a)
3025-3028	Thomas, Edith Matilda (Table P-PZ35a)
3029.T	Thomas, E. - Thomas, K.
3029.T3	Thomas, Frederick William (Table P-PZ40)
3030.T38	Thomas, Henry J., Mrs. (Table P-PZ40)
3030.T5	Thomas, Lewis Foulk (Table P-PZ40)
3030.T65	Thomes, William Henry, 1824-1895 (Table P-PZ40)
3031.T	Thompson, A. - Thompson, F.
3031.T7	Thompson, Daniel Pierce (Table P-PZ40)
3032.T	Thompson, G. - Thompson, H.
3032.T29	Thompson, George, b. 1823 (Table P-PZ40)
3033.T	Thompson, I. - Thompson, K.
3033.T4	Thompson, John Reuben (Table P-PZ40)
3034.T	Thompson, L. - Thompson, M.
3035-3038	Thompson, Maurice (Table P-PZ35a)
3039.T4	Thompson, William Tappan (Table P-PZ40)
3039.T6	Thomson, Mortimer Neal, 1832-1875 (Table P-PZ40)
	Pseudonym: Q.K. Philander Doesticks. Name sometimes spelled "Thompson
3039.T9	Thorburn, Grant (Table P-PZ40)

	Individual authors
	19th century -- Continued
	Thoreau, Henry David
3040	Collected works. By date (using date letters)
3041	Collected poems
3042	Selections. By editor
	e.g. "Autumn," "Summer," "Winter," "Early Spring in Massachusetts"
3043.A-Z	Translations. By language, A-Z
	Separate works
	Cape Cod see F72.C3
3045	Excursions (Table P-PZ41)
	"Journal" see PS3053.A2
	Letters see PS3053.A3
	The Maine woods see F27.A+
3048	Walden (Table P-PZ41)
	A week on the Concord and Merrimack Rivers see F72.A+
	A Yankee in Canada see F1052
3051.A-Z	Other, A-Z
	e. g.
3051.C5	On the duty of civil disobedience
3051.L5	Life without principle
	Biography, criticism, etc.
3052	Dictionaries, indexes, etc.
3053.A2	"Journal." By imprint date
3053.A3	Letters (Collections). By imprint date
3053.A5-Z	General works
	Criticism
3054	General works
	Special
3056	Sources
3057.A-Z	Other, A-Z
3057.A35	Aesthetics
3057.B64	Books and reading
3057.E25	Economics
3057.E6	Entomology
3057.F64	Food
3057.I5	Indians
3057.L55	Literature, Classical
3057.N3	Nature
3057.N44	New England
3057.P4	Philosophy
3057.P64	Politics
3057.R4	Religion
3057.S43	Sea
3057.S95	Symbolism

PS

	Individual authors
	19th century
	Thoreau, Henry David
	Criticism -- Continued
3058	Language. Grammar. Style
3059.T	Thoreau - Thorne
3060.T	Thornton - Thoro
3061.T	Thorp - Thr
3061.T5	Thorpe, Rose (Hartwick) (Table P-PZ40)
3061.T6	Thorpe, Thomas Bangs, 1815-1878 (Table P-PZ40)
3062.T	Thu - Ticknor
3062.T8	Ticknor, Francis Orray (Table P-PZ40)
3063-3064	Ticknor, George (Table P-PZ36)
3065.T	Ticknor - Tiernan
3066.T	Tiernan, Frances Christine Fisher, 1846-1920 (Table P-PZ39)
3067.T5	Tiffany, Francis (Table P-PZ40)
3068.T	Tig - Till
3068.T34	Tilburn, E.O. (Table P-PZ40)
3068.T63	Tillman, Katherine Davis Chapman (Table P-PZ40)
3069.T5	Tilton, Theodore (Table P-PZ40)
3070-3073	Timrod, Henry (Table P-PZ35a)
3079.T	Timrod - Torrey
3079.T15	Tincker, Mary Agnes (Table P-PZ40)
3079.T5	Toland, Mary B.M. (Table P-PZ40)
3082-3083	Torrey, Bradford (Table P-PZ36)
3085-3088	Tourgee, Albion W. (Table P-PZ35a)
3089.T2	Towle, George Makepeace (Table P-PZ40)
3089.T38	Townsend, Frederic (Table P-PZ40)
3089.T4	Townsend, George Alfred ("Gath") (Table P-PZ40)
3089.T6	Townsend, Mary Ashley (Van Voorhis) (Table P-PZ40)
3089.T645	Trafton, Mark (Table P-PZ40)
3089.T65	Trask, Kate (Nichols) (Table P-PZ40)
3089.T7	Traubel, Horace (Table P-PZ40)
3089.T8	Trent, William Peterfield (Table P-PZ40)
3090-3093	Troubetzkoy, Amelie (Rives) Chanler (Table P-PZ35a)
3095-3098	Trowbridge, John Townsend (Table P-PZ35a)
3099.T	Trowbridge - Trul
3100.T	Trum - Tucker, N.
3100.T16	Truman, O.H. (Orson Harold), b. 1850 (Table P-PZ40)
3100.T76	Tucker, George, 1775-1861 (Table P-PZ40)
3101-3102	Tucker, Nathaniel Beverley (Table P-PZ36)
3104.T	Tucker - Tuckerman, H.
3105-3108	Tuckerman, Henry Theodore (Table P-PZ35a)
3109.T	Tuckerman, H. - Turnbull
3110.T	Turner, A. - Turner, Z.
3111.T	Turney - Tyl

	Individual authors
	19th century
	Turney - Tyl -- Continued
	Twain, Mark, 1835-1910 see PS1300+
3112.T	Tyler - Tz
3113.U	U - Uz
3113.U7	Upham, Thomas Cogswell (Table P-PZ40)
3114.V	V - Van Dyke, H.
3114.V43	Van Alstyne, Frances Jane Crosby, 1820-1915 (Table P-PZ40)
3114.V78	Van Deventer, Emma Murdoch (Table P-PZ40)
3115-3118	Van Dyke, Henry (Table P-PZ35a)
3119.V2	Van Dyke, Theodore Strong, b. 1842 (Table P-PZ40)
3119.V7	Venable, William Henry (Table P-PZ40)
3120-3123	Verplanck, Guilian Crommelin (Table P-PZ35a)
3125-3128	Very, Jones (Table P-PZ35a)
3129.V2	Very, Lydia L.A. (Lydia Louisa Anna), 1823-1901 (Table P-PZ40)
3129.V54	Vickery, Sukey, 1779-1821 (Table P-PZ40)
3129.V57	Victor, Frances Fuller, 1826-1902 (Table P-PZ40)
3129.V58	Victor, Metta Victoria Fuller, 1831-1885 (Table P-PZ40)
3129.V76	Vose, John Denison (Table P-PZ40)
3129.W83	Wall, Annie Russell (Table P-PZ40)
3129.W9	Wallace, Horace Binney (Table P-PZ40)
3130-3138	Wallace, Lewis ("Lew Wallace") (Table P-PZ33)
3139.W4	Wallace, William Ross (Table P-PZ40)
3139.W6	Walsh, William Shepard (Table P-PZ40)
3139.W67	Walton, Mrs. O.F. (Table P-PZ40)
3139.W8	Walworth, Jeannette Ritchie (Hadermann) (Table P-PZ40)
3139.W84	Walworth, Mansfield Tracy, 1830-1873 (Table P-PZ40)
	Ward, Artemus, 1834-1867 see PS1140+
3140-3143	Ward, Elizabeth Stuart (Phelps) (Table P-PZ35a)
3144.W3	Ward, Samuel (Table P-PZ40)
3145.W	Ware, A. - Ware, W.
3145.W5	Ware, Eugene Fitch ("Ironquill") (Table P-PZ40)
3146-3147	Ware, William (Table P-PZ36)
3149.W	Ware, W. - Warner, C.
3149.W3	Warfield, Catherine Ann (Ware) (Table P-PZ40)
3149.W6	Warner, Anna Bartlett ("Amy Lothrop") (Table P-PZ40)
3150-3153	Warner, Charles Dudley (Table P-PZ35a)
3155-3156	Warner, Susan ("Elizabeth Wetherell") (Table P-PZ36)
3157.W2	Wasson, David Atwood (Table P-PZ40)
3157.W318	Waterloo, Stanley, 1846-1913 (Table P-PZ40)
3157.W3577	Watrous, Jerome Anthony, 1840-1922 (Table P-PZ40)
3157.W374	Watson, Robert, 1825-1913 (Table P-PZ40)
3157.W4	Watterson, Henry (Table P-PZ40)
3157.W5	Watterston, George (Table P-PZ40)

	Individual authors
	19th century -- Continued
3157.W6	Webb, Charles Henry ("John Paul") (Table P-PZ40)
3157.W635	Webber, Charles Wilkins, 1819-1856 (Table P-PZ40)
3157.W7	Webster, Noah, 1758-1843 (Table P-PZ40)
3157.W8	Weeks, Robert Kelley (Table P-PZ40)
3157.W83	Weems, M.L. (Mason Locke), 1759-1825 (Table P-PZ40)
3157.W88	Weir, James, b. 1821 (Table P-PZ40)
3157.W9	Weiss, Susan Archer (Table P-PZ40)
3158.W2	Welburn, Drummond (Table P-PZ40)
3158.W3	Welby, Amelia (Table P-PZ40)
3158.W5	Welch, Philip Henry (Table P-PZ40)
3158.W568	Welles, Henry Titus, 1821-1898 (Table P-PZ40)
3158.W664	Welsh, Mary Jane, 1846-1875 (Table P-PZ40)
3158.W7	Wendell, Barrett (Table P-PZ40)
3158.W95	West, James Harcourt (Table P-PZ40)
3159.W12	Westcott, Edward Noyes (Table P-PZ40)
3159.W28	Wetmore, Alphonso (Table P-PZ40)
3159.W3	Wetmore, Elizabeth (Bisland) (Table P-PZ40)
	Wharton, Edith see PS3545.H16
3164.W	Wharton, E. - Whaz
3165.W	Whe - Wheeler, C.
3166.W	Wheeler, D. - Wheeler, R.
3167.W	Wheeler, S. - Whipple, E.
3170-3173	Whipple, Edwin Percy (Table P-PZ35a)
3174.W	Whipple, E.P. - White, R.G.
3174.W45	Whitcher, Frances M., 1814-1852 (Table P-PZ40)
3174.W592	White, Ernest L. E. (Table P-PZ40)
3175-3178	White, Richard Grant (Table P-PZ35a)
3179.W	White, R. - Whitez
3179.W35	White, William Charles, 1777-1818 (Table P-PZ40)
3180.W	Whitf - Whiting, L.
3180.W45	Whitfield, James Monroe, 1822-1871 (Table P-PZ40)
3181-3182	Whiting, Lilian (Table P-PZ36)
3184.W	Whiting, L. - Whitl
3187.W	Whitm - Whitman, R.
3189.W	Whitman, S. - Whitman, W.
3189.W4	Whitman, Sarah Helen (Power) (Table P-PZ40)
3200-3248	Whitman, Walt (Table P-PZ31 modified)
	Collected works (Poetry and prose)
	Original editions and reprints. By date
3200.E00-.E99	1800-1899
3200.F00-.F99	1900-1999
3200.G00-.G99	2000-2099
3201	Collected poems
	Including editions of Leaves of grass, by date
3202	Prose

PS

Individual authors
19th century
Whittier, John Greenleaf
Individual genres
Individual genres
Poems -- Continued

3260	Mabel Martin, and other poems (Table P-PZ41)
3262	Maud Muller (Table P-PZ41)
3263.M3	Miriam, and other poems (Table P-PZ43)
3263.M6	Mogg Megone (Table P-PZ43)
3263.M8	Moll Pitcher (Table P-PZ43)
3264	National lyrics (Table P-PZ41)
3265.P2	Panorama, and other poems (Table P-PZ43)
3265.P4	Pennsylvania pilgrim, and other poems (Table P-PZ43)
3265.P6	Poems of nature (Table P-PZ43)
3265.P8	Prayer of Agassiz (Table P-PZ43)
3265.R4	River path (Table P-PZ43)
3265.S3	Saint Gregory's guest, and recent poems (Table P-PZ43)
3266	Snowbound (Table P-PZ41)
3267.S3	Songs of labor (Table P-PZ43)
3267.S5	Stranger in Lowell (Table P-PZ43)
3267.S7	Sycamores (Table P-PZ43)
3268	Tent on the beach, and other poems (Table P-PZ41)
3269.T62	To Oliver Wendell Holmes (Table P-PZ43)
3269.V4	Vision of Echard (Table P-PZ43)
3269.V5	Voices of freedom (Table P-PZ43)
3269.W6	Worship of nature (Table P-PZ43)
	Prose works
3271	Collected works
3272.A-Z	Separate works, A-Z
	Subarrange each by Table P-PZ43
3299.W33	Whytal, A. Russ (Table P-PZ40)
3300-3303	Wiggin, Kate Douglas (Mrs. G.C. Riggs) (Table P-PZ35a)
3304.W	Wiggin, K. - Wiggz
3305.W	Wigh - Wij
3305.W35	Wight, Orlando William, 1824-1888 (Table P-PZ40)
3308.W5	Wikoff, Henry (Table P-PZ40)
3309.W	Wil - Wilcox, E.
3310-3313	Wilcox, Ella Wheeler (Table P-PZ35a)
3315-3318	Wilde, Richard Henry (Table P-PZ35a)
3319.W2	Wilder, Marshall Pinckney (Table P-PZ40)
3319.W3	Wiley, Calvin Henderson (Table P-PZ40)
	Wilkins, Mary E. see PS1710+
3319.W44	Wilkinson, William Cleaver (Table P-PZ40)

	Individual authors
	19th century -- Continued
	Willard, Elizabeth Doten see PS1549.D53
3319.W5	Willard, Emma (Hart) (Table P-PZ40)
3319.W587	Williams, C.R. (Catherine Read), 1790-1872 (Table P-PZ40)
3319.W623	Williams, Henry Llewellyn, 1842- (Table P-PZ40)
3319.W655	Williams, Mary Lackey, 1824-1898 (Table P-PZ40)
3319.W659	Williams, Thaddeus Warsaw (Table P-PZ40)
3319.W7	Williamson, Alice Muriel (Livingstone) (Table P-PZ40)
3320-3328	Willis, Nathaniel Parker (Table P-PZ33 modified)
	Collected works
3320	By date
3320.E00-.E99	1800-1899
3320.F00-.F99	1900-1999
3320.G00-.G99	2000-2099
3329.W5	Willson, Forceythe (Table P-PZ40)
3329.W7	Wilmer, Lambert A. (Table P-PZ40)
3329.W8	Wilmshurst, Zavarr (Table P-PZ40)
3330-3333	Wilson, Augusta Jane (Evans) (Table P-PZ35a)
3334.W29	Wilson, Elizabeth Jennings, b. 1839 (Table P-PZ40)
3334.W39	Wilson, H.E. (Harriet E.), 1808-ca. 1870 (Table P-PZ40)
3334.W5	Wilson, John Byers (Table P-PZ40)
3335-3338	Wilson, Robert Burns (Table P-PZ35a)
3339.W3	Wilson, Woodrow (Table P-PZ40)
	Cf. E660.W71+ Collected works
	Cf. E767+ Biography
	Cf. J82.D2+ Speeches and messages as President
3340.W	Winn - Winter, W.
3341-3342	Winter, William (Table P-PZ36)
3343.W2	Winthrop, Theodore (Table P-PZ40)
3344.W	Wire - Wister
3344.W28	Wiren, Myra (Table P-PZ40)
3344.W3	Wirt, William (Table P-PZ40)
3344.W6	Wise, Henry Augustus ("Harry Gringo") (Table P-PZ40)
3345-3346	Wister, Owen (Table P-PZ36)
3347.W	Wister, O. - Wol
3348.W	Wolcott - Wooc
3348.W78	Wolf, Emma, 1865-1932
3349.W	Wood, A. - Wood, L.
3349.W6	Wood, George (Table P-PZ40)
	Wood, Hazel see PS2869.S2686
	Wood, Julia Amanda see PS2236.L32
3350.W	Wood, M. - Woodberry, G.
3351-3352	Woodberry, George Edward (Table P-PZ36)
3353.W	Woodberry, G. - Woodq
3354.W	Woodr - Woodworth

	Individual authors
	19th century
	Woodr - Woodworth -- Continued
3354.W5	Woods, Kate (Tannatt) (Table P-PZ40)
3355-3356	Woodworth, Samuel (Table P-PZ36)
3357.W	Woodworth - Woolf
3357.W8	Woolf, Benjamin Edward (Table P-PZ40)
3358.W	Woolg - Woolsey
3358.W4	Woolley, Celia Parker (Table P-PZ40)
3358.W6	Woolsey, Sarah Chauncey ("Susan Coolidge") (Table P-PZ40)
3360-3363	Woolson, Constance Fenimore (Table P-PZ35a)
3364.W-.Y	Woolson - Young
	Wright, Harold Bell, 1872-1944 see PS3545.R45
3364.Y19	Yandell, Enid (Table P-PZ40)
3365-3368	Young, William (Table P-PZ35a)
3369.Y-Z	Young - Z
3369.Y68	Yourell, Agnes (Table P-PZ40)
(3390)	Minor material of individual authors
	see the author
	1900-1960
	Subarrange individual authors by Table P-PZ40 unless otherwise specified
	Including usually authors beginning to publish about 1890, flourishing after 1900
	For works of fiction cataloged before July 1, 1980, except limited editions and works in the Rare Book Collection see PZ3+
3500	Anonymous works (Table P-PZ28)
3501.A-Z	A
	The author number is determined by the second letter of the name
3501.A79	Aarons, Edward S. (Edward Sidney), 1916-1975 (Table P-PZ40)
3501.B222	Abbott, Eleanor Hallowell, 1872- (Table P-PZ40)
3501.D2152	Adams, Andy, 1859-1935 (Table P-PZ40)
3501.D24	Adams, Franklin Pierce (Table P-PZ40)
3501.D317	Adams, Samuel Hopkins, 1871-1958 (Table P-PZ40)
	Addams, D.A., 1926- see PS3515.U585
3501.L23	Albery, Faxon Franklin Duane, 1848- (Table P-PZ40)
3501.L375	Aldis, Mary Reynolds, 1872- (Table P-PZ40)
	Aldon, Adair, 1884-1973 see PS3525.E2823
3501.L418	Alexander, Hartley Burr, 1873-1939 (Table P-PZ40)
	Allan, Dennis, 1900- see PS3511.O186
	Allan, Robert see PS3525.A264
3501.L526	Allen, John Edward, 1889-1947 (Table P-PZ40)
	Allen, Stephen Valentine see PS3501.L5553

Individual authors
1900-1960
A -- Continued

3501.L5553	Allen, Steve, 1921- (Table P-PZ40)
	Alsop, Mary O'Hara see PS3529.H34
3501.N4	Anderson, Sherwood, 1876-1941 (Table P-PZ40)
3501.N56145	Andrews, Annulet, 1866-1943 (Table P-PZ40)
	Andros, Phil, 1909- see PS3537.T479
	Antoninus, Brother, 1912- see PS3509.V65
	Archer, A.A., 1899- see PS3519.O712
3501.R5167	Arctander, Jno. W., 1849-1920 (Table P-PZ40)
3501.R5685	Armstrong, Margaret, 1867-1944 (Table P-PZ40)
3501.R575	Armstrong, Paul (Table P-PZ40)
	Arthur, Burt, 1899-1975 see PS3501.R77
3501.R77	Arthur, Herbert, 1899-1975 (Table P-PZ40)
	Arthur, William, 1916- see PS3527.E598
	Ashley, Ellen see PS3537.E352
	Atkins, Jack, 1922- see PS3515.A757
3501.U25	Auchincloss, Louis (Table P-PZ40)
	Auden, W.H. (Wystan Hugh) see PR6001.U4
	Austin, Brett see PS3511.L697
	Austin, Frank, 1892-1944 see PS3511.A87
3501.U8	Austin, Mary (Hunter) (Table P-PZ40)
	Ayres, Paul, 1916-1975 see PS3501.A79
3503.A-Z	B

The author number is determined by the second letter of the name

	Bagby, George, 1906- see PS3537.T3184
3503.A54115	Baker, A.Z (Alfred Zantzinger), 1870- (Table P-PZ40)
3503.A5448	Baker, Ray Stannard, 1870-1946 (Table P-PZ40)
	Baldwin, Faith, 1893- see PS3505.U97
3503.A8423	Basso, Hamilton, 1904-1964 (Table P-PZ40)
	Basso, Joseph Hamilton, 1904-1964 see PS3503.A8423
3503.A923	Baum, Lyman Frank, 1856-1919 (Table P-PZ40)
	Baxter, George Owen, 1892-1944 see PS3511.A87
	Baxter, John see PS3515.U5425
3503.E1173	Beale, Charles Willing, 1845-1932 (Table P-PZ40)
3503.E133	Beard, Daniel Carter, 1850-1941 (Table P-PZ40)
3503.E54547	Bennet, Robert Ames, 1870- (Table P-PZ40)
	Bennett, Christini, 1916- see PS3527.E598
	Bennett, Dwight, 1916- see PS3527.E9178
3503.E5475	Bennett, John, 1865-1956 (Table P-PZ40)
3503.J6	Bjorkman, Edwin (Table P-PZ40)
	Black, Ishi see PS3513.I2823
	Bligh, Norman, 1916- see PS3527.E598
3503.L65	Bliss, Sylvia Hortense, 1870-1963 (Table P-PZ40)
	Blocklinger, Betty see PS3503.O8455

	Individual authors
	1900-1960
	B -- Continued
	Blocklinger, Peggy Jeanne O'More see PS3503.O8455
	Bloomfield, Robert see PS3515.A82868
	Bookman, Charlotte, 1915- see PS3549.O63
3503.O563	Borland, Hal Glen, 1900- (Table P-PZ40)
	Boucher, Anthony, 1911-1968 see PS3545.H6172
3503.O813	Bowdoin, William Goodrich, 1860-1947 (Table P-PZ40)
3503.O8136	Bowe, John, b. 1869 (Table P-PZ40)
3503.O8193	Bower, B.M., 1874-1940 (Table P-PZ40)
3503.O8455	Bowman, Jeanne, 1897- (Table P-PZ40)
	Box, Edgar see PS3543.I26
3503.O93	Boylan, Grace Duffie, 1861? (Table P-PZ40)
3503.R2	Bradford, Gamaliel (Table P-PZ40)
3503.R2265	Bradshaw, William Richard, 1851-1927 (Table P-PZ40)
3503.R256	Branch, Anna Hempstead, 1875-1937 (Table P-PZ40)
	Branch, Florenz, 1896- see PS3537.T9246
	Brand, Max, 1892-1944 see PS3511.A87
3503.R63	Broadhurst, George H. (Table P-PZ40)
3503.R683	Brooks, Asa Passavant, b. 1868 (Table P-PZ40)
3503.R78	Brown, Abbie Farwell (Table P-PZ40)
	Brown, Bob, 1886-1959 see PS3503.R8283
	Brown, Douglas see PS3513.I2823
3503.R812	Brown, Forman George (Table P-PZ40)
3503.R8283	Brown, Robert Carlton, 1886- (Table P-PZ40)
3503.R8436	Browne, Howard, 1908- (Table P-PZ40)
3503.R937	Brush, Dorothy Hamilton, 1894-1968 (Table P-PZ40)
3503.U5647	Bunker, Ira S. (Ira Sweet), b. 1848 (Table P-PZ40)
3503.U6	Burgess, Gelett (Table P-PZ40)
3503.U6075	Burgess, Thornton Waldo, 1874-1965 (Table P-PZ40)
	Burke, Fielding see PS3507.A6
	Burns, Tex, 1908- see PS3523.A446
	Burton, Thomas see PS3523.O486
3503.U7644	Bush, Olivia, b. 1869 (Table P-PZ40)
3503.Y45	Bynner, Witter (Table P-PZ40)
3503.Y876	Byrne, James Charles, 1858-1942 (Table P-PZ40)
3505.A-Z	C
	The author number is determined by the second letter of the name
3505.A254	Caham, Abraham, 1860-1951 (Table P-PZ40)
3505.A376	Calhoun, Francis Boyd, 1867-1909 (Table P-PZ40)
3505.A53157	Campbell, William Edward March, 1894-1954 (Table P-PZ40)
	Campion, Rose see PS3523.A76
	Cannon, Curt, 1926- see PS3515.U585
3505.A763	Carr, John Dickson, 1906-1977 (Table P-PZ40)

Individual authors
   1900-1960
      C -- Continued
         Carter, Ralph see PS3527.E598

3505.A85486	Castle, William R. (William Richard), 1878-1963 (Table P-PZ40)
3505.A87	Cather, Willa Sibert (Table P-PZ40)
3505.A896	Cauldwell, Sanuel Milbank, 1862-1916 (Table P-PZ40)
3505.A97	Cayton, Susie Revels, 1870-1943 (Table P-PZ40)
	Challis, George, 1892-1944 see PS3511.A87
3505.H335	Chapin, Anna Alice, 1880-1920 (Table P-PZ40)
3505.H528	Chase, Virginia, 1902- (Table P-PZ40)
3505.H633	Chaze, Elliott (Table P-PZ40)
	Chaze, Lewis Elliott see PS3505.H633
3505.H684	Chester, George Randolph, 1869-1924 (Table P-PZ40)
3505.H716	Chetwood, John, 1859 (Table P-PZ40)
	Chin-lo-k'o, Chieh-k'o see PS3521.E735
	Clark, Alice V., 1859- see PS3535.O17944
3505.L646	Clement, Hal, 1922- (Table P-PZ40)
3505.L7872	Clifford, Carrie Williams (Table P-PZ40)
3505.O13	Coates, Florence (Earle) (Table P-PZ40)
3505.O14	Cobb, Irvin S. (Table P-PZ40)
	Cody, Al, 1899- see PS3519.O712
	Cody, C.S., 1923- see PS3545.A565
	Cody, John, 1900- see PS3535.E745
	Collins, Hunt, 1926- see PS3515.U585
	Colt, Clem see PS3527.Y33
3505.O474	Conkling, Mrs. Grace Walcott (Hazard) (Table P-PZ40)
3505.O546	Coogler, J. Gordon (Table P-PZ40)
3505.O5593	Cook, William Wallace (Table P-PZ40)
3505.O56	Cooke, Edmund Vance (Table P-PZ40)
3505.O5632	Cooke, Grace Mac Gowan, 1863-1944 (Table P-PZ40)
3505.O5695	Coolidge, Asenath Carver (Table P-PZ40)
	Coombs, Murdo, 1902- see PS3507.A728
3505.O737	Corning, Leavitt, 1870-1935 (Table P-PZ40)
3505.O77	Cort, Cyrus, 1834-1920 (Table P-PZ40)
3505.O85	Cotton, Sallie Southall, 1846-1929 (Table P-PZ40)
3505.O862	Cotter, Joseph Seaman, 1861- (Table P-PZ40)
	Courtland, Roberta see PS3513.A227
3505.O9633	Cox, Palmer, 1840-1924 (Table P-PZ40)
	Craig, Georgia see PS3513.A227
3505.R9	Crothers, Samuel McChord (Table P-PZ40)
	Cunningham, E.V., 1914- see PS3511.A784
3505.U824	Curry, Erastus S. (Table P-PZ40)
3505.U97	Cuthrell, Faith Baldwin, 1893- (Table P-PZ40)

Individual authors
1900-1960 -- Continued

3507.A-Z	D

The author number is determined by the second letter of the name

3507.A355	Dake, Charles Romyn (Table P-PZ40)
	Daniels, John S. see PS3529.V33
3507.A6	Dargan, Olive Tilford (Table P-PZ40)
	David, K., 1859- see PS3535.O17944
3507.A7118	Daviess, Maria Thompson, 1872-1924 (Table P-PZ40)
3507.A728	Davis, Frederick C. (Frederick Clyde), 1902- (Table P-PZ40)
	Cf. PS3537.T2687 Steele, Curtis
	Davis, Gordon see PS3515.U5425
3507.A87	Day, Holman Francis (Table P-PZ40)
3507.E497	Del Monte, Leon (Table P-PZ40)
3507.E5432	Deming, Alhambra G. (Alhambra Georgia), 1856- (Table P-PZ40)
	Denniston, Elinore, 1900- see PS3511.O186
	Denver, Drabe C. see PS3527.Y33
3507.E69	Derleth, August William, 1909-1971 (Table P-PZ40)
	Dern, Peggy see PS3513.A227
3507.E84	Deutsch, Babette (Table P-PZ40)
3507.E8674	Devrish, K., 1883-1963 (Table P-PZ40)
3507.E878	Dewey, John, 1859-1952 (Table P-PZ40)
	Dickson, Carter, 1906-1977 see PS3505.A763
	Dietrich, Robert see PS3515.U5425
3507.I9	Dix, Beulah Marie (Table P-PZ40)
	Dixon, Franklin W., 1862-1930 see PS3537.T817
3507.I93	Dixon, Thomas (Table P-PZ40)
3507.O726	Doolittle, Hilda, 1886-1961 (Table P-PZ40)
3507.R55	Dreiser, Theodore, 1871-1945 (Table P-PZ40)
3507.U147	Du Bois, W. E. B. (William Edward Burghardt), 1868-1963 (Table P-PZ40)
3507.U1475	Du Bois, William, 1903-1997 (Table P-PZ40)
3507.U6228	Dunbar-Nelson, Alice Moore, 1875-1935 (Table P-PZ40)
3507.U629	Duncan, Robert Edward, 1919- (Table P-PZ40)
3507.U6755	Dunne, Finley Peter, 1867-1936 (Table P-PZ40)
3509.A-Z	E

The author number is determined by the second letter of the name

3509.A63	Earle, Mary Tracy, b. 1864 (Table P-PZ40)
3509.A7469	Eastman, Alvah, 1858-1939 (Table P-PZ40)
3509.A748	Eastman, Charles Alexander, 1858-1939 (Table P-PZ40)
3509.A85	Eaton, Walter Prichard (Table P-PZ40)
3509.B453	Eberhart, Mignon Good, 1899- (Table P-PZ40)
3509.C65	Eckstorm, Frannie Hardy, 1865-1946 (Table P-PZ40)

Individual authors
1900-1960
E -- Continued

3509.D452	Edgar, William Crowell, 1856-1932 (Table P-PZ40)
	Edgley, Leslie see PS3515.A82868
	Edgley, Mary see PS3515.A82868
3509.I52	Eilshemius, Louis Michel, 1864-1941 (Table P-PZ40)
3509.L667	Ellsworth, Franklin Fowler, 1879-1942 (Table P-PZ40)
	Elshemus, Louis M. (Louis Michel), 1864-1941 see PS3509.I52
	Ericson, Walter, 1914- see PS3511.A784
	Evans, Evan, 1892-1944 see PS3511.A87
3509.V363	Evans, Florence (Wilkerson) (Table P-PZ40)
	Evans, John, 1908- see PS3503.R8436
	Everett, Gail see PS3515.A262
3509.V53	Everett, Lloyd T. (Lloyd Tilghman), b. 1875 (Table P-PZ40)
3509.V65	Everson, William, 1912- (Table P-PZ40)
3509.W3	Ewell, Alice Maude, 1860-1946 (Table P-PZ40)
3511.A-Z	F

The author number is determined by the second letter of the name

	Fair, A.A. see PS3513.A6322
3511.A738	Farrell, James T. (James Thomas), 1904-1979
	Fast, Govard see PS3511.A784
3511.A784	Fast, Howard, 1914-
	Fast, Khauard see PS3511.A784
3511.A87	Faust, Frederick, 1892-1944
	Feikema, Feike see PS3525.A52233
	Feikema, Frederick see PS3525.A52233
3511.E56	Fernald, Chester Bailey (Table P-PZ40)
	Fever, Buck see PS3501.N4
	Field, Peter, 1900- see PS3535.E745
3511.I557	Finger, Charles Joseph, 1869-1941 (Table P-PZ40)
	Finkelstein, Mark Harris, 1922- see PS3515.A757
3511.I5847	Finley, Harry T., 1866-1940 (Table P-PZ40)
3511.I725	Fish, Williston, 1858-1939 (Table P-PZ40)
3511.L15	Flagg, James Montgomery (Table P-PZ40)
	Flapdoodle, Phineas, 1891- see PS3525.I5454
3511.L4413	Fleming, Berry, 1899- (Table P-PZ40)
	Fleming, Jiles Berry, 1899- see PS3511.L4413
3511.L6	Fliesburg, Oscar Alfred, 1851- (Table P-PZ40)
3511.L697	Floren, Lee (Table P-PZ40)
3511.L8	Flower, Elliott (Table P-PZ40)
	Fogarty, Jonathan Titulescu see PS3511.A738
3511.O186	Foley, Rae, 1900- (Table P-PZ40)
3511.O4127	Ford, R. Clyde (Richard Clyde), 1870- (Table P-PZ40)

Individual authors
  1900-1960
    F -- Continued

3511.O418	Ford, Sewell, 1868-1946 (Table P-PZ40)
3511.O437	Forgue, Norman W. (Table P-PZ40)
	Forrest, Felix C., 1913-1966 see PS3523.I629
3511.O63	Fort, Charles, 1874-1932 (Table P-PZ40)
	Frederick, John, 1892-1944 see PS3511.A87
	Freeman, Dana see PS3539.A9635
	Frost, Frederick, 1892-1944 see PS3511.A87
3511.R94	Frost, Robert (Table P-PZ40)
3513.A-Z	G

The author number is determined by the second letter of the name

3513.A227	Gaddis, Peggy (Table P-PZ40)
3513.A274	Gaines, Charles Kelsey, 1854-1943 (Table P-PZ40)
3513.A34	Gale, Zona, 1874-1938 (Table P-PZ40)
	Gard, Janice, 1902-1995 see PS3523.A76
3513.A6322	Gardner, Erle Stanley, 1889-1970 (Table P-PZ40)
3513.A65	Garnett, Porter, 1871-1951 (Table P-PZ40)
	Garrison, Joan see PS3527.E598
	Garth, Will see PS3521.U87
	Gary, Dorothy Page, 1897- see PS3531.A235
3513.E2	Geisel, Theodore Seuss, 1904- (Table P-PZ40)
3513.E8679	Gerson, Noel Bertram, 1914- (Table P-PZ40)
3513.I189	Gibbons, Floyd Phillips, 1887-1939 (Table P-PZ40)
3513.I197	Gibbons, William Futhey, 1859-1936 (Table P-PZ40)
3513.I2823	Gibson, Walter Brown, 1897- (Table P-PZ40)
3513.I594	Gillmore, Inez Haynes, 1873-1970 (Table P-PZ40)
3513.L34	Glasgow, Ellen (Table P-PZ40)
3513.L68158	Glidden, Frederick Dilley, 1908-1975 (Table P-PZ40)
3513.O28	Going, Charles Buxton (Table P-PZ40)
3513.O75	Gotwalt, Helen Louise Miller (Table P-PZ40)
	Graham, Tom, 1885-1951 see PS3523.E94
	Grant, Maxwell see PS3513.I2823
	Grayson, David, 1870-1946 see PS3503.A5448
	Grendon, Stephen, 1909-1971 see PS3507.E69
3513.R6545	Grey, Zane, 1872-1939 (Table P-PZ40)
3513.R658	Grierson, Francis, 1848-1927 (Table P-PZ40)
3513.R7154	Griggs, Sutton Elhert, 1872- (Table P-PZ40)
3513.U7	Guiterman, Arthur (Table P-PZ40)
3513.U797	Gunn, James E., 1923- (Table P-PZ40)
3513.U88	Guthrie, William Norman (Table P-PZ40)
3515.A-Z	H

The author number is determined by the second letter of the name

    H.D. (Hilda Doolittle), 1886-1961- see PS3507.O726

Individual authors
  1900-1960
    H -- Continued
3515.A23	Hagedorn, Hermann (Table P-PZ40)
	Haggard, Paul see PS3523.O486
	Hai-lai-en, Lo-po, 1907- see PS3515.E288
3515.A262	Hale, Arlene (Table P-PZ40)
3515.A3146	Hall, Charles Cuthbert, 1852-1908 (Table P-PZ40)
	Hall, Claudia see PS3511.L697
3515.A315	Hall, Covington, 1871-1951 (Table P-PZ40)
	Hall, Holworthy see PS3531.O735
	Hamilton, Wade see PS3511.L697
3515.A54	Hapgood, Norman (Table P-PZ40)
3515.A722	Harris, Bernice Kelly, b. 1894 (Table P-PZ40)
	Hardin, Clement, 1916- see PS3527.E9178
	Hardin, Dave, 1895- see PS3515.O4448
3515.A757	Harris, Mark, 1922- (Table P-PZ40)
3515.A78117	Harrison, C. William (Table P-PZ40)
3515.A797	Hartman, Sadakichi (Table P-PZ40)
3515.A81	Harvey, George (Table P-PZ40)
3515.A8285	Haslett, Harriet Holmes (Table P-PZ40)
3515.A82868	Hastings, Brook (Table P-PZ40)
3515.A8297	Hasty, John Eugene (Table P-PZ40)
	Hathaway, Jan, 1916- see PS3527.E598
3515.A9	Hawthorne, Hildegarde (Table P-PZ40)
3515.A94	Hayes, John Russell (Table P-PZ40)
3515.A9547	Haynes, Arthur Edwin, 1849-1915 (Table P-PZ40)
3515.A973	Hazard, Caroline (Table P-PZ40)
3515.A982	Hazelton, George Cochrane, 1868-1921 (Table P-PZ40)
3515.E288	Heinlein, Robert A. (Robert Anson), 1907- (Table P-PZ40)
3515.E62	Herford, Oliver (Table P-PZ40)
	Hickok, Will see PS3515.A78117
3515.I486	Hill, Grace Livingston, 1865-1947 (Table P-PZ40)
3515.O4332	Holmes, Charles Elmer, 1863-1926 (Table P-PZ40)
	Holmes, H.H., 1911-1968 see PS3545.H6172
3515.O4448	Holmes, L.P. (Llewellyn Perry), 1895- (Table P-PZ40)
	Holt, Tex, 1899- see PS3519.O712
3515.O5474	Hooper, Cyrus Lauron, 1863- (Table P-PZ40)
	Hopley, George, 1903-1968 see PS3515.O6455
3515.O6455	Hopley-Woolrich, Cornell George, 1903-1968 (Table P-PZ40)
3515.O6526	Hopson, William L. (Table P-PZ40)
3515.O6578	Hord, Benjamin McCulloch, 1842-1922 (Table P-PZ40)
3515.O74	Horton, George, 1859-1942 (Table P-PZ40)
3515.O7593	Hough, Emerson, 1857-1923 (Table P-PZ40)
3515.O826	Howard, George Bronson (Table P-PZ40)

Individual authors
1900-1960
H -- Continued

3515.O858	Howe, Mark Antony De Wolfe, 1864-1960 (Table P-PZ40)
3515.U277	Hughes, Rupert, 1872-1956 (Table P-PZ40)
3515.U5425	Hunt, E. Howard (Everette Howard), 1918- (Table P-PZ40)
	Hunt, Howard, 1918- see PS3515.U5425
3515.U585	Hunter, Evan, 1926- (Table P-PZ40)
3517.A-Z	I

The author number is determined by the second letter of the name

3517.N35	Ingraham, Charles Anson, 1852-1935 (Table P-PZ40)
	Ingram, Willis J., 1922- see PS3515.A757
	Irish, William, 1903-1968 see PS3515.O6455
3517.R8	Irvine, Alexander (Table P-PZ40)
3517.R8617	Irwin, Florence, b. 1869 (Table P-PZ40)
	Irwin, Inez Haynes, 1873-1970 see PS3513.I594
3517.R87	Irwin, Wallace (Table P-PZ40)
3519.A-Z	J

The author number is determined by the second letter of the name

	James, Edwin, 1923- see PS3513.U797
	Jenkins, Will, 1896- see PS3519.E648
3519.E648	Jenkins, William Fitzgerald, 1896- (Table P-PZ40)
3519.O2	Johnson, Burges (Table P-PZ40)
3519.O2625	Johnson, James Weldon, 1871-1938 (Table P-PZ40)
3519.O3	Johnston, Annie (Fellows) (Table P-PZ40)
3519.O34	Joline, Adrian Hoffman (Table P-PZ40)
3519.O6	Jordan, Elizabeth Garver (Table P-PZ40)
	Jordan, Gail see PS3513.A227
3519.O712	Joscelyn, Archie, 1899- (Table P-PZ40)
3521.A-Z	K

The author number is determined by the second letter of the name

3521.A4347	Kane, Henry (Table P-PZ40)
3521.A73	Kaufman, Herbert (Table P-PZ40)
	Keene, Carolyn see PS3537.T817
	Keljik, Krikor Arabel, 1883-1963 see PS3507.E8674
3521.E39	Keller, Helen Adams (Table P-PZ40)
3521.E4118	Kelly, Florence Finch, 1858-1939 (Table P-PZ40)
	Kendrake, Carleton see PS3513.A6322
3521.E53	Kennedy, Charles Rann (Table P-PZ40)
	Kennedy, Joseph Charles see PS3521.E563
3521.E563	Kennedy, X.J. (Table P-PZ40)
	Kenny, Charles J. see PS3513.A6322

Individual authors
1900-1960
K -- Continued

3521.E735	Kerouac, Jack, 1922-1969 (Table P-PZ40)
	Kerouac, John, 1922-1969 see PS3521.E735
3521.E8	Kester, Paul (Table P-PZ40)
3521.I355	Kildare, Owen Frawley (Table P-PZ40)
	Kilgallen, Milton see PS3535.O176
3521.I38	Kilmer, Joyce (Table P-PZ40)
	Kineji, Maborushi see PS3513.I2823
3521.I5	King, Basil (Table P-PZ40)
3521.I76	Kiser, Samuel Ellsworth (Table P-PZ40)
	Knoblanich, Edward see PR6021.N47
3521.N75	Knowles, Frederic Lawrence, 1869-1905 (Table P-PZ40)
	Koch, Jay Kenneth, 1925- see PS3521.O27
3521.O27	Koch, Kenneth, 1925- (Table P-PZ40)
3521.R26	Král, Josef Jirí, 1870- (Table P-PZ40)
3521.U65	Kummer, Frederic Arnold, 1873-1943 (Table P-PZ40)
3521.U87	Kuttner, Henry (Table P-PZ40)
3523.A-Z	L

The author number is determined by the second letter of the name

3523.A19	Labadie, Jo, 1850-1933 (Table P-PZ40)
3523.A446	L'Amour, Louis, 1908- (Table P-PZ40)
3523.A5748	Lange, Dietrich, 1863-1940 (Table P-PZ40)
3523.A76	Latham, Jean Lee (Table P-PZ40)
3523.E313	Lee, Agnes, 1868-1939 (Table P-PZ40)
	Lee, Andrew see PS3501.U25
3523.E3158	Lee, C.Y., 1917- (Table P-PZ40)
	Lee, Caroline see PS3513.A227
	Lee, Chin Y., 1917- see PS3523.E3158
3523.E31847	Lee, Eugene, b. 1868 (Table P-PZ40)
3523.E358	Lefevre, Edwin, 1871-1943 (Table P-PZ40)
	Leighton, Lee see PS3529.V33
	Leinster, Murray, 1896- see PS3519.E648
3523.E737	Le Rossignol, James Edward, 1866-1959 (Table P-PZ40)
3523.E866	Lewis, Janet, 1899- (Table P-PZ40)
3523.E88	Lewis, Silas S., 1850- (Table P-PZ40)
3523.E94	Lewis, Sinclair, 1885-1951 (Table P-PZ40)
	Li, Chin-yang, 1917- see PS3523.E3158
3523.I46	Lincoln, Joseph Crosby (Table P-PZ40)
3523.I535	Linderman, Frank Bird, 1869-1938 (Table P-PZ40)
3523.I58	Lindsay, Nicholas Vachel (Table P-PZ40)
	Lindsay, Perry see PS3513.A227
3523.I629	Linebarger, Paul Myron Anthony, 1913-1966 (Table P-PZ40)
3523.I824	Litta-Visconti-Arese, Duke, b. 1856 (Table P-PZ40)

Individual authors
  1900-1960
    L -- Continued

	Livingston, Grace, 1865-1947 see PS3515.I486
3523.L64	Lloyd, John Uri (Table P-PZ40)
3523.O237	Lockjart, Caroline, 1879-1962 (Table P-PZ40)
3523.O27	Lodge, George Cabot (Table P-PZ40)
	Logan, Ford, 1916- see PS3527.E9178
	Lombino, Salvatore A., 1926- see PS3515.U585
3523.O46	London, Jack (Table P-PZ40)
3523.O47	Long, John Luther (Table P-PZ40)
	Long, Naomi Cornelia see PS3525.A318
3523.O486	Longstreet, Stephen, 1907- (Table P-PZ40)
3523.O545	Loomis, Charles Battell (Table P-PZ40)
3523.O64	Lorimer, George Horace (Table P-PZ40)
3523.O645	Loring, Emilie Baker (Table P-PZ40)
3523.O787	Louttit, George William, 1868- (Table P-PZ40)
3523.O85	Loveman, Robert (Table P-PZ40)
3523.O88	Lowell, Amy (Table P-PZ40)
3523.U49	Lummis, Charles Fletcher, 1859-1928 (Table P-PZ40)
3525.A-Z	M

The author number is determined by the second letter of the name

3525.A1435	McCarthy, Mary, 1912- (Table P-PZ40)
3525.A155	McClellan, George Marion, 1860- (Table P-PZ40)
3525.A1772	McCullers, Carson, 1917-1967 (Table P-PZ40)
3525.A187	McCutcheon, George Barr (Table P-PZ40)
	MacDonald, Anson, 1907- see PS3515.E288
	Macdonald, Marcia, 1865-1947 see PS3515.I486
	Macdonald, Ross, 1915- see PS3515.I486
3525.A24785	McKay, Claude, 1890-1948 (Table P-PZ40)
3525.A25	McKaye, Percy Wallace (Table P-PZ40)
3525.A264	McKuen, Rod (Table P-PZ40)
3525.A282	McNeill, John Charles, 1874-1907 (Table P-PZ40)
3525.A318	Madgett, Naomi Cornelia Long (Table P-PZ40)
3525.A52233	Manfred, Frederick Feikema, 1912- (Table P-PZ40)
	Mann, Patrick, 1923- see PS3545.A565
	Manning, David, 1892-1944 see PS3511.A87
	March, William see PS3505.A53157
3525.A625	Marean, Emma Endicott, 1854-1936 (Table P-PZ40)
	Markey, Dorothy, 1897- see PS3531.A235
	Marsh, Rebecca see PS3527.E598
3525.A72783	Marshall, Sidney John, 1866- (Table P-PZ40)
	Marsten, Richard, 1926- see PS3515.U585
	Martha, Henry, 1922- see PS3515.A757
3525.A7887	Mason, Alfred Edward Woodley, 1865-1948 (Table P-PZ40)

Individual authors
1900-1960
M -- Continued

	Mason, Tally, 1909-1971 see PS3507.E69
3525.A823	Mason, Walt (Table P-PZ40)
3525.A83	Masters, Edgar Lee (Table P-PZ40)
3525.A9775	Maynard, Francis Henry, 1853-1926 (Table P-PZ40)
	Mayo, Jim, 1908- see PS3523.A446
	McBain, Ed, 1926- see PS3515.U585
	McCall, Anthony see PS3521.A4347
	McKay, Festus Claudius see PS3525.A24785
	McKenna, Evelyn, 1899- see PS3519.O712
	McLeod, Christian, pseud. see PS3535.U22
	McNeil, Morris, 1899- see PS3525.U943
	McPherson, Jessamyn West see PS3545.E8315
3525.C58	McSpadden, J. Walker (Joseph Walker), 1874-1960 (Table P-PZ40)
	Meeker, Richard see PS3503.R812
3525.E2823	Meigs, Cornelia, 1884-1973 (Table P-PZ40)
3525.E62	Merington, Marguerite (Table P-PZ40)
	Merriman, Charles, Eustace see PS3539.I56
3525.E718	Merwin, Samuel, 1874-1936 (Table P-PZ40)
3525.E9	Meyer, Annie (Nathan) (Table P-PZ40)
3525.I33	Mighels, Phillip Verrill, 1869-1911 (Table P-PZ40)
3525.I486	Millar, Kenneth, 1915- (Table P-PZ40)
	Miller, Helen Louise see PS3513.O75
3525.I5454	Miller, Henry, 1891- (Table P-PZ40)
3525.I548	Miller, Lewis, B., b. 1861 (Table P-PZ40)
3525.I6986	Miniter, Edith, 1869- (Table P-PZ40)
	Modell, Merriam see PS3531.I76
3525.O13	Moffett, Cleveland, 1863-1926 (Table P-PZ40)
	Monroe, Lyle, 1907- see PS3515.E288
	Moody, William Vaughn see PS2425+
3525.O5815	Moorehead, Warren King, 1866-1939 (Table P-PZ40)
3525.O6	More, Brookes, 1859- (Table P-PZ40)
	Morland, Peter Henry, 1892-1944 see PS3511.A87
3525.O71	Morley, Christopher Darlington (Table P-PZ40)
3525.O7368	Morris, Clara, 1848-1925 (Table P-PZ40)
3525.O825	Morton, Frederic (Table P-PZ40)
	Morton, Leah, 1890- see PS3537.T444
3525.O8298	Morton, Mary A. (Table P-PZ40)
3525.U943	Musselman, Morris McNeil, 1899- (Table P-PZ40)
3527.A-Z	N
	The author number is determined by the second letter of the name
3527.A6365	Nash, N. Richard (Table P-PZ40)
3527.E35	Neihardt, John Gneisenau (Table P-PZ40)

	Individual authors
	1900-1960
	N -- Continued
	Nelson, Alice Ruth Moore Dunbar, 1875- see PS3507.U6228
	Nelson, Marguerite see PS3511.L697
3527.E598	Neubauer, William Arthur, 1916- (Table P-PZ40)
	Newcomb, Norma see PS3527.E598
	Newman, Thomas see PS3525.A264
3527.E917	Newton, A. Edward (Alfred Edward), 1864-1940 (Table P-PZ40)
3527.E9178	Newton, Dwight Bennett, 1916- (Table P-PZ40)
3527.E928	Newton, Harry L. (Harry Lee), b. 1872 (Table P-PZ40)
3527.I35	Nicholson, Meredith (Table P-PZ40)
3527.I87	Nirdlinger, Charles Frederic (Table P-PZ40)
3527.O2	Nock, Albert Jay, 1872 or 3-1945 (Table P-PZ40)
3527.O575	North, Frank Mason, 1850-1935 (Table P-PZ40)
	Norton, Alice Mary see PS3527.O632
3527.O632	Norton, Andre (Table P-PZ40)
	Nusbaum, Nathan Richard see PS3527.A6365
3527.Y33	Nye, Nelson Coral, 1907- (Table P-PZ40)
3529.A-Z	O
	The author number is determined by the second letter of the name
3529.D47	Odland, Martin Wendell, 1875-1949 (Table P-PZ40)
	O'Donnell, Lawrence see PS3521.U87
3529.H34	O'Hara, Mary (Table P-PZ40)
	Olivieri, David, 1862-1937 see PS3545.H16
	O'More, Peggy, 1897- see PS3503.O8455
3529.P4	Opdycke, John Baker (Table P-PZ40)
3529.P6	Oppenheim, James (Table P-PZ40)
	Ormsbee, David see PS3523.O486
3529.S86	O'Sullivan, Vincent, 1872-1940 (Table P-PZ40)
3529.V33	Overholser, Wayne D. (Table P-PZ40)
	Owen, Philip, 1903- see PS3531.H442
3531.A-Z	P
	The author number is determined by the second letter of the name
	Padgett, Lewis see PS3521.U87
	Page, Dorothy Myra, 1897- see PS3531.A235
3531.A235	Page, Myra, 1897-. (Table P-PZ40)
3531.A27	Paine, Albert Bigelow (Table P-PZ40)
3531.A275	Paine, Ralph Delahaye (Table P-PZ40)
3531.A28	Painton, Edith F.A.U., b. 1878 (Table P-PZ40)
3531.A667	Parry, David M. (David Maclean), 1852-1915 (Table P-PZ40)
	Patrick, Q. see PS3545.H2895

Individual authors
  1900-1960
    P -- Continued

3531.E13	Peabody, Josephine Preston (Table P-PZ40)
3531.E18	Peake, Elmore Elliott, 1871- (Table P-PZ40)
3531.E214	Pears, Fanny Carleton (Table P-PZ40)
	Pentecost, Hugh, 1903- see PS3531.H442
	Perkins, Virginia Chase see PS3505.H528
	Perry, Mignon Good Eberhart, 1899- see PS3509.B453
3531.E8	Peters, Arthur Anderson, 1913- (Table P-PZ40)
	Peters, Fritz, 1913- see PS3531.E8
3531.H442	Phillips, Judson Pentecost, 1903- (Table P-PZ40)
3531.H5	Phillips, David Graham (Table P-PZ40)
3531.I7133	Pinkerton, Colin McKenzie (Table P-PZ40)
3531.I76	Piper, Evelyn (Table P-PZ40)
3531.L2	Plummer, Mary Wright (Table P-PZ40)
	Porter, Donald Clayton, 1914- see PS3513.E8679
3531.O7345	Porter, Gene Stratton, 1863-1924 (Table P-PZ40)
3531.O735	Porter, Harold Everett ("Holworthy Hall") (Table P-PZ40)
3531.O76427	Post, Melville Davisson, 1871-1930 (Table P-PZ40)
3531.O82	Pound, Ezra, 1885-1972 (Table P-PZ40 modified)
3531.O82A61- .O82Z458	Separate works. By title
	e. g.
	Cantos
3531.O82C24	Texts (Collected). By date
3531.O82C2412- .O82C2419	Translations (Collected). By language
3531.O82C259	Concordances. By date
3531.O82C28- .O82C2899	Criticism
3531.O82C29	Selected Cantos. By date
3531.O82C2912- .O82C2919	Translations. By language
3531.O82C292- .O82C299	Criticism
	Powell, El Sea see PS3531.O954
3531.O954	Powell, Lawrence Clark, 1906-
3531.R66	Prinsen, G.E. (Table P-PZ40)
3531.R988	Pryor, George Langhorn (Table P-PZ40)
	Putnam, Edith Palmer see PS3531.A28
3533.A-Z	Q
	The author number is determined by the second letter of the name
3533.U4	Queen, Ellery (Table P-PZ40)
	Quentin, Patrick see PS3545.H2895
3533.U53	Quick, Herbert, 1861-1925 (Table P-PZ40)
	Quint, Wilder Dwight, l863-l936 see PS3539.I56

Individual authors
1900-1960 -- Continued
3535.A-Z   R
The author number is determined by the second letter of the name
3535.A385   Raine, William Macleod, 1871-1954 (Table P-PZ40)
Randolph, Georgianna Ann, 1908-1957 see PS3535.I2236
Ransom, Stephen, 1902- see PS3507.A728
3535.A849   Rawson, Gertrude E. Gilchrist (Gertrude Elizabeth Gilchrist), 1870-1930 (Table P-PZ40)
3535.E3   Reed, Myrtle (Table P-PZ40)
3535.E745   Repp, Ed. Earl, 1900- (Table P-PZ40)
3535.H68   Rhodes, Eugene Manlove, 1869-1934 (Table P-PZ40)
3535.I2145   Rice, Alice Caldwell Hegan, 1870-1942 (Table P-PZ40)
3535.I22   Rice, Cale Young (Table P-PZ40)
3535.I2236   Rice, Craig, 1908-1957 (Table P-PZ40)
Richardson, George Tilton, I863-1938 see PS3539.I56
3535.I4224   Richmond, Grace Smith, 1866-1959 (Table P-PZ40)
3535.I654   Riis, Jacob A. (Jacob August), 1849-1914 (Table P-PZ40)
3535.I88   Rittenhouse, Jessie Belle (Table P-PZ40)
Riverside, John, 1907- see PS3515.E288
3535.O15   Robbins, Reginald Chauncey (Table P-PZ40)
3535.O176   Roberts, Kenneth Lewis, 1885-1957 (Table P-PZ40)
3535.O17944   Robertson, Alice Alberthe, 1859- (Table P-PZ40)
3535.O25   Robinson, Edwin Arlington (Table P-PZ40)
3535.O26613   Robinson, William Henry, 1867- (Table P-PZ40)
3535.O4125   Rogers, Bruce, 1870-1957 (Table P-PZ40)
3535.O514   Rollit, Carter, 1863-1935 (Table P-PZ40)
Rollit, Charles Carter, 1863-1935 see PS3535.O514
Ronns, Edward, 1916-1975 see PS3501.A79
3535.O5394   Roman, Sallie Rhett, 1844-1921 (Table P-PZ40)
Roos, Audrey Kelley, 1912- see PS3535.O54665
3535.O54665   Roos, Kelley (Table P-PZ40)
Roos, William, 1911- see PS3535.O54665
Ross, Barnaby see PS3533.U4
Ross, Dana Fuller, 1914- see PS3513.E8679
3535.U22   Ruddy, Anna Christian, 1861- (Table P-PZ40) (Christian McLeod)
3535.U47   Runkle, Bertha (Table P-PZ40)
3535.U67   Russell, Charles Edward (Table P-PZ40)
3535.Y45   Rye, Edgar (Table P-PZ40)
3535.Y53   Rygh, George Taylor, 1860-1942 (Table P-PZ40)
3537.A-Z   S
The author number is determined by the second letter of the name

Individual authors
1900-1960
S -- Continued

3537.A694	Sanford, John B., 1904- (Table P-PZ40)
	Saundering, Silas see PS3505.O737
	Saunders, Caleb, 1907- see PS3515.E288
3537.C71176	Schultz, James Willard, 1859-1947 (Table P-PZ40)
3537.C975	Scudder, Vida Dutton, 1861-1954 (Table P-PZ40)
3537.E23	Sedgwick, Henry Dwight (Table P-PZ40)
3537.E26	Seeger, Alan (Table P-PZ40)
3537.E3514	Seid, Ruth, 1913- (Table P-PZ40)
3537.E352	Seifert, Elizabeth, 1897- (Table P-PZ40)
	Semple, Gordon see PS3527.E598
	Seuss, Dr., 1904- see PS3513.E2
3537.H12	Shackelford, Otis M., 1871- (Table P-PZ40)
	Shapiro, Julian L., 1904- see PS3537.A694
	Shappiro, Herbert Arthur, 1899-1975 see PS3501.R77
3537.H3	Sharp, Dallas Lore (Table P-PZ40)
3537.H618	Sheldon, Charles Monroe, 1857-1946 (Table P-PZ40)
3537.H62	Sheldon, Edward Brewster (Table P-PZ40)
	Shepard, Florence, 1896- see PS3537.T9246
	Shepperd, Eli, b. 1868 see PS3547.O5
	Sherman, Gail see PS3513.A227
	Sherman, Joan see PS3513.A227
	Short, Luke, 1908-1975 see PS3513.L68158
3537.I47	Sill, Louise Morgan (Smith) (Table P-PZ40)
	Sims, John see PS3515.O6526
	Sinclair, B.M. (Bertha Muzzy), 1874- see PS3503.O8193
	Sinclair, Bertha, Muzzy, 1874-1940 see PS3503.O8193
	Sinclair, Jo, 1913- see PS3537.E3514
3537.I85	Sinclair, Upton Beall (Table P-PZ40)
3537.J6	Sjolander, John Peter, 1851-1939 (Table P-PZ40)
3537.L38	Slaughter, Frank Gill, 1908- (Table P-PZ40)
	Smith, Carmichael, 1913-1966 see PS3523.I629
	Smith, Cordwainer, 1913-1966 see PS3523.I629
3537.M36	Smith, Effie Waller, 1879-1960 (Table P-PZ40)
	Smith, Lew see PS3511.L697
	Smith, Lula Carson, 1917-1967 see PS3525.A1772
3537.M836	Smith, Titus K. (Titus Keiper), b. 1859 (Table P-PZ40)
3537.O83	Sousa, John Philip, 1854-1932 (Table P-PZ40)
3537.P652	Spillane, Frank Morrison, 1918- (Table P-PZ40)
	Spillane, Mickey, 1918- see PS3537.P652
	Squires, John Radcliffe, 1917- see PS3537.Q68
3537.Q68	Squires, Radcliffe, 1917- (Table P-PZ40)
	St. John, David see PS3515.U5425
	St. Luz, Berthe, 1859- see PS3535.O17944
	Stagge, Jonathan see PS3545.H2895

Individual authors

1900-1960

S -- Continued

3537.T1757	Standing Bear, Luther, 1868?-1939 (Table P-PZ40)
3537.T2687	Steele, Curtis (Table P-PZ40)
3537.T313	Steffens, Lincoln, 1866-1936 (Table P-PZ40)
3537.T3184	Stein, Aaron Marc, 1906- (Table P-PZ40)
3537.T323	Stein, Gertrude (Table P-PZ40)
3537.T3533	Stephens, Charles Asbury, 1844-1931 (Table P-PZ40)
3537.T42	Sterling, George, 1869-1926 (Table P-PZ40)
3537.T444	Stern, Elisabeth G., 1890- (Table P-PZ40)
	Stevens, Dan J., 1906- see PS3529.V33
	Stevens, William Christopher see PS3501.L5553
3537.T479	Steward, Samuel M. (Table P-PZ40)
3537.T483	Stewart, Charles David (Table P-PZ40)
	Stewart, Will see PS3545.I557
3537.T667	Stone, Grace (Zaring) (Table P-PZ40)
	Stone, Hampton, 1906- see PS3537.T3184
	Stone, Thomas, 1896- see PS3537.T9246
	Stonebaker, Florence, 1896- see PS3537.T9246
	Storm, Diedric see PS3527.A6365
	Story, Josephine see PS3523.O645
3537.T817	Stratemeyer, Edward, 1862-1930 (Table P-PZ40)
	Stratton-Porter, Gene, 1863-1924 see PS3531.O7345
3537.T845	Stringer, Arthur (Table P-PZ40)
3537.T8534	Strobridge, Idah M. (Idah Meacham), 1855-1932 (Table P-PZ40)
3537.T9246	Stuart, Florence, 1896- (Table P-PZ40)
	Stuart, Matt, 1895- see PS3515.O4448
	Stubbs, Harry C. see PS3505.L646
	Sture-Vasa, Mary O'Hara Alsop see PS3529.H34
3537.U53	Sullivan, William Laurence, 1872-1935 (Table P-PZ40)
3537.U89	Sutherland, Evelyn Greenleaf Baker, 1855-1908 (Table P-PZ40)
3537.U9	Sutherland, Howard Vigne (Table P-PZ40)
3537.U946	Sutphen, William Gilbert van Tassel, 1861-1945 (Table P-PZ40)
3537.U948	Sutro, Alfred, 1869-1945 (Table P-PZ40)
	Sweet, Florence, 1896- see PS3537.T9246
	Symmes, Robert, 1919- see PS3507.U629
3539.A-Z	T

The author number is determined by the second letter of the name

	Taine, Ted, 1926- see PS3515.U585
3539.A39	Talman, John, 1851-1936 (Table P-PZ40)
3539.A889	Taylor, Edward Dewitt (Table P-PZ40)
3539.A89	Taylor, Edward Robeson, 1838-1923 (Table P-PZ40)

Individual authors
1900-1960
T -- Continued

3539.A9635	Taylor, Phoebe Atwood, 1909-1976 (Table P-PZ40)
3539.E15	Teasdale, Sara (Table P-PZ40)
	Temple, Dan, 1916- see PS3527.E9178
3539.E48	Templeton, Rinny (Table P-PZ40)
	Tepperman, Emile C. see PS3537.T2687
3539.E65	Terhune, Albert Payson (Table P-PZ40)
	Terry, C.V. see PS3537.L38
3539.H149	Thatcher, Maurice Hudson, 1870-1973 (Table P-PZ40)
	Thomas, Dee see PS3539.H573
3539.H573	Thomas, Dorothy, 1898- (Table P-PZ40)
	Thomas, Lee see PS3511.L697
	Thompson, James Myers, 1906-1977 see PS3539.H6733
3539.H6733	Thompson, Jim, 1906-1977 (Table P-PZ40)
	Tilton, Alice, 1909-1976 see PS3539.A9635
3539.I56	Tilton, Dwight (Table P-PZ40)
3539.I648	Tinley, J.W. (James Walter), b. 1866 (Table P-PZ40)
3539.O56	Tope, J. LeRoy, b. 1870 (Table P-PZ40)
3539.O63	Torrence, Frederic Ridgely (Table P-PZ40)
3539.O793	Toulmin, George Bowers, 1853- (Table P-PZ40)
3539.R715	Trites, W. B. (William B.) (Table P-PZ40)
	Turner, Len see PS3511.L697
3541.A-Z	U
	The author number is determined by the second letter of the name
3541.L4	Ullman, Samuel, 1840-1924 (Table P-PZ40)
3541.N55	Underwood, Edna Worthley, 1873-1961 (Table P-PZ40)
3541.N72	Untermeyer, Louis (Table P-PZ40)
3541.P7	Upson, Arthur Wheelock (Table P-PZ40)
3543.A-Z	V
	The author number is determined by the second letter of the name
	Van Dine, S.S. see PS3545.R846
3543.A6578	Van Zandt, Earl C. (Earl Christian), b. 1894 (Table P-PZ40)
	Vance, Ethel, 1891- see PS3537.T667
	Vasa, Mary O'Hara Alsop Sture see PS3529.H34
	Vidal, Eugene Luther see PS3543.I26
3543.I26	Vidal, Gore, 1925- (Table P-PZ40)
3543.I32	Viereck, George Sylvester (Table P-PZ40)
3543.O88	Vorse, Mary Marvin Heaton (Table P-PZ40)
3545.A-Z	W
	The author number is determined by the second letter of the name

Individual authors
1900-1960
W -- Continued

3545.A565	Waller, Leslie, 1923- (Table P-PZ40)
	Walmsley, Dorothy Brush, 1894-1968 see PS3503.R937
3545.A59	Walsh, Thomas (Table P-PZ40)
3545.A61	Walter, Eugene (Table P-PZ40)
3545.A724	Waren, Helen (Table P-PZ40)
3545.A74335	Warren, Charles, 1868-1954 (Table P-PZ40)
	Washington, Alex, 1922- see PS3515.A757
3545.A8	Waterman, Nixon (Table P-PZ40)
	Watson, Will see PS3511.L697
	Wayne, Joseph, 1906- see PS3529.V33
3545.E533	Wells, Carolyn (Table P-PZ40)
3545.E8315	West, Jessamyn (Table P-PZ40)
	West, Mary Therese, 1912- see PS3525.A1435
	West, Ward, 1900- see PS3503.O563
	Westland, Lynn, 1899- see PS3519.O712
3545.H16	Wharton, Edith, 1862-1937 (Table P-PZ40)
	Wharton, Edith Newbold Jones see PS3545.H16
	Wheeler, Hugh, 1912- see PS3545.H2895
3545.H2895	Wheeler, Hugh Callingham, 1913- (Table P-PZ40)
3545.H484	Whitcomb, Charlotte, b. 1841 (Table P-PZ40)
3545.H53	White, Hervey (Table P-PZ40)
3545.H6	White, Stewart Edward (Table P-PZ40)
3545.H617	White, William Allen, 1868-1944 (Table P-PZ40)
3545.H6172	White, William Anthony Parker, 1911-1968 (Table P-PZ40)
3545.H75	Whitlock, Brand, 1869-1934 (Table P-PZ40)
3545.H83	Whitney, Helen (Hay) (Table P-PZ40)
3545.I175	Widdemer, Margaret (Table P-PZ40)
	Wiener, Henri see PS3523.O486
	Wiener, Philip see PS3523.O486
	Wiener-Longstreet, Stephen Henri see PS3523.O486
	Wiggen, Henry J., 1922- see PS3515.A757
3545.I342	Wilder, Laura Ingalls, 1867-1957 (Table P-PZ40)
3545.I36	Wiley, Sara King (Table P-PZ40)
	Williams, Coe see PS3515.A78117
3545.I557	Williamson, Jack, 1908- (Table P-PZ40)
	Wilson, Dave see PS3511.L697
	Wilson, Mary Therese, 1912- see PS3525.A1435
3545.I68157	Windson, William, b. 1857 (Table P-PZ40)
	Winfield, Arthur, M., 1862-1930 see PS3537.T817
	Winters, Janet, 1899- see PS3523.E866
	Witherspoon, Naomi Long see PS3525.A318
3545.O465	Wood, Charles Erskine Scott, 1852-1944 (Table P-PZ40)
3545.O742	Woodward, William E., 1874-1950 (Table P-PZ40)

Individual authors
1900-1960
W -- Continued
Woolrich, Cornell, 1903-1968 see PS3515.O6455

3545.R33	Wright, Ernest Vincent, 1872-1939 (Table P-PZ40)
3545.R45	Wright, Harold Bell (Table P-PZ40)
	Wright, Jack R., 1922- see PS3515.A757
3545.R8	Wright, Philip Green, 1861-1934 (Table P-PZ40)
3545.R846	Wright, Willard Huntington, 1888-1939 (Table P-PZ40)
3545.Y3	Wyatt, Edith Franklin, 1873-1958 (Table P-PZ40)
3546.A-Z	X

The author number is determined by the second letter of the
name

3547.A-Z	Y

The author number is determined by the second letter of the
name

3547.A748	Yates, Frederick Benjamin, b. 1848 (Table P-PZ40)
	York, Simon, 1907- see PS3515.E288
3547.O4745	Young, Ella, 1867-1956 (Table P-PZ40)
3547.O5	Young, Martha, b. 1868 (Table P-PZ40)
3549.A-Z	Z

The author number is determined by the second letter of the
name

3549.O63	Zolotow, Charlotte, 1915- (Table P-PZ40)

1961-2000
Subarrange individual authors by Table P-PZ40 unless
otherwise specified
Including usually authors beginning to publish about 1950,
flourishing after 1960
For works of fiction cataloged before July 1, 1980, except
limited editions and works in the Rare Book
Collections see PZ4

3550	Anonymous works (Table P-PZ28)
3551.A-Z	A

The author number is determined by the second letter of the
name
"A", Dr., 1920- see PS3551.S5
Abbot, Rick see PS3569.H3427

3551.D34	Adams, Clifton (Table P-PZ40)
	Adams, Laura, 1960- see PS3561.A41665
3551.I2	Ai, 1947- (Table P-PZ40)
	Aimé, Albert Du see PS3573.H32
	Akhnaton, Askia see PS3555.C53
	Alcade, Miguel see PS3568.E4754
3551.L346	Aldyne, Nathan (Table P-PZ40)
3551.L362	Alicia (Table P-PZ40)
	Allan, Dennis, 1900- see PS3511.O186

	Individual authors
	1961-2000
	A -- Continued
	Allan, John B. see PS3573.E9
	Allen, Clay, 1916- see PS3566.A34
3551.L3922	Allen, Dick, 1939- (Table P-PZ40)
3551.L393	Allen, Henry Wilson, 1912- (Table P-PZ40)
	Allen, Marcus, 1946- see PS3551.L3963
3551.L3963	Allen, Mark, 1946- (Table P-PZ40)
	Allen, Mary Elizabeth see PS3557.R482
	Allen, Richard Stanley, 1939- see PS3551.L3922
	Allyson, Kym, 1929- see PS3561.I417
	Almonte, Rosa, 1916- see PS3566.A34
3551.L84	Alurista (Table P-PZ40)
	Ames, Joye see PS3562.A8479
3551.N384	Anderson, Roberta (Table P-PZ40)
	Cf. PS3563.I27 Michaels, Fern
	Andress, Lesley see PS3569.A5125
	Andrews, A.A., 1916- see PS3566.A34
	Andrews, Elton see PS3566.O36
3551.N464	Angelou, Maya (Table P-PZ40)
	Anthony, Florence, 1947- see PS3551.I2
3551.N73	Anthony, Piers (Table P-PZ40)
3551.N76	Antler, 1946- (Table P-PZ40)
	Archer, Dennie, 1916- see PS3566.A34
	Arden, William, 1924- see PS3562.Y44
	Armour, John, 1916- see PS3566.A34
3551.R49	Arnett, Carroll, 1927- (Table P-PZ40)
	Arrow, William see PS3568.O873
	Ascher, Sheila see PS3551.S33
3551.S33	Ascher/Straus (Table P-PZ40)
	Ashley, Steven see PS3563.A2555
	Ashton, Ann, 1929- see PS3561.I417
	Ashton, Harry see PS3563.A31166
3551.S5	Asimov, Isaac, 1920- (Table P-PZ40)
	Askia, Akhnaton see PS3555.C53
	Austin, Harry see PS3563.A31166
3551.U838	Austin, John Osborne, 1849-1918 (Table P-PZ40)
3552.A-Z	B
	The author number is determined by the second letter of the name
	Bache, Ellyn see PS3563.A845
	Bachman, Richard, 1947- see PS3561.I483
	Bagby, George, 1906- see PS3569.T34
3552.A4278	Baker, James Robert (Table P-PZ40)
	Ball, Pat see PS3558.A4434
3552.A4733	Bamford, Susannah (Table P-PZ40)

Individual authors
1961-2000
B -- Continued

3552.A476	Banis, Victor J. (Table P-PZ40)
3552.A583	Baraka, Imamu Amiri, 1934- (Table P-PZ40)
3552.A59177	Barba, Harry (Table P-PZ40)
	Baron, Mikan see PS3552.A59177
	Barr, Lily see PS3553.O6454
	Bartlett, Kathleen, 1916- see PS3566.A34
	Bass, Madeline Tiger, 1934- see PS3570.I3377
	Batchelor, Reg, 1916- see PS3566.A34
	Beck, Harry, 1916- see PS3566.A34
3552.E2568	Becker, Robert D. (Table P-PZ40)
3552.E26	Becker, Stephen D., 1927- (Table P-PZ40)
	Bedford, Kenneth, 1916- see PS3566.A34
3552.E345	Beeler, Janet (Table P-PZ40)
	Beldone, Cheech see PS3555.L62
	Beldone, Phil see PS3555.L62
	Bennet, Laura see PS3558.A624283
3552.E54765	Bensen, D.R. (Donald R.), 1927- (Table P-PZ40)
	Benton, Will, 1916- see PS3566.A34
3552.I3	Bickham, Jack M. (Table P-PZ40)
3552.I449	Biller, Elizabeth (Table P-PZ40)
	Birdwell, Cleo see PS3554.E4425
	Blaisdell, Anne see PS3562.I515
	Blake, Jennifer, 1942- see PS3563.A923
	Bleeck, Oliver see PS3570.H58
	Bloom, John see PS3552.R458
3552.L77	Blue Cloud, Peter (Table P-PZ40)
3552.L79	Blue Ring Dave (Table P-PZ40)
	Bond, Evelyn, 1926- see PS3558.E78
3552.O754	Borland, Kathryn Kilby (Table P-PZ40)
3552.O79	Boswell, Barbara (Table P-PZ40)
	Bosworth, Frank, 1916- see PS3566.A34
	Bovee, Ruth, 1916- see PS3566.A34
3552.O8756	Bowman, Craig C. ("C.C.B.") (Table P-PZ40)
	Bowman, Eric, 1953- see PS3556.R599
	Boyer, Richard see PS3552.O895
	Boyer, Richard L. see PS3552.O895
3552.O895	Boyer, Rick (Table P-PZ40)
	Bradford, Will, 1916- see PS3566.A34
	Bradley, Concho, 1916- see PS3566.A34
3552.R2298	Bradley, Rodrick (Table P-PZ40)
	Bramwell, Charlotte, 1929- see PS3561.I417
	Brand, Rebecca, 1939- see PS3553.H325
	Breit, William see PS3560.E88
	Brennan, Will, 1916- see PS3566.A34

Individual authors
1961-2000
B -- Continued

3552.R458	Briggs, Joe Bob (Table P-PZ40)
	Brisco, Patty, 1927- see PS3563.A853
	Brock, Stuart, 1917- see PS3570.R519
3552.R656	Bronte, Louisa (Table P-PZ40)
	Brown, Joseph A. see PS3562.U457
	Brown, William F. see PS3573.A7713
	Browne, Robert see PS3561.A63
	Buettner, Kristeen T. Von (Kristeen Tadich) see PS3572.O423
	Bummer, Stanley see PS3557.R2918
	Buning, Sietze, 1930- see PS3573.I358
	Burdick, Brad, 1946- see PS3551.N76
	Burgess, Michael Roy see PS3568.E4754
3552.U7234	Burke, Phyllis, 1951- (Table P-PZ40)
3552.U725	Burkholz, Herbert, 1932- (Table P-PZ40)
	Cf. PS3562.U255 Luckless, John
3552.U75	Burroughs, William S., 1914- (Table P-PZ40)
	Byer, Kathryn Stripling see PS3569.T6965
3553.A-Z	C
	The author number is determined by the second letter of the name
	C.C.B. see PS3552.O8756
	Callahan, Pete, 1965- see PS3570.E447
3553.A434	Cameron, Lou, 1924- (Table P-PZ40)
	Camp, John see PS3569.A516
	Campion, Emma see PS3568.O198
3553.A583	Capella, Raul Garcia (Table P-PZ40)
	Capella, Ray see PS3553.A583
	Carbury, A.B. see PS3553.A7627
3553.A686	Cariño, Maria Luisa B. Aguilar-, 1961- (Table P-PZ40)
	Carney, John Otis see PS3553.A757
3553.A757	Carney, Otis (Table P-PZ40)
	Carpenter, John Jo see PS3568.E43
	Carr, A.H.Z. see PS3553.A7627
3553.A7627	Carr, Albert H.Z. (Table P-PZ40)
	Carrel, Mark, 1916- see PS3566.A34
	Carroll, Mary, 1929- see PS3569.H5792
	Carter, Nevada, 1916- see PS3566.A34
3553.A7952	Casper, Linda Ty (Table P-PZ40)
	Cassady, Claude, 1916- see PS3566.A34
	Castle, Jayne see PS3561.R44
	Chandler, Mark see PS3569.H3427
	Chapman, Virginia Hathaway see PS3563.O871644
	Chapman, Walker see PS3569.I472

	Individual authors
	1961-2000
	C -- Continued
	Charbonneau, Louis H. see PS3575.O7
3553.H325	Charnas, Suzy McKee (Table P-PZ40)
3553.H3534	Cherkovski, Neeli (Table P-PZ40)
	Cherry, Neeli see PS3553.H3534
	Chow, Shirley R. see PS3573.O5968
	Cid see PS3553.O65
	Clark, Badger, 1916- see PS3566.A34
	Clark, Curt see PS3573.E9
	Clark, Katharine see PS3556.L5838
	Clarke, Boden see PS3568.E4754
	Clarke, Richard, 1916- see PS3566.A34
	Clarke, Robert, 1916- see PS3566.A34
	Clinton, Jeff see PS3552.I3
	Cloud, Peter Blue see PS3552.L77
	Coe, Tucker see PS3573.E9
	Collins, Jim, 1945- see PS3563.I4125
	Collins, Michael, 1924- see PS3562.Y44
	Colton, James, 1923- see PS3558.A5132
	Coltrane, James see PS3573.O39
	Coltrane, James, 1961- see PS3565.N316
	Cooper, C. Everett see PS3568.E4754
3553.O64	Coppel, Alfred (Table P-PZ40)
3553.O6454	Corderman, Esther Boyce (Table P-PZ40)
3553.O65	Corman, Cid (Table P-PZ40)
	Coy, Stanley Miller see PS3563.I37655
	Coyne, P.J. see PS3563.A82
	Craig, Alisa see PS3563.A31865
3553.R34	Creeley, Bobbie, 1930- (Table P-PZ40)
	Crichton, John Michael, 1942- see PS3553.R48
3553.R48	Crichton, Michael, 1942- (Table P-PZ40)
	Cross, Amanda, 1926- see PS3558.E4526
	Crowe, John, 1924- see PS3562.Y44
3553.R789	Cruz, M. (Table P-PZ40)
3554.A-Z	D
	The author number is determined by the second letter of the name
	D., Ra'mola, 1964- see PS3554.H27
3554.A3	Daimler, Harriet (Table P-PZ40)
3554.A47	D'Ambrosio (Table P-PZ40)
	D'Ambrosio, Joseph J. see PS3554.A47
	Dana, Amber, 1916- see PS3566.A34
	Dana, Richard, 1916- see PS3566.A34
	Dangler, Sue see PS3553.R789
	Danton, Rebecca see PS3552.R656

	Individual authors
	1961-2000
	D -- Continued
	David, Jay see PS3556.I812
	Davis, Audrey see PS3566.A34
	Davis, Jennie see PS3563.O517
	De Wetering, Janwillem van, 1931- see PS3572.A4292
3554.E13	Deal, Borden, 1922- (Table P-PZ40)
	Deal, Loyse Youth see PS3554.E13
3554.E174	DeAndrea, William L. (Table P-PZ40)
3554.E4	DeFrees, Madeline (Table P-PZ40)
	DeGrave, Philip see PS3554.E174
3554.E4425	DeLillo, Don (Table P-PZ40)
	Demijohn, Thom see PS3569.L25
3554.E48	Deming, Richard (Table P-PZ40)
3554.E537	Dennis, Patrick, 1921-1976 (Table P-PZ40)
	Denniston, Elinore, 1900- see PS3511.O186
	DeWeese, Eugene see PS3554.E929
3554.E929	DeWeese, Gene (Table P-PZ40)
	DeWeese, Jean see PS3554.E929
3554.H27	Dharmaraj, Ramola, 1964- (Table P-PZ40)
3554.I223	Dial, Joan, 1937- (Table P-PZ40)
3554.I24	Diamond, Jacqueline (Table P-PZ40)
	Dillinger, James see PS3552.A4278
3554.I8	Disch, Thomas M. (Table P-PZ40)
3554.O32	Dodd, Wayne, 1930- (Table P-PZ40)
	Dodge, Steve see PS3552.E26
	Dominic, R.B. see PS3562.A755
	Dominique, Meg see PS3569.H5792
	Donicht, Mark, 1946- see PS3551.L3963
	Douglas, Michael, 1942- see PS3553.R48
	Dr. "A," 1920- see PS3551.S5
3554.R183	Dragonwagon, Crecent (Table P-PZ40)
	Drennen, Lynne see PS3569.C695
	Drexler, J.F., 1916- see PS3566.A34
	Drummond, Walter see PS3569.I472
	Dublin, Martin David see PS3552.L79
	Duchesne, Antoinette see PS3566.A34
3554.U279	Ducornet, Erica, 1943- (Table P-PZ40)
	Durham, John see PS3566.A34
3555.A-Z	E
	The author number is determined by the second letter of the name
3555.A39	Eagle Walking Turtle (Table P-PZ40)
	Ebmeier, L. Paul see PS3557.R188
3555.C53	Eckels, John (Table P-PZ40)
3555.C54	Ecker, Ronald L. (Table P-PZ40)

	Individual authors
	1961-2000
	E -- Continued
	Egan, Lesley see PS3562.I515
3555.L378	Elethea, Abba (Table P-PZ40)
3555.L56	Ellin, Stanley (Table P-PZ40)
	Ellin, Stanley Bernard see PS3555.L56
3555.L62	Ellison, Harlan (Table P-PZ40)
3555.L84	Elward, James (Table P-PZ40)
	English, Arnold, 1926- see PS3558.E78
	Ericson, David see PS3561.E388
3555.R58	Ernenwein, Leslie (Table P-PZ40)
	Ernenwein, Leslie Charles, 1900- see PS3555.R58
3555.V27	Evans, Tabor (Cameron, Lou, 1924- or Knot, Bill, 1927- or Tobin, Greg as house pseud.) (Table P-PZ40)
	Cf. PS3553.A434 Cameron, Lou, 1924-
	Cf. PS3561.N645 Knott, Bill, 1927-
	Cf. PS3570.O29 Tobin, Greg
3556.A-Z	F
	The author number is determined by the second letter of the name
	Fain, Michael see PS3563.I254
	Falconer, Sovereign see PS3569.T6935
3556.A72	Farmer, Philip José (Table P-PZ40)
	Farrell, John Wade see PS3563.A28
3556.A87	Father Gander (Table P-PZ40)
	Feinberg, Bea see PS3556.R384
	Feldman, Ellen see PS3572.I38
	Fernandes, 1938- see PS3565.A8
	Ferrand, Georgina see PR6053.A824138
	Ferris, Monk see PS3569.H3427
	Fisher, Clay, 1912- see PS3551.L393
3556.I812	Fisher, David, 1946- (Table P-PZ40)
	Fisher, Margot, 1916- see PS3566.A34
3556.I828	Fitzgerald, Amber, 1951- (Table P-PZ40)
3556.I93	Five Lesbian Brothers (Theater troupe) (Table P-PZ40)
	Fleck, Betty, 1916- see PS3566.A34
3556.L49	Fletcher, Cora C. (Table P-PZ40)
3556.L5838	Flora, Kate, 1949- (Table P-PZ40)
3556.O67	Forbes, Stanton, 1923- (Table P-PZ40)
	Foster, John, 1917- see PS3556.U72
	Foxx, Jack see PS3566.R67
	Franklin, Max see PS3554.E48
	Frayer, Andrew, 1928- see PS3563.A674
3556.R37	Frede, Richard (Table P-PZ40)
	Frederies, Macdowell see PS3556.R37
3556.R384	Freeman, Cynthia (Table P-PZ40)

	Individual authors
	1961-2000
	F -- Continued
	Freeman, Jean K., 1929- see PS3561.E48
	French, Paul, 1920- see PS3551.S5
3556.R518	Friedman, H.L. (Table P-PZ40)
	Friedman, Harry see PS3556.R518
	Friedman, Linda see PS3556.R518
	Frost, Joni, 1916- see PS3566.A34
3556.R599	Frost, Mark, 1953- (Table P-PZ40)
	Frost, P. R. see PS3568.A325
3556.U72	Furcolo, Foster (Table P-PZ40)
3557.A-Z	G
	The author number is determined by the second letter of the name
3557.A715	Garfield, Brian, 1939- (Table P-PZ40)
3557.A7238	Garrett, Randall (Table P-PZ40)
	Cf. PS3568.A497 Randall, Robert
3557.H63	Ghose, Zulfikar, 1935- (Table P-PZ40)
	Gilbert, Sister see PS3554.E4
	Gill, Bartholomew, 1943- see PS3563.A296
	Gilman, Robert Cham see PS3553.O64
	Gladstone, Arthur M., 1921- see PS3569.E28
	Gladstone, Maggie, 1921- see PS3569.E28
	Glendenning, Donn, 1916- see PS3566.A34
	Glenn, James, 1916- see PS3566.A34
	Gogisgi, 1927- see PS3551.R49
3557.O384	Goldman, William, 1931- (Table P-PZ40)
	Goodman, George J.W. see PS3569.M443
	Gordon, Angela, 1916- see PS3566.A34
	Gorman, Beth, 1916- see PS3566.A34
3557.R188	Graham, Clayton R. (Table P-PZ40)
	Granback, Marilyn see PS3558.E487
	Grandower, Elissa see PS3573.A9
3557.R2918	Gray, Darrell, 1945- (Table P-PZ40)
	Green, Hannah see PS3557.R3784
3557.R356	Greber, Judith (Table P-PZ40)
3557.R3784	Greenberg, Joanne (Table P-PZ40)
3557.R482	Grey, Kitty, 1961- (Table P-PZ40)
3557.R583	Gross, Kenneth G. (Table P-PZ40)
3557.R8	Gruenfeld, Lee (Table P-PZ40)
3557.U43	Gulick, Bill, 1916- (Table P-PZ40)
	Gulick, Grover C. see PS3557.U43
3558.A-Z	H
	The author number is determined by the second letter of the name
3558.A3117	Haddad, C.A. (Table P-PZ40)

Individual authors
1961-2000
H -- Continued

	Haddad, Carolyn see PS3558.A3117
3558.A373	Hall, Oakley M. (Table P-PZ40)
	Hamady, Mary see PS3562.A36
3558.A4429	Hamilton, Jane, 1972- (Table P-PZ40)
3558.A4434	Hamilton, Nan (Table P-PZ40)
	Hamrick, S.J. see PS3570.Y53
	Han, Ling-ku see PS3558.A5132
3558.A513	Hansen, Joseph, 1923- (Table P-PZ40)
3558.A5132	Hansen, Paul (Table P-PZ40)
	Hargrave, Leonie see PS3554.I8
3558.A624283	Harlowe, Justine (Table P-PZ40)
	Harris, MacDonald, 1921- see PS3558.E458
3558.A6558	Harris, Thomas (Table P-PZ40)
	Harris, William Thomas, 1940- see PS3558.A6558
	Hart, Francis, 1916- see PS3566.A34
	Harvey, Jean see PS3558.A624283
	Harvey, Kathryn see PS3573.O5877
	Hawkins, Bobbie Louise see PS3553.R34
3558.A824	Hawthorne, Violet (Table P-PZ40)
	Hayden, Jay, 1916- see PS3566.A34
	Healey, Ben see PS3560.E45
3558.E4526	Heilbrun, Carolyn G. (Table P-PZ40)
3558.E458	Heiney, Donald W., 1921- (Table P-PZ40)
3558.E487	Henderson, M.R. (Table P-PZ40)
	Henissart, Martha see PS3562.A755
	Henry Elyssa see PS3562.A8479
	Henry, Will, 1912- see PS3551.L393
3558.E78	Hershman, Morris, 1926- (Table P-PZ40)
3558.I227	Hickey, Dr. 1909- (Table P-PZ40)
3558.I366	Highsmith, Patricia, 1921- (Table P-PZ40)
	Hill, Fiona, 1952- see PS3566.A463
	Hillerman, Anthony G. see PS3558.I45
3558.I45	Hillerman, Tony (Table P-PZ40)
3558.O3473	Hogan, Ray (Table P-PZ40)
	Hogan, Robert Ray, 1908- see PS3558.O3473
	Holt, Helen, 1916- see PS3566.A34
	Houston, Will, 1916- see PS3566.A34
	Howard, Elizabeth, 1916- see PS3566.A34
	Howard, Troy, 1916- see PS3566.A34
3558.U323	Huff, T.E. (Table P-PZ40)
	Huff, Tom see PS3558.U323
	Hughes, Jeffrey, 1942- see PS3553.R48
	Hughes, Matilda see PS3563.A31865
	Hunt, John, 1916- see PS3566.A34

	Individual authors
	1961-2000
	H -- Continued
	Hyman, Jackie see PS3554.I24
	Hyman, Tom see PS3558.Y49
3558.Y49	Hyman, Vernon Tom (Table P-PZ40)
3559.A-Z	I

The author number is determined by the second letter of the name

Igloria, Luisa A. see PS3553.A686

Ingersoll, Jared, 1916- see PS3566.A34

3559.R79	Irving, Clifford
	Cf. PS3562.U255 Luckless, John
3560.A-Z	J

The author number is determined by the second letter of the name

Jacob, Piers Anthony Dillingham see PS3551.N73

3560.A37	Jakes, John, 1932- (Table P-PZ40)

James, Rebecca see PS3555.L84

James, Stephanie see PS3561.R44

Jamison, Amelia see PS3569.I57

Jans, Miriam see PS3570.H65

Jaxon, Milt, 1929- see PS3561.I417

3560.E45	Jeffreys, J.G. (Table P-PZ40)
3560.E88	Jevons, Marshall (Table P-PZ40)

Johnson, Marguerite see PS3551.N464

Johnson, Mike, 1931-1992 see PS3569.H3427

Johnson, Shirley see PS3565.V44

Jones, LeRoi, 1934- see PS3552.A583

Jorgenson, Ivar see PS3569.I472

3561.A-Z	K

The author number is determined by the second letter of the name

3561.A41665	Kallmaker, Karin, 1960 (Table P-PZ40)

Kamien, Marcia see PS3568.O7639

Kantor, Herman see PS3558.I227

3561.A63	Karlins, Marvin (Table P-PZ40)
3561.A675	Karmel-Wolfe, Henia (Table P-PZ40)

Keimberg, Allyn, 1929- see PS3561.I417

Keith, Carlton see PS3568.O2493

3561.E388	Kelley, Leo P. (Table P-PZ40)

Kelley, Ray, 1916- see PS3566.A34

3561.E3975	Kelton, Elmer (Table P-PZ40)
3561.E425	Kennedy, Adam (Table P-PZ40)
3561.E48	Kenny, Jean Lenore, 1929- (Table P-PZ40)
(3561.E5192)	Kent, Katherine, 1937-
	see PS3554.I223

	Individual authors
	1961-2000
	K -- Continued
	Kenyon, Bruce see PS3572.I86
	Ketchum, Jack, 1916- see PS3566.A34
	Khanshendel, Chiron see PS3568.O7644
	Kilgore, John, 1916- see PS3566.A34
	Kimbro, Jean, 1929- see PS3561.I417
3561.I417	Kimbro, John M., 1929- (Table P-PZ40)
	Kimbrough, Kathryn, 1929- see PS3561.I417
3561.I483	King, Stephen, 1947- (Table P-PZ40)
	Knight, J.Z. see PS3568.A475
3561.N645	Knott, Bill, 1927- (Table P-PZ40)
3561.N65	Knott, Bill, 1940- (Table P-PZ40)
	Knox, Calvin M. see PS3569.I472
3561.O363	Kohn, Robert Rothenberg, 1925- (Table P-PZ40)
	Kong see PS3561.O46
	Konigsberger, Hans see PS3561.O46
3561.O46	Koning, Hans, 1921- (Table P-PZ40)
	Koningsberger, Hans see PS3561.O46
3561.O8	Kosinski, Jerzy N., 1933- (Table P-PZ40)
3561.R44	Krentz, Jayne Ann (Table P-PZ40)
3561.U23	Kuczkir, Mary (Table P-PZ40)
	Cf. PS3563.I27 Michaels, Fern
3562.A-Z	L
	The author number is determined by the second letter of the name
3562.A36	Laird, Mary (Table P-PZ40)
	Lambec, Zoltan, 1929- see PS3561.I417
	Land, Jane see PS3552.O754
	Lange, John, 1942- see PS3553.R48
	Larche, Douglas W. see PS3556.A87
3562.A755	Lathen, Emma (Table P-PZ40)
	Latsis, Mary J. see PS3562.A755
3562.A8479	Lavene, Joyce (Table P-PZ40)
	LaVoie, Phyllis see PS3552.U7234
	Lawhead, Stephen R. see PS3562.A865
3562.A865	Lawhead, Steve (Table P-PZ40)
3562.A916	Lawrence, Steven C. (Table P-PZ40)
3562.A98	Lazarus, Mell, 1927- (Table P-PZ40)
3562.A995	Lazowick, Louis, 1912- (Table P-PZ40)
	Lebak, Jane, 1972- see PS3558.A4429
	Lee, William, 1914- see PS3552.U75
	LeSourd, Catherine, 1914- see PS3563.A7212
	Lesser, Milton, 1928- see PS3563.A674
	Lester, Lewis, 1912- see PS3562.A995
	Liggett, Hunter, 1916- see PS3566.A34

Individual authors
1961-2000
L -- Continued

	Lillo, Don De see PS3554.E4425
	Lillywhite, Eileen Silver-, 1953- see PS3569.I4717
3562.I515	Linington, Elizabeth (Table P-PZ40)
3562.O75	Lorde, Audre (Table P-PZ40)
	Lore, Phillips see PS3569.M538
3562.O759	Loring, Emilie Baker (Table P-PZ40)
	Lucas, J.K., 1916- see PS3566.A34
3562.U255	Luckless, John (Table P-PZ40)
	Cf. PS3552.U725 Burkholz, Herbert, 1932-
	Cf. PS3559.R79 Irving, Clifford
3562.U26	Ludlum, Robert, 1927- (Table P-PZ40)
3562.U457	Luke, 1944-
	Luria-Sukenick, Lynn see PS3569.U3
3562.Y44	Lynds, Dennis, 1924- (Table P-PZ40)
	Lyon, Buck, 1916- see PS3566.A34
3563.A-Z	M

The author number is determined by the second letter of the name

	McAllister, Troon see PS3557.R8
	MacCreigh, James see PS3566.O36
	Mackey, Eman see PS3563.A31166
3563.A2555	McCaig, Donald (Table P-PZ40)
	McCaig, Snee see PS3563.A2555
3563.A28	MacDonald, John D. (John Dann), 1916- (Table P-PZ40)
3563.A296	McGarrity, Mark, 1943- (Table P-PZ40)
3563.A31166	McInerny, Ralph M. (Table P-PZ40)
3563.A31865	MacLeod, Charlotte (Table P-PZ40)
	Makaira, Robert R. see PS3561.O363
	Manor, Jason see PS3558.A373
	Mardette, Q see PS3563.E239
	Marin, A.C. see PS3553.O64
	Marlow, Edwina see PS3558.U323
3563.A674	Marlowe, Stephen, 1928- (Table P-PZ40)
	Marquand, John, 1924- see PS3566.H4793
3563.A7212	Marshall, Catherine, 1914- (Table P-PZ40)
	Martin, Bruce, 1916- see PS3566.A34
3563.A723274	Martin, Charles Morris, 1891- (Table P-PZ40)
	Martin, Chuck see PS3563.A723274
3563.A725	Martin, Malachi (Table P-PZ40)
	Martin, Tom, 1916- see PS3566.A34
	Mary, Sister see PS3554.E4
3563.A82	Masters, Hilary (Table P-PZ40)
3563.A845	Mathews, Ellen (Table P-PZ40)
3563.A853	Matthews, Patricia, 1927- (Table P-PZ40)

Individual authors
1961-2000
M -- Continued

3563.A899	Maxwell, A.E. (Table P-PZ40)
	Maxwell, Ann, 1944- see PS3563.A899
	Maxwell, Evan, 1943- see PS3563.A899
3563.A923	Maxwell, Patricia, 1942- (Table P-PZ40)
	Maynard, Suzanne see PS3563.I421447
(3563.C3343)	McCall, Wendell
	see PS3566.E234
	McClain, Gary see PS3555.A39
	McDonnell, Margie see PS3563.I2733
	McElroy, Lee see PS3561.E3975
	McKinnon, K.C. see PS3566.E42
	McNab, Oliver see PS3556.R37
3563.E239	Medill, Dorothy
	Mell see PS3562.A98
3563.E747	Mertz, Barbara (Table P-PZ40)
3563.I254	Michael, Judith (Table P-PZ40)
	Michaels, Barbara see PS3563.E747
3563.I27	Michaels, Fern (Table P-PZ40)
	Cf. PS3551.N384 Anderson, Roberta
	Cf. PS3561.U23 Kuczkir, Mary
3563.I2733	Michaels, Margie (Table P-PZ40)
	Michaels, Richard, 1965- see PS3570.E447
3563.I37655	Miller, Cissie (Table P-PZ40)
3563.I379	Miller, Dallas (Table P-PZ40)
	Miller, Harry Dallas, 1930- see PS3563.I379
3563.I4125	Miller, Jim, 1945- (Table P-PZ40)
	Miller, Susan R. Pecastaing (Susan Reed Pecastaing)
	see PS3566.E243
3563.I421447	Miller, Suzanne Maynard (Table P-PZ40)
	Milton, Jack, 1929- see PS3561.I417
3563.O517	Moncure, Jane Belk (Table P-PZ40)
	Morgan, Arlene, 1916- see PS3566.A34
	Morgan, Claire, 1921- see PS3558.I366
	Morgan, John, 1916- see PS3566.A34
	Morgan, Valerie, 1916- see PS3566.A34
	Morgenstern, S. see PS3557.O384
3563.O871644	Moriconi, Virginia (Table P-PZ40)
	Murphy, Lawrence A. see PS3562.A916
3564.A-Z	N
	The author number is determined by the second letter of the
	name
	Neal, Vickie Theobald, 1958- see PS3570.H373
3564.E457	Nelson, Casey (Table P-PZ40)
	Nelson, Marilyn, 1946- see PS3573.A4795

Individual authors

1961-2000

N

	Norcross, Lisabet, 1921- see PS3569.E28
3564.O886	Novak, Barbara (Table P-PZ40)
	Novak, Joseph see PS3561.O8
	Novak, Rose see PS3568.O7639
3564.Y84	Nyuka (Table P-PZ40)
3565.A-Z	O

The author number is determined by the second letter of the name

3565.A8	Oates, Joyce Carol, 1938- (Table P-PZ40)
	O'Connor, Clint, 1916- see PS3566.A34
3565.C57	O'Connor, Flannery (Table P-PZ40)
	O'Connor, Mary Flannery see PS3565.C57
	O'Doherty, Barbara see PS3564.O886
	Ogawa, Pelorhankhe Ai, 1947- see PS3551.I2
	O'Hara, Scott see PS3563.A28
	Ohon see PS3552.A59177
	Oliphant, B.J. see PS3570.E673
3565.L458	Oliver, Chad, 1928- (Table P-PZ40)
	Oliver, Symmes Chadwick see PS3565.L458
3565.L77	Olsen, Jack (Table P-PZ40)
	Olsen, John Edward see PS3565.L77
3565.L8	Olsen, Theodore V. (Table P-PZ40)
	Olson, Merle Theodore see PS3565.L84
3565.L84	Olson, Toby (Table P-PZ40)
3565.N316	O'Nan, Stewart, 1961- (Table P-PZ40)
	O'Neill, Egan see PS3562.I515
	O'Neill, Jude see PS3552.A4733
	Orde, A.J. see PS3570.E673
	Ortner-Zimmerman, Toni see PS3576.I512
	Osborne, Betsy see PS3552.O79
	Osborne, David see PS3569.I472
3565.S53	Osgood, Charles (Table P-PZ40)
3565.S813	Oster, Jerry (Table P-PZ40)
3565.V44	Ovesen, Ellis (Table P-PZ40)
	Owens, Iris see PS3554.A3
3566.A-Z	P

The author number is determined by the second letter of the name

3566.A34	Paine, Lauran, 1916- (Table P-PZ40)
3566.A463	Pall, Ellen, 1952- (Table P-PZ40)
	Papier, Judith Barnard see PS3563.I254
	Parker, Beatrice see PS3558.U323
	Parsons, Ellen see PS3554.R183
	Patrick, Maxine, 1942- see PS3563.A923

Individual authors
1961-2000
P -- Continued

	Patton, Lee see PS3564.E457
3566.E234	Pearson, Ridley (Table P-PZ40)
3566.E243	Pecastaing, Susan Reed (Table P-PZ40)
3566.E42	Pelletier, Cathie (Table P-PZ40)
	Pelletier, Lynne B. see PS3551.L362
	Perry, Max see PS3565.S813
	Pershing, Marie see PS3569.C5532
	Peters, Elizabeth see PS3563.E747
3566.H4793	Phillips, John, 1924- (Table P-PZ40)
	Phillips, R.B., 1943- see PS3552.R2298
3566.L3	Platty, Jeno (Table P-PZ40)
	Platty, Jane see PS3566.L3
3566.O36	Pohl, Frederick (Table P-PZ40)
3566.O5348	Pollock, J.C. (Table P-PZ40)
	Pollock, James see PS3566.O5348
	Ponder, Patricia, 1942- see PS3563.A923
	Pridgen, William see PS3555.C54
3566.R575	Prince Charming (Table P-PZ40)
3566.R67	Pronzini, Bill (Table P-PZ40)

| 3567.A-Z | Q |

The author number is determined by the second letter of the name

Quick, Amanda see PS3561.R44
Quill, Monica see PS3563.A31166
Quinn, Simon, 1942- see PS3569.M5377

| 3568.A-Z | R |

The author number is determined by the second letter of the name

3568.A243	Rachie, Elias, 1875-1950 (Table P-PZ40)
	Radcliffe, Jeanette see PS3552.R656
3568.A325	Radford, Irene (Table P-PZ40)
	Rainone, Christopher see PS3558.A824
	Rampling, Anne see PS3568.I265
3568.A475	Ramtha, the enlightened one (Table P-PZ40)
	Randall, Clay see PS3551.D34
3568.A497	Randall, Robert (Table P-PZ40)
	Cf. PS3557.A7238 Garrett, Randall
	Cf. PS3569.I472 Silverberg, Robert
3568.E27	Rebeta-Burditt, Joyce (Table P-PZ40)
	Redgate,John see PS3561.E425
	Reed, Barry, 1939- see PS3557.R583
3568.E367	Reed, Kit (Table P-PZ40)
	Reed, Lillian Craig see PS3568.E367
	Reed, Peter see PS3563.A28

Individual authors
1961-2000
R -- Continued

3568.E43	Reese, John Henry (Table P-PZ40)
3568.E4754	Reginald, R. (Table P-PZ40)
	Reynolds, Dallas McCord see PS3568.E895
3568.E895	Reynolds, Mack (Table P-PZ40)
	Rhoades, Jonathan see PS3565.L77
3568.I265	Rice, Anne, 1941- (Table P-PZ40)
	Ridgeway, Jason, 1928- see PS3563.A674
	Rikki, 1943- see PS3554.U279
	Ringo, Clay, 1908- see PS3558.O3473
3568.O198	Robb, Candace M. (Table P-PZ40)
	Roberts, Gillian, 1939- see PS3557.R356
	Roberts, Janet Louise see PS3552.R656
3568.O2493	Robertson, Keith (Table P-PZ40)
	Rollins, Audre Lorde see PS3562.O75
	Roquelaure, A.N. see PS3568.I265
3568.O7639	Rose, Marcia (Table P-PZ40)
3568.O7644	Rose, Wendy (Table P-PZ40)
3568.O873	Rotsler, William (Table P-PZ40)
	Rowans, Virginia see PS3554.E537
	Ruminonds, Richard-Gabriel see PS3556.L49
	Russ, Lisa see PS3569.P25
	Ryder, Jonathan, 1927- see PS3562.U26
3569.A-Z	S

The author number is determined by the second letter of the name

	Sadler, Mark, 1942- see PS3562.Y44
	Saint Geraud see PS3561.N65
	Samuels, Victor see PS3552.A476
3569.A5125	Sanders, Lawrence, 1920-1998 (Table P-PZ40)
3569.A516	Sandford, John, 1944- (Table P-PZ40)
	Sanford, Annette see PS3569.H5792
	Saxon, Alex see PS3566.R67
3569.C5532	Schultz, Pearle Henriksen (Table P-PZ40)
	Scotland, Jay see PS3560.A37
	Scott, Amana see PS3569.C695
3569.C695	Scott-Drennan, Lynne (Table P-PZ40)
3569.E1763	Seare, Nicholas (Table P-PZ40)
	Searls, Hank, 1922- see PS3569.E18
3569.E18	Searls, Henry (Table P-PZ40)
	Sebastian, Lee see PS3569.I472
3569.E28	Sebastian, Margaret, 1921- (Table P-PZ40)
	Serafian, Michael see PS3563.A725
	Shannon, Dell see PS3562.I515
3569.H3427	Sharkey, Jack (Table P-PZ40)

	Individual authors
	1961-2000
	S -- Continued
	Sharp, Helen, 1916- see PS3566.A34
	Shaw, Janet Beeler, 1937- see PS3552.E345
	Sheldon, Alice B., 1915- see PS3570.I66
3569.H3928	Sheldon, Walter J. (Table P-PZ40)
	Shepherd, Michael, 1927- see PS3562.U26
3569.H5792	Shore, Anne (Table P-PZ40)
3569.I4717	Silver-Lillywhite, Eileen, 1953- (Table P-PZ40)
3569.I472	Silverberg, Robert (Table P-PZ40)
	Cf. PS3568.A497 Randall, Robert
3569.I565	Singer, Rochelle (Table P-PZ40)
3569.I57	Singer, Sally M. (Table P-PZ40)
	Singer, Shelley see PS3569.I565
	Sister Mary Gilbert see PS3554.E4
3569.L25	Sladek, John Thomas (Table P-PZ40)
	Slaughter, Jim, 1916- see PS3566.A34
3569.L3	Slavitt, David R., 1935- (Table P-PZ40)
3569.M443	Smith, Adam, 1930- (Table P-PZ40)
	Smith, Martin, 1942- see PS3569.M5377
3569.M5377	Smith, Martin Cruz, 1942- (Table P-PZ40)
	Smith, Nancy, 1951- see PS3556.I828
	Smith, Rosamond see PS3565.A8
3569.M538	Smith, Terrence Lore (Table P-PZ40)
	Somtow, S.P. see PS3569.U23
3569.P25	Spaar, Lisa Russ (Table P-PZ40)
	Sparer, Laurie Taylor see PS3570.A943
	St. Clair, Katherine see PS3558.U323
	St. George, Arthur, 1916- see PS3566.A34
	St. John, Lisa, 1929- see PS3569.H5792
	Standish, Buck, 1916- see PS3566.A34
	Stark, Joshua see PS3565.L8
	Stark, Richard see PS3573.E9
	Starr, Anne see PS3569.H5792
3569.T34	Stein, Aaron Marc, 1906- (Table P-PZ40)
	Stevens, E.M. see PS3560.E88
	Stone, Hamilton see PS3569.T34
	Storm, P. W., 1965- see PS3570.E447
	Story, Josephine see PS3562.O759
	Stowe, Alden see PS3569.I57
	Straus, Dennis see PS3551.S33
3569.T6935	Strete, Craig (Table P-PZ40)
3569.T6965	Stripling, Kathryn (Table P-PZ40)
	Stuart, Margaret, 1916- see PS3566.A34
3569.T875	Sturgeon, Theodore (Table P-PZ40)
3569.U23	Sucharitkul, Somtow (Table P-PZ40)

Individual authors
1961-2000
S -- Continued

3569.U3	Sukenick, Lynn (Table P-PZ40)
	Sutton, Henry, 1935- see PS3569.L3
3570.A-Z	T

The author number is determined by the second letter of the name

3570.A49	Tan, Teresa (Table P-PZ40)
	Tanner, Edward Everett, 1921- see PS3554.E537
	Taylor, Jane see PS3561.R44
3570.A943	Taylor, Laurie (Table P-PZ40)
3570.E447	Telep, Peter, 1965- (Table P-PZ40)
	Templeton, Janet, 1926- see PS3558.E78
3570.E673	Tepper, Sheri S. (Table P-PZ40)
	Thames, C.H., 1928- see PS3563.A674
	Thatcher, Julia see PS3552.E54765
3570.H373	Theobald-Neal, Vickie, 1958- (Table P-PZ40)
	Thomas, Rosanne Daryl see PS3566.R575
3570.H58	Thomas, Ross, 1926- (Table P-PZ40)
	Thompson, James W. see PS3555.L378
	Thompson, Russ, 1916- see PS3566.A34
	Thorn, Barbara, 1916- see PS3566.A34
3570.H65	Thorne, Evelyn (Table P-PZ40)
3570.I3377	Tiger, Madeline, 1934- (Table P-PZ40)
	Tiger, John see PS3573.A35
3570.I66	Tiptree, James (Table P-PZ40)
3570.O29	Tobin, Greg (Table P-PZ40)
	Townsend, Augusta Tucker, 1904- see PS3570.U237
3570.R339	Traver, Robert, 1903- (Table P-PZ40)
	Travis, Gerry, 1917- see PS3570.R519
	Treahearne, Elizabeth, 1942- see PS3563.A923
3570.R519	Trimble, Louis, 1917- (Table P-PZ40)
	Trout, Kilgore see PS3556.A72
3570.U237	Tucker, Augusta, 1904- (Table P-PZ40)
	Ty-Casper, Linda see PS3553.A7952
3570.Y53	Tyler, W.T. (Table P-PZ40)
3571.A-Z	U

The author number is determined by the second letter of the name

	Upton, Mark, 1920-1998 see PS3569.A5125
	Urista Heredia, Alberto Baltazar see PS3551.L84
3572.A-Z	V

The author number is determined by the second letter of the name

3572.A398	Valerie, 1908- (Table P-PZ40)
3572.A4292	Van de Wetering, Janwillem, 1931- (Table P-PZ40)

	Individual authors
	1961-2000
	V -- Continued
3572.I38	Villars, Elizabeth (Table P-PZ40)
3572.I86	Vivian, Daisy (Table P-PZ40)
	Voelker, John, 1903- see PS3570.R339
3572.O423	Von Buettner, Kristeen T. (Kristeen Tadich) (Table P-PZ40)
3573.A-Z	W
	The author number is determined by the second letter of the name
3573.A35	Wager, Walter H. (Table P-PZ40)
	Waldo, Edward Hamilton see PS3569.T875
	Walker, Harry see PS3573.A9
3573.A44	Wallop, Douglas, 1920- (Table P-PZ40)
	Wallop, John Douglas, 1920- see PS3573.A44
	Walters, Shelly see PS3570.I66
3573.A4795	Waniek, Marilyn Nelson, 1946- (Table P-PZ40)
	Wannamaker, Bruce see PS3563.O517
	Warner, Valerie, 1908- see PS3572.A398
3573.A7713	Warren, Christopher (Table P-PZ40)
3573.A9	Waugh, Hillary (Table P-PZ40)
	Wayne, Donald, 1930- see PS3554.O32
	Weaver, Ben, 1965- see PS3570.E447
	Webb, Lionel, 1926- see PS3558.E78
	Webb, Lucas see PS3568.E4754
3573.E3979	Weisbecker, A.C. (Alan C.) (Table P-PZ40)
	Weisbecker, Alan see PS3573.E3979
	Wells, Tobias see PS3556.O67
3573.E9	Westlake, Donald E. (Table P-PZ40)
	Wetering, Janwillem van, 1931- see PS3572.A4292
3573.H32	Wharton, William (Table P-PZ40)
	Whitaker, Rod see PS3569.E1763
	Whitmore, Cilla, 1921- see PS3569.E28
3573.I358	Wiersma, Stanley M. (Table P-PZ40)
	Wilcox, Jess, 1926- see PS3558.E78
	Wilde, Jennifer see PS3558.U323
3573.O39	Wohl, James P. (Table P-PZ40)
	Wolfe, Henia Karmel see PS3561.A675
3573.O5877	Wood, Barbara (Table P-PZ40)
	Wood, Charles Osgood see PS3565.S53
3573.O5968	Wood, Shirley R. (Table P-PZ40)
	Wylie, Dirk see PS3566.O36
	Wynne, Frank, 1939- see PS3557.A715
3574.A-Z	X
	The author number is determined by the second letter of the name

	Individual authors
	1961-2000 -- Continued
3575.A-Z	Y
	The author number is determined by the second letter of the name
	Young, Axel see PS3551.L346
3575.O7	Young, Carter Travis (Table P-PZ40)
3576.A-Z	Z
	The author number is determined by the second letter of the name
3576.I512	Zimmerman, Toni (Table P-PZ40)
	Zulfikar, Ghose, 1935- see PS3557.H63
	2001-
	Subarrange each author by Table P-PZ40 unless otherwise specified
3600	Anonymous works (Table P-PZ28)
3601.A-Z	A
	The author number is determined by the second letter of the name
3601.L36	Alfonsi, Alice
	For works written with Marc Cerasini under the joint pseudonym Cleo Coyle see PS3603.O94
3602.A-Z	B
	The author number is determined by the second letter of the name
	Barrett, Lorna see PS3602.A83955
3602.A83955	Bartlett, L. L. (Lorraine L.) (Table P-PZ40)
	Benjamin, Melanie see PS3608.A876
	Bentley, C. F. see PS3568.A325
3603.A-Z	C
	The author number is determined by the second letter of the name
3603.O94	Coyle, Cleo
	This is a joint pseudonym of Alice Alfonsi and Marc Cerasini.
	For works by Alice Alfonsi alone see PS3601.L36
3604.A-Z	D
	The author number is determined by the second letter of the name
3605.A-Z	E
	The author number is determined by the second letter of the name
3606.A-Z	F
	The author number is determined by the second letter of the name
3606.A727	Faro, R. E. (Table P-PZ40)

Individual authors
2001- -- Continued

3607.A-Z	G
	The author number is determined by the second letter of the name
3608.A-Z	H
	The author number is determined by the second letter of the name
3608.A876	Hauser, Melanie
3609.A-Z	I
	The author number is determined by the second letter of the name
3610.A-Z	J
	The author number is determined by the second letter of the name
3611.A-Z	K
	The author number is determined by the second letter of the name
3612.A-Z	L
	The author number is determined by the second letter of the name
3613.A-Z	M
	The author number is determined by the second letter of the name
3613.A4358	Malin, Libby (Table P-PZ40)
	Miscione, Lisa, 1970- see PS3621.N486
3614.A-Z	N
	The author number is determined by the second letter of the name
3615.A-Z	O
	The author number is determined by the second letter of the name
3616.A-Z	P
	The author number is determined by the second letter of the name
3617.A-Z	Q
	The author number is determined by the second letter of the name
3618.A-Z	R
	The author number is determined by the second letter of the name
3619.A-Z	S
	The author number is determined by the second letter of the name
	Schwarzenberger, Richard see PS3606.A727
	Sternberg, Libby see PS3613.A4358

Individual authors
2001- -- Continued

3620.A-Z	T

The author number is determined by the second letter of the name

3621.A-Z	U

The author number is determined by the second letter of the name

3621.N486	Unger, Lisa, 1970-
3622.A-Z	V

The author number is determined by the second letter of the name

3623.A-Z	W

The author number is determined by the second letter of the name

3624.A-Z	X

The author number is determined by the second letter of the name

3625.A-Z	Y

The author number is determined by the second letter of the name

3626.A-Z	Z

The author number is determined by the second letter of the name

<8001-8599>   Canadian literature
                               This span of alternative class numbers for Canadian literature was
                                   developed by Mr. T.R. McCloy under contract to the National
                                   Library of Canada. Its purpose is to provide a more specific
                                   treatment of the topic than that provided by the regular class
                                   numbers, PR9180-9199.4, PQ3900-3919.3, and PM30-2711, of
                                   the Library of Congress Classification System. In the Canadian
                                   context a comprehensive classification scheme for Canadian
                                   literature regardless of language is considered preferable to the
                                   LC System which separates Canadian literature by language
                               It is not possible for the Library of Congress to adopt these class
                                   numbers and incorporate them into its own system because
                                   they differ in principle from LC practice in their assembling of
                                   Canadian literature together regardless of language. The
                                   Library of Congress, however, recognizes a need for the
                                   PS8000 area and endorses its use as an official alternative
                                   classification scheme. In order to eliminate the danger of a
                                   conflict in numbers, the PS8000 area will not be developed by
                                   LC in the future for other purposes.
                               Libraries desiring to use the alternative numbers may obtain copies
                                   of the schedule "Class PS8000: a classification for Canadian
                                   literature" from the National Library of Canada, Standards and
                                   Support, Acquisitions and Bibliographic Services, 395
                                   Wellington Street, Ottawa, Ontario, K1A ON4.

Fiction and juvenile belles lettres
  Fiction in English
      A special collection of standard and current fiction including
        English translations of foreign authors. In the Library of
        Congress, fiction in English selected for the rare book
        collection, including but not restricted to first and limited
        editions of certain designated authors, as well as all fiction in
        English cataloged after June 30, 1980, is classed in PR, PS,
        or other literature classes
    Collections of novels, short stories, etc.
        Including Tales from Blackwood's
(1.A1)   Periodicals. Serials
(1.A2-Z)   General collections
    Individual authors
(3)   1750 through 1950
              For authors who did not publish fiction after 1750, see PR,
                PS, or other literature classes
(4)   1951-
              Class here authors who have not published any works of
                fiction prior to 1951
  Juvenile belles lettres
      For works of noted authors in foreign languages, see PQ, PT,
        etc., e.g. Andersen, Lagerlof, etc.
      For translations see PZ5+
    Periodicals see AP200+
    History see PN1009.A1
    American and English
5   Collections
6   Early to 1860/1870
7   General juvenile belles lettres, 1870-
7.5   Novels in verse
            Class here juvenile and young adult novels written as a series
              of poems, not necessarily in rhyme
            For stories that are not novels but are written in rhymed
              text see PZ8.3
7.7   Graphic novels
8   Fairy tales
            Including juvenile editions of Arabian nights
            Cf. PJ7715+ English translations of Arabian nights
8.1   Folklore, legends, romance
            Including juvenile editions of Arthurian romance
            Cf. PN-PT, Folk literature sections
8.2   Fables
            Including AEsop in English versions for children

Juvenile belles lettres
American and English -- Continued

| 8.3 | Anonymous nursery rhymes (including Mother Goose). Stories in rhyme |

For Library of Congress practice on poetry for children see PN6109.97

| (8.7) | Humorous works |

see subclass PN

| (8.9) | Miscellaneous stories |

see PZ7

| (9) | Historical and geographical tales |

This class number is no longer used. All juvenile non-fiction is classed with the topic in the regular subject classes

Biography see CT107

| (10) | Science and industry |

This class number is no longer used. All juvenile non-fiction is classed with the topic in the regular subject classes

| 10.3 | Animal stories |

For verse see PZ8.3
Cf. PZ8.2 Fables

Juvenile drama
see subclasses PR, PS

| 10.4 | Sign language and braille |

Class here juvenile belles lettres and folklore accompanied by sign language diagrams or braille text

| 10.5 | Polyglot |

Class here children's books in three or more languages
For bilingual editions, see the lesser known languages

Arabic
Collections

10.72	General works
10.721	For boys
10.722	For girls
10.73	Early works to 1860/1870
10.731	General juvenile belles lettres, 1870-
10.74	Fairy tales
10.741	Folklore, legends, romance
10.742	Fables
(10.743)	Verses for children

For Library of Congress practice, see PN6109.97

10.747	Humorous works
10.749	Miscellaneous stories
(10.75)	Historical and geographical tales

This class number is no longer used. All juvenile non-fiction is classed with the topic in the regular subject classes

	Juvenile belles lettres
	Arabic -- Continued
(10.76)	Science and industry
	This class number is no longer used. All juvenile non-fiction is classed with the topic in the regular subject classes
10.763	Animal stories
10.77	Juvenile drama
10.78	Miscellaneous
	Chinese
	Collections
10.82	General works
10.821	For boys
10.822	For girls
10.83	Early works to 1860/1870
10.831	General juvenile belles lettres, 1870-
10.84	Fairy tales
10.841	Folklore, legends, romance
10.842	Fables
(10.843)	Verses for children
	For Library of Congress practice, see PN6109.97
10.847	Humorous works
10.849	Miscellaneous stories
(10.85)	Historical and geographical tales
	This class number is no longer used. All juvenile non-fiction is classed with the topic in the regular subject classes
(10.86)	Science and industry
	This class number is no longer used. All juvenile non-fiction is classed with the topic in the regular subject classes
10.863	Animal stories
10.87	Juvenile drama
10.88	Miscellaneous
11-18	Dutch. Flemish. Afrikaans (Table PZ1)
21-28	French (Table PZ1)
31-38	German (Table PZ1)
	Hebrew
39	Collections
40.A-Z	Individual authors, A-Z
41-48	Italian (Table PZ1)
	Japanese
	Collections
49.2	General works
49.21	For boys
49.22	For girls
49.3	Early works to 1860/1870
49.31	General juvenile belles lettres, 1870-
49.4	Fairy tales
49.41	Folklore, legends, romance

Juvenile belles lettres
Japanese -- Continued
49.42 Fables
(49.43) Verses for children
For Library of Congress practice see PN6109.97
49.47 Humorous works
49.49 Miscellaneous stories
(49.5) Historical and geographical tales
This class number is no longer used. All juvenile non-fiction is
classed with the topic in the regular subject classes
(49.6) Science and industry
This class number is no longer used. All juvenile non-fiction is
classed with the topic in the regular subject classes
49.63 Animal stories
49.7 Juvenile drama
49.8 Miscellaneous
Korean
Collections
50.52 General works
50.521 For boys
50.522 For girls
50.53 Early works to 1860/1870
50.531 General juvenile belles lettres, 1870-
50.54 Fairy tales
50.541 Folklore, legends, romance
50.542 Fables
(50.543) Verses for children
For Library of Congress practice, see PN6109.97
50.547 Humorous works
50.549 Miscellaneous stories
(50.55) Historical and geographical tales
This class number is no longer used. All juvenile non-fiction is
classed with the topic in the regular subject classes
(50.56) Science and industry
This class number is no longer used. All juvenile non-fiction is
classed with the topic in the regular subject classes
50.563 Animal stories
50.57 Juvenile drama
50.58 Miscellaneous
Scandinavian
51-54.3 Danish (Table PZ2)
Including Danish-Norwegian
For works in Norwegian published after ca. 1900, including
works in Landsmal or Nynorsk, prefer PZ54.4+
Norwegian
Including Landsmal or Nynorsk
Collections

	Juvenile belles lettres
	Scandinavian
	Norwegian
	Collections -- Continued
54.4	General works
54.41	For boys
54.42	For girls
54.5	General works
54.6	Fairy tales
54.9	Verses for children
	Icelandic
55	Collections
56	Individual authors
	Faroese
56.2	Collections
56.3	Individual authors
57-60.3	Swedish (Table PZ2)
	Slavic
61-68	Russian (Table PZ1)
69	Polish
69.A2	Collections
70.A-Z	Other, A-Z
	Belarusian see PZ70.W49+
	Bulgarian
70.B7	Collections
70.B8	Individual authors
	Czech
70.C8	Collections
70.C9	Individual authors
	Macedonian
70.M2	Collections
70.M3	Individual authors
	Serbo-Croatian
70.S4	Collections
70.S42	Individual authors
	Slovak
70.S45	Collections
70.S46	Individual authors
	Slovenian
70.S5	Collections
70.S6	Individual authors
	Ukrainian
70.U7	Collections
70.U72	Individual authors
	Wendic. Sorbian
70.W39	Collections
70.W4	Individual authors

	Juvenile belles lettres
	Slavic
	Other, A-Z -- Continued
	White Russian. Belarusian
70.W49	Collections
70.W5	Individual authors
71-78	Spanish (Table PZ1)
81-88	Portuguese (Table PZ1)
90.A-Z	Other languages, A-Z
90.A2	Abkhaz
90.A28	Adygei
90.A4	Albanian
90.A6	Amharic
90.A72	Armenian
90.A723	Aromanian
90.A73	Assamese
90.A9	Azerbaijani
90.B36	Bashkir
90.B37	Basque
90.B39	Bemba
90.B4	Bengali
90.B77	Buriat
90.B8	Burmese
90.C3	Catalan
90.C45	Chechen
	Chewa see PZ90.N88
90.C52	Choctaw
90.C55	Chuvash
90.C73	Creole
90.D96	Dzongkha
90.E68	Erzya
90.E69	Eskimo
	Esperanto see PM8285.A2+
90.E7	Estonian
90.E93	Even
(90.F3)	Faroese
	see PZ56.2+
90.F5	Finnish
	Gaelic (Irish) see PZ90.I7
90.G2	Gaelic (Scottish Gaelic)
90.G25	Gagauz
90.G3	Gallegan
90.G35	Ganda
90.G45	Georgian
90.G7	Greek, Modern
90.G8	Gujurati
90.H27	Hawaiian

	Juvenile belles lettres
	Other languages, A-Z -- Continued
(90.H3)	Hebrew
	see PZ39+
90.H5	Hindi
90.H55	Hmong
90.H8	Hungarian
90.I2	Iban
90.I52	Indonesian
90.I54	Ingush
90.I56	Inuit
	Including Inuit dialects
90.I7	Irish (Gaelic)
90.J35	Javanese
90.K23	Kabardian
90.K29	Kamba
90.K3	Kannada
90.K33	Kara-Kalpak
90.K332	Karachay-Balkar
90.K334	Kasena
90.K337	Kashmiri
90.K34	Kavirondo
90.K35	Kazakh
90.K43	Ket
90.K47	Khanty
90.K49	Khasi
90.K493	Khmer
90.K495	Kikuyu
90.K5	Kirghiz
90.K55	Komi
90.K57	Konkani
90.K87	Kurdish
90.L23	Ladino
90.L25	Lamut
90.L27	Lao
90.L28	Lapp
90.L3	Latin
90.L4	Latvian
90.L5	Lithuanian
90.L6	Logooli
90.L64	Lozi
90.L78	Luo
90.L8	Luyia
90.M222	Madurese
90.M225	Maithili
90.M23	Malagasy
90.M25	Malay

Juvenile belles lettres

Other languages, A-Z -- Continued

90.M3	Malayalam
90.M32	Maltese
90.M33	Mangulasi
90.M34	Maori
90.M35	Marathi
90.M38	Mari
90.M4	Meru
90.M45	Michif
90.M5	Minangkabau
90.M6	Moksha
90.M7	Moldavian
90.M75	Mongolian
90.N34	Nahuatl
90.N38	Navajo
90.N44	Ndebele (Zimbabwe)
90.N45	Nepali
90.N5	Niuean
90.N67	Northern Altai
90.N88	Nyanja. Chewa
90.O7	Oriya
90.O88	Ossetic
90.P34	Papiamento
90.P4	Persian
90.P54	Pitjandjara
90.R3	Raeto-Romance
90.R6	Romanian
90.S3	Sanskrit
	Scottish Gaelic see PZ90.G2
90.S48	Sindhi
90.S5	Sinhalese
90.S57	Somali
90.S6	Sotho
90.S77	Suk
90.S8	Sundanese
90.S94	Swahili
90.T27	Tagalog
90.T28	Tajik
90.T3	Tamil
90.T35	Tatar
90.T4	Telugu
90.T5	Thai
90.T58	Tibetan
90.T65	Tonga (Zambesi)
90.T7	Tshi
90.T77	Tulu

PZ

Juvenile belles lettres
Other languages, A-Z -- Continued

90.T8	Turkish
90.T85	Turkmen
90.T88	Tuvinian
90.U65	Udmurt
90.U68	Ukrainian
90.U7	Urdu
90.U9	Uzbek
90.V4	Venda
90.V5	Vietnamese
90.W4	Welsh (Celtic)
90.W54	Wik-Munkan
90.W6	Worora
90.X48	Xhosa
90.Y3	Yakut
90.Y5	Yiddish
90.Y6	Yoruba
90.Z84	Zulu

1	Treatises
2	Documents. Contemporary records. Historical sources
3	Collected essays
4	Addresses, essays, lectures
5.A-Z	Special topics, A-Z
	For topics that apply to a special period, see topics under that period
5.A33	Adolescence
5.A34	Aesthetics
5.A4	Allegory
5.A44	Allusions
5.A48	American Revolution
5.A49	Androgyny
5.A493	Angels
5.A55	Antiquities
5.A59	Anxiety
5.A66	Apocalypse
5.A78	Art
5.A79	Arthurian romances
5.A84	Association of ideas
5.A88	Authority
5.A9	Authors and readers
5.B37	Bards and bardism
5.B44	Belief and doubt
5.B54	Birthdays
5.C3	Catullus, C. Valerius
5.C45	Children
5.C67	Classicism
5.C675	Contemplation
5.C677	Cosmography
5.C678	Cosmopolitanism
5.C68	Country homes
5.C687	Courtesy
5.C69	Courts and courtiers
5.C75	Crime
5.C77	Crises
5.D36	Dante Alighieri, 1275-1321
5.D38	Darwin, Erasmus, 1731-1802
5.D42	Death
	Doubt see PR1 5.F74
5.D45	Devil
5.D47	Devotion
5.D57	Disappointment
5.D59	Displacement (Psychology)
5.E44	Elizabeth I, Queen of England, 1533-1603
5.E5	Emblems
5.E55	Emotions

Special topics, A-Z -- Continued

5.E6	Enthusiasm
5.E85	Epiphanies
	Epithalamia see PR1 5.M29
5.F34	Failure (Psychology)
5.F37	Farewells
5.F55	Flowers
5.F74	Free will and determinism
5.F8	French Revolution
5.G35	Gardens
5.G46	Geology
5.G7	Greek literature
5.H3	Happiness
5.H5	History and politics
5.H65	Homosexuality, Male
5.H86	Humanism
5.H87	Humorous poetry
5.I25	Iconoclasm
5.I33	Identity (Psychology)
5.I56	Imagination
5.I6	Imagism
5.I65	Indifferentism (Ethics)
5.I67	Inheritance
5.J47	Jesuit influence
5.K56	Kings and rulers
5.L27	Landscape
5.L3	Language. Poetic diction, etc.
5.L38	Laudatory poetry
5.L54	Life
5.L64	London (England)
5.L7	Love
5.L89	Luxury
5.M29	Marriage
5.M34	Melancholy
5.M37	Metaphor
5.M54	Millennialism
5.M85	Music
5.M9	Mysticism
5.M93	Myth. Mythology
5.N26	Narrative poetry
5.N27	Nationalism
5.N28	Naturalism
5.N3	Nature
5.N66	Nostalgia
5.O6	Optics
5.O74	Originality
5.P33	Particularity. Preoccupation with detail

	Special topics, A-Z -- Continued
5.P36	Paternity
5.P63	Platonism. Neoplatonism
	Poetic diction see PR1 5.L3
	Politics see PR1 5.H5
5.P68	Power (Social Sciences)
	Preoccupation with detail see PR1 5.P33
5.P75	Primitivism
5.P77	Prophecy
5.P85	Psychology
5.R33	Radicalism
5.R37	Realism
5.R4	Religion
5.R57	Rivers
5.R87	Rural conditions
5.S25	Satire
5.S28	Scandinavia
5.S33	Science
5.S44	Self
5.S46	Sentimentalism
5.S48	Sex
5.S52	Sincerity
5.S53	Slavery and slaves
5.S6	Social problems
5.S65	Speech
5.S74	Style
5.S77	Sublime
5.S85	Supernatural
5.S9	Symbolism
5.T47	Textual criticism
5.T6	Totalitarianism
5.T75	Transcendentalism
5.T78	Truth
5.T94	Typology
5.V4	Versification
5.V62	Vocation
5.W3	War
5.W34	Water
5.W45	Will
5.W5	William III
5.W58	Women
5.W6	Women authors
9.A-Z	Special forms, A-Z
9.B8	Burlesque
9.C6	Comic verse
9.E45	Elegies
9.E64	Epics

TABLES

	Special forms, A-Z -- Continued
9.E75	Epistolary
9.F2	Fables
9.H34	Haiku
9.L8	Lyrics
9.M6	Monologues
9.N3	Narratives
9.N65	Nonsense verses
9.P3	Pastorals
9.S7	Sonnets
9.V4	Vers de société. Society verse

	History
0	Periodicals. Societies. Serials
1	General works
4	Biography (Collective)
10	Poetry
11	Drama
12	Other
	Collections
13	General collections
14	Poetry
15	Drama
16	Other

TABLES

1	All's well that ends well
2	Antony and Cleopatra
3	As you like it
4	Comedy of errors
5	Coriolanus
6	Cymbeline
7	Hamlet
8	Julius Caesar
9	King Henry IV, parts 1 and 2
10	King Henry IV, part 1
11	King Henry IV, part 2
12	King Henry V
13	King Henry VI, parts 1, 2, and 3
14	King Henry VI, part 1
15	King Henry VI, part 2
16	King Henry VI, part 3
17	King Henry VIII
18	King John
19	King Lear
20	King Richard II
21	King Richard III
22	Love's labour's lost
23	Macbeth
24	Measure for measure
25	Merchant of Venice
26	Merry wives of Windsor
27	Midsummer night's dream
28	Much ado about nothing
29	Othello
30	Pericles
31	Romeo and Juliet
32	Taming of the shrew
33	Tempest
34	Timon of Athens
35	Titus Andronicus
36	Troilus and Cressida
37	Twelfth Night
38	Two gentlemen of Verona
39	Winter's tale
40	Lost play: Love's labour's won

	Texts
.A1	By date
	For original quartos and facsimiles or reprints, see PR2750
.A2A-.A2Z	By editor or actor
.A23	Adaptations for radio, TV, or film
.A25	Adaptations for school performance, juvenile versions in dramatic form
	For other adaptations of individual works, see PR2878
.A3A-.A3Z	Selections. By editor
	Translations
	For French, see PR2779; for German, see PR2782; for other languages (by language), see PR2776, PR2784, etc.
.A8-.Z	Criticism

TABLES

.x	Collected works. By translator
.x2A-.x2Z	Separate works, A-Z
	Subarrange by translator
	Poems
.x2X1	Collected poems
	Subarrange by date
.x2X2	Selections. Anthologies
.x2X3	Songs
	Special poems or songs
.x2X5	Venus and Adonis
.x2X6	Rape of Lucrece
	Passionate pilgrim
	see PR2873.P3
	Sonnets
.x2X8	Collections. Selections
.x2X84	Separate sonnets. By number
	e.g.
.x2X84 no. 91	Sonnet number 91
.x2X9	Other

1	General works
2	Documents, contemporary records, etc.
3	Collected essays
4	Addresses, essays, lectures
5	Sources, relations, foreign influences
8.A-Z	Special topics, A-Z
8.A37	Actors
8.A38	Adultery
8.A4	Africa
8.A43	Aging
8.A45	Aliens
8.A73	Art
8.A77	Assassins
8.A8	Astrology
8.A88	Audiences
8.A89	Authority
8.A897	Authors and patrons
8.A9	Authorship
8.A95	Autobiography
8.B63	Body, Human
8.C4	Censorship
8.C47	Characters and characteristics
8.C49	Cities and towns
8.C55	Collaboration
8.C6	Comedy
8.C62	Commercial products
8.C64	Country life
8.C7	Courts and courtiers
8.D35	Dandies
8.D4	Death
8.D43	Deception
8.D47	Devil
8.D5	Dialect
8.D54	Dinners and dining
8.D56	Discontent
8.D65	Domestic drama
8.D76	Drugs
8.D84	Dueling
8.E35	Economics
8.E38	Education
	Epilogues see PR5 8.P68
8.E85	Ethics
8.E88	Ethnicity
8.F33	Face painting
8.F335	Fairies
8.F34	The Fantastic

TABLES

	Special topics, A-Z -- Continued
8.F35	Farce
8.F45	Feminism
8.F7	Fools and jesters
8.F74	France
8.G46	Geography
8.H42	Heroes
8.H44	Heterosexuality
8.H5	History
8.H58	Homosexuality
8.H6	Honor
8.H64	Hospitality
8.I33	Identity (Psychology)
8.I43	Illegitimacy
8.I45	Imperialism
8.I47	Incest
8.I48	Interludes
8.I7	Irish
	Jesters see PR5 8.F7
8.J4	Jews
8.J8	The Jurist
8.K54	Kings and rulers
	Knaves see PR5 8.V5
8.L35	Landscapes
8.L37	Laughter
8.L38	Law
8.L5	Libel and slander
8.L52	Libertines
8.L58	London (England)
8.L6	Lost plays
8.L63	Love
8.M25	Machiavellianism
8.M27	Magic
8.M275	Masculinity
8.M3	Masques
8.M33	Master and servant
8.M35	Medicine
8.M4	Melodrama
8.M45	Memory
8.M5	Mental illness
8.M56	Metaphor
8.M68	Motherhood
8.M87	Muslims
8.O3	Occultism
8.P25	Pageantry
8.P28	Pantomime

	Special topics, A-Z -- Continued
8.P29	Parody
8.P297	Patriarchy
8.P48	Philosophy
8.P5	Physicians
8.P55	Play within a play
8.P6	Plots
8.P63	Poetic justice
8.P65	Politics
8.P66	Praise
8.P665	Prejudices
8.P67	Prodigal son (Parable)
8.P675	Professions
8.P68	Prologues and epilogues
8.P7	Property
8.P72	Prostitution
8.P724	Protestantism
8.P73	Proverbs
8.P8	Puns
8.P9	Puritans
8.R34	Race
8.R4	Realism
8.R43	Religion
8.R45	Revenge
8.R55	Romances
8.R86	Rumor
8.S3	Satire
8.S39	Sex
8.S4	Sex crimes
8.S42	Sex role
	Slander see PR5 8.L5
8.S46	Social history
8.S47	Social ideals
8.S5	Social problems
8.S59	Stage directions
8.S597	Stage props
8.S6	Stage quarrel of Ben Jonson and others
8.S7	Style
8.S79	Subjectivity
8.S82	Supernatural
8.S85	Swordplay
8.S94	Symbolism
8.T35	Technique
8.T4	Textual criticism
8.T5	Time, Presentation of
8.T7	Tragedy

TABLES

	Special topics, A-Z -- Continued
8.T72	Tragicomedy
8.T75	Travel. Travelers
8.T77	Treason
8.U65	The usurer
8.U7	Utopias
8.V4	Verse drama
8.V5	Villians. Knaves
8.V52	Virginity
8.V55	Vision
8.V65	Voice
8.W53	Widows
8.W58	Witchcraft
8.W6	Women
8.W65	Work
8.W7	Writing
8.Y6	Youth

1	General works
2	Documents, contemporary records, etc.
3	Collected essays
4	Addresses, essays, lectures
5	Sources, relations, foreign influences
8.A-Z	Special topics, A-Z
8.A38	Aesthetics
8.A5	Animals
8.A9	Autobiography
8.B56	Biography
8.C56	Confession
8.C9	Country life
8.C93	Criticism (as a theme)
8.C96	Culture
8.D52	Dialogues
8.D58	Divorce
8.H57	History
8.H95	Hysteria
8.I4	Illegitimacy
8.I46	Infanticide
8.M36	Masculinity
8.M37	Material culture
8.M95	Mysticism
8.N38	Natural history
8.O43	Oedipus complex
8.P55	Philosophy
8.P64	Polemics
	Rhythm
	see PE1561
8.R65	Romanticism
8.S33	Science
8.S38	Self
8.S39	Sentimentalism
8.S46	Social history
8.S47	Social ideals
8.S62	Social problems
8.T45	Theater
8.T72	Travel
8.U86	Utopias
8.W65	Women
8.W67	World War I

TABLES

.x	General works. History
.x2	Collections
.x3A-.x3Z	Individual authors, A-Z

1	Texts. By date
2	School texts. By editor
3	Translations
4	Criticism. By author

TABLES

	Texts
.A1	By date
.A11-.A2	By editor
	Translations
.A21-.A39	Modern English versions
.A4-.A49	French
.A5-.A59	German
.A6-.A69	Other languages. By language
.A7-.Z	Criticism

	Texts
.xA1	By date
.xA11-.xA2	By editor
	Translations
.xA21-.xA39	Modern English versions
.xA4-.xA49	French
.xA5-.xA59	German
.xA6-.xA69	Other languages. By language
.xA7-.xZ	Criticism

TABLES

	Texts
.A1	By date
.A3A-.A3Z	By editor
	Translations
.A5A-.A5Z	Modern English versions. By translator, A-Z
.A6A-.A6Z	Other languages, A-Z
	Subarrange by translator
.A7-.Z	Criticism

	Texts
.A1	By date
.A3A-.A3Z	By editor
	Translations
.A4A-.A4Z	Modern English versions. By translator, A-Z
.A6A-.A6Z	Other languages, A-Z
	Subarrange by translator
.A7-.Z	Criticism

TABLES

	Text
1.A2	By date
1.A3-Z	By editor, A-Z
2	Criticism

.A1	Editions. By date
.A2	Selections. By editor or publisher
.A3	Selections for schools
	Translations
.A4-.A49	French. By translator, if given, or date
.A5-.A59	German. By translator, if given, or date
.A6-.A69	Other. By language
.A7-.Z	Criticism

TABLES

	Collections
1	General works
1.1	For boys
1.2	For girls
2	Early works to 1860/1870
3	General juvenile belles lettres, 1870-
3.7	Graphic novels
4	Fairy tales
	Including juvenile editions of Arabian nights
4.1	Folklore, legends, romance
4.2	Fables
4.3	Anonymous nursery rhymes (including Mother Goose). Stories in rhyme
	For Library of Congress practice see PN6109.97
4.7	Humorous works
	Prefer PZ1 3
4.9	Miscellaneous stories
	Including stories of dolls, toys, etc.
(5)	Historical and geographical tales
	This class number is no longer used. All juvenile non-fiction is classed with the topic in the regular subject classes
	Biography
	see CT107
(6)	Science and industry
	This class number is no longer used. All juvenile non-fiction is classed with the topic in the regular subject classes
6.3	Animal stories
	For verse see PZ1 4.3
	Cf. PZ1 4.2 Fables
(7)	Juvenile drama
	For Library of Congress practice see PN6119.9
8	Miscellaneous

	Collections
1	General works
1.1	For boys
1.2	For girls
2	Early works to 1860/1870
3	General juvenile belles lettres, 1870-
4	Fairy tales
	Including juvenile editions of Arabian nights
4.1	Folklore, legends, romance
4.2	Fables
4.3	Anonymous nursery rhymes (including Mother Goose). Stories in rhyme
	For Library of Congress practice see PN6109.97

TABLES

African Americans in literature
  American
    Literary history
      Prose fiction: PS374.N4
Africans in literature
  English
    Literary history
      Fiction: PR830.A39
Age groups in literature
  American
    Collections
      Poetry: PS595.A33
Aggressiveness in literature
  American
    Literary history
      Prose fiction: PS374.A38
Aging in literature
  American
    Collections: PS509.A37
      Drama: PS627.A35
      Prose: PS648.A37
  English
    Literary history
      Fiction: PR830.A394
Agriculture in literature
  American
    Collections: PS509.A4
    Literary history
      20th century: PS228.A52
AIDS (Disease) in literature
  American
    Collections: PS509.A43
      Drama: PS627.A53
      Poetry: PS595.A36
      Prose: PS648.A39
    Literary history: PS169.A42
      Poetry: PS310.A4
      Prose fiction: PS374.A39
  English
    Collections
      Poetry: PR1195.A44
Air in literature
  English
    Collections
      Poetry: PR1195.A46

Airplanes in literature
  American
    Literary history
      20th century: PS228.A57
Alchemy in literature
  American
    Literary history
      19th century: PS217.A43
  English
    Literary history
      20th century: PR478.A43
      Elizabethan era: PR428.A44
      Fiction: PR830.A397
Alcoholics in literature
  American
    Collections
      Prose: PS648.A42
Alcoholism in literature
  American
    Collections
      Poetry: PS595.A39
    Literary history
      20th century: PS228.A58
      Prose fiction: PS374.A42
  English
    Literary history
      Fiction: PR830.A4
Alexander (English metrical romances):
  PR2065.A15+
Alienation (Social psychology) in
  literature
  American
    Collections
      Poetry: PS595.A4
    Literary history
      19th century: PS217.A45
      20th century: PS228.A6
      Poetry: PS310.A44
      Prose: PS366.A44
      Prose fiction: PS374.A44
  English
    Literary history
    Drama
      20th century: PR739.A44
      Elizabethan era: PR428.A45
      Fiction: PR830.A42

Allegory in literature
  American
    Literary history: PS169.A47
      19th century: PS217.A46
      Prose fiction: PS374.A45
  English
    Literary history: PR149.A647
      18th century: PR448.A44
      Medieval: PR275.A4
      Modern: PR408.A4
      Poetry: PR509.A6
        Medieval: PR317.A52
        Renaissance: PR418.A4
Alliteration in literature
  English
    Literary history
      Poetry
        Medieval: PR317.A55
Allusions in literature
  English
    Literary history
      Fiction: PR830.A44
      Poetry: PR508.A44
Alphabet in literature
  English
    Literary history
      Poetry: PR508.A45
Alternative histories (Fiction) in literature
  English
    Literary history: PR830.A46
Alzheimer's disease in literature
  American
    Collections
      Poetry: PS595.A42
Amadas (English metrical romances):
  PR2065.A18+
Amazons in literature
  English
    Literary history
      Elizabethan era: PR428.A47
America in literature
  American
    Collections
      Poetry: PS595.A43
  English
    Collections
      Poetry: PR1195.A5

America in literature
  English
    Literary history: PR149.A67
American Dream in literature
  American
    Literary history: PS169.A49
American Indians
  Authors
    American
      Collections: PS508.I5
        Poetry: PS591.I55
        Prose: PS647.I5
      Literary history: PS153.I52
American Indians in literature
  American
    Collections: PS509.I5
    Literary history: PS173.I6
      19th century: PS217.I49
      Drama: PS338.I53
      Poetry: PS310.I52
      Prose fiction: PS374.I49
American literature: PS1+
Amis and Amiloun (English metrical
  romances): PR2065.A2+
Amish in literature
  American
    Collections
      Prose: PS648.A45
Amnesia in literature
  English
    Literary history
      Fiction: PR830.A49
Anarchism in literature
  English
    Literary history
      19th century: PR468.A5
      20th century: PR478.A53
Ancients and moderns, Quarrel of, in
  literature
  English
    Literary history
      17th century: PR438.A53
Androgyny (Psychology) in literature
  English
    Literary history
      Fiction: PR830.A52

INDEX

Blushing in literature
  English
    Literary history
      Fiction: PR830.B58
Boadicea, Queen, d. 62, in literature
  English
    Literary history
      Elizabethan era: PR428.B6
Boadicea, Queen, in literature
  English
    Literary history: PR153.B63
Boats and boating in literature
  American
    Collections: PS509.B63
Body fluids in literature
  English
    Literary history
      Fiction: PR830.B62
Body, Human, in literature
  American
    Literary history
      19th century: PS217.B63
      Prose fiction: PS374.B64
  English
    Literary history: PR149.B62
      18th century: PR448.B63
      Elizabethan era: PR428.B63
      Fiction: PR830.B63
Bohemianism in literature
  American
    Literary history
      19th century: PS217.B65
      20th century: PS228.B6
Boke of Mawndeville (English metrical romances): PR2065.B57+
Bone Florence of Rome (English metrical romances): PR2065.B6+
Book reviewing
  English
    Literary history
      18th century: PR448.B67
Books
  English
    Literary history
      Renaissance: PR418.B66

Books and reading in literature
  American
    Collections: PS509.B66
    Literary history
      Poetry: PS595.B65
      Prose fiction: PS374.B67
Bookstore employees as authors
  American
    Collections: PS508.B66
Boredom in literature
  English
    Literary history
      Fiction: PR830.B66
      Modern: PR408.B67
Boston (Mass.) in literature
  American
    Collections: PS509.B665
Botany in literature
  English
    Literary history
      Fiction: PR830.B68
Boundary disputes in literature
  English
    Literary history
      19th century: PR468.B68
Boxing in literature
  American
    Collections
      Prose: PS648.B67
Boys in literature
  American
    Literary history
      Prose fiction: PS374.B69
Boys, Poetry for
  English
    Collections: PR1195.B7
Brainwashing in literature
  English
    Literary history
      Fiction: PR830.B72
Breast cancer in literature
  American
    Collections
      Poetry: PS595.B73
Breast cancer patients as authors
  American
    Collections: PS508.B74

Character sketches
  English
    Literary history
      17th century: PR438.C45
Characters and characteristics in
literature
  American
    Literary history
      Drama: PS338.C43
      Prose: PS366.C4
      Prose fiction: PS374.C43
  English
    Collections
      Prose: PR1309.C47
    Literary history
      17th century: PR438.C45
      By period
        18th century: PR448.C52
      Drama: PR635.C47
        18th century: PR719.C47
      Fiction: PR830.C47
      Medieval: PR275.C42
Charity in literature
  English
    Literary history
      Fiction: PR830.C475
      Medieval: PR275.C45
Charles I in literature
  English
    Literary history
      Poetry
        17th century: PR545.C4
Charms in literature
  American
    Collections: PS593.C43
Chartism in literature
  English
    Collections: PR1111.C515
    Poetry: PR1195.C455
Chaucer, Geoffrey: PR1850+
Chester plays
  English
    Collections: PR1261.C54
Cheuelere, Assigne (English metrical
  romances): PR2065.C39+
Chevalier au Cygne (English metrical
  romances): PR2065.C39+

Chevy Chase (English metrical
  romances): PR2065.C4+
Chiasmus in literature
  English
    Literary history
      Elizabethan era: PR428.C35
Chicago (Ill.) in literature
  American
    Literary history
      Prose fiction: PS374.C44
Chick lit
  American
    Collections
      Prose: PS648.C415
Child authors
  American
    Collections: PS508.C5
    Drama: PS628.C55
    Prose: PS647.C42
  English
    Collections: PR1110.C5
    Poetry: PR1178.C5
    Literary history: PR120.C55
Childbirth in literature
  American
    Collections: PS509.C5154
    Literary history
      Poetry: PS310.C48
  English
    Collections
      Poetry: PR1195.C46
    Literary history
      Fiction: PR830.C48
      Medieval: PR275.C48
Childlessness in literature
  American
    Collections: PS509.C518
Children
  English
    Literary history
      Prose: PR756.C48
Children and politics in literature
  American
    Collections: PS509.C519
Children, Anthologies of poetry for
  English: PR1175.3

Dramatic monologues in literature
American
    Literary history
      Poetry: PS309.D73
    English
    Literary history: PR509.M6
Dreams in literature
American
    Collections: PS509.D73
      Poetry: PS595.D76
    Literary history
      Poetry: PS310.D74
English
    Collections: PR1111.D7
    Literary history
      Elizabethan era: PR428.D74
      Modern: PR408.D7
      Poetry: PR508.D8
        Medieval: PR317.D7
Drinking and drinking customs in
literature
American
    Collections: PS509.D75
    Literary history
      19th century: PS217.D75
English
    Collections: PR1111.D75
    Poetry: PR1195.D7
Drinking of alcoholic beverages in
literature
American
    Literary history
      20th century: PS228.D74
Drug abuse in literature
English
    Collections
      Poetry: PR1195.D72
Drugs in literature
English
    Collections
      Prose: PR1309.D78
Dryden, John, in literature
English
    Collections
      Poetry: PR1195.D73

Dutch Americans in literature
American
    Literary history: PS173.D88
Dwellings in literature
English
    Collections
      Prose: PR1309.D84
Dystopias in literature
American
    Literary history
      Prose fiction: PS374.D96
English
    Literary history: PR149.D96
      Fiction: PR830.D96

E

Earth in literature
English
    Collections
      Poetry: PR1195.E17
East Anglia (England)
    Literary history
      Drama
        Medieval: PR644.E28
East Asia in literature
English
    Literary history
      17th century: PR438.E363
East European American authors
American
    Literary history: PS153.E37
East (Far East) in literature
English
    Literary history: PR149.E28
Easter in literature
American
    Collections
      Drama: PS627.E37
      Poetry: PS595.E34
English
    Collections: PR1111.E25
Eating disorders in literature
English
    Literary history
      Drama
        Elizabethan era: PR428.E37

Feminine influence in literature
  English
    Collections
      Poetry: PR1195.F45
    Literary history: PR119
      19th century: PR468.F46
    Drama
      20th century: PR739.F45
    Fiction: PR830.F45
Femininity in literature
  English
    Literary history: PR149.F46
Feminism in literature
  American
    Collections
      Poetry: PS595.F45
    Literary history
      20th century: PS228.F45
  English
    Literary history
      18th century: PR448.F45
      20th century: PR478.F45
    Drama
      Elizabethan era: PR428.F45
Femmes fatales in literature
  English
    Literary history
      Fiction: PR830.F46
Ferries in literature
  American
    Collections: PS509.F46
Ferumbras (English metrical romances): PR2065.F4+
Festivals in literature
  English
    Literary history
      Fiction: PR830.F47
Fetishism in literature
  American
    Collections
      Fiction: PS648.F43
    Literary history
      20th century: PS228.F48
  English
    Literary history
      Fiction: PR830.F48

Fiction
  American
    Collections: PS642+
    Literary history: PS360+
  English
    Collections: PR1281+
      Poetry: PR1195.P74
    Literary history: PR751
      Drama: PR635.P7
      Poetry: PR509.P7
Figures of speech in literature
  English
    Literary history
      Modern: PR408.F5
Filipino American authors
  American
    Collections: PS508.F53
Finance in literature
  English
    Literary history
      19th century: PR468.F56
Financial crises in literature
  American
    Collections
      Poetry: PS595.F56
Finn MacCumhaill in literature
  English
    Literary history
      Modern: PR408.F55
Finnish American authors
  American
    Collections: PS508.F55
Fire in literature
  American
    Collections
      Poetry: PS595.F57
Fishing in literature
  American
    Collections: PS509.F5
      Fiction: PS648.F57
  English
    Collections: PR1111.F53
Flagellants and flagellation in literature
  English
    Collections: PR1111.F54

Grandparents in literature
  American
    Collections: PS509.G7
      Poetry: PS595.G75
      Prose: PS648.G73
Graphic novels
  Juvenile belles lettres: PZ7.7
Greece in literature
  American
    Collections
      Poetry: PS595.G77
Greed in literature
  American
    Collections
      Prose: PS648.G74
Greek American authors
  American
    Collections
      Poetry: PS591.G74
Greek Americans in literature
  American
    Literary history
      Prose fiction: PS374.G73
Greek civilization in literature
  English
    Collections
      Prose: PR1309.G73
Greek romances
  English
    Literary history
      Elizabethan era: PR839.G7
Grief in literature
  American
    Literary history
      19th century: PS217.G75
      Prose fiction: PS374.G75
  English
    Literary history
      Elizabethan era: PR428.G74
      Fiction: PR830.G67
Grotesque in literature
  American
    Literary history: PS169.G75
      Prose fiction: PS374.G78
  English
    Collections: PR1111.G7

Grotesque in literature
  English
    Literary history
      Fiction: PR830.G7
Guardian and ward in literature
  English
    Literary history
      Poetry
        Medieval: PR317.G83
Guardian, The
  English
    Collections
      Essays: PR1369.G8
Gui de Warewic (Romance):
  PR2065.G6+
Guilt in literature
  English
    Literary history
      Fiction: PR830.G84
Guy of Warwick (English metrical
  romances): PR2065.G6+

H

Hagar (Biblical character) in literature
  American
    Literary history
      Prose fiction: PS374.H27
Haiku
  American
    Collections: PS593.H3
  English
    Collections
      Poetry: PR1195.H25
Hair in literature
  American
    Collections: PS509.H28
    Poetry: PS595.H34
  English
    Literary history
      19th century: PR468.H35
Haitian American authors
  American
    Collections: PS508.H33
    Poetry: PS591.H33

Mennonite authors
  American
    Collections
      Poetry: PS591.M43
    Literary history: PS153.M35
  English
    Collections
      Poetry: PR1178.M45
Mennonites in literature
  American
    Collections
      Prose: PS648.M37
Menstruation in literature
  American
    Literary history
      Prose fiction: PS374.M437
Mental illness in literature
  American
    Collections
      Prose: PS648.M38
    Literary history
      Prose fiction: PS374.M44
  English
    Literary history
      18th century: PR448.M45
      Fiction: PR830.M46
Mental patients as authors
  American
    Collections
      Poetry: PS591.M45
Mentally ill authors
  American
    Collections: PS508.M37
  English
    Collections
      Poetry: PR1178.M46
Mentally ill in literature
  American
    Collections: PS509.M47
    Literary history
      Prose fiction: PS374.M44
  English
    Literary history
      18th century: PR448.M45

Mentoring in literature
  American
    Literary history
      Prose fiction: PS374.M47
  English
    Literary history
      18th century: PR448.M47
      Fiction: PR830.M47
Merlin in literature
  English
    Literary history: PR153.M47
      Modern: PR408.M47
      Renaissance: PR418.M45
Mesmerism in literature
  American
    Literary history
      19th century: PS217.M47
  English
    Literary history
      Modern: PR468.M47
Metamorphosis in literature
  American
    Literary history
      Poetry: PS310.M37
Metaphor in literature
  American
    Literary history
      Poetry: PS310.M4
  English
    Literary history
      Fiction: PR830.M475
      Poetry: PR508.M43
Metaphysical poets
  English
    Literary history
      17th century: PR545.M4
Methodist authors
  American
    Collections
      Drama: PS628.M34
Mexican American authors
  American
    Collections: PS508.M4
      Drama: PS628.M4
      Essays: PS683.M49
      Poetry: PS591.M49
      Prose: PS647.M49

O

Obama, Barack, in literature
American
Collections
Poetry: PS595.O23
Object (Philosophy) in literature
English
Literary history: PR149.O18
Obsessive-compulsive disorder in
literature
English
Literary history: PR149.O2
Fiction: PR830.O28
Occasional verse
American
Literary history: PS309.O25
English
Literary history: PR509.O24
Occult fiction
American
Literary history: PS374.O28
Occultism in literature
American
Collections
Prose: PS648.O33
Literary history
19th century: PS217.O33
Poetry: PS310.O33
English
Literary history
Fiction: PR830.O33
Ocean in literature
American
Collections: PS509.S34
English
Collections: PR1111.O24
Ocean travel in literature
English
Collections: PR1111.O25
Literary history
Elizabethan era: PR428.O24
Octavian (English metrical romances):
PR2065.O3+
Odes
American
Collections: PS593.O33

Odes
American
Literary history: PS309.O33
English
Collections: PR1195.O3
Literary history: PR509.O3
Odors in literature
English
Literary history
Fiction: PR830.O46
Oedipus complex in literature
English
Literary history
Prose: PR756.O43
Offices in literature
American
Literary history
Prose fiction: PS374.O34
Oklahoma City Federal Building
Bombing, 1995, in literature
American
Collections
Poetry: PS595.O47
Old age in literature
American
Collections
Poetry: PS595.O5
Literary history
Prose fiction: PS374.O43
English
Literary history: PR149.O44
Elizabethan era: PR428.O43
Older authors
American
Collections: PS508.A44
Poetry: PS591.A35
Older men in literature
American
Literary history: PS173.A35
Older people in literature
American
Collections
Drama: PS627.A35
Literary history
Poetry: PS310.A34

INDEX

INDEX

Rivers in literature
  English
    Collections
      Poetry: PR1195.R55
    Literary history
      20th century: PR478.R58
Robert of Sicily (English metrical
  romances): PR2065.R6+
Robin Hood (Legendary character) in
  literature
  English
    Collections
      Prose: PR1309.R58
Rock music in literature
  American
    Collections
      Poetry: PS595.R57
      Prose: PS648.R63
  English
    Collections
      Prose: PR1309.R6
Rock musicians as authors
  American
    Collections
      Prose: PS647.R63
Rocky Mountain region in literature
  American
    Collections
      Poetry: PS595.R6
Rogues and vagabonds in literature
  English
    Collections
      Poetry: PR1195.V2
      Prose: PR1309.R64
    Literary history: PR151.V3
      Elizabethan era: PR428.R63
      Modern: PR408.R6
      Renaissance: PR418.R6
Roland and Vernagu (English metrical
  romances): PR2065.R8+
Romance in literature
  English
    Literary history: PR149.R65
Romances
  English
    Literary history
      Elizabethan era: PR428.R65

Romances
  English
    Literary history
      Fiction: PR830.R7
Romances, Medieval, in literature
  English
    Literary history
      Renaissance: PR418.R7
Romanies in literature
  English
    Literary history
      19th century: PR468.R63
Romanticism
  English
    Collections: PR1139
      Poetry: PR1222
      Prose: PR1302
    Literary history
      Drama: PR716+
      Poetry: PR571+
        19th century: PR590
Romanticism in literature
  American
    Literary history: PS169.R6
      19th century: PS217.R6
      Poetry: PS310.R66
      Prose fiction: PS374.R6
  English
    Collections
      Poetry (19th century): PR1222
    Literary history: PR146
      19th century: PR468.R65
      20th century
        Poetry: PR605.R64
      Fiction: PR830.R73
      Poetry
        Medieval: PR317.R6
      Prose: PR756.R65
      Victorian era
        Poetry: PR595.R6
Romany poetry
  English
    Collections: PR1195.G485
Rome (City) in literature
  American
    Collections: PS509.R6

Swamps in literature
American
Literary history
19th century: PS217.S95
Swan-Knight (English metrical
romances): PR2065.C39+
Swindlers and swindling in literature
American
Literary history
Prose: PS366.S95
Swine in literature
American
Collections
Poetry: PS595.S96
Switzerland in literature
English
Collections: PR1111.S9
Symbolism in literature
American
Literary history: PS169.S9
20th century: PS228.S9
Poetry: PS310.S9
Prose fiction: PS374.S95
English
Literary history
18th century: PR448.S94
19th century: PR468.S9
Fiction: PR830.S9
Symbolism of numbers in literature
English
Literary history
Fiction: PR830.S93
Symmetry in literature
American
Literary history
Prose fiction: PS374.S96
Sympathy in literature
American
Literary history: PS169.S93
Prose fiction: PS374.S97
English
Literary history: PR149.S95
18th century: PR448.S95
Syntax in literature
English
Literary history
Poetry: PR508.S95

T

Taboo in literature
English
Literary history: PR149.T33
Taste in literature
English
Literary history
Modern: PR408.T37
Tatler, The
English
Collections
Essays: PR1369.T2
Tattooing in literature
American
Collections
Prose: PS648.T37
Tea in literature
American
Collections
Poetry: PS595.T4
Teacher-student relationships in
literature
American
Literary history: PS169.T37
Teachers as authors
American
Collections
Poetry: PS591.T4
Prose: PS647.T43
Teachers in literature
American
Literary history
Prose fiction: PS374.T43
Technology in literature
American
Collections: PS509.T37
Literary history: PS169.T4
19th century: PS217.T43
20th century: PS228.T42
Drama: PS338.T43
Prose fiction: PS374.T434
English
Literary history
19th century: PR468.T4
Elizabethan era: PR428.T43

Z

GPO U.S. GOVERNMENT PRINTING OFFICE: 2012–372–396/40020